Inflation

Issues and Concerns

Inflation

Issues and Concerns

K.R. Gupta

ATLANTIC

PUBLISHERS & DISTRIBUTORS (P) LTD

Published by

ATLANTIC

PUBLISHERS & DISTRIBUTORS (P) LTD

7/22, Ansari Road, Darya Ganj,
New Delhi-110002
Phones : +91-11-40775252, 23273880, 23275880, 23280451
Fax : +91-11-23285873
Web : www.atlanticbooks.com
E-mail : orders@atlanticbooks.com

Branch Office
5, Nallathambi Street, Wallajah Road,
Chennai-600002
Phones : +91-44-64611085, 32413319
E-mail : chennai@atlanticbooks.com

ISBN 978-81-269-1631-3

Printed in India at Nice Printing Press, A-33/3A, Site-IV, Industrial Area, Sahibabad, Ghaziabad, U.P.

Preface

Inflation can be defined as disproportionate and relatively sharp or sudden increase in the quantity of money or credit, or both, as well as incomes and purchasing power relative to goods available for purchase. It always brings a rise in the price levels. There is erosion in the value of the internal medium of exchange and unit of account in the economy as money income is expanding relative to the output of work done by the productive agents, and too much money chases too few goods.

The chief measure of inflation is the inflation rate, i.e. the annualized percentage change in the general price index, normally the consumer price index, over a period of time. In order to measure overall inflation, the price changes of a large basket or collection of representative goods and services is measured. The weighted average prices are combined for calculating the overall price. To better relate the price changes over a period of time, indexes choose a 'base year' price and assign it a value of 100. Index prices in subsequent periods are expressed in relation to the base year price.

Inflation can be broadly categorized into food inflation and non-food inflation. Food inflation affects poor people more because a high percentage of their meager earnings is spent on food. Thus, rising prices of food hold special social, political and economic significance in countries like India, where large masses live in poverty and destitution and the government is hard pressed to provide foodgrain to the poor at reasonable prices under social safety nets. Non-food inflation reveals, among other things, the rising prices of oil, which in turn increase the prices of a large number of commodities due to increase in transportation costs; increase in the prices of steel, some other metals and cement, which affects the budget earmarked for building of infrastructure, like roads, bridges, airports, ports, power stations, etc.; escalation of prices of manufactured goods, particularly consumer durables; and the latest price trends in real estate, which contributes more than nine per cent of national employment in India.

Inflation is of great concern for people, as prices of various types of goods and services have direct bearing on the purchasing power of their earnings, which determines their living standard. Rising prices are always a cause of worry for governments, officials and policymakers as they are invariably criticized for poor policies and are faced with the challenges of controlling malpractices like hoarding and black marketing of essential goods, particularly food items, improving the public distribution system (PDS), importing goods which are in short supply, putting in abeyance the export of certain goods and controlling money supply through monetary measures while not letting the fiscal deficit go beyond the acceptable level. High inflation may bring a wage increase spiral which is detrimental to the growth of the economy.

The book, *Inflation: Issues and Concerns,* explains various definitions of inflation, price indexes, types of inflation, like demand-pull and cost-push inflation and major characteristics thereof as well as the states of inflation such as hyperinflation, deflation, disinflation and stagflation. Different methods of measurement of inflation prevalent in India and other major countries like the US and UK have been explained.

An exclusive chapter has been devoted to food inflation discussing all pertinent issues including poor agricultural yield in India; wastage of foodgrain due to lack of proper storage facilities; poverty of farmers which prevents them to buy inputs like quality seeds, fertilizers, pesticides, farm implements, etc.; lack of adequate marketing facilities; growing crops like jatropha to make bio-fuel and using grown crops like maize to make bio-fuel; and a large and increasing population in India and therefore a huge demand for food. Various types of programs and schemes brought by the government, including food, fertilizer and oil subsidies under social safety nets for the poor to fight inflation have been included. Similarly, non-food inflation and various issues related to it have been taken up separately to give focused attention.

Discussion on inflation these days focuses mainly on the effects of price increase rather than on its causes. This book however, not only describes the effects of inflation on developing economies like India's but also on advanced economies like America's. It delves deep into the major causes of inflation and explains its likely effects on the socio-economic life of people of India. Giving examples from countries like Zimbabwe which tried to tide over high inflation by making more currency and aggravated the situation further, it explains how, by adopting the gold standard, a country can control inflation because gold, unlike paper currency, cannot be created at will. The issues like inflation vs gold, money vs gold, rise in the price of gold, gold exchange rate, gold as investment, inflation-indexed securities, income bonds, inflation-linked derivatives, etc. have been discussed, which the readers will not only find interesting but also enriching.

Inflation-growth trade-off is an interesting empirical question for economists and policymakers. A.W. Phillips was the first to propose that there may be a trade-off between inflation and real economic performance, which was encapsulated in the Phillips curve. This has been explained with the help of diagrams and equations and will be particularly useful for the students of economics.

Since inflation is a major concern for the government, apart from addressing the supply side bottlenecks, it has initiated many monetary management measures. The Reserve Bank of India has increased the key policy rates several times during the past one year and a half to control money supply. But it was seen that reserve money (M0), narrow money (M1) and broad money (M3) increased during 2010-11. Various reasons responsible for this have been discussed, besides giving an account of liquidity management measures taken by the apex bank through monitoring the money market and financial instruments like certificates of deposit, commercial papers, treasury bills and other securities.

Inflation this time around is not limited to any single country or region, but is a global phenomenon though its impact varies across countries. Global inflation may be linked to oil, real economy or monetary shocks, or a combination of these. The common factors that affect inflation across countries are industrial production, wage rates, interest rates, money supply, quantity of imports and exports, foreign direct investment, among other things. All these aspects have been discussed to give the readers a wider picture relating to the subject.

The book has a wide coverage as it elaborates on all the important aspects of inflation. The current scenario of inflation in India has been studied in the light of various underlying reasons, suggesting some anti-inflationary measures. The book is the result of analysis of the current situation, various reports, surveys and observations of experts. I hereby acknowledge all the sources on which it has drawn though most of them have been mentioned in the Notes given at the end of chapters and below the tables, graphs, etc. reproduced to supplement and enrich the text. Figures and equations have been given as per requirement of the topic. The data given is latest, while additional information has been given in Appendices in some chapters. Ideas have been presented in simple language and lucid manner for easy comprehension by the readers.

The book will be useful for a wide cross-section of people. It will help government officials, parliamentarians and economists in understanding different aspects of inflation and framing right policies to control it. Besides, it will benefit the students, teachers and researchers of Economics. Chapters like "Prices and Monetary Management" and "Inflation vs. Growth Trade-off will be of special interest for them. Those preparing for various competitive examinations will also draw benefit from the book's rich contents. To common readers who wish to know about inflation and various issues related to it, the book will provide for a richly rewarding and intellectually stimulating reading.

K.R. Gupta

Contents

1

Inflation, Price Indices, Types, States and Measurement of Inflation

What is Inflation

According to Wyplosz and Burda, inflation can be defined as a rise in the general level of prices of goods and services in an economy over a period of time. When the general price level rises, each unit of currency is able to buy fewer goods and services. Consequently, inflation, as per Paul H. Walgenbach et al. also reflects the erosion in the value of internal medium of exchange and unit of account in the economy. According to Mankiw, the chief measure of price inflation is the inflation rate, the annualized percentage change in a general price index (normally the Consumer Price Index) over time.

All these definitions show that the basic phenomenon is that of quantity of money in circulation exceeding the total amount of goods and services, which leads to an extraordinary increase in prices. Inflation is a situation in which the general level of prices keeps on rising primarily due to stimulus that is continuously being administered by the ever-rising demand in the face of inadequate physical supplies. Thus, inflation refers to a persistent rise in the general level of prices over a certain period owing to the continuous growth of demand very much in excess of the supply of goods and services.

No doubt, a rise in prices is an important characteristic of inflation, but every rise in prices may not be inflationary. A rise in prices resulting from a rise in production costs, for instance, cannot be regarded as inflation. Further, as some writers have pointed out, inflation may exist without a rise in prices. When costs are falling but prices are kept stable (as happened in United States during 1924-29), or when the decline in prices is less than that in costs, the country may develop all symptoms of inflation. Such a phenomenon is described by Keynes as "profit inflation" to distinguish it from "commodity inflation" (meaning a rise in prices). In a state of repressed inflation, prices are prevented from rising by an efficient system of controls and rationing. The inflationary pressure is held strictly under control and hidden from public view but the pressure is still there, dormant, but ready to manifest itself in the form of high prices the moment controls are relaxed or removed. Nevertheless, a rise in the general price level is a common characteristic of inflation and any definition of the term inflation must explain this phenomenon.

On this basis, inflation can be defined in two ways. Earlier writers based their definition on the well known Quantity Theory of Money and explained inflationary trends in prices in terms of an increase in the supply of money. Irving Fisher is of the view that the prices are affected much more by the supply of money than by the supply of goods. After an examination of the price trends in Europe and the United States in the nineteenth and the earlier part of the twentieth century, he concludes that "price level almost invariably shifts with monetary factors—gold, silver, paper, credit and very little with commodity factors. The latter control only the deviations of individual prices from average price movement. In a word, supply and demand dictate each individual price level itself."[1]

But this definition, according to which expansion of money is the cause and rise in prices the effect is open to question. It is commonly known that during the inflation of early 1920s in Germany, prices, far from being pushed up by the volume of money, actually constituted the active factor drawing out into circulation an ever increasing volume of money. The prices were increasing at such a fast rate that the rate of expansion of money supply could not keep pace with the demand for it. As such the relationship between the money supply and prices was reversed. The writers at that time did not hold increase in money supply responsible for inflation. On the contrary, they emphasized the relative deficiency in the supply of money and attributed the rise in prices to the unfavourable balance of payments position of Germany and the consequent depreciation of Mark in terms of foreign currencies. Thus, this definition of inflation is not very appropriate in a situation of hyper-inflation. This led Paul Einzig to distinguish between money inflation and price inflation, the first relates to that stage as it were, in which over-expansion of money beyond normal requirement for it pushes up prices; the second relates to the next stage in which prices get out of control and rise so rapidly that money supply lags behind. Paul Einzig defines inflation "as a state of disequilibrium in which an expansion of purchasing power tends to cause, or is the effect of, an increase of the price level."[2] This definition of inflation covers not only the familiar phenomenon of too much money chasing too few goods but also the other and the more vicious aspect of the problem of a wage, cost of production and price spiral in which each becomes at the same time the cause and effect.

A definition which attempts to explain inflation in terms of a relationship between money supply and price is at best a statement of one aspect of the problem. While mentioning the factors which help in an inflationary price movement, it does not explain the root cause of the trouble. A proper definition of inflation should indicate not only the factors responsible for an exceptional rise in the price level but also show how these factors work themselves out and produce an inflationary situation. In other words, it should cover not only the static but also the dynamic aspect of the problem.

This definition has another drawback. During the peroid of depression, if the government undertakes monetary and fiscal measures which lead to an expansion of money supply and a recovery in the price level, it would obviously be wrong to call such a situation as an inflationary one.

The second approach to the problem of inflation has been put forward by economists like Wicksell, Bent Hansen and

J.M. Keynes. According to this approach, "general price level is determined by the total demand for and total supply of the group of goods concerned, the prices of which determine the general price level."[3] And the inflation is defined as that situation in which the total demand for goods, indicated by the volume of money offered, is in excess of the supply of goods at prevailing prices. Excess of demand over supply is a common factor to both repressed and open inflation. In the former case, it is concealed by devices like controls and rationing while in the latter it appears apparent in the form of excessive money prices.

It can easily be seen that there is not much difference in the basic premises of the two approaches mentioned above insofar as excess demand, which forms the cornerstone of the analysis of the latter approach, can become effective only by means of increased money supply. The basic difference between the two approaches is that while the earlier quantity theory approach explains the position as it is, it fails to point out the origin of the trouble, while the latter supply and demand approach not only indicates the source of the problem but also helps in visualizing the means by which the causal factors work themselves out in an inflationary process.

Keynes makes a distinction between semi-inflation and full or true inflation. According to him, an expansion of the supply of money in circulation before the state of full employment is reached will exhaust itself partly in increasing employment and partly in increasing prices through an increase in production costs. He calls it the state of semi-inflation. Theoretically speaking, so long as full employment is not reached, any increase in the quantity of money should wholly exhaust itself in raising the level of employment and output and not in price level. Because of the existence of various frictions and bottlenecks in the economic system, however, a part of the increased supply of money exhausts itself in raising prices while the remaining part finds its way into productive channels raising the volume of employment and production in the country. It is only after full employment is reached through a series of inflationary waves occasioned by an increase in the quantity of money that there is established a direct nexus between the increments in the quantity of money and the price level, such that an increase in the quantity of money causes a direct and proportionate increase in the price levels. It is here that the true or full inflation comes into operation. Before the full employment is reached, prices rise on account of rising costs associated with higher wages and diminishing returns as the scale of output increases in the short period.

The effects of inflation on an economy are various and can be simultaneously positive and negative. The negative effects include a decrease in the real value of money and other monetary items over time, uncertainty over future inflation may discourage investment and savings, while high inflation may lead to shortages of goods if consumers begin hoarding out of concern that prices will increase in the future. The positive effects of inflation include ensuring that central banks, e.g. Reserve Bank of India, Federal Reserve, Bank of England can adjust nominal interest rates, and encouraging investment in non-monetary capital projects.

Robert Barro and Vittorio Grilli are of the opinion that the economists generally agree that high rates of inflation and hyperinflation are caused by an excessive growth of the money supply.[4] The views on which factors determine low to moderate rates of inflation are more varied. Low or moderate inflation may be due to fluctuations in real demand for goods and services, or changes in available supplies such as during periods of shortage, as well as to growth in the money supply. However, there is consensus of opinion, as per Abel and Bernanke, that a long sustained period of inflation is caused by money supply growing faster than the rate of economic growth.

According to Geffrey Rogers Hummel, most mainstream economists these days favour a low, steady rate of inflation.[5] As opposed to zero or negative inflation, low inflation may reduce the severity of economic recessions by enabling the labour market to adjust more quickly in a downturn, and reduce the risk that a liquidity trap prevents monetary policy from stabilizing the economy. Roger Dobson, in his interesting article, "How Alexander Caused a Great Babylon Inflation" states that the task of keeping the rate of inflation low and stable is usually given to monetary authorities. Generally, these monetary authorities are the central banks that control the size of the money supply through the setting of interest rates, open market operations, and the fixing of banking reserve requirements.

Originally, the term 'inflation' referred to increases in the amount of money in circulation, and some economists still use the word in this way. However, most economists nowadays use it to refer to a rise in the price level. An increase in the money supply may be called monetary inflation, to distinguish it from rising prices, which may also for clarity be called 'price inflation'.[6] Economists generally agree that in the long run, inflation is caused by increases in the money supply, which has a direct effect on demand for various types of goods and services. However, in the short and medium term, inflation is largely dependent on supply and demand pressures in the economy.

Most frequently, the term 'inflation' is used for a rise in a broad price index representing the overall price level for goods and services in the economy. The Consumer Price Index (CPI), the Personal Consumption Expenditures Price Index (PCEPI) and the GDP deflator are some examples of broad price indices. Inflation however may also be used to describe a rising price level within a narrower set of assets, goods or services within the economy such as commodities including food, fuel, metals; financial assets like stocks, bonds and real estate; and services such as entertainment, banking, insurance, transportation and health care. The Reuters-CRB Index (CCI), the Producer Price Index, and Employment Cost Index (ECI) in some countries are examples of narrow price indices used to measure price inflation in particular sectors of the economy.

Main Characteristics of Inflation

In spite of the differences of opinion among economists in regard to the meaning of the term inflation, there is substantial consensus of opinion regarding the characteristics exhibited by the economic system as symptomatic of an inflationary situation. In the first place, inflation is popularly associated with a rise in prices. This is based on observation of facts and is by and large correct. Barring recovery of prices from the depression as a result of monetary and fiscal measures adopted by the government, it would be agreed that an excessive rise in prices has generally been the hallmark of inflation.

The second important characteristic of inflation is an excessive supply of money. In times of war or other national emergency when the tax resources of the state are not sufficient to meet the needs for funds, governments resort to banks which make advances on the basis of government bonds and securities. This results in an expansion in the volume of paper currency as well as of bank credit in the country.

An inflationary spiral once in operation has strong tendencies to feed upon itself. Since the prices are generally expected to rise, the incentive to save is diminished and the incentive to spend is increased. Consumers have a tendency to postpone savings and to buy goods which they do not require in the immediate period. During periods of rising prices, money increasingly becomes a less desirable mode of holding assets. When the value of money is declining, people have a tendency to economise on their cash balances by increasing their spending. This leads to a spending spree and hence an increase in the velocity of money which reinforces increase in the supply of money and thereby further raises prices. Businessmen likewise have a tendency to anticipate their growth requirements. Thus, spending is increased on both accounts. But since the economy is already operating at more or less full capacity, further increases in spending result not in increased production but in rising prices, wages and costs. Rising prices and costs increase the demand for bank creuit. More bank credit means more money to spend. Thus, the vicious circle once started continues, ever afterwards.

How is Inflation Measured

According to Taylor and Hall, inflation is estimated by calculating the inflation rate of a price index, usually the Consumer Price Index, which measures prices of a selection of goods and services purchased by a 'typical consumer'. The inflation rate is the percentage rate of change of a price index over period of time.

For instance, in January 2007, the U.S. Consumer Price Index was 202.416, and in January 2008 it was 211.080. The formula for calculating the annual percentage rate inflation in the CPI over the course of 2007 is

$$\left(\frac{211.080-202.416}{202.416}\right)\times 100\% = 4.28\%$$

The resulting inflation rate for the CPI in this one year period is 4.28 per cent, meaning the general level of prices for typical U.S. consumers rose by approximately four per cent in 2007.[7]

Some other price indices widely used for calculating price inflation are briefly described below:

Producer Price Index (PPI): It is an index which measures average changes in prices received by domestic producers for their output. It is different from the CPI in that price subsidization, profits, and taxes may cause the amount received by the producer to differ from what the consumer actually paid. There is also a delay between an increase in the PPI and any eventual increase in the CPI. Producer price index measures the pressure being put on producers by the costs of their raw materials. The increase in costs of inputs, etc. could be passed on to consumers, or it could be absorbed by profits, or offset by increasing productivity. In India and the United States, an earlier version of the PPI was called the Wholesale Price Index.

Wholesale Price Index (WPI): The Wholesale Price Index (WPI) can be described as the price of a representative basket of wholesale goods. Countries like India and the Philippines use WPI changes as a central measure of inflation. However, India and the United States now report a producer price index instead.

The WPI is the price of a representative basket of wholesale goods. Some countries, including India, use the changes in this index to measure inflation in their economies. The Indian WPI figure is released weekly on every Thursday and influences stock and fixed price markets. The WPI focuses on the price of goods traded between corporations, rather than goods bought by consumers, which is measured by the CPI. The purpose of the WPI is to monitor price movements that reflect supply and demand in industry, manufacturing and construction. This helps in analyzing both macroeconomic and microeconomic conditions.

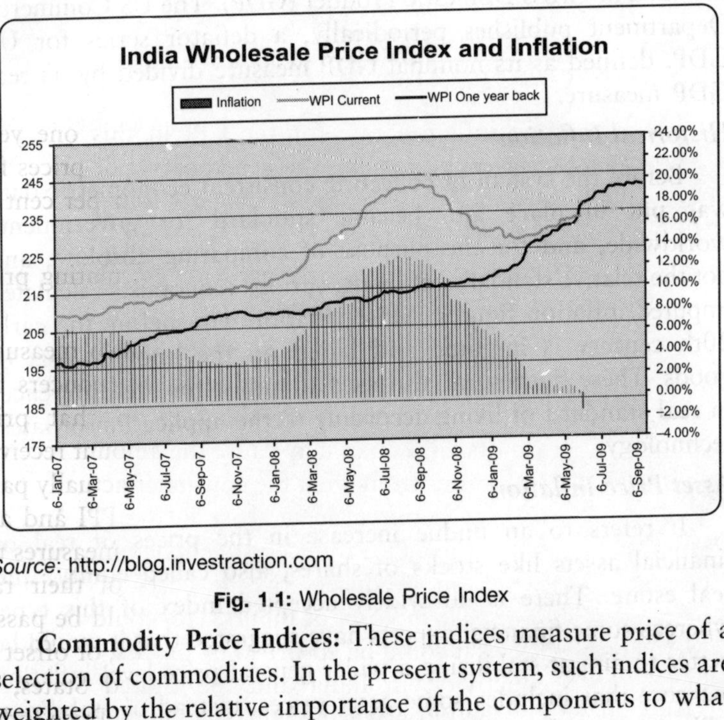

Source: http://blog.investraction.com

Fig. 1.1: Wholesale Price Index

Commodity Price Indices: These indices measure price of a selection of commodities. In the present system, such indices are weighted by the relative importance of the components to what is termed as the 'all in' cost of an employee.

Core Price Indices: The prices of food articles as well as of oil usually change quickly due to changes in supply and demand conditions in the food and oil markets. It is therefore difficult to detect the long-run trend in price levels when those prices are included. Thus, most statistical agencies separately report a measure of 'core inflation', which removes the most volatile components such as food and oil, from a broad price index like the CPI. Since core inflation is less affected by short-term supply and demand conditions in specific markets, central banks rely on it to measure adequately the inflationary impact of current monetary policy.

Other common measures of inflation are mentioned below:

GDP Deflator

It is a measure of the price of all the goods and services included in Gross Domestic Product (GDP). The US Commerce Department publishes periodically, a deflator series for US GDP, defined as its nominal GDP measure divided by its real GDP measure.

Historical Inflation

Before the system of collecting consistent econometric data was put in place and became standard for governments worldwide, and for the purpose of comparing absolute, and not the relative standards of living, various economists calculated imputed inflation figures. Most inflation data before the early 20th century is imputed and based on the known costs of goods. These figures are also used to adjust for the differences in real standard of living according to the application of latest technology.

Asset Price Inflation

It refers to an undue increase in the prices of real or financial assets like stocks of shares, also called equity, and real estate. There is no widely accepted index of this type, whereas some financial experts have suggested that it would be better to aim at stabilizing a wider general price level inflation measure that includes some asset prices, instead of stabilizing CPI or core inflation only. The main reason is that by raising interest rates when stock prices or real estate prices rise, and lowering them when these asset prices fall, central banks are able to avoid bubbles and crashes in asset prices.

Issues in Measuring Inflation

Measuring inflation in an economy necessitates that an objective means of differentiating changes in nominal prices on a common set of goods and services be adopted, and the same be distinguished from those price shifts that result from changes in value such as volume, quality, or performance. For example, if the price of one kg of sugar changes from ₹ 35 to ₹ 32 over the course of a year, with no change in quality, then this price difference represents inflation. This single price change would not, however, represent general inflation in an overall economy. In order to measure overall inflation, the price change of a large basket or collection of representative goods and services is measured. This is the purpose of a price index, which is the combined price of a basket of many goods and services. The combined price is the sum of the weighted average prices of items in the basket. A weighted price is calculated by multiplying the unit price of an item to the number of those items the average consumer purchases. Weighted pricing is a necessary means to measure the impact of individual unit price changes on the overall inflation in the economy. For instance, the CPI uses data collected by surveying households for determining what proportion of the typical consumer's overall spending is spent on specific goods and services, and it weights the average prices of those items accordingly. Those weighted average prices are combined for calculating the overall price. To better relate price changes over a period of time, according to Timothy Taylor, indices typically choose a 'base year' price and assign it a value of 100. Index prices in subsequent years are then expressed in relation to the base year price.[8]

Inflation measures are modified over periods of time, either for the relative weight of goods in the basket, or in the way in which goods and services from the present are compared with goods and services from the past. Adjustments are made as to the type of goods and services selected in order to reflect changes in the sorts of goods and services normally purchased by 'typical consumers'. New products may be introduced, while older products are done away with. The quality of existing products may change, and consumer preferences can also shift over a period of time. Both the sorts of goods and services which are included in the basket and the weighted price used in inflation measures are changed over time intervals in order to keep pace with the changing marketplace and make the index more representative of the existing state of affairs.

The inflation numbers are also seasonally adjusted in order to differentiate the expected cyclical cost shifts. For example, the air conditioning costs of residences and offices are expected to rise in summer months, while the demand and costs of woollens rise in winter months in India. The seasonal adjustments are often used while measuring inflation to compensate for cyclical changes in energy or fuel demand. Inflation numbers may be averaged or otherwise subjected to statistical techniques to account for volatility of individual prices.

It has also been pointed out that while having a look at inflation, economic institutions may focus only on certain kinds of prices, or special indices such as the core inflation index which is used by central banks to formulate monetary policy.

Another issue relating to the measurement of inflation is that most of the inflation indices are calculated from weighted averages of selected price changes. This invariably brings distortion, and may lead to disputes about what the true inflation rate is. It has been suggested that this problem can be addressed by including all available price changes in the calculation, and then choosing the median value.

Difference between Wholesale Price Index (WPI) and Consumer Price Index (CPI)

For a complete understanding of inflation, it is necessary to know the difference between WPI and CPI, which are two of the many indices that play the major part in setting the price of a good in the market. Without these two indices, the market would fall into chaos. These indices are necessary tools for different businesses in keeping track of the price of their goods.

WPI

WPI is used in some countries as a basis for the inflation or deflation rate in the market. The traded goods and services amidst different manufacturers and corporations is the core of the WPI. The WPI can be established using the status of the five groups in basic human commodities, namely manufacturing, agriculture, quarrying, mining, and in the export/import industry.

CPI

CPI measures the average prices of goods and services that the consumers have paid for. There are eight groups in which CPI is used. They are: education, apparel, foods and beverages, communication, transportation, recreation, housing, and medical care. Other services like school and government registration fees and electricity and water bills are also sometimes included in the CPI.

To put it simply, the WPI is the middle point of all the prices that the merchants pay for certain goods or services from the manufacturers or traders. CPI, on the other hand, is also the middle point of all the prices that the consumers, homeowners and the entire private sector have paid for particular products and services. These two indices are very important factors in determining how strong a country's economy is. WPI measures the deflation while CPI is for inflation.

Types of Inflation

Inflation is of different types. These different types may be looked at by dividing them into different categories on different considerations. In the first place, we may distinguish between different types of inflation on the basis of degree or speed with which the prices rise. Secondly, the distinction may be based on the processes through which inflation is induced. Thirdly, different types of inflation may be distinguished on the basis of time. Fourthly, inflation may be either sporadic or comprehensive. Fifthly, inflation may be open or suppressed. On the basis of rapidity with which prices increase, inflation may be divided into four types: (i) creeping inflation, (ii) walking inflation, (iii) running inflation, and (iv) jumping or galloping or hyper-inflation. The speed at which prices rise is significant from the point of view of the dangerous effects on the economy. Creeping inflation is the most mild form of inflation and some economists do not consider it to be dangerous for the economy. In fact, some economists consider it to be an important instrument of economic development. It is argued that it keeps the national economy free from the cankering effects of stagnation. Creeping inflation in which prices rise imperceptibly over a long period has been attracting a good deal of attention in Germany and the United States since 1956.

There is another school of thought which considers creeping inflation to be dangerous for the economy. According to this school, inflation is like conception which when once takes place goes on increasing till the baby is delivered. In course of time, the baby ceases to creep. It learns to walk, run and finally gallop. It should, therefore, be nipped in the bud.

In case of walking inflation, the rise in prices becomes more marked as compared with the situation obtaining under creeping inflation; in fact, it is danger signal of the occurrence of running and jumping inflation under which the rise in prices takes place by fits and starts. In hyper or galloping inflation, prices rise every moment and there is no limit of the height to which the prices might rise. The post-war inflation in Germany and Austria, when the quantity of money increased many hundred quintillion times over the pre-war quantity and the prices increased many trillions over the pre-war prices, is a classic example of the runaway or hyperinflation.

Hyperinflation is an indication of the highest degree of abnormality in the monetary system of a country. After the First World War (1914-18), prices in Germany rose at one time by one million times the pre-war level.[9] Under the condition of such an inflation, all assets having a fixed income lose there real value. The best examples of such assets and incomes are provided by salaries, savings, mortgages, insurance policies, bonds, etc. Hyperinflation ruined millions of German families; it more or less wiped out the German middle class. Hyperinflation was also experiened in Hungary, Poland, Greece, Austria, Russia, etc. The question may be raised as to why the government issued such a large quantity of currency that led to hyperinflation. The answer is that the large issue of currency served as a major source of funds for government expenditure. Statistical data has revealed beyond any doubt that in the final stage of hyperinflation

(1923) the half-yearly index of output in Germany declined by one-third in less than six months.[10]

On the basis of different processes through which it is induced, inflation is of three types:

(i) Deficit-induced inflation, which is caused by the adoption of deficit financing or by government spending in excess of its revenue receipts.

(ii) Wage-induced inflation, which results from an increase in money wages.

(iii) Profit-induced inflation, which occurs on account of an increase in the profits of the manufacturers.

Coming to the third category, we may have war-time inflation which emerges from the exigencies of war during the war period and the post-war inflation which exists in immediate post-war period and more often is the legacy of war. The hyperinflation of Germany during the 'twenties' provides the classical example of war and post-war inflation. There is also peace time inflation which refers to the rise in prices during periods of peace resulting from increased government oulays.

Inflation is comprehensive or economy-wide when the price of every commodity rises throughout the economy. Sporadic inflation is of ephemeral and sectional nature. It occurs when a group of prices rises as a result of sporadic increases in individual prices owing to abnormal shortage of specific goods. The condition of sporadic inflation does not mean more market shortages of goods caused by distortions of price structure such as might take place when the prices of raw materials or wages increase but the prices of finished products are not adjusted in upward direction. It results in situations where supply is restricted by physical conditions and cannot be expanded quickly. The shortages of current production are further accentuated by the backlog of deferred demand. Under such conditions, a rise in prices does not help in restoring supply in a high level of demand. A typical case of sporadic inflation would be an increase in prices of food products as a result of crop failure or a rise in the prices of manufactured goods resulting from the formation of a successful monopoly which aims at the curtailment of output, or rise in the prices of those goods whose production has been interrupted and capacity curtailed by war.

Inflation may be open or suppressed. It is open when prices rise without any interruption. The hyperinflation during the 'twenties' in Germany, Austria, Russia, etc. and in China in the 'forties' provides an example of such an inflation. Suppressed inflation, in contrast, refers to conditions in which as a result of adoption of certain policies (e.g. price control and rationing) by the government, prices are prevented from rising. When price control and rationing or other physical controls are removed, suppressed inflation bursts into an open inflation with vengeance. War-time controls are an example of suppressed inflation developed into an open inflation. The word suppression here means: (i) the postponement of the present demand to some future date; and (ii) the diversion of demand from one kind of goods to another—from those goods which are subject to price-control and rationing—to those whose prices are uncontrolled and which are not rationed.

Suppressed inflation suffers from a number of evils. It gives rise to administrative problems. It leads to a hierarchy of price controllers and rationing officers whose duty is to administer rationing and controls. Efficient administration of rationing and controls requires that the administrative machinery should be competent, experienced and honest. War-time experience of actual working of controls and rationing even in advanced countries, however, shows that the administrative machinery is inefficient and easily corruptible. Under such conditions, there grows the most unpleasant phenomenon of black market through which the rationed and price-controlled goods are sold. The administrative machinery being a party to the activities of black-marketers, there soon develops hidden price inflation which is worse than open inflation. To cite Halm, "Excess purchasing power then causes a violent price inflation in the black markets, while the legal markets are drained of merchandise. Once the population finds that it cannot even buy its modest rations, black-market operations become the preoccupation of everybody. Where one such black-market transaction earns more money than a week's or a month's hard work, productivity will decline enormously."[11] Black-market demoralises national character.

Apart from all this, suppressed inflation causes uneconomic diversion of productive resources from essential goods industries whose prices are statutorily fixed to those industries which produce relatively less essential goods but whose prices, being not subject to price control, are free to rise. Thus, the scarce resources of the community have a tendency to move from more productive fields to less productive but monetarily more profitable channels. Such a deviation from the optimum utilisation of resources is very harmful for the community.

Sometimes, economists talk of the demand-pull, demand-shift and cost-push inflation.

Demand-Pull Inflation

It emerges when the aggregate demand exceeds the level of full employment output. Consumers and investors seek to buy more than the total amount of output that can be produced. This type of inflation is also known as excess demand inflation. Excess demand may arise either in the public or private sector. The demand-pull inflation may be caused by an increase in the quantity of money. All increase in the quantity of money would lower the rate of interest which would stimulate investment. This will also lead to an increase in consumption expenditure through the multiplier. The demand-pull inflation can also occur without an increase in money supply. This would occur when aggregate demand increases either because of a rise in the marginal efficiency of capital or a rise in the propensity to consume.

Figure 1.2 illustrates the demand-pull inflation. In this diagram D curves show aggregate demand function and S curve shows the given supply function. As D curve rises higher and higher from D_1 to D_5, the price level rises higher and higher from P_1 to P_5. When the aggregate demand function rises from D_1 up to D_3, there takes place an increase both in the price level and the aggregate output because the full-employment level is not yet reached. This is known as bottleneck inflation. Full employment is reached at point C and, therefore, beyond C or

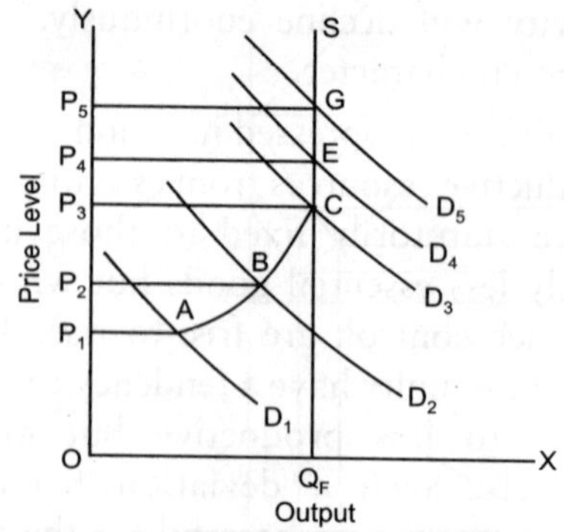

Fig. 1.2: Demand-Pull Inflation

above D_3, rise takes place only in the price level. This is known as true inflation.

Cost-Push Inflation

For a long time before the fifties, inflation theory ran mainly in terms of the generalised excess demand, explained either by quantity theory or Keynesian theory. During the fifties, there occurred a revival of supply, or cost, theories of inflation. The general notion that price inflation can arise on the supply, or cost, side is not new. To cite M. Bronfenbrenner and F.D. Holzman, "Cost inflation has been the layman's instinctive explanation of general price increases since the dawn of the monetary system. We know of no inflationary movement that has not been blamed by some people on 'profiteers', 'speculators', 'hoarders', or workers and peasants 'living beyond their station'."[12]

Figure 1.3 illustrates the cost-push inflation. The full employment output equilibrium is determined at the point where the demand curve D_1 and the supply curve S_1 intersect each other. This is point A at which output is OQ_1 and price is OP_1. When the aggregate supply function shifts to S_2, output declines to OQ_2 and the price level rises to OP_2. Similarly, when the supply function further rises to S_3, output declines to OQ_3 and price level rises to OP_3. The process will continue for still further upward shifts in the supply function.

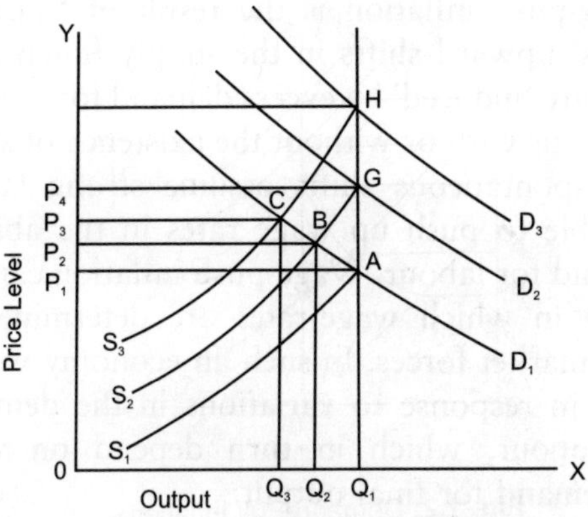

Fig. 1.3: Cost-Push Inflation

There are two main causes of inflationary shifts in the aggregate supply function, viz. (i) higher money wages secured by labour unions and (ii) higher prices secured by business firms in monopolistic or oligopolistic industries. The inflation caused by the first factor is known as wage-push inflation while that caused by the second factor is known as profit-push inflation.

Wage-Push Inflation

If the increase in wage-rate is faster than the increase in productivity, there will occur an upward shift in the aggregate supply function. One cause of a rise in wage rates is an excess demand for labour. Once the economy has reached full employment, any increase in the level of money income will reflect only in a rise in prices and no rise in output. Higher prices mean greater profits, and greater profits induce employers to expand output. For this purpose they seek more labour which is not available. Competition among employers leads to a rise in the wage rate. Thus, there occurs a rise in wage rates without any rise in the productivity of labour. But it may be pointed out that this rise in the labour cost per unit of output is not the cause of the rise in the price level but the result. Wage rates rose because of an excessive demand for labour; this would have happened whether labour was organised or not.

The concept of wage-push inflation is restricted to increase in labour costs which are the cause and not the result of higher prices. Wage-push inflation is the result of 'spontaneous' or 'autonomous' upward shifts in the supply function as against those which are 'induced' by excess demand for labour. Induced shifts may occur with or without the existence of strong labour unions but spontaneous shifts assume strong labour unions which are able to push up wage rates in the absence of any excess demand for labour. Wage-push inflation cannot occur in an economy in which wage-rates are determined by purely competitive market forces. In such an economy wage rates rise or fall only in response to variations in the demand for and supply of labour, which in turn depend on variations in aggregate demand for final output.

Profit-Push Inflation

This is another form of supply inflation. Just as labour unions may exercise their market power by forcing wage increases, so oligopolists and monopolists may, in order to increase their profits, raise prices more than needed to offset any increase in costs. Again just as labour unions are a prerequisite to a generalised wage-push inflation, so the existence of imperfectly competitive markets in the sale of goods and services is a pre-requisite to profit-push inflation. Where prices are determined by the competition among buyers and sellers, as is the case with agricultural commodities and raw material, the seller cannot influence the price significantly. But many goods are not sold through such markets and the sellers of these goods manipulate prices. In an economy where so-called administered prices abound, there is at least the possibility that these prices may be administered upward faster than costs in an effort to increase profits.

The cost-push hypothesis, however, rarely considers autonomous attempts to increase profits as an important inflationary element. In the first place, since profits are generally a small fraction of the total price, an increase in profits would not have much impact on prices. Secondly, monopolists and oligopolists generally hesitate to raise prices in the absence of obvious demand-pull elements. Finally, the motivation for a profit-push is weak since, at least in corporations, those who make the decision to raise prices are not the direct beneficiaries of increase in price. The cost-push is, therefore, generally conceived as being synonymous with wage-push.

Demand-Shift Inflation

A rise in the price level may occur without an increase in aggregate demand if the structure of demand changes so rapidly that the resources cannot be shifted equally fast. The year 1946 provides a typical example of demand-shift inflation in the United States. With the end of the War, there developed a simultaneous reduction in government expenditure and an increase in private consumption and private investment. Further, during the year, real net national product declined below the 1945 level, although money national product continued to rise. Thus, while the real output declined, the price level rose up. In this way, it is possible for changes in the structure of demand to affect the general price level even though there is no increase in aggregate demand. The basic idea behind demand shift inflation is that a shift in demand would raise wages and prices in fields in which demand has increased. But since wages and prices are inflexible in the downward direction, the rising wages and prices in some sectors are not matched by corresponding reductions in wages and prices in the sectors in which demand has declined. As such the general level of prices rises in spite of the fact that no increase in the over-all aggregate demand has taken place.

Demand-Pull Versus Cost-Push Inflation

According to some economists, inflation is neither demand-pull alone nor cost-push alone and, in actual practice, it possesses elements of both. They point out that there cannot be such a thing as cost-push inflation because, without an increase in the purchasing power and demand, cost increases would lead to unemployment and depression and not to inflation. Similarly, there are assumptions for which it would be appropriate to say that demand-pull cannot cause inflation unless it is produced by cost-push. In other words, it is contended that there are conditions under which 'effective demand' is not effective and would not pull up prices unless cost-push produces inflation.

But this position ignores an important distinction, namely whether the cost-push is 'equilibrating' in the sense that it 'absorbs' a previously excess demand or whether it is 'disequilibrating' in the sense that it creates an excess supply (of labour and productive capacity) which would have to be prevented or removed by an increase in effective demand. To cite Prof. Harry G. Johnson, "The issue of cost-push versus demand-pull was...a spurious one.... Neither cost-push nor demand-pull inflation models can generate a sustained inflation unless it is assumed either that the demand for money can be compressed indefinitely without adverse effects on demand and employment, which runs contrary to the theory and fact of monetary behaviour, or that the monetary authority permissively provides the additional money required to circulate the national income at ever-increasing prices, in which case the behaviour of the monetary authority becomes the crucial factor in inflation (and, in addition, the question arises for the cost-push theory as to what determines the pace of inflation). The two theories are therefore not independent and self-contained theories of inflation, but rather theories concerning the mechanism of inflation in a monetary environment that permits it."[13] Further, in actual practice, it is very difficult to devise a test capable of determining whether a particular inflation is of the demand-pull or cost-push variety.

No doubt the distinction between demand-pull and cost-push inflation is not very scientific, it cannot be denied that it does help in separating two forces which might be in simultaneous and interdependent operation in any actual inflation. The distinction is also important for its policy implications. According to Harry G. Johnson, "The importance of the debate stems largely from the difference between the recommendations for anti-inflationary policy to which the two views of the cause of inflation lead, the demand-pull explanation leading to the recommendation of monetary restraint and fiscal orthodoxy and the cost-push explanation leading to the rejection of macroeconomic measures of this sort in favour of policies directed at the processes of price formation and wage determination."[14]

Inflationary Gap

Inflationary gap was defined by the Chancellor of the Exchequer in England in his budget speech of April 1941 as "the amount of the government's expenditure against which there is no corresponding release of real resources of manpower or material by some other member of the community". As such it indicates an excess of total demand for goods over their total supply measured at constant prices. The concept of inflationary gap may be viewed in relationship to full employment level of real income and defined as the excess of the amount of aggregate spending over the amount of aggregate output at full employment level at the existing prices. Prof. Kurihara defines the inflationary gap as "an excess of anticipated expenditure over available output at base prices". According to Klein, this gap "is the difference between what the population will try to consume out of income (which is determined by the interaction of consumption function and the level of the government expenditure) and the amount available for consumption at pre-inflation prices".

Even if it is assumed that there exist some unemployed resources which can be commissioned to raise the level of income above the present level, an excess of demand over supply will lead to a rise in prices because production cannot be increased instantaneously. It takes time to build new factories and commission new plants. Increased raw materials have to be obtained by increasing agricultural and mineral production. Workers have to be trained in new skills. All this requires time. Thus, even when production can be increased, such an increase would take place with a time-lag. As such when expenditure increases, prices would rise and inflationary gap would exist till the supply of goods is expanded.

To illustrate how the inflationary gap arises and how it is measured, we may consider the example of a war economy which is more or less a full-employment economy. The aggregate real national income would be equal to the sum of government and private expenditures incurred on investment and consumption. Let us suppose this amounts to ₹ 1200 crores in money terms calculated at the existing price level. Now if, out of this total output, the government takes away output worth ₹ 300 crores for war purposes, output only worth ₹ 900 crores would be available for civilian consumption. This output worth ₹ 900 crores constitutes the supply side. Let us suppose that the money income paid to the community during the same period is ₹ 1200 crores, out of which the government takes away ₹ 100 crores in the form of taxes. This leaves a disposable income of ₹ 1100 crores with the community. Obviously, the community would not spend the entire disposable money income on the purchase of goods and save a part of it. If people are in the habit of saving 10 per cent of their disposable income, the money income that would actually be spent on goods would amount to ₹ 990 crores (e.g. ₹ 1100 crores – ₹ 110 crores saved). As such, the inflationary gap at the current level of prices would be ₹ 90 crores, i.e. ₹ 990 crores – ₹ 900 crores. Thus, when disposable income of ₹ 990 crores chases goods available for civilian consumption worth ₹ 900 crores, there arises an inflationary gap to the tune of ₹ 90 crores. The process may be summarised as below:

Demand Side	₹ Crores	Supply Side	₹ Crores
Money income paid to community	1200	Gross national product (GNP) at existing price (or at pre-inflation prices)	1200
Taxes	100		
Total disposable income	1100	War expenditure, i.e. value of GNP appropriated for war purposes	300
Savings by community at the rate of 10 per cent	110		
Net disposable income (which represents total amount of anticipated expenditure)	990	Value available for civilian consumption at pre-inflation prices	900

A similar inflationary gap can arise during a period of development planning. The amount of money expenditure (and as such money income) may be high because of expenditure on development projects but there may not be a corresponding increase in the production of consumption goods because of the time-lag between the investment on development projects and the flow of goods from them. Thus, the basic fact is that so long as the amount of disposable income in the community and the amount of goods available are equal, price level could remain stable, but if the former exceeds the latter, an inflationary gap would appear. If, in contrast, the amount of goods is in excess of the disposable money incomes, a deflationary gap would appear.

Figure 1.4 shows the concept of inflationary gap. In this figure, total anticipated expenditure is measured along the vertical axis while the real income (gross national product) is measured along the horizontal axis. C represents consumption expenditure, I private investment expenditure and G government expenditure, so that the total expenditure of the economy is shown by the C + I + G function. The 45° line OE is the equilibrium line showing that the economy is in equilibrium when the supply of goods and services (as reflected in real income) equals the demand for them (as reflected in the total spending function). The C + I + G curve intersects the curve OE (equilibrium line) at point E_f which gives the equilibrium income Y_f, which may be assumed as the full employment income at current prices. At this point the aggregate monetary demand reflected by the C + I + G function amounts to E_fY_f which is equal to the total amount of goods available, that is, OY_f. As such, there is no excess demand and no question of inflationary gap.

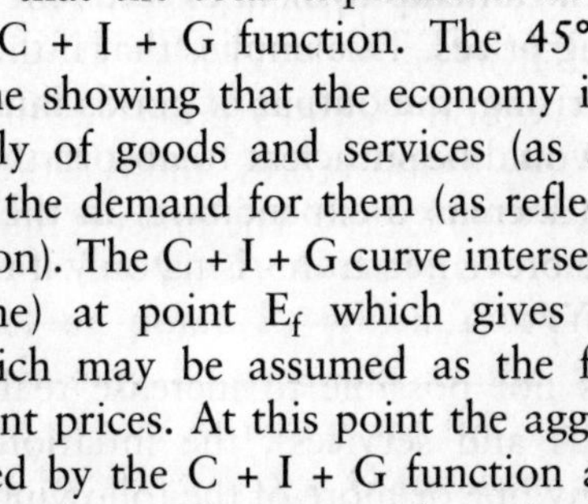

Fig. 1.4: Inflationary Gap

Now, suppose, for some reasons, the government expenditure increases by E_fE_0 which gives the economy new function C + I + G′. Since Y_f is the real income at full employment level, it does not increase with the increase in government expenditure by E_fE_0. Thus, E_fE_0 represents an excess of monetary demand over the available quantity of goods (OY_f). In this case, E_fE_0 is the extent of inflationary gap which forces up prices. Thus, inflationary gap occurs when, with the economy at full employment, the money income rises faster than the output of goods and services. When the expenditures are rising faster than the output of goods and services, prices will necessarily rise to equate expenditures with the money value of output at a higher price level. The inflationary gap is, therefore, defined as the amount by which full employment exceeds the value of current output at existing prices. This implies that if the prices are to be prevented from rising, the output of goods must increase by an amount which would be sufficient to absorb the excess demand generated by an increased expenditure. In the above diagram, the prices can be prevented from rising only if the real income is increased from Y_f to Y_n.

In case it is not possible to increase real income (or the volume of goods and services), the inflationary gap can be bridged up by any one or more of the following three measures: (i) inducing the public to save more, (ii) mopping up the surplus purchasing power with the public through additional taxation, and (iii) raising the value of the available output to the level of disposable income by permitting the prices to rise. Among these three alternative measures, a good government tries to bridge up the inflationary gap by the first two measures, viz. by inducing the public to save more and by increasing taxes. But a bad government may allow the prices to rise and thus expose the economy to inflation.

Significance of Inflationary Gap

The concept of inflationary gap is a highly useful analytical device because it indicates the direction and extent to which the various anti-inflationary measures should be carried out by the monetary and fiscal authorities. To cite Kurihara, "Analysis of the inflationary gap in terms of such aggregates as national income, investment outlays, and consumption expenditures clearly reveals what determines public policy with respect to taxes, public expenditures, savings campaigns, credit control, wage adjustments—in-short, all the conceivable anti-inflation measures affecting the propensities to consume, to save, and to invest, which together determine the general price level. It is by influencing those propensities, directly or indirectly, that the monetary-fiscal authorities hope to wipe out the inflationary gap and therefore prevent further price increases."[15]

Unemployment-Inflation Dilemma (Phillips Curve)

With remarkable prescience, both Keynes and Mrs. Robinson foresaw in the pre-war period the dilemma which most of the Western countries face today; the possibility of attaining simultaneously, and without price or wage controls, the twin goals of full employment and price stability. The experience of many countries with strong producer pressure groups shows that as unemployment is reduced below a certain critical level, prices begin to rise, and that, when prices are stable, unemployment is above the level that is considered "socially tolerable" by countries committed in principle to a full employment goal.

Thus, we cannot have price stability and full employment at one and the same time. If we want stable prices, we have to forgo a high level of employment. And if we want a high level of employment, we have to sacrifice stable prices. Thus, we have to trade between unemployment and inflation.

A.W. Phillips has made an empirical study of the relationship between unemployment and the rate of change of money wage rates, which is known as "the Phillips Curve". The objective of his study is to investigate whether statistical evidence supports the hypothesis that the rate of change of money wage rates in the United Kingdom can be explained by the level of unemployment and the rate of change of unemployment and if so, to form some quantitative estimate of the relation between unemployment and the rate of change of money wage rates. The empirical study appears in general to support the hypothesis that the rate of change of money wage rates can be explained by the level of unemployment and the rate of change of unemployment. The relation between unemployment and the rate of change of wage rates is likely to be curvilinear and not linear. Phillips has used this curve to determine that for the United Kingdom, a rate of 5½ per cent unemployment is needed if wages are to be held steady, and a rate of 2½ per cent unemployment is needed if prices are to be held steady. This means that wages would rise by the same percentage as the increase in productivity, which is estimated to be 2 per cent per annum. Samuelson and Solow have estimated a similar curve for the United States and have found a more pessimistic figure of 5½ per cent unemployment necessary for price stability, assuming that productivity increases at 2½ per cent per annum.[16]

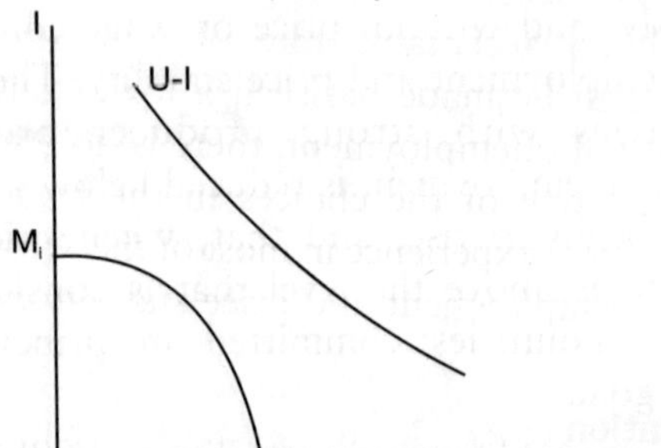

Fig. 1.5: Phillips Curve

In Fig. 1.5, the curve U-I represents the Phillips relationship. The curve can be derived from an economy's data for a period of years by plotting for each year the percentage money wage increase (vertical axis) against the percentage labour force that is unemployed (horizontal axis). The curve M_iM_u represents the acceptable trade-off between inflation and unemployment. This curve is concave indicating that as unemployment reaches low levels, more inflation is acceptable only if a relatively large decrease in unemployment can be traded for it and as the rate of inflation reaches low levels higher unemployment is acceptable only if increasingly large cuts in the rate of inflation can be traded for it. M_i is assumed to be the maximum rate of inflation which would be tolerated by the authorities concerned; this rate is associated with zero unemployment. Similarly, M_u represents the maximum tolerable rate of unemployment and is associated with complete price stability. The curve M_iM_u represents the maximum tolerable rate of inflation for every rate of unemployment up to M_u and conversely. All the U-I points located on or within the M_iM_u curve are acceptable, each point representing a combination of an acceptable rate of inflation and an acceptable rate of unemployment. All points inside the curve, however, are not equally desirable.

If the U-I limit curve neither touches nor intersects M_iM_u curve, the goals of full employment and price stability would be in effective conflict. A tolerable rate of unemployment would have to be paid for by an unacceptable rate of inflation and conversely. In contrast, if the macro boundary intersects the M_iM_u curve, an acceptable rate of unemployment can be combined with an acceptable rate of inflation. Although a trade-off must still be made between a lower rate of inflation and a lower rate of unemployment, there is no effective conflict in the sense that one of the choices in the trade-off must be unacceptable. Actual experience in most of the Western countries shows that high employment and price stability are in effective conflict.

Critical Evaluation

The Phillips curve has not been accepted by all economists and the empirical evidence is still a matter of great controversy. Many economists do not approve of an explanation of inflation which does not pay adequate consideration to the monetary conditions. Even if Phillips relation does exist, it does not necessarily imply that it will usefully lend itself to macroeconomic decision-making. They feel that changes in prices are at least as important as unemployment in determining changes in the wage rate. This is ignored in the Phillips Curve. The 'money illusion' among workers as suggested by Keynes is largely absent in today's bargaining because wage-earners would make every effort to retain their share of national income, if this has been eroded by rising prices. To cite Harry G. Johnson, "...there are some serious doubts about the applicability of the Phillips curve to the formulation of economic policy. On the one hand, the curve represents only a statistical description of the mechanics of adjustment in the labour market, resting on a simple model of economic dynamics with little general and well-tested monetary and value theory behind it. On the other hand, it describes the behaviour of the labour market in a combination of periods of economic fluctuation and varying rate of inflation, conditions which presumably influenced the behaviour of the labour market itself, so that it may reasonably be doubted whether the curve would continue to hold its shape if an attempt were made by economic policy to pin the economy down to a point on it."[17]

Friedman holds the view that a function relating the volume of employment to the rate of change in money prices is fallacious because it implies a relationship between real and nominal magnitudes.[18] Since the former is determined by real forces in the economy, and only temporarily influenced by the monetary variable, while the latter is determined entirely by monetary forces, it is obvious that there is no reason to assume any relationship between the two.

It has been pointed out that the degree of non-linearity between changes in the wage rate and unemployment is an empirical question which needs further examination. Profits have often been suggested as another important determinant of the change in wage rates. This point needs serious consideration.

Phillips Curve and Control of Inflation

If we succeed in achieving full employment, we must find some way other than the use of monetary and fiscal policy to prevent the inflation which Phillips Curve suggests may well result. One of the ways is to link increase in wages to increases in productivity of the workers. Other measures include various forms of anti-union legislation, which at the extreme would abolish collective bargaining or prohibit industry-wide bargaining. Although all such measures have implications which go far beyond their possible anti-inflationary applicability, it may be emphasized that some such measures would be absolutely necessary if we want to attain full employment and rapid economic growth and at the same time avoid inflation.

States of Inflation

There are different states of inflation based on its value as well as variation from the previous value, as stated below.

Hyperinflation

It is a very high rate of inflation, generally a rate in excess of 50 per cent. History has some good examples of hyperinflation. In Germany, inflation exceeded 1 million per cent in 1923. It was said that a cart full of money would not buy even a newspaper. A few years ago, Zimbabwe was having an inflation of 1 million per cent. However, hyperinflation is a very very rare phenomenon and can be termed as out-of-control inflationary spirial.

Deflation

It can be described as the decrease in the general price level of goods and services only when annual inflation is below zero per cent, resulting in the real value of money. Hence, it is sometimes called 'negative inflation'. Japan suffered from deflation for almost in the entire decade of 1990s. In order to control recession, the Central Bank of Japan was forced to have a negative interest rate on deposit for over a decade.

Disinflation

It is a time when the rate of change of prices is falling while the inflation rate is positive. For example, if the inflation rate comes down from five per cent to four per cent we would say it is disinflation.

Stagflation

It is an economic situation in which inflation and economic stagnation occur at the same time and remain unchecked for a period of time. It can result when an economy is slowed by an unfavourable supply shock, like an increase in the price of oil in an oil importing country, which tends to raise prices at the same time slowing down the pace of growth of economy by making production less profitable. Thus, stagflation is a combination of inflation, slow economic growth and high unemployment.

Reflation

It can be stated as an attempt to raise the general level of prices to counteract deflationary pressures.

New Inflation Index

The Indian Government unveiled in the first week of February 2011 a national consumer price index (CPI) that incorporates the price of several key services including telephone bills, education, recreation, catering, fashion designing, etc.

The Statistics and Programme Implementation Ministry released the methodology of the new CPI that will come into effect for the prices of January 2011. The base for the new series will temporarily have calendar 2010 as the base year, which will be shifted to 2011-12 when the 68th round of consumer expenditure survey is completed. Data is being collected from 1,183 villages and 310 towns across India.

The new consumer price series for rural, urban and combined for January 2011, reflecting the impact of price rise on common man, were released later in February. Work for a comprehensive CPI started in 2008 when the country saw an inflationary surge as measured by WPI. The Finance Ministry was of the view that WPI-based inflation overstated the level of the price rise in the economy.

The present four CPI numbers do not encompass all the segments of the population and as such they, according to the Chief Statistician, T.C.A. Anant, "do not reflect the true picture of the price behaviour in the country". He said on the sidelines of the 15th Conference of Commonwealth Statisticians, "It is, therefore, necessary to compile a CPI which takes into account the consumption patterns of all segments of the population".

The government proposes to release provisional indices for a period of one year. "These provisional numbers will be subsequently revised and final numbers with complete data for all-India and also for all the state and Union Territories would be released with a time lag of two months", Mr. Anant said.

Central banks rely mostly on CPI data to decide monetary policy, unlike RBI, which uses WPI as the key inflation index. In a 2009 report of a committee on financial sector assessment, chaired by then RBI deputy governor Rakesh Mohan, said: "Relying on a single index might result in loss of information on some crucial sectors and might be less useful in tackling the diversity of issues." Hence, the changes like this are being effected.

Table 1.1: Items and Their Weightage in the New Consumer Price Index

Items	Rural	Urban	Combined
Food, beverages and tobacco	59.3	37.2	49.7
Fuel and lighting	10.4	8.4	9.5
Clothing, bedding and footwear	5.4	3.9	4.7
Housing	—	22.5	9.8
Education	2.7	4.2	3.8
Medical care	6.7	4.3	5.7
Recreation	1.0	2.0	1.4
Transport and communication	5.8	9.8	7.6
Personal care	3.1	2.7	2.9
Household requisties	4.5	3.9	4.3
Others	1.1	1.1	0.6
Total	100	100	100

Source: *Hindustan Times*

WPI is the index used to measure the change in the average price level of goods traded in wholesale market. In India, the data relating to the price level of a total of 435 commodities is tracked through WPI, which is an indicator of movement in prices of commodities in all trades and transactions. The Indian Government considers WPI as an indicator of the rate of inflation in the economy.

How is WPI Calculated in India

As stated above, a set of 435 commodities and their price changes are used for the calculation of WPI in India. The selected commodities are supposed to represent various strata of the economy and are supposed to give a comprehensive WPI value for the economy.

WPI is calculated on a base year and WPI for the base year is assumed to be 100. The data of wholesale prices of all the 435 commodities in the base year and the time for which WPI is to be calculated is gathered.

If we have the WPI values of two time zones, say, beginning and end of year, the inflation rate for the year will be, as under:

WPI of end of year – WPI of beginning of year/WPI of beginning of year × 100

For example, WPI on Jan 1st 2010 was 107, and WPI of Jan 1st 2011 was 113, then inflation rate for the year 2010 is,

113–107/107×100 = 6% and we say the inflation rate for the year 2010 is 6%.

Since WPI figures are available every week, inflation for a particular week, which usually means inflation for a period of one year ended on the given week, is calculated based on the above method using WPI of the given week and WPI of the week one year before. This is how we get weekly inflation rates in India.

Calculation of Inflation in Developed Countries

Most of the developed countries use the Consumer Price Index (CPI) to calculate inflation. CPI is a statistical time-series measure of a weighted average of prices of a specified set of goods and services purchased by consumers. It is a price index that tracks the prices of a specified basket of consumer goods and services, providing a measure of inflation.

India is the only major country that uses WPI to measure inflation. Most countries use the CPI as a measure of inflation, as it actually measures the increase in price that a consumer will ultimately have to pay. Economists however say that it is high time India abandoned WPI and adopted CPI to calculate inflation.

According to V. Shunmugam and D.G. Prasad, CPI is the official barometer of inflation in many countries such as the United States, the United Kingdom, Japan, France, Canada, Singapore and China. The governments there review the commodity basket of CPI every 4-5 years to factor in changes in consumption pattern. They have pointed out that WPI does not properly measure the exact price rise an end-consumer will be asked to pay because, as the name suggests, it is at the wholesale level. The main problem with WPI calculation according to Shunmugam and Prasad is that more than 100 out of the 435 commodities included in the Index have ceased to be important from the consumption point of view.

In countries like the America, WPI is determined through the averaging principle. The main methods used to compute the WPI are mentioned below:

Laspeyres Formula

It is the weighted arithmetic mean based on the fixed value-based weights for the base period.

Ten-Day Price Index

It is a method under which 'sample prices' with high intra-month fluctuations are selected and surveyed every ten days through phone. Utilizing the data retrieved by this procedure and assuming that other non-surveyed sample prices remain unchanged, a ten-day price index is compiled.

Calculation Method

In this method, monthly price indexes are compiled by calculating the simple arithmetic mean of three ten-day sample prices in the month.

Core Inflation

Core inflation is a measure of inflation that excludes certain items which face volatile price movements, particularly food and energy. The concept of core inflation as aggregate increase in price of goods excluding food and energy was introduced by Robert J. Gardon in his article "Alternative Responses of Policy to External Supply Shocks", published in *Brookings Papers on Economic Activity*. The concept was further developed by Otto Eckstein. Gordon's and Eckstein's ideas on core inflation are extensively used.

According to Michael J. Kiley, core inflation is a measure of inflation for a subset of consumer prices that excludes food and energy prices, which rise and fall more than other prices in the short term. The US Federal Reserve Board pays particular attention to the core inflation rate to get a better estimate of overall long-term future inflation trends.

The preferred measure of core inflation by the Federal Reserve in the US is the core Personal Consumption Expenditures Price Index (PCEPI), abbrivated PCI in short, based on what is termed as "chained dollars".

Since February 2000, the Federal Reserve Board's semi-annual monetary policy reports to Congress have described the Board's outlook for inflation in terms of the PCE. Prior to that, the inflation outlook was presented in terms of the CPI. In explaining its preference for the PCE, the Board in its Monetary Policy Report stated that the chain-type price index for PCE draws heavily on data from the consumer price index but, while not entirely free of measurement problems, it has several advantages relative to the CPI.

The PCE chain-type index is constructed from a formula that reflects the changing composition of spending and thereby avoids some of the upward bias associated with the fixed-weight nature of the CPI. Additionally, weights are based on a more comprehensive measure of expenditures. Finally, historical data used in the PCE price index can be revised to make adjustments for newly available information and for improvements in measurement techniques, including those that affect source data from the CPI, the result being a more consistent series over a period of time.

Previously, the Federal Reserve has used the US Consumer Price Index as its preferred measure of inflation. The CPI is still used for many purposes, for instance, for indexing social security. The equivalent of the CPI is also commonly used by central banks of other countries like UK and France for measuring inflation. The CPI is presented monthly in the US by the Bureau of Labor Statistics. This index tends to change more on a month-to-month basis than does core inflation. This is because core inflation eliminates products that can have temporary price shocks such as energy, food products. Core inflation is thus intended to be an indicator and predictor of underlying long-term inflation.

Food Inflation

Food inflation can be simply put as the relative rise or fall in food prices including wheat, rice, maize, soyabean, milk, meat, vegetables, fruits, etc., either raw or processed. Variations in food inflation occur due to demand-supply mismatch for whatever reason. Food inflation is also taken as rise in the prices of food items. Rapid financialisation of food market, unchecked flow of speculative capital into the derivatives market for major food crops, vagaries of weather adversely impacting agriculture production, poor storage facilities, bottlenecks like hoarding and black marketing, faulty distribution system, bio-fuel policies of the government, rising demand for food due to populations increase, etc. are the major causes of spiralling food prices in India.

Measuring Inflation in India: Limitations of the WPI

The Wholesale Price Index (WPI) is widely used as a measure of inflation. Many important monetary and fiscal policy changes are often linked to it. The WPI indices are also used for the purpose of escalation clauses in the supply of raw materials, machinery, etc. Over a period of time, the weekly index numbers of wholesale prices have acquired considerable significance as this is the only index which gives an idea of the week-to-week fluctuations in the prices of all the traded commodities.

However, the WPI in its role as a guide to policy formulation suffers from several limitations. The main limitations relate to (i) non-inclusion of services; (ii) following a fixed weighting scheme while the economy is undergoing major structural changes; and (iii) use of gross transactions data rather than data on final purchases. The first and third problems can only be addressed by including services and transactions not at the wholesale stage but only at the stage of final transactions, while the second problem can be taken care of through either changing the weighting methodology or by revising the base year more frequently. While choosing the base year it must be ensured that it is a normal year and does not contain abnormal output or wide price fluctuations.

Further, in case services are included in the WPI, the modified measure should look like the national income deflator, which incorporates all activities in the economy. The Working Group on WPI highlighted in its report the following practical problems in the context of including services in the ambit of WPI.

(i) The problem of availability of data on different services sectors on a continuous basis;

(ii) The problem of identifying services purchased by producers and services purchased by consumers;

(iii) The need for mixing and matching data collected from administered prices as well as from market prices for services rendered; and

(iv) Problem of services which are not tradable.

The Working Group also recommended that initially, an attempt should be made to prepare a separate index, incorporating indices from the following sub-sectors:

(i) Financial intermediation, including banking, insurance, etc.;

(ii) Transport services road and rail;

(iii) Postal communications and telecommunication;

(iv) Water supply; and

(v) Construction activities in addition to the material inputs which go into them.

It has been argued by some experts that a measure of inflation should measure the prices only at the "final demand level" and not at "intermediate demand" level. The sum total of final goods corresponds to the national income which is the sum total of final consumption plus trade. Therefore, the weighting diagram must exclude inter-industry transactions that are not central to the measurement of the price of final goods and services in the system.

WPI in India is widely used for short-term policy intervention. The inflation needs to be managed with respect to changes in prices of final goods or consumer prices. A number of consumer price indices such as Consumer Price Index for Industrial Workers (CPI-IW), for Agricultural Labourers (CPI-AL), and for Urban Non-Manual Employees (CPI-UNME) are compiled on a monthly basis.

The Labour Bureau of Government of India prepares the CPI-IW. It attempts to measure changes in the retail prices of fixed baskets of goods and services being consumed by the target group, viz. the average working class family. This index is based on the Income and Expenditure survey by National Sample Survey Organisation (NSSO) in 78 selected centres, and is constructed on a monthly basis. The weighting diagram for this index is constructed on the basis of average monthly family expenditures on consumption groups comprising food, pan, supari and tobacco, fuel and light, housing, cloth, bedding and miscellaneous, including medical care, education, recreation, transport, communication, etc. This index is also used for determining the dearness allowances to be paid to Central and State Government employees and to industrial workers, besides fixation and revision of minimum wages to scheduled employments. The coverage of CPI-IW is broader than that for CPI-AL. The CPI-AL and CPI-UNME are designed for specific groups of population for measuring the impact of increase in prices on rural and urban poverty. The CPI-IW depicts the price increase in the service sector.

Another alternative measure for inflation comes from the implicit price deflator of GDP. This is an annual series, which is available with a lag of two years. Nowadays, the quarterly series of GDP have become available. For these reasons, the WPI continues to be used extensively for measuring inflation and for related policy interventions.

In general, the rate of inflation represents the widespread rise in prices of various types of goods and services. The true depiction of inflation is a macroeconomic tasks. One of the measures of fighting inflation is to raise the interest rates. The higher the interest rates are, the stronger the support for local currency is supposed to be. That is why the traders watch the movement of inflation very closely. Even public which is becoming more and more aware of the impact of inflation on their pockets is following inflation with concern. Higher interest rates, though may arrest the upward movement of prices by luring people to save more through bank deposits and thus decreasing demand for goods and services, they are not considered good for industrial growth. Thus, there is always a limit upto which inflation can be controlled.

Since normal interest rates, the Gross National Product (GNP) and Gross Domestic Product (GDP) are deflated to their real values by means of rate of inflation, a more accurate measure of data is achieved. For money managers, traders of international financial instruments like commercial papers, certificates of deposit, Treasury bills, Eurodollar deposits, etc. the representation of real values of GNP and GDP is quite important, because they can accurately compare trade opportunities worldwide and take right policy decisions based on these values.

Notes

1. Irving Fisher, *Inflation*, 1933, p. 45.
2. Paul Einzig, *Inflation,* 1952, p. 22.
3. Bent Hansen, *A Study in the Theory of Inflation* (1951), p. 2.
4. Robert Burro and Vittorio Grilli (1994), *European Macroeconomic.* Macmillan: p. 139.
5. Jeffrey Rogers Hummel (2007), "Death and Taxes, Including Inflation: The Public versus Economists."
6. Michael F. Bryan, "On the Origin and Evolution of the Word 'Inflation'".
7. The numbers are from US Consumer Price Index, from base level 100 in the base year 1982 (FRED database, through Wikipedia).
8. Timothy Taylor (2008), *Principles of Economics*. Freeload Press.
9. Crowther, *An Outline of Money,* p. 108.
10. Philip Cagan, *Studies in the Quantity Theory of Money* (ed. Friedman), p. 53.
11. G.N. Halm, *Economics of Money and Banking,* p. 417.

12. M. Bronfenbrenner and F.D. Holzman, "Survey of Inflation Theory", *American Economic Review* (September 1963), p. 613.
13. Harry G. Johnson, *Essays in Monetary Economics* (London, 1967), p. 128.
14. *Ibid.*, p. 127.
15. Kenneth K. Kurihara, *Monetary Theory and Public Policy* (London, 1956), p. 45.
16. Samuelson and Solow, "Analytical Aspects of Anti-Inflation Policy", *American Economic Review* (May, 1960), pp. 177-94.
17. Harry G. Johnson, *Essays in Monetary Economics* (London, 1967), pp. 132-33.
18. Milton Friedman, "The Role of Monetary Policy", *American Economic Review* (March 1969).

2

Causes and Effects of High Inflation

There have been discussions, debates and studies on the causes of inflation. Historically, a great deal of economic literature has been concerned with the question of what causes inflation. There are different schools of thought as to the causes of inflation and they can be divided into two broad areas: (i) Quality Theory of Inflation and; (ii) Quantity Theory of Inflation.

The Quality Theory of Inflation rests on the expectation of a seller accepting currency to be able to exchange that currency at a later time for goods that are desirable as a buyer. It explains inflation mainly arising due to sudden increase in demand or sudden shortage of supply.

The Quantity Theory of Inflation is more widely accepted based on the quantity equation of money, that relates the money supply, its velocity, and the nominal value of exchanges. It argues that increase in the quantity of money available in the economy is the main cause of inflation. Adam Smith and David Hume proposed a Quantity Theory of Inflation for money, and a Quality Theory of Inflation for production.

The concept of the Quantity Theory of Money began in the 16th century, when Jean Bodin argued that among the reasons for the rise in French prices were abundance of gold and silver, monopolies, scarcity, the pleasure of princes, and debasement of the coinage. He contended that prices had risen higher than they were in France fifty years earlier. He was primarily interested in determining the causes of the price rise, and believed that the amount of gold and silver, which was used as currency at that time had increased substantially and that, consequently, prices had risen. His was one of the first statements that linked price movement to movements in money stock (Klein, 1970). He noted that the increase in the supply of money caused an increase in demand for French goods, resulting in the increase of prices at home and abroad.[1]

It is believed that the Quantity Theory of Inflation was intended as a weapon against mercantilism. Drawing a distinction between money and wealth, advocates of the quantity theory argued that if the accumulation of money by a nation merely raised prices, the mercantilist emphasis on a favourable balance of trade would only increase the supply of money without increasing wealth. The Theory contributed to the ascendancy of free trade over protectionism. In the 19th and 20th centuries it played a part in the analysis of business cycles and in the Theory of Rates of Foreign Exchange.[2]

Currently, the Quantity Theory of Money is considered as an accurate model of inflation in the long run. There is now a broad agreement among economists that in the long run, the inflation rate is very much dependent on the growth rate of money supply. In the short and medium term, however, inflation may be affected by supply and demand pressures in the economy, and influenced by the relative elasticity of wages, prices and interest rates.[3] The question of whether the short-term effects last long enough to be important is the central topic of debate between monetarist and Keynesian economists. It is pertinent to mention here that in monetarism, prices and wages adjust quickly enough to render other factors merely marginal, following a general trend-line. In the Keynesian view, prices and wages adjust at different rates, and these differences have enough effects on real output to constitute "long term" in the view of people in an economy. Both these views are discussed below.

Keynesian View

Keynesian economic theory believes that changes in money supply do not directly affect prices, and that visible inflation is often the result of pressures in the economy which express themselves in prices. The supply of money is a major, but not the only cause of inflation. There are three major types of inflation, as part of what Robert J. Gordon calls the "triangle model".[4]

As already stated in the previous chapter, demand-pull inflation is caused by increases in aggregate demand due to increased private and government spending, etc. Demand inflation is considered to be constructive and brings a faster rate of economic growth since the excess demand and favourable market conditions are said to generally stimulate investment and expansion.

Cost-push inflation, also known as "supply shock inflation", is caused by a drop in aggregate supply. This may be due to natural disasters, particularly those affecting production and therefore supply of goods and services, or increased prices of inputs. A sudden decrease, for example, in the supply of oil, leading to increased oil prices, can cause cost-push inflation as producers for whom oil is a part of their costs pass this increase on to consumers in the form of increased prices. It may be mentioned here that some commodities such as oil are inflation sensitive. An increase in the price of oil due to its short supply not only causes increase in the price of oil for consumers when producers pass on the price increase to the former, but also leads to increase in the price of several other commodities. This happens because when the producers of oil increase its price, the transportation costs of goods increases for manufacturers, traders and distributors of those goods, who in turn, pass on such increase to the consumers.

Built-in inflation is a type of inflation that results from past events and persists in the present. It is one of three major determinants of the current inflation rate. In Robert J. Gordon's triangle model of inflation, the current inflation rate equals the sum of demand-pull inflation, cost-push inflation, and built-in inflation. Built-in inflation originates from either persistent demand-pull or large cost-push (supply-shock) inflation in the past. It then becomes a normal aspect of the economy, through inflationary expectations and the price-wage spiral. Built-in inflation is induced by adaptive expectations, and is often linked to the price/wage spiral. It involves workers trying to keep their wages up with prices, viz. above the rate of inflation, and firms passing these higher labour costs on to their customers as higher prices, leading to a vicious circle. Built-in inflation reflects events in the past and so, it might be seen as hangover inflation.

Demand-pull theory states that the rate of inflation accelerates whenever aggregate demand is increased beyond the ability of the economy to produce, i.e. its potential output. Hence, any factor that increases aggregate demand can cause inflation.[5] However, in the long run, aggregate demand can be held above productive capacity only by increasing the quantity of money in circulation faster than the real growth rate of the economy. Another cause can be a rapid decline in the demand for money, as happened in the Japanese occupied territories just before the defeat of Japan in 1945. However, this cause is less common.

The effect of money on inflation is believed to be most obvious when governments finance spending in a crisis such as a civil war, by printing money excessively. This sometimes leads to hyperinflation, which, as already explained, is a condition where prices can double in a month or so. Money supply is also thought to play a major role in determining moderate levels of inflation, although there are differences of opinion on the magnitude of the role of money supply in this regard. For example, monetarist economists believe that the link between money supply and inflation is very strong, while Keynesian economists, on the contrary, emphasize the role of aggregate demand in the economy, rather than the money supply in determining inflation. For Keynesians, the money supply is only one determinant of aggregate demand.

Some Keynesian economists do not agree with the opinion that central banks fully control the money supply, and argue that these banks have little control, since the money supply adapts to the demand for bank credit issued by commercial banks. This is known as the Theory of Endogenous Money, and has been advocated strongly by post-Keynesians. This position is not accepted by many economists who argue that banks create money by making loans, but the aggregate volume of these loans diminishes as real interest rates increase. Thus, central banks can influence the money supply by making money cheaper or more expensive, thus increasing or decreasing its production and circulation.

Another concept worthy of note is the potential output, sometimes called the natural gross domestic product, a level of GDP, where the economy is at its optimal level of production, given institutional and natural constraints. This level of output corresponds to the Non-Accelerating Inflation Rate of Unemployment (NAIRU), or the 'natural' rate of unemployment, or the full-employment unemployment rate. According to David T. Coe, if the GDP of a country exceeds its potential and unemployment is below the NAIRU, the inflation will accelerate as suppliers increase their prices and built-in inflation will worsen. But in case the GDP falls below its potential level, and unemployment is above the NAIRU, inflation will decelerate as suppliers attempt to fill excess capacity, cutting prices and undermining built-in inflation.[6]

However, it has been argued that the exact level of potential output and of the NAIRU is generally unknown and tends to change over a period of time. Inflation also seems to act in an asymmetric way, rising more quickly than it falls. Moreover, it can change because of policy. For example, high unemployment in the UK when Margaret Thatcher was the country's Prime Minister might have led to a rise in the NAIRU and a fall in potential, because many of the unemployed people found themselves as structurally unemployed, unable to find jobs that fit their skills. A rise in structural unemployment implies that a smaller percentage of the labour force can find jobs at the NAIRU, where the economy avoids crossing the threshold into the realm of accelerating inflation.

The Monetarist View

Monetarists, according to Paul Lagassé, believe the most significant factor influencing inflation or deflation is how fast the money supply grows or shrinks. They consider fiscal policy, or government spending and taxation, as ineffective in controlling inflation.[7] Well-known monetarist economist Milton Friedman states: “Inflation is always and everywhere a monetary phenomenon.”[8] Some monetarists, however, will qualify this by making an exception for very short-term circumstances.

Monetarists assert that the empirical study of monetary history shows that inflation has always been a monetary phenomenon. The Quantity Theory of Money, simply stated, says that any change in the amount of money in a system will change the price level.

Monetarists assume that the velocity of money is unaffected by monetary policy, at least in the long run, and the real value of output is determined in the long run by the productive capacity of the economy. Under these assumptions, the primary driver of the change in the general price level is changes in the quantity of money. With exogenous velocity, i.e. the velocity being determined externally and not being influenced by monetary policy, the money supply determines the value of nominal output (which equals final expenditure) in the short run. However, in the long run, changes in velocity are assumed to be determined by the evolution of the payments mechanism. If velocity is relatively unaffected by monetary policy, the long-run rate of increase in prices, i.e. the inflation rate is equal to the long run growth rate of the money supply, plus the exogenous long run rate of velocity of growth, minus the long run growth rate of real output (Mankiw, 2002).

It is also argued that inflation slows the economy, thus serving as a natural economy balancer, as well as a crucial indicator. The reason why growing inflation moderates economic growth, and also potential overheating of the economy is that when prices increase, people, as well as companies start to buy less. This function of inflation decreases the needs of central bank base rates’ hikes, which in itself has many negative side effects such as increasing the interest payment obligations of governments.

Inflation and exchange rate of the currency of a country move more or less parallel. This means that if inflation increases, the exchange rate of the currency of the country against foreign currency is likely to remain strong, and the currency will not devalue. The exchange rates are important because they affect the competitiveness of exporting companies. The importance of exporting lies in the arrival of new money into the economy of a country. For example, if a country has, say, 100 billion dollars of national economic output, 1 billion more means that companies have 1 billion more to spend in the country, and also the government has more tax income which it can spend on various projects of development. Thus, inflation, in this aspect, is a significant economic indicator.

As seen above, basically speaking, the inflationary pressures arise when money income and corresponding expenditure or demand increase without being accompanied by a corresponding increase in the supply of goods and services. In other words, inflation results from factors which give rise to 'excess demand'. Broadly speaking, excess demand may be caused by two sets of factors, viz. (i) those which shift the demand upwards and (ii) those which shift the supply downwards. These two sets of factors are briefly described below.

Factors Causing an Upward Shift in Demand

Deficit Financing

In recent years, there has been a tendency. Particularly in developing countries, to heavily resort to deficit financing to obtain funds for executing development plans. Deficit financing increases money in the hands of people and thereby increases demand for goods and services.

Increase in the Velocity of Money

This factor is particularly important during boom periods. The velocity of circulation of money increases on account of an increase in the marginal efficiency of capital or reduction in liquidity preference, or an increase in the propensity to consume.

Credit Expansion

The credit structure of a country is determined by the policy of the government as well as that of the commercial banks. The central bank of the country can cause an expansion of credit by lowering the bank rate or by purchasing government securities. Similarly, the commercial banks can expand credit by lowering their cash reserves; but they can do so only when there is demand for loans from borrowers. It may be pointed out that once the credit expands, as a result of either the policy of the government or the initiative of the commercial banks, it continues for a sufficiently long period of time.

Rapidly Increasing Public Expenditure

In recent years public expenditure has been growing fast, particularly because of increasing defence expenditure and expanding role of the state in economic activities; this considerably increases the demand for goods and services.

Expansion of exports

An increase in exports would mean less available for domestic consumption. This would make the existing unchanged domestic demand excessive for the commodities whose exports increase and thus cause a rise in their prices.

Rapid Growth of Population

A rapidly growing population increases the demand for goods and services and thus pushes up their prices. To cite Prof. Coulborn, "If population increases rapidly, while the aggregate of money remains stable, the consequent rise in the velocity of circulation is likely to outweigh the countervailing decrease in the volume of money per head; further, a rapid increase of population may increase output less than proportionately—another factor tending to raise prices."[9]

War

This has been one of the most common causes of inflation. Financing of war leads to a considerable expansion in the supply of money. Further, it leads to a diversion of productive resources from the production of consumer goods to that of war materials and thus causes a shortage of consumer goods.

Trade Union Activities

The trade unions continuously agitate for higher wages, shorter hours of work, more holidays with pay and other amenities. In a democratic country, the government is often compelled to accept even some unreasonable demands of the labourers. The increase in wages of labourers and other amenities provided to them beyond the increase in their productivity raises the cost of production and hence prices. Further, increase in wage increases purchasing power in the hands of labourers and reduction in working hours leads to a decline in the volume of production. This adds to the rise in prices.

Excise and Sales Taxes

Increased taxation is generally disinflationary because it mops up the purchasing power of the public. But if taxes are levied on the production and sale of goods which can be shifted to consumers, the prices of such goods, will rise and add to inflationary pressures.

International Factors

Inflation in one country may be transmitted to other countries through trade. When prices are rising abroad, the importing country has to pay higher and higher prices for its imports. The rise in the prices of imported goods leads to a sympathetic rise in the prices of goods produced within the country.

Devaluation

Devaluation of the domestic currency increases the prices of imported goods. It stimulates foreign demand for export goods, which raises their prices. Rise in the prices of imported goods and exported goods causes a rise in the prices of non-traded goods also.

Factors Causing a Downward Shift in Supply

Natural Calamities

They can take a number of forms like floods, earthquakes, epidemics, etc. They decrease production and thereby lead to a rise in prices.

Stage of Production

If the production has reached a stage where the law of diminishing returns begins to operate, the cost of production and hence the prices would start rising.

Hoarding

During periods of rising prices, dealers as well as consumers have a tendency to hoard commodities which aggravates shortages.

Shortage of Factors of Production

Non-availability of certain factors like capital equipment, land, skilled labour, raw materials, etc. makes it difficult to expand production in response to an increase in demand and thus leads to shortages.

Inflation in an Underdeveloped Economy

Basically speaking, inflation arises owing to a gap between effective demand and output. Inflation is normally considered to be a post full employment phenomenon because so long as unemployed resources exist, increase in effective demand is expected to lead to an increase in output and employment rather than to a rise in the prices. Theoretically, inflation starts only after the full employment stage is reached. But in actual practice, prices may start rising much before the full employment is reached because of lack of perfect elasticity of supply of goods and services and because of other factors which assist in raising the cost of production. Keynes mentions the following factors which cause an inflationary situation before full-employment is reached.[10]

(a) Effective demand will not change in exact proportion to the money supply.

(b) Since the resources are not homogeneous and as such not perfectly substitutable, the law of diminishing returns starts operating as the employment of resources gradually increases.

(c) Since various factors are not perfect substitutes for each other, some commodities will reach a condition of inelastic supply, while there are still unemployed resources available for the production of other are still unemployed resources available for the production of other commodities.

(d) The wage-unit will tend to rise before the full employment has been reached.

(e) The remunerations of the factors entering into marginal cost will not change in the same proportion.

Because of the bottlenecks mentioned above at various levels in the structure of the economy, an increase in the supply of money, and hence in demand, has a tendency to lead to a rise in the price level before the full employment stage is reached. In addition to these general bottlenecks, an underdeveloped economy is characterised by various other forms of bottlenecks which cause a relative rigidity in the supply of goods and thus lead to a sharper rise in prices. Importance of these is briefly mentioned below:

(a) There exist several market imperfections which present an optimum allocation of resources and thereby extension of the actual production frontier to the maximum possible frontier. The important market imperfections include imperfect knowledge, imperfect mobility, specificity of factors and imperfect divisibility of factors.

(b) In advanced countries, the existence of unemployment leads to increased output as a result of increased demand. In underdeveloped countries, what exists is not unemployment but disguised unemployment or underemployment which does not lead to increased production with an increase in effective demand. To the extent supply does not respond to an increase in effective demand caused by monetary expansion, the prices would tend to rise.

Apart from the bottlenecks mentioned above, there are other factors which cause inflationary pressures in underdeveloped countries. Because of lack of other sources of financing development plans, resort has to be made to deficit financing. High priorities given to the production of capital goods in development plans lead to a shortage of consumer goods. Thus, while money incomes increase leading to a rise in demand, the consumer goods become inadequate, which results in a general rise in the price level.

Inflation and Economic Development

There exists great controversy as to whether inflation promotes or retards economic development. Some economists, including Keynes, hold the opinion that inflation, in one form or the other, helps economic development. It is held that inflation helps in the mobilisation of resources by redistributing income and wealth away from wage-recipients towards the profit-recipients. Since the marginal propensity to save of the profit-earners is much higher than that of the wage-earners, transfer of income from the latter to the former class increases the volume of savings which can profitably be invested by the entrepreneurial class in productive channels, thereby raising the rate of economic development. Keynes favours mild inflation on the ground that slowly rising prices create an optimistic atmosphere resulting in high profit expectation which stimulates investment. Maurice Dobb remarks, "Inducements are necessary for large-scale movements of labour and for increased supplies of foodstuffs and raw materials to be made available by the village for the town."[11] Prof. Kaldor also remarks, "a slow and steady rate of inflation provides a most powerful aid to the attainment of a steady rate of economic progress".[12] Prof. Robertson too favours a mild inflation for economic growth. Such a policy is particularly important in the developing economies where a great part of the labour force is self-employed and price incentives (through mild inflation) assume greater importance than wage incentives (at least in the initial stages of breakthrough). Professor Rostow believes that several 'take-off' processes have been assisted by inflation. Hamilton holds the view that inflation has been a powerful stimulant in a large number of historical instances and can perform a similar function in the developing countries.

Many economists believe that a mild inflation is not necessarily an undesirable thing because the alternative to this would be unemployment and impaired economic growth. The argument is that since prices are flexible only in the upward direction in our present institutional set-up, resource allocation through the price system must operate through price increases in the sectors of the economy which are growing rather than through price decreases in the sectors which are stagnating. It is argued that since the monopoly power of unions and enterprises is such that price increases are inevitable, it is better for authorities not to adopt deflationary policies which might cause unemployment rather than a decline in the price level. Prof. Lewis believes that inflation for the purpose of creating useful capital is often ultimately self-terminating because sooner or later it would increase the supply of goods in the market.[13]

Some economists believe that inflation is a product of economic growth. Some inflation is considered to be unavoidable in the process of economic development. At least in the initial stages of development process, there is bound to be a time-lag between the increases in money incomes and the availability of consumption goods in the country and hence a rise in the price level. The inflationary pressures are considered to be almost certain if the planned investment exceeds the volume of real savings.

Another group of economists holds the view that inflation does not facilitate economic growth and, on the contrary, hinders the process of economic growth. Milton Friedman, for instance, completely disagrees with the policy of 'development through inflation'. He also holds the view that "inflation is not inevitable in the course of development".[14] He does not find much substance in the argument that inflation tends to stimulate development through its redistributive effects. No doubt, there were some circumstances in the past in which redistributive effects were favourable to development; but there is no guarantee that these favourable effects would operate in all cases.[15] The reason inflation had favourable effects in the past was that it was unexpected. The process of inflation was unanticipated because it was not planned by anybody. Friedman believes that favourable effects cannot be obtained by a deliberate expansion in the supply of money without its degenerating into hyperinflation. When the process of inflation is deliberate, many people would know about it and act in a way which prevents the occurrence of redistributive effects. Prof. Nurkse also observes that "the success of inflation as an instrument of capital formation depends largely on the degree of which rise in prices is unforeseen and unexpected. When a further rise in price is expected and seems certain, the velocity of circulation of money increases, saving gives place to dissaving and inflation loses its capital-forming power".[16] Further, inflation "invites development, if any, only through manipulation of markets rather than efficient production". This is obvious from the deterrent effects of inflation on productive enterprise, increasing cost of development, depreciating real value of cash holdings, accumulation of investment in real estates, decreasing investment in the export sector, speculation and hoarding resulting from rising prices.[17]

The decline in the real value of money resulting from inflation destroys the saving habits of the people and places a premium on improvidence and careless spending. Inflation may not only obstruct the process of capital formation but may drive the available capital out of the country. During inflationary periods, business skill and efficiency tends to be used for speculative purposes rather than for productive purposes. Rising prices lead to a decline in the demand for export-goods resulting in unemployment in the export industries and balance of payments difficulties.[18]

According to Mankiw, an increase in the general level of prices implies a decrease in the purchasing power of the currency, i.e. when the general level of prices rises, each monetary unit buys fewer goods and services. It is widely known that the effect of inflation is not evenly distributed in the economy. As a result, there are hidden costs to some and benefits to others, from this decrease in the purchasing power of money. Thus, with inflation, the depositors of money who are paid a fixed rate of interest on deposits will be at a disadvantage in terms of loss of purchasing power from their interest earnings, while the borrowers will benefit as they enjoy a higher current purchasing power of the money borrowed by them than it will be when they return that money. The erosion of purchasing power of money over a period of time may be more than the amount of interest paid by the borrowers of money. Timothy Taylor states that individuals or institutions with cash assets will experience a decline in the purchasing power of their holdings. Increases in payments to workers and pensioners often lag behind inflation, especially for those with fixed payments.[19]

Umit and Arsoy are of the opinion that increases in the price level, viz. inflation, erode the real value of money, i.e. the functional currency and other items with an underlying monetary nature such as loans and bonds. However, inflation has no effect on the real value of non-monetary items, e.g. goods and commodities, gold, real estate, etc. According to them, "The purchasing power of non monetary items does not change in spite of variation in national currency value."[20]

Debtors, i.e. people who borrowed money at a fixed nominal rate of interest will see a reduction in the 'real' interest rate as the inflation rate rises. The real interest on a loan is the nominal rate minus the inflation rate, viz. R = N – I. For instance, if you take a loan where the stated interest rate is 9 per cent and the inflation rate is at 5 per cent, the real interest rate that you are paying for the loan is 4 per cent. It would also hold true that if you had a loan at a fixed interest rate of 9 per cent and the inflation rate goes to as high as 16 per cent you would have a real interest rate of –7 per cent, or in other words, an advantage of 7 per cent. Banks and other lenders adjust for this inflation risk by including an inflation premium in the costs of lending the money, by creating a higher initial stated interest rate. But such adjustment is usually small and does not fully account for the inflation rate. There are two major reasons for this adjustment being small. One, it is difficult to correctly anticipate the exact amount of inflation, say after one year or two, if the adjustment is deemed big and the rate of interest fixed goes too high, the lender may lose business as people will hesitate to borrow money, or borrow to the minimum extent.

The other method used by the lenders of money to account for the inflation rate is to set the interest at variable rate instead of the fixed rate. But this also does not go well with the borrowers as most of them prefer a fixed rate of interest, which is considered more transparent as the borrowers know their exact liability in terms of the amount of interest to be paid by them, and secondly, it cannot be increased at any time as per the will of the lender, which is often the case with variable rate of interest. Similarly, when the rate of inflation decreases, this has the opposite, i.e. negative effect on borrowers.

High or unpredictable inflation rates invariably prove harmful to an overall economy as they add inefficiencies in the market, and make it difficult for companies to budget or plan long-term. In his book, *Principles of Economics*, Timothy Taylor writes that inflation can act as a drag on productivity as companies are forced to shift resources away from products and services in order to focus on profit and losses from currency inflation. Uncertainty about the future purchasing power of money, according to George Bulkley, discourages investment and saving.[21] It is also believed that inflation can impose hidden tax increases, as inflated earnings push taxpayers into higher income tax rates unless the tax brackets are indexed to inflation.

Timothy Taylor has also pointed out that with high inflation, purchasing power is redistributed from those on fixed nominal income such as some pensioners whose pensions are not indexed to the price level, towards those with variable incomes whose earnings may better keep pace with inflation. This redistribution of purchasing power will also occur between international trading partners. Where fixed exchange rates are imposed, higher inflation in one country's economy in comparison with another's may cause the first country's exports to become more expensive and affect the balance of trade. There can also be negative effects on trade from an increased instability in currency exchange prices caused by unpredictable inflation.

Effect of Cost-push Inflation

Many economists are of the view that high inflation can prompt employees to demand rapid wage increases, to get some relief from the spiraling consumer prices. However, this may prove more harmful for the economy, because, as per cost-push theory of inflation, rising wages in turn can help fuel inflation due to the fact that higher wages will give more purchasing power to the workers and thus, increase demand for goods and services in the market, pushing the prices further up.

In the case of collective bargaining, wage growth will be set as a function of inflationary expectations, which will be higher when inflation is high. This can cause a wage spiral, which is detrimental to the growth of economy. Higher wages increase the cost of production for the manufacturers. If they do not increase the price of goods they produce, their profit margin decreases, which kills the motive to produce. Some goods may not even remain economically viable to produce. In case the increasing wages are passed on to the consumers in the form of increase in the price of goods, inflation will rise further with all its attendant consequences. In a sense, inflation begets further inflationary expectations, which lead to further high inflation.

Raising the price of goods and services to account for an increase in wages does not always work for the producer. Setting higher prices affects demand which may decrease, necessitating changes in production strategies relating to the quantities of particular goods to be produced, raw material to be purchased, the number of workers to be engaged, among other things. This may, in turn, lead to the problem of underutilization of the plant, etc. If the number of workers is reduced and there is a lay-off, there may be labour-management conflicts and pressures from the labour union.

Setting higher prices also gives an advantage to the competitors who may have an increased sale of their products because the prices thereof are lower. In today's market conditions of fierce competition, this may have far-reaching consequences. The companies spend a lot of money and time to build a brand and establish its products in the market. It can ill afford to take any decision which may adversely affect the sale of any of its products, because, once the market is captured by some other product of the competitor, it becomes extremely difficult to regain the market. Customers' preferences and tastes may be built around the competitor's product which may be hard to change.

For those engaged in the export of goods and services, there may be bigger challenges associated with increasing the prices because of increase in the cost of producing those goods and services. International market is highly competitive as a large number of countries come up with their products. The importers prefer goods and services which are of good quality and come at a cheaper rate than others. The point can be driven home by the fact that China has captured international markets in various types of goods and services during the last decade or so. A market survey released in 2010 by Brain and Company, a US consulting firm, showed that during the financial year 2009-10, the sale of Chinese luxury goods in the international market increased by 23 per cent.

Goldman Sachs predicted that in 2011-12, the sale of luxury goods from China would be at US$ 6.5 billion—putting the country on top of the world for major brand sales, after three consecutive years of double digit growth. Zhu Mingxia, Director of the Research Centre for Luxury Goods at Beijing's University of International Business and Economics declared at the 2011 Summit on Luxury Market Trends held in Beijing, that the country has overtaken the US as the world's second largest consumer of luxury goods.

More leading brands are tailoring their goods and services to suit the needs of Chinese consumers. It is pertinent to mention here that the robust sale of Chinese goods in international markets is not just confined to luxury goods. A whole lot of other goods including digital cameras, mp3 players, computer accessories, cell phones, and other electronic goods that are manufactured in China are gaining tremendous popularity and capturing international market.

In recent times, Chinese electronic products industry has dominated international trade in such goods. There is no doubt that the Chinese wholesale electronic goods feature good quality that is far better in comparison to other electronic products available in international market. But an important factor of these goods experiencing high sales is their low price as compared to those from most other countries. If the prices of Chinese goods are increased, it is quite possible that they will lose some markets and the sale will not rise as much as it has risen during the last few years. In domestic as well as in international markets, the competitors always look for opportunities to have an edge over others. Thus, increasing the price of goods and services to pass on the cost of production to the buyers is at times a dangerous option.

It may however be mentioned that more often than not, the producers of goods and services are able to pass on the increase in costs of goods and services they produce to the buyers. This is true of consumer goods for which there is a ready and ever-increasing market because of growing population in many countries including India, and because of increase in the incomes of people generally over periods of time. Many economists are of the view that so long as the demand remains high, an increase in prices will not harm the producers.

Hoarding

Hoarding is defined as the excessive collection of goods and the inability to discard them. In times of inflation, people tend buy durable and/or non-perishable commodities and other goods as stores of wealth, to avoid the losses expected from the declining purchasing power of money. This creates shortages of the hoarded goods.

Hoarding and Speculation

One of the adverse effects of high inflation is that it leads to bottlenecks like hoarding and speculation. It has been seen that in India, a large number of hoarders and speculators, especially of food items, keep large stocks and do not bring them out until prices thereof rise because of artificial shortage of those items thus created. The prices of sugar, onion, garlic, etc. rose sharply in India in the latter half of 2010, which can be attributed to short supplies vis-à-vis demand, as also to the speculation and hoarding. High prices also lead to black marketing of essential goods.

Despite claims to bring the hoarders, speculators and black marketers to book, the government failed to stop these illegal practices. It was felt that it should have acted with more firmness to curb hoarding and speculation of food articles. According to Planning Commission Member Abhijit Sen, "Whenever prices start rising, some people see opportunity to make money. So, there is bound to be certain degree of speculation and that must have happened. On that front, probably, the government did not act with resoluteness that it could have." Driven by rising prices of sugar, pulses and vegetables, food inflation in India soared to a decade's high of nearly 20 per cent in 2010.

Effects of Hyperinflation

As already stated in the previous chapter, hyperinflation is very high inflation, or upward spiral of inflation that does not seem to relent. If inflation gets totally out of control in the upward direction, i.e. turns into hyperinflation, it can grossly interfere with the normal working of the economy, hurting its ability to supply goods. In economics, hyperinflation is inflation that is very high or 'out of control'. According to Arthur O'Sullivan and Steven M. Sheffrin, while the real values of the specific economic items generally stay the same in terms of relatively stable foreign currencies, in hyperinflationary conditions, the general price level within a specific economy increases rapidly as the functional or internal currency, as opposed to a foreign currency, loses its real value very quickly, normally at an accelerating rate.[22] The monthly and annual low inflation and deflation are mostly reported per month, while under hyperinflation, the general price level could rise by 5 or 10 per cent or even much more every day. A vicious circle is created in which more and more inflation is created with each iteration of the ever-increasing money printing cycle.

Hyperinflation becomes visible when there is an unchecked increase in the money supply, as seen during hyperinflation in Zimbabwe recently, usually accompanied by a widespread unwillingness on the part of the local population to hold the hyperinflationary money for more than the time needed to trade it for something non-monetary to avoid further loss of real value. Hyperinflation is a highly abnormal situation and is often associated with wars or their aftermath, currency meltdowns, political or social upheavals, or aggressive bidding on currency exchanges.

Phillip Cagan, in his book entitled *The Monetary Dynamics of Hyperinflation*, widely regarded as the first serious study of hyperinflation and its effects, defined hyperinflation as a monthly inflation rate of at least 50 per cent. International Accounting Standard (IAS) establishes special accounting rules for use in hyperinflationary environments, and lists the following four factors which can trigger application of these rules:

1. People prefer to keep their wealth in non-monetary assets or in a relatively stable foreign currency. The amounts of local currency held are immediately invested to maintain purchasing power.
2. People regard monetary amounts not in terms of the local currency but in terms of a relatively stable foreign currency. Prices may be quoted in that foreign currency.
3. Sales and purchases on credit take place at prices that are increased by an amount that will compensate for the expected loss of purchasing power during the credit period, even if the period is short.
4. Interest rates, wages and prices are linked to a price index and the cumulative inflation rate over three years approaches, or exceeds 100 per cent.

Hyperinflation wipes out the purchasing power of private and public savings, distorts the economy in favour of extreme consumption and hoarding of real assets, causes the monetary base, whether specie or hard currency, to flee the country, and makes the afflicted area "anathema to investment". Drastic measures are taken to address hyperinflation, which includes imposing the shock therapy of slashing government expenditures or altering the currency basis. An example was the dollarization in Ecuador, initiated in September 2000 in response to a massive 75 per cent loss of value of the Sucre currency in early January 2000.

The aftermath of hyperinflation is equally complex. Since hyperinflation always brings turmoil and traumatic experiences for the country, its people and economy which endure it, the government enacts policies to prevent its recurrence. Often this means making the central bank very aggressive about maintaining price stability, as was the case with the German Bundesbank, or moving to some hard basis of currency such as a currency board. Many governments, in such stiuations, have enacted extremely stiff wage and price controls in the wake of hyperinflation but this does not prevent further inflating of the money supply by its central bank, and invariably leads to widespread shortages of consumer goods if the controls are rigidly enforced.

Inflation has often been called "a regressive consumption tax", but less overt than levied taxes and therefore harder to understand by ordinary citizens. It has also been argued hat inflation can obscure quantitative assessments of the true cost of living, as price indices only look at data in retrospect. Monetary inflation can become hyperinflation if monetary authorities fail to fund increasing government expenses from taxes, government debt, cost cutting, or by other means, because of any of the reasons that follow: (i) During the time between recording or levying taxable transactions and collecting the taxes due, the value of the taxes collected falls in real value to a small fraction of the original taxes receivable; (ii) Government debt issues fail to find buyers except at very deep discounts; or (iii) A combination of the above.

Effect on Efficiency in Allocation of Sources

A change in the supply or demand for a commodity usually causes its relative price to change, signaling to buyers and sellers that they should re-allocate resources in response to the new market conditions and they are able to do so when fluctuation in price is not frequent, and thus achieve what is termed as allocative efficiency. But when prices are constantly changing due to inflation, price changes due to genuine relative price signals are hard to distinguish from price changes due to general inflation, and hence, agents are slow to respond to them. This results in a loss of allocative efficiency.

Shoe Leather Cost High Inflation Effect

It is believed that inflation makes people spend more time in knowing about the prices of goods and services as well as about the securities where they can put their money for better returns to negate the effect of inflation on their means. Inflation increases the opportunity cost of holding cash balances and can induce people to hold a greater portion of their assets in interest paying accounts. In times of high inflation, people usually do not prefer to spend money on productive activities, and tend to invest rather on inflation-hedging activities.[23] However, since cash is still needed in order to carry out transactions, this means that more trips to the bank are necessary in order to make withdrawals, proverbially wearing out the "shoe leather" with each trip. This is known as shoe leather cost high inflation effect.

Menu Costs Effect

With high inflation, particularly where prices of goods and services change frequently, the firms have to change their prices often in order to keep up with economy-wide changes. But changing prices often is itself a costly activity whether explicitly, as with the need to print new menus, or implicitly with changes in the prices of inputs. The problem is not limited to changing the menus as the term seems to suggest. Where projects involving high expenditure are undertaken, changes in prices of goods and services to be used may make the project unprofitable or even unviable if allotment of funds is not increased commensurately. If financial resources are limited, it may create problems like delay, or compromise on the quality of inputs being used, with dangerous consequences.

Business Cycles

The most damaging effect of inflation, according to the Austrian Business Cycle Theory, is that it sets off the business cycle. Thorsten Polleit, an Austrian economist, believes that artificially low interest rates and the associated increase in the money supply lead to reckless, speculative borrowing, resulting in the clusters of malinvestments, which eventually have to be liquidated as they become unsustainable.[24] Businesses tend to overproduce during times of inflation as prices of goods are higher. Going for borrowing more money from banks as interest rates are low, traders often indulge in overtrading. This may lead to overheating of the economy, which may follow a period of slackness. Such business cycles are not good for the sustained and steady growth of the economy, because it is not easy to change policies within a short time according to the situation. Implementing the existing policies without making changes as per demands of the situation also does not bring the desired results. Thus, the business cycles brought by inflation do not provide conducive environment for framing long-term policies of growth like Five-Year Plans in India.

Positive Effects of Inflation

Inflation is often decried as a situation which is harmful and a cause of whole lot of negative effects on the country, its economy and individuals. It may be true only to some extent, because inflation is neither as dangerous and damaging as it is often stated to be, nor without positive effects. Some important effects of inflation are discussed below.

Labour Market Adjustments

The economists who belong to the Keynesians school of economics believe that nominal wages are slow to adjust downwards. This can lead to prolonged disequilibrium and high unemployment in the labour market. Since inflation would lower the real wage if nominal wages are kept constant, these economists argue that some inflation is good for the economy, as it would allow labour markets to reach equilibrium faster.

Room to Maneuver

The main tools for controlling the money supply include the ability to set the discount rate, i.e. the rate at which banks borrow from the central bank like RBI in case of India, and open market operations, which can be described as the central bank's interventions into the bonds market with the purpose of affecting the nominal interest rate. If an economy finds itself in a recession with already low, or even zero nominal interest rates (as was seen in 2008-09 and 2009-10 in most parts of the world), then the bank cannot cut these rates further (since negative nominal interest rates are impossible) in order to stimulate the economy, and this situation is known as liquidity trap. A moderate level of inflation helps in ensuring that nominal interest rates stay sufficiently above zero so that the central bank can cut the nominal interest rate in case there is need to do so.

Mundell-Tobin Effect

Robert Mundell, Professor of Economics at Columbia University and the recipient of Nobel Prize in Economics in 1999, noted that moderate inflation would induce savers to substitute lending for some money holding as a means to finance future spending. That substitution would cause market clearing real interest rates to fall.[25] The lower real rate of interest would induce more borrowing to finance investment. Another American Nobel laureate, James Tobin, who served on the Council of Economics and the Board of Governors of the Federal Reserve System, taught at Harvard and Yale universities and developed the ideas of Keynesian economics, noted that such inflation would make businesses to substitute investment in physical capital such as plant, equipment, and inventories, for money balances in their asset portfolios. That substitution would mean choosing the making of investments with lower rates of real return. It may be noted that the rates of return are lower because the investments with higher rates of return were already being made before.[26] The two related effects combined are known as the Mundell-Tobin effect. Unless the economy is already overinvesting according to models of economic growth theory, that extra investment resulting from the effect would remain positive.

Instability with Deflation

Deflation, according to Prof. Paul Einzig, is a state of disequilibrium in which, a concentration of purchasing power tends to cause, or is the effect of, a decline of the price level. Thus, deflation is the state of declining prices when the output by productive agents is increasing relative to the money income. Deflation arises when the total expenditure of the community falls short of the value of output at the existing prices. As such, the the value of money goes up and the prices fall. S.C. Tsaing, an emeritus professor at Cornell University, Ithaca, New York, and the main architect of Taiwan's economic development, noted that once substantial deflation is expected, two important effects will appear—both a result of money holding substituting for lending as a vehicle for saving.[27] The continually falling prices and the resulting incentive to hoard money will cause instability resulting from the likely increasing fear that while money held grows in value, the value of such money is at risk, as people realize that a movement to trade those money hoards for real goods and assets will quickly drive the prices up. The movement to spend large amount of money "once started would become a tremendous avalanche, which could rampage for a long time before it would spend itself".[28] Thus, a regime of long-term deflation is likely to be interrupted by periodic spikes of rapid inflation, causing real economic disruptions with adverse consequences. Moderate and stable inflation on the other hand would avoid such a see-sawing of price movements and let the economy function rather smoothly.

Deflation Brings Financial Market Inefficiency

The other effect noted by Tsaing is that in conditions of deflation when people holding money substitute such money for lending in financial markets, the role of those markets in channeling savings into investment is undermined. With nominal interest rates driven to zero, or near zero level, from the competition with a high return money asset, there would be no price mechanism in whatever is left of those markets. With financial markets effectively put down, the remaining goods and physical asset prices would move in perverse directions. For instance, an increased desire to save could not push interest rates further down (and thereby stimulate investment), but would instead cause additional money hoarding, driving consumer prices further down and making investment in consumer goods production less attractive. On the other hand, moderate inflation, once its expectation is incorporated into nominal interest rates, gives those interest rates room to go both up and down in response to shifting investment opportunities, or savers' preferences, and is thus instrumental in allowing financial markets to function in a more normal fashion.

Effects of Inflation

Though inflation implies a general rise in the price level, this rise is not uniform throughout the economy. If the rate of increase in the prices of goods and services were uniform in all sectors of the economy, the relative position of the various earning groups would remain unchanged and as such, the economic effects of inflation would be neutral. But in reality, during the inflationary process, the prices of different goods and services rise at different rates. This results in a change in the pattern of income distribution in the community which is the source of many evil effects normally attributed to inflation.

Inflation resulting from excess demand of the government in a state of national emergency, as during a war, amounts to a forced levy on the community and helps in the mobilisation of resources to meet the emergency by restricting civilian consumptions. From this special point of view, inflation is useful. In addition to this, it is claimed that inflation benefits two important classes of people in the community who form the backbone of the nation's economy, viz. (i) farmers and (ii) entrepreneurs. It can easily be observed that both these classes of people gain from a rise in prices because they are primarily a debtor class. In an inflationary period, repayment of debt becomes easier because the real burden of debt falls with the rise in prices of goods and services. Farmers gain partly because the products which they sell are highly inflation-sensitive and partly because the costs which they incur in connection with their productive operations such as interest charges, taxes, wages, etc. rise only to a small extent, at least in the early stages of inflation, in comparison with the prices of the product which they offer for sale. Businessmen gain from a similar lagging of costs behind prices. They also gain from an appreciation in the value of their inventories. It is claimed that an increase in the profits of the entrepreneurial class stimulates capital formation, helps in the drawing up of idle resources for economic utilisation and in expanding production to the maximum capacity of the economy.

Though the advantages mentioned above have some validity in the short period, yet it cannot be disputed that ultimately inflation has harmful effects on the economy. The very forces which are helpful in stimulating capital formation start retarding investment after a stage is reached. A study[29] conducted by an economist of the International Monetary Fund points out that while no definite conclusions can be drawn, the evidence available broadly indicates that among the underdeveloped countries the rate of growth of the economy was higher when the rate of inflation was lower. In his study of the course of inflation in Europe in the 1920s, Professor Nurkse points out that the "success of inflation as an instrument of capital formation depends largely on the degree to which rise in prices is unforeseen and unexpected".[30] When a further rise in prices is expected and seems certain, velocity of circulation of money rises, saving gives place to dissaving and inflation loses its power of stimulating investment. Thereafter, there is cumulative process of inflation.

The declining value of the money and the failure of the wage level to adjust itself to the price level leaves the workers with a sense of frustration which impairs their incentives to work more with a view to earn more. Declining value of money also impairs the incentives to save and places a premium on improvidence and careless spending. Continued inflation or the knowledge that the government budgetary or monetary policy would maintain inflationary forces for long drives out capital from the country as happened in France and Germany at the end of the First World War. Thus, beyond a certain stage, inflation not only obstructs domestic capital accumulation but also drives available capital out of the country. Nor is the attitude and behaviour of the entrepreneurial class in an inflationary period favourable to increased production. Cost accounting which is an important instrument of measuring efficiency, loses its meaning, when the value of money changes very frequently. There is a tendency to employ business skill and efficiency for speculative purposes rather than for productive purposes. The chances of earning windfall profits out of the rapidly rising prices of existing supplies encourage business community to indulge in hoarding and helps in the growth of black markets. When producers do not find much difficulty in transferring higher costs on to consumers, they have a tendency to be wasteful and lethargic. The transfer of income from the middle and lower income groups to higher income groups resulting from inflation leads to a decline in the aggregate consumption and thus generates instability.

During an inflationary period, the revenues of government fail to respond to the growing responsibilities of the state. The result is the starvation of developmental services like public works, education and public health, on which depends largely the growth and prosperity of the national economy.

Inflation affects different classes of society against the sound maxims of social justice. Comparing inflation to robbery, C.N. Vakil states, "Both deprive the victim of some possession with the difference that the robber is visible, inflation is invisible; the robber's victim may be one or a few at a time, the victims of inflation are the whole nation; the robber may be dragged to a court of law, inflation is legal."[31]

The people worst hit by inflation are those who are least able to protect themselves. Inflation causes hardships to all who live on fixed incomes, e.g. pensioners, widows, teachers, civil servants, factory workers, etc. Among the workers, the worst sufferers are those who are ill-organised. Long and sustained inflation corrupts the foundations of society. It erodes savings and undermines the provision for sickness, education and old age. It undermines the incentive for hard work and thrift. The investors in equities gain while those who invest in fixed interest yielding bonds are adversely affected. Since most of the middle class investors choose fixed interest bearing securities, insurance and saving accounts, inflation adversely affects the small investors. Angell describes the sufferings of the middle class during the post-war German inflation as follows: "The group which suffered most from the inflation, however, was the group which was also least able to defend itself; the middle classes among the town-dwellers...composed largely of people with small fixed incomes, such as salaried officials and clerks, recipients of pensions, and little investors living on interest and rent of whom the latter group were hit especially hard by the government control of city rentals—they were precisely the group most exposed to the evil consequences of currency depreciation, while they lacked both the knowledge and the opportunity to combat it."[32] Kemmerer makes similar observations about the impact of inflation on the middle class. "The middle class, however, which by hard work and thrift has built up a fund of savings to educate its children and to provide a livelihood for times of sickness and for old age, finds itself in a desperate situation in a time of serious inflation. The cost of living rises disproportionately to income; savings are wiped out; and hard work, independence, and thrift seem to be false gods. Under such conditions the middle class is all too often overwhelmed by a sense of futility and desperation."[33] Thus, the people worst hit by inflation are those belonging to the middle class who form the backbone of modern democracy. The hyperinflation in Germany, Austria, Poland and France after the First World War completely ruined the middle class.

Though businessmen, debtors and producers gain from continuously rising prices, creditors are hit hard. The creditors are affected adversely because the purchasing power of the money which is returned to them is much lower than that of the money which they had lent.

Although slowly rising prices stimulate economic activity and increase the volume of employment, yet if they start rising fast, they may lead to depression and cause widespread unemployment. To cite William McChesney Martin Jr., "If inflation is allowed to pursue its course it feeds upon itself in such a way that, when the inevitable correction finally comes, unemployment will be that much worse. It should not be difficult to see how inflation leads to unemployment. The danger becomes manifest when, as costs go up, it becomes increasingly hard to pass those costs along to the customer in the form of price increases, and it becomes increasingly easy to misjudge or miscalculate the market. Then for the first time volume dips, there is price-profit squeeze, and, at some point the profit-squeeze leads to a cutback in investment, income and production. The cutback in production leads to a cutback in employment."

Inflation makes business planning and long-term investment risky. It upsets calculations about depreciation costs and profits and thereby poses a threat to the solvency and sound growth of business. It deprives the economy of the benefits of a stable unit of account and store of value. It raises interest rates and creates a chaos in the money market. It causes a disequilibrium in the balance of payments.

Inflation lowers the moral standards of the people, particularly of business community and government officials. Black market, bribery and corruption become rampant. When people are robbed of their savings accumulated through hard work, they lose all confidence in the government. Andrew D. While depicts the impact of inflation on public morale at the time of fiat money inflation in France during the French Revolution as follows: "...with such masses of money and with such uncertainty as to its future value, the ordinary motives for saving and care are diminished, and a loose luxury spreads throughout the country. A still worse out-growth was the increase of speculation and gambling. In the leading French cities now arose a luxury and licence which was a greater evil than the plundering that ministered to it. In the country the gambling spirit spread more and more.... Nor was this reckless and corrupt spirit confined to businessmen; it began to break out in official circles, and public men who a few years before, had been thought above all possibility of taint became luxurious, reckless, cynical and finally corrupt."[34]

A severe inflation not only disrupts the economy of the country but also sometimes leads to social and political upheavals. The hyperinflation in Germany was one of the important factors which led to the fall of Dr. Cuno's liberal government and coming into power of Hitler. Constantino Bresciani Turroni beautifully describes the social and political consequences of inflation as follows: "The depreciation of the mark of 1914-23...is one of the outstanding episodes in the history of the twentieth century. It was the most colossal thing of its kind in history; and next probably to the Great War itself, it must bear responsibility for many of the political and economic difficulties of our generation. It destroyed the wealth of the more solid elements in German society; and it left behind a moral and economic disequilibrium, apt breading ground for the disasters which have followed. Hitler is the foster-child of the inflation. The financial convulsions of the great depression were, in part at least, the product of the distortions of the system of international borrowing and lending to which its ravages had given rise. If we are to understand correctly the present position of Europe, we must not neglect the study of the great German inflation. If we are to plan for greater stability in the future, we must learn to avoid the mistakes from which it sprang."[35]

Anti-inflationary Measures

The measures for controlling inflation can be divided into three broad categories: (i) monetary measures, (ii) fiscal measures, and (iii) direct controls and other measures.

Monetary Measures

The central bank of the country can curb inflation by restricting the supply of money and credit with the help of three important weapons available to it, viz. (i) bank rate policy, (ii) open market operations and (iii) varying the reserve requirements of the member banks. Monetary measures, however, are not very effective in the developing countries which do not have a well-developed and integrated money market. In such countries, selective credit control is preferable to the general credit control. Care should be taken that the credit control measures do not restrict the supply of credit for development projects.

Not to talk of developing countries, monetary policy has not been very effective in curbing inflation even in advanced countries. Prof. Hansen assigns monetary policy only a secondary role in controlling inflation. It cannot be the primary measure. No doubt, a sufficiently sharp reduction in the supply of money may quickly end inflation. But stopping an inflationary development simply by reducing the quantity of money may involve dangerous consequences. To cite Hansen, "Moderately used, monetary policy courts the failure of ineffectiveness; pushed to the needed fanatical extremes, it courts disaster."[36]

Fiscal Measures

The limitations of monetary measures make it important to make use of fiscal measures to curb inflation. Fiscal measures refer to taxation, government spending and public borrowing. Government should try to mop up through taxation as much purchasing power as possible without adverse effects on incentives to enterprise and invest. In developing countries, there exists considerable evasion of taxes. Measures should be taken to check this evasion.

Today, the government accounts for a considerable portion of the total expenditure. It should cut down all its unnecessary and wasteful expenditure and try to work in the most economical manner.

Private savings have a strong disinflationary effect. The government should take measures to promote private savings. A strong savings drive reduces the spendable incomes of the people without involving harmful effects of the type associated with higher taxation. Further, public debt should be managed in such a manner that the supply of money in the country is controlled. The government should avoid paying back any of its past loans during inflationary periods so as to prevent an increase in the circulation of money.

Voluntary saving schemes may, however, be of limited success, particularly among poor classes who may not be able to avoid the temptation of spending their increased incomes on goods which they could not afford to buy for long. Keynes, therefore, suggested a programme of compulsory saving like "deferred pay" or "forced savings" to control inflation. "Deferred pay" implies that a part of the pay of the workers is credited to their savings account and would not be available for spending so long as the inflation lasts. Such compulsory saving schemes are expedient during war-time, or during post-war hyperinflation, but are not practicable in peace time, particularly in democratic societies.

Direct Controls and Other Measures

Many countries have resorted to price control and rationing for checking a rise in prices, particularly in case of essential commodities. Rationing and price control, however, have not been very effective in the developing countries because of a lack of competent and honest machinery to administer these. These have often led to the disappearance of goods from the market, black marketing, bribery and corruption. Keynes objects to price control on the ground that it fails to bring about equilibrium between purchasing power and available output.[37] Further, it is also detrimental to the consumer's sovereignty, freedom and welfare. Prof. Kurihara observes that when administrative difficulties in enforcing price control and legal restrictions against black marketing are considered, price control becomes dim by the side of monetary-fiscal policy.[38] Keynes also objects to rationing because it "involves a great deal of waste, both of resources and of enjoyment".[39] Kurihara, however, suggests that "a sensible progress of rationing should aim at diverting consumption from particular articles whose supply is below normal rather than at controlling aggregate consumption".[40]

Measures should be taken to expand the production of necessary goods at the expense of luxury goods because a shortage of the former type of goods raises the prices much more rapidly than a shortage of the latter type of goods.

Control of wages has often been suggested to check a wage-price spiral. During galloping inflation it may be necessary to apply a wage-profit freeze. Control of wages and profits keeps down disposable income and hence, the level of effective demand for goods and services.

Efforts should be made to obtain as much foreign capital as possible. Investment financed by foreign capital is less inflationary.

In some cases, relaxation of restrictions on imports may lighten inflationary pressures by increasing the supply of essential goods available in the country. Similar effects may be obtained by a curtailment of exports. But increase in imports and curtailment of exports are possible only if the country is having a very easy balance of payments position.

Every effort should be made to increase production. Preference should be given to investment in those projects which start yielding production earlier.

It is now widely believed that inflation can easily be controlled in the initial stages but when it goes beyond a certain stage, it assumes such dimensions that it becomes very difficult to control it. Hyperinflation, for instance, can be removed only by replacing the old currency by a new currency.

Inflation is a hydra-headed monster and should be fought with many weapons. Dependence on a single measure may not help much in curbing inflation.

Conclusion

It is quite clear that the effects of inflation on an economy are manifold and can be positive as well as negative. Negative effects of inflation include a decrease in the real value of money and other monetary items over time, uncertainty about future inflation which may discourage investment and saving, or it may lead to reductions in investment of productive capital and increase savings in non-producing assets, e.g. selling stocks and buying gold. This can reduce overall economic productivity rates due to shortage of capital. High inflation may lead to shortages of goods if consumers begin hoarding out of concern that prices will increase in the future. Positive effects include a mitigation of economic recession, and debt relief by reducing the real level of debt.

High inflation is caused by an excessive growth of the money supply. Low or moderate inflation may be attributed to fluctuations in real demand for goods and services, or changes in available supplies such as during scarcities, as well as to growth in the money supply. A long sustained period of inflation is caused by money supply growing faster than the rate of economic growth. Most mainstream economists favour a low and steady rate of inflation, which is said to reduce the severity of economic recessions by enabling the labour market to adjust more quickly in a downturn, and reduce the risk of a liquidity trap. The task of keeping the rate of inflation low and stable usually rests with monetary authorities including the central banks that control the size of the money supply through the setting of interest rates, open market operations, and the setting of banking reserve requirements. However, there are some external causes and bottlenecks which cannot be easily addressed. Also, the policy actions have some side effects which prove harmful for growth. For example, raising the interest rates to control money supply to bring down inflation rates may be detrimental to industrial growth. Thus, inflation trends have to be watched carefully and remedial measures to keep it under acceptable levels need to be taken after taking into account their short- and long-term effects.

Notes

1. Emmanuel I.S. Ajuzie et al., "Import Response and Inflationary Pressures in the New Economy: The Quality Theory of Money Revisited", *Journal of Business Quantity and Economic Research*, May 2008; Vol. 6, No. 5.
2. http://www.answers.com/topic/quantity-theory-of-money#ixzz1FEsII CQb
3. Jean-Qaude Trichat, "Introductor Statement." Federal Reserve Board's Semiannual Monetary Policy Report to the Congress. July 2004.
4. Robert J. Gordon (1988), *Macroeconomics: Theory and Policy* (2nd ed.), McGraw Hill.
5. Arthur O'Sullivan and Steven M. Sheffrin (2003), *Economics: Principles in Action*, Addison Wesley Longman, p. 341.
6. David T. Coe, *National Wages: The Nairu and Wage Flexibility*. (http://www.mufad.org/index2.php?option=cin_dicynebtiftasj=dic).
7. Paul Lagassé (2000), "Monetarism", *The Columbia Encyclopedia* (6th ed.). New York: Columbia University Press.
8. Milton Friedman (1963), *A Monetary History of the United States 1867-1960*.
9. W.A.L. Coulborn, *A Discussion of Money*, p. 159.
10. J.M. Keynes, *The General Theory of Employment, Interest and Money* (London, 1936), p. 296.
11. Maurice Dobb, *Some Aspects of Economic Development*, p. 48.
12. Nicholas Kaldor, 'Economic Growth and Problem of Inflation", *Economica*, 1959.

13. W.A. Lewis, *The Theory of Economic Growth.*
14. Milton Friedman, *Inflations—Causes and Consequences* (Bombay, 1963), p. 17.
15. *Ibid.*, p. 13.
16. Ragnar Nurkse, *League of Nations: Course and Control of Infation,* p. 13.
17. Indian Merchants Chamber, *Inflation in a Developing Economy,* 1961, p. 82.
18. Also see section on Deficit Financing and Economic Development in the Chapter on Deficit Financing.
19. Timothy Taylor (2008), *Principles of Economics.* Freeload Press.
20. Unit Gucenme and Aylin Poroy Arsoy, "Changes in Financial Reporting in Turkey: Historical Development of Inflation Accounting 1960-2005".
21. Gorge Bulkley, "Personal Savings and Anticipated Inflation", *The Economic Journal* (91) 261: pp. 124-35.
22. Arthur O'Sullivan and Steven M. Sheffrin (2003), *Economics Principles in Action.* Pearson Prentice Hall: pp. 341, 444.
23. Michael R. Pakko, "Shoe-Leather Cost of Inflation and Policy Credibility". *Review*: November/December 1998.
24. Thornsten Polleit, "Inflation is a Policy that cannot Last." (http://mises.org/story/2901), Mises Institute.
25. James Mundel, "Inflation and Real Interest", *Journal of Political Economy,* LXXI.
26. James Tobin, "Money and Economic Growth", *Economictrice,* V. 33 (1965), pp. 671-84.
27. S.C. Tsaing, "A Critical Note on the Optimum Supply of Money", *Journal of Money, Credit and Banking* (1969), pp. 266-80.
28. *Ibid.*, p. 274.
29. U. Tun Wai (1959), "The Relation between Inflation and Economic Development", *International Monetary Fund Staff Papers,* October, p. 302.
30. League of Nations (1947), *Course and Control of Inflation,* p. 6.
31. C.N. Vakil, *Financial Burden of War on India.*
32. J.W. Angell (1929), *The Recovery of Germany* (New Haven), p. 38.
33. Edwin Walter Kemmerer, *The ABC of Inflation,* p. 94.
34. Andrew D. While, *Flat Money Inflation in France,* pp. 27-28.

35. Constantino Bresciani, *The Economics of Inflation*, p. 5.
36. A.H. Hansen, *Monetary Theory and Fiscal Policy* (New York, 1949), p. 163.
37. J.M. Keynes, *How to Pay for the War*, p. 57.
38. Kenneth K. Kurihara (1956), *Monetary Theory and Public Policy* (London), p. 100.
39. Keynes, *op. cit.*, pp. 51-54.
40. Kurihara, *op. cit.*, p. 101.

3

Inflation: A Global Phenomenon

Inflation is not limited to any single country or region, but is a global phenomenon. However, global inflation varies largely, owing to the trend components of inflation as well as due to the fluctuations arising in the frequencies of the commercial cycles. Moreover, the impact of global inflation varies in different countries across the world. For example, a country like Germany which is dedicated towards stabilization of prices is less troubled by inflation compared to nations like Italy which have feeble inflation discipline.

Inflation and Globalization

While some economists say that globalization encourages inflation, few others express opinion on the contrary. According to the former, globalization results in trade expansion which might lead to domestic inflation. This happens because trade expansion depends to a large extent on cost of goods, which are imported. Another factor is the competitive pressure brought forth by globalization. It results in utilization of resources in economies of foreign countries which, in turn, could influence domestic inflation. Economists who hold the latter viewpoint feel that globalization does not affect the rate of inflation as the changes brought forth by globalization affect relative costs of services and goods.

In the era of globalization, practically even single-country firms have to contend with both the positive and negative effects of offshore outsourcing, the influx of cheap products from producer countries, the importation and use of raw materials from resource provider countries, or even the glut in the supply of money in consumer countries. In other words, globalisation poses a peculiar situation. While unemployment may increase due to outsourcing of certain jobs to low-wage countries, goods can be bought more cheaply that are imported from countries like China. In turn, Chinese firms that profit from the exportation of goods to a consumer country like the US plow back their profits into the US economic system as investments. Thus, a consumer country like the US may have more money to spend on cheaper goods, and yet its workforce may be significantly reduced with unemployment. This workforce is the same consumer that fuels the US economic system. Moreover, since most jobs are outsourced to low-wage countries, the purchasing power of the US consumer gets greatly diminished. As a result, the US economy may have too much money on its hands and yet so many consumers who can no longer afford to spend it.

Causes of Global Inflation

Global inflation may be linked to oil, real or monetary shock or a combination of these and perhaps other shocks. Common factors that affect inflation across countries are industrial production, nominal wages, short-term interest rates, long-term interest rates, the yield curve, and nominal and real money. Although these factors are not exhaustive, these are the most likely determinants of inflation. Money and the short-term interest rates are associated with monetary policy, either as instruments or as operating targets. The long-term interest rate is particularly interesting given that it reflects long-run inflation expectations. Wage inflation is a central link in propagating inflation shocks into persistent changes. Finally, industrial production is a factor that is the most readily available indicator of the business cycle.[1]

Indicators of the fiscal discipline are not very successful in forecasting global inflation. Two variables, oil and commodity price, tend to fluctuate significantly and their sign is not always positive. When measured at the global level, real and monetary determinants are sensitive to global inflation. The response of global inflation to both real determinants (at short horizons) and monetary determinants (at longer horizons) invite central banks to monitor both categories of inflation determinants. This surveillance, however, should be done not only at the level of countries, but also more globally to account for the spill over of these determinants across countries.

Monetary and financial conditions may spill over across countries, but in theory such spill over is less likely when exchange rates are floating. Since monetary policy concepts are effectively spreading among central banks, similar monetary policy strategies, either good or bad, dominate for a majority of countries.

Global inflation responds to commodity prices, the global business cycle and the growth of the global liquidity. This has two important policy implications. First, given the importance of global inflation for local inflation, the nature of global inflation brings support to the monetary policy strategies that give importance both to real and monetary developments in their assessment of inflationary pressures. Second, there may be a powerful externality between country inflation records. Even if some countries were clearly less affected by global inflation than others, none, not even Switzerland, can claim to have been completely immune from global inflation shocks.

At present, the surging prices of many raw materials, agricultural produce, and oil are the main cause of higher inflation across the globe. They are also related, at least in part, to structural changes in the global economy. The world economy is increasingly powered by countries such as China and India, whose growth is far more energy- and commodity-intensive than that of rich countries. Since 2001, China has accounted for about half of the increase in the world's demand for metals and almost two-fifths of the increase in oil demand. The surge in raw material prices in recent years reflects the fact that few foresaw the pace of emerging-market growth.

A similar view was expressed at the 2011 G20 Summit in Davos, where top global CEOs listed out potential dangers that ranged from asset bubbles in emerging economies to soaring global commodity prices and large sovereign debt problems in Europe. Domnic Barton, worldwide MD of consulting firm McKinsey & Co. said that massive urbanisation in emerging markets like China, India, Indonesia and Brazil is driving a lot of changes. It becomes hard to pick where the next bubble is when there is such unlimited growth.[2]

Many economists put part of the blame for regional imbalances on China, which tightly controls the yuan's movements. Some developing countries in turn blame ultraloose monetary policy in the developed world which prompts a surge in capital inflows into higher-yielding emerging nations.

Global Inflation and Oil Prices

Despite fluctuations, the international prices of oil have remained high and rising. For example, the prices of the two varieties of crude oil that India imports have moved from less than $25 in May 2003 to close to or well above $100 in a span of few years. Moreover, since 2006, nominal oil prices having risen further at rates much higher than the average level of prices. Underlying this buoyancy in prices is the closing gap between global petroleum demand and supply at a time when the spare capacity is more or less fully utilised. Though much of the increase in demand is from China, it is affecting stockpiles everywhere. This trend, combined with the turmoil in the Middle-East due to an array of events, has created a situation where any destabilising influence such as political uncertainty and attacks on the oil supply chain in Nigeria triggers a sharp rise in prices.

Another reason for increase in oil prices is the involvement of speculators. Since 2004, and especially after the global financial crisis of 2008-09, energy markets have attracted substantial financial investor interest. Due to the worldwide decline in stock markets as well as the value of the dollar, investors have moved into speculative investments in commodities in general and oil in particular. The Organisation of the Petroleum Exporting Countries (OPEC), which is normally held responsible for all oil price increases, has repeatedly asserted that oil has crossed the $100-a-barrel mark not because of a shortage of supply but because of financial speculation.

Global Inflation and Commodity Prices

A look at the FAO annual food price indices shows the extent to which the prices of commodities have risen since 1990. In fact, globally the prices of many basic commodities have been rising faster than they ever did during the last three decades. It may be argued that these developments are largely demand driven, being the result of several years of rapid global growth and the voracious demand from some fast-growing countries such as China. Certainly, there is some element of truth in this. But this is not the only cause of commodity price inflation and there are other, more worrying tendencies in operation, that suggest that the global inflationary process has other factors pushing it which will not be so easily controlled.

Table 3.1: Annual Food Price Indices (2002-2004=100)

Date	Food Price Index	Meat Price Index	Dairy Price Index	Cereals Price Index	Oils Price Index	Sugar Price Index
1990	105.4	124.0	74.8	97.6	74.0	178.1
1991	103.6	125.4	79.6	96.9	79.1	127.2
1992	108.4	125.2	95.4	102.3	84.3	128.5
1993	104.6	118.1	84.6	99.5	86.0	142.2
1994	110.5	115.0	82.3	104.5	113.4	171.8
1995	123.2	118.4	109.6	119.4	125.0	188.5
1996	129.1	128.4	109.4	140.7	111.2	169.7
1997	118.4	123.2	105.1	112.1	112.5	161.4
1998	107.1	103.2	99.1	99.8	129.9	126.6
1999	92.3	97.8	86.3	90.2	91.6	89.0
2000	90.2	95.8	95.4	84.5	67.8	116.1
2001	93.3	96.5	107.1	86.2	67.6	122.6
2002	89.9	89.5	82.2	94.6	87.0	97.8
2003	97.7	96.8	95.1	98.1	100.8	100.6
2004	112.4	113.7	122.6	107.4	112.2	101.7
2005	117.3	120.1	135.4	103.4	103.6	140.3
2006	126.5	118.5	128.0	121.5	112.0	209.6
2007	158.6	125.1	212.4	166.8	169.1	143.0
2008	199.6	153.2	219.6	237.9	225.4	181.6
2009	156.8	132.9	141.6	173.7	150.0	257.3
2010	185.1	152.1	200.4	182.6	193.0	302.0
2011	230.7	165.9	221.3	244.8	277.7	420.2

Source: FAO

In the case of food, although it is certainly true that rising incomes in Asia and other parts of the developing world have led to increased demand, there are five major aspects affecting supply conditions.[3] First, high oil prices affect agricultural costs directly because of the significance of energy as an input in the cultivation process through fertiliser and irrigation costs as well as in transportation of food. The reduction in protection and subsidies on agriculture by governments across the world also directly translate into higher costs of cultivation, and therefore higher prices of output.

Second, the promotion of bio-fuels as an alternative to petroleum, especially in the US, Europe, Brazil and elsewhere has led to significant shifts in acreage as well as use of certain grains. For example, in 2006 the US diverted more than 20 per cent of its maize production to the production of ethanol; Brazil used half of its sugarcane production to make bio-fuel, and the European Union used the greater part of its vegetable oil production as well as imported vegetable oils, to make bio-fuel. This has naturally reduced the available land for producing food, thus resulting in higher food prices.

Third, changes in market structure have resulted in a small number of agribusiness companies worldwide controlling all aspects of cultivation and distribution, from supplying inputs to farmers to buying crops and even in some cases to retail food distribution. This has led to an increase in marketing margins as well as greater speculation in food, with more centralized storage. Thus, the rising food prices do not automatically benefit farmers.

Fourth, there are several issues that are largely ignored by policymakers in most countries in spite of being highlighted by analysts. These include the prolonged agrarian crisis in many parts of the developing world; the shifts in acreage from food crops to cash crops relying on purchased inputs; the excessive use of groundwater and inadequate attention to preserving or regenerating land and soil quality; the lack of attention to relevant agricultural research and extension; the overuse of chemical inputs that have long-run implications for both safety and productivity; the ecological implications of both pollution and climate change, including desertification and loss of cultivable land.

Finally, commodity speculation is increasingly emerging as an important alternative investment market. It has also affected the minerals and metals sector. This has been further fueled by the growing imbalance between world supply and demand.

Inflation and Economic Growth

Inflation and economic growth are parallel lines and the twain can never meet. Inflation reduces the value of money and makes it difficult for the common people. It affects all sectors of an economy, the consumer price index as well as the gross domestic product. It adversely effects investment, interest rates, exchange rates, employment, stocks, and various fiscal and monetary policies.

In practice, however, low inflation rate and an upward economic growth is never possible. Low inflation rate leads to slow economic growth. Whenever money is in excess, there is bidding by the consumers due to which the costs of goods escalate. For developing countries, inflation remains a big issue. In the growth versus inflation debate, it would not necessarily be worthwhile to sacrifice some growth now for better growth in the future. Pressures on domestic demand growth can be removed by rebalancing in the deficit economies towards external demand.

IMF on Inflation

In the midst of price increases across Asia, the International Monetary Fund (IMF) has urged policymakers to let their currencies rise to address accelerating inflation. The depth of concern at the IMF can be understood as the curve of inflation in the world's fastest-growing region could threaten the global recovery.

According to the IMF, inflation has taken hold in some of Asia's high-speed economies as extreme weather conditions and supply constraints drive food, oil and commodity prices higher, prompting central banks to tighten policy. There are increasing signs of inflation because of wider structural economic shifts, not just one-off volatility; something that requires broader reforms in order to contain price pressures. Monetary policy alone will not be enough to contain these price pressures and necessitate exchange-rate reforms.[4]

The IMF sees flexibility and appreciation of many currencies in Asia as part of the process of normalizing the policy stance. In the words of Anoop Singh, IMF's Asia Chief, some governments are reluctant to allow their exchange rates to float freely, in order to protect their exporters. He adds that monetary policy cannot be effective as long as exchange rates remain tightly controlled.[5] In the same vein, IMF's first deputy MD John Lipsky opines that export ban is a sign of a system that is not working well and is not serving the needs of all the people.[6] Instead, better ways of fixing the problem should be found through alternative set of macroeconomic policies. In other words, price controls need to be carried out in a better manner.

Europe needs to strengthen its financial rescue fund to reduce the risk of renewed global instability as US tax cuts and buoyant emerging economies help propel the recovery elsewhere, according to the IMF. It has asked the rich nations to nurture their slower growth rates by keeping monetary policy loose, while inflation pressures may force a number of emerging economies to raise borrowing costs. In an update to its Global Financial Stability Report, the Fund said the effective size of Europe's financial rescue fund should be increased and that its banks needed rigorous stress-testing to help restore market confidence.[7]

The IMF's Special Drawing Rights (SDR) at present has only four constituents: the euro, sterling, dollar and yen. The process to add yuan to the list is being considered as one of the steps to curtail inflation.

Inflation and Central Banks

Since inflation has never done any good, governments around the world take appropriate steps to minimize its ill effects, whenever inflation is expected to rise. Otherwise, the rise in the cost of services coupled with goods has the potential to disrupt the entire economy. One reason for people to expect that the long-term inflation will remain low is today, in contrast to the situation in the 1970s, the central banks have earned a reputation as inflation fighters.

The responsibility to fight inflation lies with central bankers, as it is a monetary phenomenon. Any upswing in inflation poses awkward questions. It necessitates determining the factors that drive inflation up. Pessimists point out that monetary conditions have been loose in recent years, with real interest rates low and credit growth rapid, particularly in emerging economies. Others worry that the task of central bankers has become harder as globalisation has shifted from being a disinflationary phenomenon to an inflationary one.[8]

Inflation Rates Across Countries

While the US, Canada, the UK and Spain have inflation rates below 3 per cent, several countries in the world have a much higher rate of inflation. Zimbabwe has the most shocking inflation rate in the world at 12,563 per cent. Table 3.2 gives inflation figures of some countries as of January 2011. All the figures are in consumer price index, which is often viewed as a country's most important inflation figure.

Inflation and Emerging Powers

The sting of global inflation has led the G-20's emerging powers—China, Brazil, India, Indonesia and South Korea—to raise borrowing costs in 2011. The biggest economies were not spared either. China's inflation accelerated to nearly 5 per cent, exceeding the government's 2011 target while Europe's inflation rate of 2.4 per cent was higher than the European Central Bank's ceiling of 2 per cent.[9]

In some emerging economies monetary laxness is clearly fuelling inflation in the Gulf states, for instance, as the direct consequence of their dollar pegs. A more direct link between developing countries such as China and inflationary pressure comes through commodity prices.

Table 3.2: Inflation Figures of Some Important Countries

(in percentage)

Country/Region	Monthly Basis	Yearly Basis
Belgium	0.574	3.222
Brazil	0.830	5.993
Canada	0.255	2.346
Chile	0.283	0.570
Czech Republic	0.693	1.750
Denmark	0.081	2.662
Estonia	–0.056	5.223
Finland	0.259	3.036
France	–0.238	1.755
Germany	–0.365	1.961
Great Britain	0.086	3.967
Greece	–0.715	5.203
Hungary	0.733	3.950
Iceland	–0.912	1.851
India	1.622	9.303
Indonesia	0.895	7.016
Ireland	–0.196	1.700
Japan	–0.201	0.000
Luxembourg	–0.443	3.165
Mexico	0.487	3.782
Norway	–0.537	2.045
Portugal	0.586	3.641
Russia	2.372	9.553
Slovakia	1.918	3.008
Slovenia	–0.820	1.835
South Africa	0.532	3.562
South Korea	0.934	4.116
Spain	-0.733	3.269
Sweden	-0.836	2.121
Switzerland	-0.353	0.278
The Netherlands	0.019	1.943
Turkey	0.412	4.900
United States	0.476	1.631

Source: http://www.global-rates.com/economic-indicators/inflation/inflation.aspx

Inflation in Asian Countries

After a period of falling prices in 2009, inflation has returned to nearly every major Asian economy, with the exception of Japan. Excluding Japan, which remains mired in seemingly chronic deflation, Asian inflation rose to 5.3 per cent in the 12 months ending in November 2010, up markedly from the 3.5 per cent rate a year earlier. Inflationary trends in the region's two giants remain worrisome. While inflation has pierced the 5 per cent threshold in China, it has been in excess of 8 per cent in India. Price growth is worrisome in Indonesia (7 per cent), Singapore (3.8 per cent), Korea (3.5 per cent), and Thailand (3 per cent) as well. At the same time, annual core inflation for Asia (excluding Japan) was running at a 4 per cent rate in late 2010, which was up about one percentage point from late 2009.[10]

Trends in international food and oil prices tend to have a big impact on inflation in Asia. For example, when food and oil prices surged in 2008, inflation across the region rose sharply. It is also equally important to note that both food and oil prices have been very volatile over the past few years, which do not let prices stabilise.

Another factor that could cause inflation to overshoot is the rapid economic recovery which is now under way in Asia. In the first quarter of 2010, every major economy in the region grew at a faster pace than would normally be regarded as its long-term sustainable rate. However, with policy set to remain very supportive of growth, and with stories of labour shortages being reported in factories across the region, falling unemployment, and other capacity constraints starting to emerge, there is a risk that inflation could soon emerge as a more serious problem.[11]

According to another analysis, some of the underlying demand in Asia can be attributed to a widening middle class, which means the price increases may not be temporary. Sharp rise in food prices is not a trivial matter for low-income families in the developing world, as the share of foodstuffs in household budgets is 2-3 times the ratio in developed countries.

The share of food related expenditure is 46 per cent in India and 33 per cent in China.

Asian countries heavily rely on exports and external demand. Hence, the fear of a relapse of end-market demand acts as a break on the willingness of these countries to tackle inflation. In fact, most of the region's monetary authorities have been generally slow in tightening their policies.

Policy Options

In the post-crisis scenario, when there are uncertain demand prospects in the major markets of the developed world, Asia has to face a classic policy trap to risk the negative impact of stronger currencies while dragging its feet on monetary tightening. In such a situation the only way out for Asian countries is to significantly increase real or inflation-adjusted policy interest rates. In this regard, the efforts of China focus mainly on increasing banks' mandatory reserve ratios while introducing administrative measures to deal with food price pressures, approving a couple of token interest-rate hikes, and managing a modest upward adjustment in the currency.

China's dilemma is emblematic of one of developing Asia's greatest challenges—the need to tilt the growth model away from external towards internal demand. For this to happen there should be increased wages and purchasing power for workers. But in an increasingly inflationary environment, any such efforts could fuel an outbreak of the dreaded wage-price spiral—the same thing that wreaked havoc in the United States in the 1970s. To avoid this problem and get on with the heavy lifting of pro-consumption rebalancing, Asia definitely needs to nip inflation in the bud.

Central banks and government policymakers in Asia have two main policy options available to control inflation, either raise interest rates or allow currencies to appreciate. In the recent past, central banks across the region, including in Vietnam, India, South Korea, Thailand, Taiwan and Malaysia, have raised their main policy rates. Raising interest rates is typically the most effective way of cooling economic growth and curbing inflationary pressures. However, if interest rates in the US, Japan and the euro zone remain at ultra-low levels, Asia's higher interest rates could attract inflows of short-term hot money. This could lead to the creation of destabilising asset bubbles and make monetary policymaking even more difficult.[12]

The other policy option allowing currency appreciation would help slow inflation by reducing the local currency prices of imports, and by reducing demand for exports of those countries with appreciating currencies, thus slowing overall economic growth. Until recently, central banks were wary of allowing their currencies to appreciate against the US dollar, fearing that the Chinese renminbi's peg to the US currency would mean a loss of export competitiveness vis-à-vis China. The Chinese government's decision in the middle of June 2010 to allow the renminbi to start appreciating again against the US dollar will have eased some of these fears. A stronger renminbi would not only increase the policy tools available for central banks to tackle inflation, but could also mean a faster rate of currency appreciation across the region.[13]

China

China is giving fighting inflation higher priority in 2011 after its inflation crossed the 5 per cent mark driven by sensitive food articles, higher rental prices and increased labour costs. In 2010, the Chinese GDP grew at a higher than the estimated rate at 11.9 per cent during the second quarter and 9.6 per cent in third quarter, which was above the comfort zone of their central bank.[14] Among other things, China has imposed tightened mortgage rules and stricter norms on outside investment to limit the amount of foreign investments which was seen as fuelling the bubble scenario in their property market. In the event of inflation crossing the 6 per cent mark, the People's Bank of China might curb expansion by hiking interest rates to put brakes on fast growing markets.

Indonesia

In Indonesia, where food articles comprise a fifth of its inflation basket, inflation has neared 7 per cent, well above the comforts of Bank of Indonesia. Besides its reliance on imports of sugar, wheat and rice, Indonesia had been hard hit by prolonged wet weather and strong winds in 2010. In such a situation, Indonesia's central bank might not be able to keep interest rates on hold for long, as it would like to in order to stave off from greater inflows from hot money. Meanwhile, the government has urged Indonesians to go for home-grown vegetables to reduce reliance on expensive imports and cool down inflation.

Thailand

Powered by transportation, energy and food price increases, Thailand's inflation heated up fuelling concerns of hike in interest rates going further. In 2010, Thailand had raised interest rates three times in an effort to unwind the stimulus measures provided during the 2008-crash.

Vietnam

The country relies on exports of low-value stuff like processed seafood and rice which leads to huge current account deficit. This, in turn, puts pressure on its currency. Hence, in its effort to drag inflation lower, the State Bank of Vietnam is aiming to stifle the credit growth in the region to 23 per cent from 27 per cent in 2010. Further, the central bank is also likely to hike interest rates and go for currency devaluation.

Malaysia

Unlike other countries in Asia, inflation has not surged at a draconian pace in Malaysia. In the midst of slow-paced withdrawal of subsidies and the prospects of ringgit (Malaysian currency) staying strong, Bank Negara Malaysia raised its interest rates three times in 2010 to 2.75 per cent in order to combat rising inflation.[15] As inflationary pressures are perceived at stable levels for the Malaysian economy, the policymakers may not hike interest rates at a brisk pace in 2011.

Pakistan

In the aftermath of devastating 2010 summer floods, Pakistan is suffering from hyperinflation. Consumer inflation has remained in double digits for more than a year, despite the policy tightening. In the midst of high government borrowing following delays in tax reforms, lack of foreign inflows and higher international commodity prices, the State Bank of Pakistan (SBP) has raised its policy rate for the fourth consecutive increase for the fiscal year ending in June 2011.

The government has aggravated the problem of rising food prices through its heavy borrowings from the central bank, which the SBP subsequently funds by printing money. In such a scenario, the central bank is unlikely to loosen its monetary policy. Besides raising rates, the SBP could raise statutory reserves for banks, but it appears loath to do so because of the burden government borrowing is placing on the banking system, causing yields to rise. Six-month bill yields are above 13 per cent.[16]

Inflation in Advanced Countries

Europe

Vibrant growth in the euro zone and British services sectors has brought with it new evidence of surging inflation pressures during January 2011. The Market Services Purchasing Managers' Indexes (PMIs), which measure the activity of thousands of companies from banks to hotels, showed accelerating growth among the service sector firms that power the bulk of the European economy. PMIs showed the costs paid by companies for raw materials and fuel grew at the fastest rate in more than two years in the euro zone and UK. While these costs were largely absorbed by euro zone firms, British firms passed on price hikes to consumers at the fastest rate since September 2008, suggesting room for growing inflation expectations. Bank of England is inching closer to tightening policy by increasing interest rates, if inflation, which hit 3.7 per cent in December 2010, becomes embedded.

European Central Bank President Jean-Claude Trichet has also suggested that price pressures are not expected to ease for some time. He said inflation could rise further owing to commodity and energy price rises, and remain above two per cent for most of 2011 before moderating around the turn of the year.[17]

In theory, the European Central Bank should be starting to think about raising its benchmark interest rate soon to cool down the euro zone economy. But in practice, the central bank cannot raise the benchmark rate from a record low of one per cent without making life even more difficult than it already is for the so-called peripheral countries, like Greece, Ireland and Spain. It is because a rate increase would push up borrowing costs for the governments of those countries even more. And it would add to the burden on millions of homeowners, particularly in Spain and Ireland, who have variable-rate mortgages and would face higher monthly payments.

The blame for the spike in inflation has been put by the central bank on higher energy prices. European factories are still not operating at capacity, and unemployment in most of the continent remains above levels seen before the financial crisis. In addition, demand by companies for credit remains weak. All these factors mean that the European Central Bank may leave rates untouched for some time. However, the central bank will come under much more pressure if higher prices for food or fuel feed into prices of other goods, prompting workers to demand higher wages.

The central bank's other big problem is that it continues to prop up ailing European banks by providing unlimited low-interest loans. The European Central Bank is also granting *de facto* aid to Greece, Portugal and Ireland by buying their bonds on the open market as a way of stabilizing prices. While the central bank has maintained that these so-called non-standard measures are separate from interest-rate policy and do not preclude a tighter monetary policy, the ECB may have to wind down the measures before it can risk a rate increase. The special measures are upsetting the usual mechanisms that the ECB uses to control market rates.[18] Seeing the situation, the central bank may announce steps to wean banks from their dependence on cheap central bank loans.

Australia

As early as May 2010, the Reserve Bank of Australia (RBA) upwardly revised its forecasts for inflation and economic growth. It signaled that more interest rate increases will be needed to temper a surge in activity that has been fuelled by a hefty upswing in commodity prices and limited spare capacity. Through 2012, inflation may remain at or above the upper end of the RBA's 2-3 per cent target band. The expected rise in consumer price index (CPI) inflation is partly due to the government's decision to sharply increase taxes on tobacco.

The RBA expects economic growth to accelerate to 4 per cent through the year to December 2012, well above the 3-3.25 per cent band that economists would like to see. The forecasts will be troubling for the RBA, and imply that tighter monetary policy conditions will be needed as the economy surges well beyond its long-term average rates of growth.

While the RBA is expecting some deterioration in the outlook for inflation, it is not detecting a strong wages upswing despite tightening of the labour market. The RBA's attention, however, is clearly drawn towards the commodity price surge.[19] The RBA has, in fact, firmly established its place as one of the most aggressive central banks among developed economies by raising its cash rate target several times since October 2009. The central bank identified inflationary risks on many fronts and said price increases have been seen for a number of services.

United States

Like Europe and Australia, inflationary pressures are also building up in the United States, but its central bank will be extremely reluctant to raise interest rates for fear of jeopardising its fragile economic recovery. People like Marc Faber, author of the GloomBoomDoom report, have claimed that the US authorities have continually lied about the country's inflation rate. They estimate that inflation in the US to be between 5 and 8 per cent.[20]

The ISM report on manufacturing in the US supports Faber's argument. According to the report, the price pressures are widespread, with prices for 30 commodities rising, while none fell. It may be noted here that the increasing price pressures are not being caused by excess demand. Even there is no difficulty in securing supplies of commodities.

Since the US Federal Reserve is not yet half-way through its latest exercise in monetary expansion—the US$ 600 billion bond buying program, aimed at boosting a lacklustre economic recovery and reducing stubbornly high unemployment levels—it is extremely unlikely that the bank will suddenly change track and start raising interest rates. This reluctance of the central bank in the United States to raise rates will mount global inflationary pressures.

Inflation in Other Countries

Brazil

Brazil—the land of commodities—has also seen a spurt with its consumer inflation nearing 6 per cent in 2010. This rise in prices has largely been on account of rising food prices, especially meat and beans. Inflation is likely to be driven higher due to clothing and transportation costs, apart from soaring food prices. Hence, the country's central bank raising its key interest rates cannot be ruled out.

South Africa

Gill Marcus, Governor of Reserve Bank of South Africa predicts that inflation may reach the upper end of the central bank's 3 per cent to 6 per cent target range "sooner than expected" due to increase in oil and food prices. While there is limited scope for the bank to cut its benchmark interest rate further, raising the rate may undermine the economy's recovery.

In 2010, three rate cuts helped to spur consumer spending and food and energy costs climbed. Some of the gains made by rand in 2010 have been reversed, leading to its weakening against the dollar and adding to price pressures.

The central bank has made an inflation forecast for 2011 at an average of 4.6 per cent, and its 2012 estimate at 5.3 per cent. The Reserve Bank expects economic growth to average 3.4 per cent in 2011 and 3.6 per cent in 2012. Still, the growth in the Africa's biggest economy is not fast enough to cut the jobless rate significantly and it has unemployment rate of 25.3 per cent among the highest in the world.[21]

Inflation Targeting

In the 21st century, the rise in the rate of inflation has forced a number of countries in the world to take measures that restrict the growing pace of inflation. It is because the experience of both the developed and developing countries has shown that high and unpredictable inflation is not good for growth, employment, and equal distribution of real income in the long run. Also, it cannot patronize stronger growth, external competitiveness or employment on a sustainable basis.

Many advanced countries have started targeting inflation rather than a monetary aggregate as the correlation between money and inflation is getting unstable, especially in the short run. The global integration of goods and financial markets has also impacted the changes, in monetary policies. In the developing countries volatile inflation leads to an unstable price rates, and inflation targeting becomes necessary to stabilize price rates. Inflation targeting has helped to reduce the average inflation even in the emerging market economies like Brazil, Chile, Colombia, Hungary, Israel, Mexico, Peru, South Korea, and Thailand.

Case for Global Monetary Reserve Board

In an increasingly interconnected world, it is difficult for a single-country monetary board like the Reserve Bank of India to keep the inflation rate down through the traditional ways of regulating the supply of money. Single-country central banks are yet to evolve a strategy to regulate the lending activities of global banks, especially when these global banks have enough funds from all over the world to flood a country's economic system through its credit products like credit cards, and automobile and housing loans. Further, it is equally difficult for single-country monetary boards to regulate the investing activities of its financial institutions that use heavy leverage instruments like over-the-counter derivatives, real estate investment trusts, options and other complex financial devices which result in a glut of money.

In short, it is no longer possible to effectively manage global inflation by increasing or decreasing the reserve requirements on banks or buying and plowing back money into the financial markets through debt instruments. Hence, a case arises for setting up of a global monetary reserve board to control global inflation, i.e. to make it less volatile. In fact, the financial markets that serve each or all areas of the macroeconomic triangle—consumer markets, producer markets and resource provider markets—need a global inflation economic indicator to help keep global inflation fairly stable for businesses, both large and small, to sustain growth and survive profitably.[22]

Overview and Future Outlook

The global recovery after the financial crisis of 2008-09 has led to a significant increase in prices of metals and energy. Changing weather conditions accompanied by rising demand has pushed prices of soft commodities higher. There are no visible signs that price increases are about to stop and any new weather disturbances could trigger a further sharp rise in soft commodities. Among other reasons for inflation returning as a market theme are the strengthening global recovery and the sharp rise in commodity prices. In fact, commodities are increasingly becoming the scarce resource in global production. This means headline inflation will be harder to control. For emerging markets, rising food prices have the greatest impact as food is a larger share of the consumer basket.

It is a well-documented fact that inflation is causing serious problems in many countries, especially in the emerging economies such as India and China. The scenario in the developed world, though is not as worrisome as it is in the emerging countries, they are still struggling to shake off recession. Besides, unemployment also remains alarmingly high. If, however, the governments of these countries continue with ineffective policies then inflation would certainly cause a lot of problem in these countries when their economies fully recover.

Inflation was at historic lows throughout most of the period of global financial crisis in the US and Europe. But it has shown increasing trend thereafter, which is partly attributed to higher commodity prices. Oil especially has touched the US$ 100 a barrel mark and the crisis in the oil-rich countries like Egypt and Libya has only worsened matters further. Since energy forms a larger part of the inflation number as compared to food for the developed countries, rise in crude prices is definitely going to push inflation upwards.

Excessive money supply has also been contributing to this rise in inflation, especially in the developed world. As the governments keep printing money, there is more and more money chasing lesser goods and hence the prospect of an increase in inflation becomes imminent. Further, a lot of this money finds its way to emerging markets, causing asset bubbles there. Also, as inflation rises, expectations of higher wages increase in order to maintain the purchasing power.[23]

Thus, the fluctuations of inflation have been strikingly similar around the world. In the absence of a key adjustment mechanism to isolate an economy from foreign shocks to prices, inflation might be determined, at least to some extent, at an international level increase. Moreover, even if exchange rates partially adjust for accumulated inflation differentials, there are other reasons for co-movement of inflation across countries, some of them being relevant for the trend component of inflation, others for inflation fluctuations at business cycle or higher frequencies. The trend component of inflation might reflect the objective of the central banks which is not defined in vacuum.

There could also be some international pressures among or on top of monetary authorities. These 'peer pressures' can arise through several channels. For example, the continuous exchange of views among central banks of various countries through official meetings, conferences and publications can lead to such a peer pressure. Hence, the dominant approach on the best monetary policy practice, irrespective of whether it is good or bad, may be reflected in the level of inflation throughout the world. The spread of inflation targeting monetary policy strategy in the early 1990s is perhaps a more striking example of the potential power of this 'peer pressure' channel.

Another channel could potentially be identified with the endogenous equilibrium mechanisms that make a community of central banks (or of groups of central bank watchers) converge to relative rather than absolute benchmarks of success. Typically, performing badly on the inflation record is more tolerable when others perform badly as well.

Beyond the trend of inflation, it is a fact that countries are also subject to shocks. Many scholars associate the 1970s great inflation to the two oil shocks of 1973 and 1979 and several also consider that the mid-1980's disinflation is linked to the 1986 counter oil shock. In the short run, the changes in the price of commodities, which are traded worldwide, have a systematic effect on the price of raw materials and energy that make up a significant share of consumer price indices.

The key drivers for surge in commodity prices are the business cycle, the weather and the so-called super-cycle of commodities. The prices of raw materials are headed northwards due to both the effects of climate change and the structural changes in the world economy. The structural changes are especially related to the increasing demand in emerging markets coupled with waning supply in a range of sectors. Hence, it will not be naïve to visualize a scenario where ever-increasing commodity prices may become the order of the day for decades to come. It may be also marked by a heightened volatility.

The energy prices are also expected to remain high as oil majors are facing an increasingly uncertain environment on the supply side as the prospects of expanding output in non-OPEC countries are growing bleaker. Oil prices above US$ 100 per barrel pose a risk to global growth. It is because higher oil prices add to heating and transport costs and thus reduced consumers' disposable income. This in turn results in a depressed consumer confidence, retail sales and eventually economic activity. The International Energy Agency (IEA) has said that oil prices are entering a "danger zone" in which the oil burden defined as nominal oil expenditures relative to GDP could increase significantly.

The rise in prices of food and agricultural commodities is chiefly due to unfavourable weather conditions in key growing regions. These include droughts in Russia and the Black Sea region, the La Nina effects, dry weather in South America, and erratic monsoons in South Asia. These events have shown that adverse weather conditions in key growing areas have the potential to exert massive impact on grains prices as the sector operates with little spare capacity. Hence, the medium-term outlook for global commodity prices, while uncertain, is that they are likely to remain high even if the world economy slows down in terms of output growth.

No doubt, several measures have been taken by different countries to fight high food price. While a range of producing countries have introduced export bans, consumer countries have cut import tariffs. Some countries have even resorted to cracking down on speculators who are charged with driving prices to excessive levels. But all these measures fall short of addressing the central cause of rising prices and the limited capacity in the agricultural sector amidst rising consumption.

To compound the problem, investment in agriculture has been very limited for many years and the global capital stock has seen only very small additions. Actually, the price signals that farmers have received over the years have not really been incentivizing an increase in production. Indeed, margins of farmers have been squeezed by a combination of rise in costs and stalling prices. While the labour costs have increased on the one hand, there has been limited access to increase the amount of farm land globally on the other. This is in spite of better machinery and fertilizers.

The rising human and livestock population, plus the changing dietary habits of people in developing areas towards more refined foods, including meat products, act as a catalyst for increasing demand of agricultural products. Further adding to this demand is the increasing need of food crops for bio-fuels. As if this is not enough, some crops diseases such as wheat stem rust have revived, increasing the threat to supplies. All these factors, clearly point towards only one thing, that the prices of agricultural and food products may rise substantially over time.

Two factors out of the many—the scarcity of raw materials and the rising demand from emerging economies—are bound to supersede all other factors in keeping the prices high for decades to come. The implementation of massive infrastructure projects including rail networks and power grids along with the ongoing urbanization process in the emerging countries is bound to increase these countries' need for raw materials. An increase in inflation suggests that price pressure has seeped beyond commodities. In more than two-thirds of countries, core consumer prices, excluding food and fuel have been rising.

The global growth in the 21st century is increasingly been driven by emerging markets rather than developed economies. Prior to 1990s, developed countries accounted for two-thirds of global growth while the emerging markets accounted for the remaining one-third. Two decades later, the scenario has changed drastically with the emerging markets driving three-fourths of global growth whereas the developed countries are responsible for the remaining one-fourth.

To achieve a one percentage point growth in developing countries, it requires more commodities than needed for a similar growth in a developed country. It is because the growth in the developing countries is more driven by infrastructure and industrial production, whereas in the advanced countries the growth is more driven by the service sector. Also, the fact that emerging countries are less energy-effective compared to the advanced countries implies higher energy consumption. For example, producing automobiles in Brazil is less energy-effective than producing them in the US.

Hence, it may not be entirely wrong to say that the world is entering a new inflation regime. The factors that drive inflation are no more based on local economy, understood in terms of unemployment rate and output gap. Globalisation has brought in a condition where countries vie for resources needed for production that are not local in nature. It may appear that there are sufficient resources in the ground for the global economy for many years. But the demand growth is outpacing supply growth, mainly due to the rapid pace of growth in emerging markets. Thus, a new regime of inflation marked by pushing prices higher seems to have ushered in.

Notes

1. Matteo Ciccarelli and Benoît Mojon. "Global Inflation", Working Paper Series, No. 537, October 2005, European Central Bank.
2. "Wheres next shock coming from: Global CEOs Discuss Asset Bubbles, Soaring Commodity Prices." *The Times of India*, January 28, 2011, http://articles.timesofindia.indiatimes.com/2011-01-27/india-business/28356830_1_asset-bubbles-asset-prices-financial-crisis
3. "Global Inflation and India", Apr 08, 2008, http://www.thehindubusinessline.in/2008/04/08/stories/2008040850360900.htm
4. "IMF Official Says Asian Governments Need to Fight Inflation With Freer Currencies." ENDA CURRAN, Feb. 15, 2011, http://online.wsj.com/article/SB10001424052748703361904576142901753380400.html?mod=googlenews_wsj
5. *Ibid.*, http://online.wsj.com/article/SB10001424052748703361904576142901753380400.html?mod=googlenews_wsj
6. "Price distortions troublesome: IMF". Jan. 28, 2011. *Times of India*, http://articles.timesofindia.indiatimes.com/2011-01-28/india-business/28374404_1_export-ban-rise-in-food-prices-economies
7. "Recovery builds but Europe, inflation pose risks: IMF." Jan. 25 2011, Phumza Macanda and Ed Cropley, http://www.reuters.com/article/2011/01/25/us-imf-idUSTRE70O36L20110125
8. Global inflation, Jan. 17 2008, Hong Kong and Washington, DC. *The Economist.*
9. "The sting of global inflation". Feb. 22, 2011, http://www.asiaone.com/Business/News/Story/A1Story20110222-264727.html
10. "Asia's Inflation Trap." (THE ASIA PORTFOLIO), Stephen S. Roach, Project Syndicate, 2011. www.project-syndicate.org
11. Asia Economy: Inflation Redux, 2 Aug. 2010, The Economist Intelligence Unit
12. Asia Economy: Inflation Redux, 2 Aug. 2010, The Economist Intelligence Unit
13. Asia Economy: Inflation Redux, 2 Aug. 2010, The Economist Intelligence Unit
14. "High Inflation-Its not just India, but across Asia!" Viral Dholakia, http://trak.in/tags/business/2011/01/08/high-inflation-asia-india/

15. *Ibid.*

16. http://www.dawn.com/2011/01/29/pakistan%E2%80%99s-double-digit-inflation-and-policy-responses.html

17. "Surging inflation marks Europe services rebound." Andy Bruce, http://in.reuters.com/article/2011/02/03/idINIndia-54637920110 203, 3 Feb. 2011

18. "Risk of Inflation Puts Europe in a Tough Spot." Jack Ewing, February 1, 2011, http://www.nytimes.com/2011/02/02/business/global/02euro.html?_r=1&partner=rss&emc=rss

19. "Reserve Bank of Australia lifts forecasts for inflation, economic growth." James Glynn, May 07, 2010, http://www.theaustralian.com. au/business/markets/rba-lifts-inflation-economic-growth-forecasts/story-e6frg926-1225863583990

20. "Fed lies on inflation." Karen Maley, 3 Feb. 2011, http://www.business spectator.com.au/bs.nsf/Article/Fed-lies-on-inflation-pd20110203-DPSHM?opendocument&src=rss

21. "South Africa Inflation May Hit Top End of Central Bank Target." Marcus Says, Nasreen Seria and Renee Bonorchis, Feb. 6, 2011, http://www.bloomberg.com/news/2011-02-06/south-african-inflation-may-reach-upper-end-of-target-update1-.html

22. "Global Inflation Measurement and Regulation: World Inflation Affects Single-country Economics." http://www.suite101.com/content/global-inflation-measurement-and-regulation-a220262#ixzz1F2 nazEPO

23. "The dilemma of inflation." http://www.equitymaster.com/tm/tm.asp?date=02/08/2011&title=The-dilemma-of-inflation

Table A.1: Composition of Exports by Major Markets

	Percentage share					CAGR	Growth rate[a]			
	2000-01	2008-09	2009-10	2009-10 (Apr.-Sept.)	2010-11 (Apr.-Sept.)	2000-01 to 2007-08	2008-09	2009-10	2009-10 (Apr.-Sept.)	2010-11 (Apr.-Sept.)
I Primary Products										
World	16.0	13.9	14.9	13.4	12.7	19.7	1.7	3.8	-27.8	23.2
USA	9.4	7.2	6.8	7.0	7.7	7.9	2.9	-13.5	-27.4	42.6
EU	13.1	8.4	8.6	9.0	8.5	12.7	1.7	-5.7	-23.5	15.8
Others	19.8	16.7	18.0	15.7	14.5	22.8	1.6	6.6	-28.5	23.0
(a) Agri & Allied Products										
World	14.0	9.6	10.0	9.3	8.5	14.6	9.7	1.1	-28.4	18.7
USA	9.0	6.0	5.8	5.9	6.6	4.4	13.1	-12.1	-25.9	45.1
EU	11.9	6.9	7.1	7.4	7.1	10.6	6.6	-6.4	-23.5	17.1
Others	16.8	11.0	11.6	10.4	9.1	17.1	10.0	3.8	-29.5	16.6
(b) Ores and Minerals (excl. coal, incl. mica)										
World	2.0	4.3	4.9	4.1	4.2	38.9	-12.5	9.9	-26.5	33.5
USA	0.4	1.2	1.0	1.1	1.1	37.9	-29.6	-21.1	-34.5	29.8
EU	1.3	1.4	1.5	1.6	1.4	26.0	-16.7	-2.5	-23.3	9.5
Others	3.0	5.7	6.5	5.3	5.4	40.7	-11.4	11.9	-26.5	35.7
II Manufactured Goods										
World	78.8	68.9	67.2	71.1	68.9	16.7	23.1	-5.9	-21.4	26.1
USA	90.6	90.2	89.1	88.5	88.7	11.3	7.1	-8.7	-24.9	30.4
EU	86.8	79.3	73.2	77.3	73.5	15.8	20.6	-15.4	-29.5	15.7
Others	70.9	62.0	62.0	66.5	64.5	19.3	28.9	-1.3	-17.3	28.7
(a) Textiles incl. RMG										
World	23.6	10.2	10.5	11.3	9.5	8.1	4.4	-1.2	-8.4	9.7
USA	27.2	18.4	18.4	19.1	16.9	7.1	-4.8	-7.6	-14.1	15.1
EU	29.2	18.2	18.5	19.9	15.7	11.4	7.9	-6.7	-10.5	-4.1
Others	19.8	6.4	6.9	7.5	6.7	6.3	6.2	6.9	-3.9	18.1
(b) Gems & Jewellery										
World	16.6	15.1	16.2	17.0	14.9	15.0	42.1	3.7	-20.9	14.2
USA	29.3	21.7	24.2	24.2	20.3	8.9	-7.7	2.8	-23.3	8.9
EU	11.5	8.3	6.7	6.9	6.4	11.3	24.8	-26.2	-48.5	12.8
Others	13.9	16.1	17.8	18.7	16.3	19.8	66.2	8.8	-15.5	15.4
(c) Engineering Goods										
World	15.7	21.8	18.2	19.5	21.8	25.2	18.7	-19.6	-32.1	46.0
USA	13.4	23.9	17.1	16.4	22.2	19.5	16.1	-33.9	-48.7	75.8
EU	14.0	25.4	20.8	22.2	22.1	27.1	25.7	-25.1	-41.0	21.1
Others	17.2	20.0	17.6	19.2	21.7	26.0	16.6	-13.1	-24.7	50.2
(d) Chemical & Related Products										
World	10.4	12.3	12.8	12.7	12.1	24.3	7.2	0.9	-18.1	23.8
USA	5.7	14.8	17.2	15.8	17.6	26.8	12.8	7.4	-9.9	45.5
EU	9.7	13.0	12.5	12.4	13.0	24.4	7.4	-11.8	-26.4	27.5
Others	12.5	11.6	12.2	12.3	11.0	23.7	6.0	4.0	-16.9	18.2
(e) Leather & leather mnfrs										
World	4.4	1.9	1.9	2.0	1.7	8.7	1.5	-5.5	-20.2	14.1
USA	3.7	1.7	1.5	1.6	1.4	-1.5	16.1	-17.8	-24.4	14.5
EU	11.4	5.9	6.3	6.7	6.0	9.5	1.0	-2.1	-16.9	8.2
Others	1.6	0.7	0.6	0.7	0.7	12.6	-2.1	-9.4	-26.8	31.1
(f) Handicrafts including Handmade Carpets										
World	2.8	0.6	0.5	0.5	0.5	2.3	-25.8	-10.6	-30.4	22.6
USA	6.0	1.6	1.5	1.5	1.4	-1.7	-30.6	-14.7	-32.2	21.6
EU	4.4	1.1	1.1	1.1	0.9	1.9	-18.0	-7.5	-29.4	3.2
Others	0.8	0.2	0.2	0.2	0.2	10.6	-30.2	-10.6	-29.4	56.4
III Petroleum, Crude & Products (incl. coal)										
World	4.3	14.9	15.8	13.3	16.9	46.8	-3.0	2.3	-42.5	66.0
USA	0.0	0.8	2.3	2.2	2.7	214.9	-76.2	180.3	21.5	61.4
EU	0.0	10.6	16.9	12.6	17.4	683.2	5.7	45.4	-10.9	67.9
Others	7.9	18.6	18.1	15.8	19.5	43.7	-5.0	-3.9	-47.8	64.5
Total Exports										
World	100.0	100.0	100.0	100.0	100.0	20.4	13.6	-3.5	-25.7	30.1
USA	100.0	100.0	100.0	100.0	100.0	12.1	2.0	-7.6	-23.5	30.1
EU	100.0	100.0	100.0	100.0	100.0	18.3	13.9	-8.4	-26.8	21.7
Others	100.0	100.0	100.0	100.0	100.0	23.5	15.7	-1.3	-25.7	32.6

Source: Computed from DGCI&S data

Note: Totals of I, II, and III may not add up to total exports due to some unclassified items.

[a] Growth rate in US dollar terms

Table A.2: Domestic and Global Y-o-Y Inflation Trend (per cent)

(base: 2004-05=100)

Commodity	Domestic Dec-09	Global Dec-09	Domestic Mar-10	Global Mar-10	Domestic Dec-10	Global Dec-10
Agriculture	18.5	28.5	20.6	17.8	15.3	27.8
Beverages	6.5	27.8	8.2	23.0	5.3	32.4
Energy	4.6	55.4	13.8	60.1	11.2	19.7
Fats & Oils	-0.7	34.6	3.3	18.2	5.0	35.4
Fertilizers	7.0	-41.7	6.2	-27.1	5.5	39.6
Food	20.2	23.8	18.5	8.5	8.6	25.3
Grains	19.5	5.0	13.2	-10.3	-2.6	25.3
Metal & Minerals	-7.1	42.8	3.4	41.4	12.4	38.6
Non-fuel	7.4	27.8	9.6	23.0	7.9	32.4
Raw Materials	11.1	36.5	26.1	44.0	24.1	45.8
Timber	-1.3	-9.2	8.8	-5.6	50.3	13.4
Other Raw Materials	18.3	88.4	44.2	91.1	33.6	63.5
Other Food	16.3	30.7	7.0	16.9	-0.5	10.2

Sources: Pink sheet of the World Bank and the Office of the Economic Adviser, Ministry of Commerce and Industry.

Table A.3: Commodity Composition of Imports

Commodity Group	Percentage Share				CAGR	Growth Rate (per cent)[a]			
	2000-01	2009-10	2009-10 (Apr.-Sept.)	2010-11 (Apr.-Sept.)	2000-01 to 2007-08	2008-09	2009-10	2009-10 (Apr.-Sept.)	2010-11 (Apr.-Sept.)
I Food and Allied Products, of which	**3.3**	**3.7**	**3.5**	**3.2**	**19.3**	**9.1**	**69.0**	**59.8**	**13.7**
1. Cereals	0.0	0.0	0.0	0.0	73.8	-93.3	123.1	-2.7	237.5
2. Pulses	0.2	0.7	0.6	0.5	42.6	-2.4	58.8	47.1	4.2
3. Edible Oils	2.6	1.9	1.9	1.8	9.7	34.4	62.3	69.7	17.6
II Fuel, of which	**33.5**	**33.2**	**32.5**	**33.2**	**26.0**	**17.7**	**-5.5**	**-39.7**	**28.9**
4. POL	31.3	30.2	29.2	30.1	25.8	17.4	-7.0	-40.8	29.7
III Fertilizers	**1.3**	**2.3**	**2.6**	**2.4**	**33.3**	**156.8**	**-48.3**	**-55.4**	**14.4**
IV Capital Goods, of which	**10.5**	**15.0**	**15.9**	**13.1**	**37.2**	**-3.9**	**-8.2**	**-20.0**	**4.2**
5. Machinery except electrical & machine tools	5.9	7.4	8.0	7.3	33.1	7.7	-10.2	-24.3	15.7
6. Electrical machinery	1.0	1.1	1.2	1.0	28.7	27.7	-15.1	-28.9	7.4
7. Transport equipment	1.4	4.1	4.2	2.1	61.1	-34.3	-11.6	-18.1	-36.1
V. Others, of which	**46.3**	**42.6**	**42.5**	**43.2**	**22.6**	**23.8**	**1.3**	**-27.8**	**28.0**
8. Chemicals	5.9	5.2	5.6	5.7	22.1	23.0	0.0	-22.9	26.7
9. Pearls, Precious, Semi-precious Stones	9.6	5.6	4.3	7.7	7.2	107.7	-2.4	-47.8	128.9
10. Gold & Silver	9.3	10.3	9.1	8.1	20.8	26.4	32.8	-23.9	12.1
11. Electronic Goods	7.0	7.3	8.3	6.3	28.1	15.3	-10.0	-17.7	-5.3
Total Imports	**100.0**	**100.0**	**100.0**	**100.0**	**25.6**	**20.7**	**-5.0**	**-30.7**	**26.0**

Source: Calculated from DGCI&S data

Note: * Growth rate in US dollar terms.

Totals of I, II, III, IV, and V may not add up to total imports due to some unclassified items.

4

Inflation in India: Food Inflation

Food inflation can be defined as the relative rise or fall in the prices of food items, particularly of essential items like wheat, rice, maize, soyabean, pulses, vegetables, meat, milk, sugar, cooking oil, etc., either raw or processed. In common parlance, food inflation has come to mean a rise in the price of food items. Variations in the price of food items occur due to a mismatch between demand and supply for various reasons. The Government of India has acknowledged that inflation continues to be a cause for concern.

Food Inflation Scenario in India

The year-on-year WPI inflation that started trending up in Dec. 2009 continued through 2010-11. The financial year 2010-11 started with a double-digit headline inflation of 11 per cent in Apr. 2010. After remaining in double digits from April to July 2010, headline inflation came down to single digits and stood at 8.8 per cent in Aug. 2010. Headline inflation in November 2010 was 7.5 per cent, though the falling trend reversed and in Dec. 2010 it rose to 8.4 per cent. The early 2011 again saw an increase. In spite of having a good monsoon during 2010, headline inflation at elevated levels owed to high levels of food inflation. The inflation in food articles which had moderated to single digit in November 2010 again jumped to double digits and stood at 13.6 per cent in Dec. 2010.[1]

High inflation in Dec. 2010 could be attributed to supply bottlenecks especially in vegetables, onions, tomatoes, fruits, milk, eggs, and fish. A sudden spurt in prices of onions during Dec. 2010 was witnessed because of damage to the onion crop. It is pertinent to mention here that food price inflation during the last financial year was mainly driven by high inflation in pulses, cereals, and sugar due to poor monsoon. It will be right to assume that the rise in the purchasing power owing to the rapid growth of the economy and inclusive programs like the Mahatma Gandhi National Rural Employment Guarantee Act (MNREGA) might have contributed to the upward trend in inflation. The inflation in primary articles was reported at 18 per cent on an average during the period Apr. 2010 to Dec. 2010 as compared to 10 per cent in the previous year for the same period. Recovery in the domestic economy led to demand-side pressure on inflation. The inflationary pressure persisted both from domestic demand and higher global commodity prices on account of the global recovery.[2]

Table 4.1: Main Drivers of Food Inflation

		WPI			y-o-y Inflation	y-o-y WC	*Financial year inflation	Financial year WC
Items	Weight%	Dec. 2009	Mar. 2010	Dec. 2010	Dec. 2010	Dec. 2010	Apr.-Dec. 2010	Dec. 2010
All Commodities	100.00	132.9	135.8	144.1	8.43	100.00	6.11	100.00
Primary Articles	20.12	162.2	165.9	188.9	16.46	47.96	13.86	55.75
Primary Food Articles	14.34	164.6	163.6	186.9	13.55	28.55	14.24	40.25
Rice	1.79	164.5	163.3	166.4	1.16	0.30	1.90	0.67
Wheat	1.12	180.8	172.8	171.6	-5.09	-0.92	-0.69	-0.16
Pulses	0.72	212.1	198.9	189.0	-10.89	-1.48	-4.98	-0.85
Vegetables	1.74	180.0	132.0	224.9	24.94	6.96	70.38	19.43
Potatoes	0.20	240.1	105.4	176.3	-26.57	-1.15	67.27	1.72
Onions	0.18	268.2	171.3	391.1	45.82	1.95	128.31	4.71
Fruits	2.11	136.0	145.6	163.8	20.44	5.23	12.50	4.62
Milk	3.24	151.0	167.2	178.5	18.21	7.95	6.76	4.41
Eggs, Meat, & Fish	2.41	164.3	172.1	195.9	19.23	6.81	13.83	6.92
Condiments & Spices	0.57	202.7	204.9	270.6	33.50	3.45	32.06	4.50
Tea	0.11	165.8	129.1	156.7	-5.49	-0.09	21.38	0.37
Manufactured Food	9.97	142.2	141.7	142.7	0.35	0.45	0.71	1.20
Sugar	1.74	185.7	183.6	167.3	-9.91	-2.85	-8.88	-3.41
Vanaspati	0.71	107.3	108.5	119.6	11.46	0.79	10.23	0.96
Oil, Groundnut	0.30	133.0	131.5	147.8	11.13	0.40	12.40	0.60
Oil, Sunflower	0.17	115.8	112.5	128.4	10.88	0.20	14.13	0.33
Rice Bran Extraction	0.09	210.3	210.4	231.2	9.94	0.17	9.89	0.23
Tea & Coffee Process	0.71	148.6	140.7	160.4	7.94	0.75	14.00	1.69
Malt Liquor	0.15	150.9	150.4	167.1	10.74	0.22	11.10	0.31

Source: The Office of the Economic Adviser, Ministry of Commerce and Industry.

Note: WC – weighted contribution.

Food has higher weight in consumer price indices than in the WPI. In Aug. 2010, inflation in terms of all price indices had come down to single digit after 15 consecutive months of double-digit inflation. Year-on-year inflation in the CPI-IW was 9.47 per cent in Dec. 2010 as compared to 14.97 per cent in Dec. 2009. On year-on-year basis, inflation in the consumer price indices for agriculture workers (CPI-AL) and rural workers (CPI-RL) was 7.99 per cent and 8.01 per cent respectively in Dec. 2010 as compared to 17.21 and 16.99 per cent respectively in Dec. 2009.

In the WPI, primary articles have a weightage of 20.12 per cent, that of primary food articles like rice, wheat, pulses, vegetable, etc. is 14.34 per cent, while that of manufactured food like sugar, edible oils, etc. is 9.97 per cent. Table 4.1 provides a detail of weightage of items in the WPI. It also gives a comparison of WPI for Dec. 2009 Mar. 2010 and Dec. 2010. In case of all commodities the WPI went from 132.9 in Dec. 2009 to 144.1 in Dec. 2010. Primary articles registered an increase from 162.2 to 188.9, and primary food articles rose from 164.5 to 186.9, while manufactured food went from 142.2 to 142.7 during that period. These are yearly comparisons and it may be mentioned here that in case of some commodities the prices cooled off a little after remaining high for several months.

The sharp hike in the price of vegetables seen during December 2010 and January 2011, especially of onions, reveals defects in our food production and marketing systems. What came to light during this period was the great difference in prices for the same product at the farm gate and in city retail outlets, and also across different cities and towns. On 7 January 2011, for instance, onions were selling for ₹ 30 kg in Agra and ₹ 57.5 in Delhi; for ₹ 35 kg in Nagpur and ₹ 62 in Mumbai; for ₹ 23 in Thiruvananthapuram and ₹ 60 kg in Dindigul. This bears testimony to the fact that our markets were neither functioning efficiently nor they were competitive. What these price differentials suggest more than anything else is not so much hoarding as the cartelization of trade resulting in the prevention of entry of new traders. Such problems need to be tackled using our Competition Act, 2002.[3]

Food inflation has been a big worry in India for the last few years as consumers are paying more for food. Table 4.2 shows that the index number of wholesale prices in India for foodgrains was 139.3 points in 1997-98, which rose to 270.5 in 2009-10, an increase of nearly 100 per cent. In the index, cereals showed an increase from 138.4 in 1997-98 to 261.7 in 2009-10. All major cereals, viz. rice, wheat, jowar, bajra, maize, barley and ragi registered a substantial increase. Pulses rose from 145.9 to 334.3, while sugar, khandsari and gur went from 134.4 to 242.4 during the same period.

It can be seen from Table 4.3 that the index numbers for vegetables rose from 113.7 in 2005-06 to 161.8 in 2009-10 and showed an increasing trend in 2010-11. Similarly, fruits rose from 103.3 to 136.2 in 2009-10 and showed an increasing trend in 2010-11. Index for milk went from 101 in 2005-06 to over 177 in Nov. 2010, while eggs, meat and fish went higher from 106.3 to 194.6 in the said period.

Table 4.4 reveals that the WPI index for foodgrains showed a growth of 9.1 in 1998-99 and 16.1 in 1999-2000, before coming down slightly during the next two financial years, viz. 2000-01 and 2001-02. But in the next eight financial years, i.e. from 2002-03 to 2009-10 it kept on increasing. The cereals showed a steady percentage increase except in a few years when their numbers declined marginally. A distinct feature of the rising trend is that this rise became sharper in percetage terms during 2009-10, over the previous year, i.e. 14.4 for rice, 10.5 for wheat, 14.4 for jowar, 30.0 for bajra, 14.0 for maize and 31.3 for ragi. The trends for 2010-11 are also on the higher side as reported in various newspapers and journals. The numbers for pulses also showed an increase during the period 1998-99 to 2009-10 except for the years 2002-03 to 2004-05 and in 2007-08. However, the increase in the year 2009-10 was as high as 29.7. The index for sugar went up a whopping 45.4 in 2009-10. The rising trend of index number of food articles clearly shows that people are facing high food inflation.

Table 4.2: Trends in Wholesale Price Index of Foodgrains

(Base year-1993-94=100)

Commodity	Weight	1997-98	1998-99	1999-2000	2000-2001	2001-2002	2002-2003	2003-2004	2004-2005	2005-2006	2006-2007	2007-2008	2008-2009*	2009-2010p
1	2	3	4	5	6	7	8	9	10	11	12	13	14	15
(I) All Commodities	100.00	132.8	140.7	145.3	155.7	161.3	166.8	175.9	187.3	195.6	206.2	215.7	233.9	242.7
(a) Primary Articles	22.03	139.4	156.2	158.0	162.5	168.4	174.0	181.5	188.1	193.6	208.7	224.4	247.3	273.6
(b) Fuel, Power & Lubricants	14.23	143.8	148.5	162.0	208.1	226.7	239.2	254.5	280.2	306.8	323.9	327.0	351.4	343.1
(c) Manufactured Products	63.75	128.0	133.6	137.2	141.7	144.3	148.1	156.5	166.3	171.4	179.0	187.8	203.1	209.6
(II) Foodgrains	5.01	139.3	152.0	176.4	173.8	172.4	174.3	176.3	177.5	187.0	206.0	215.5	234.1	270.5
(a) Cereals	4.41	138.4	150.9	177.8	173.0	170.1	173.5	176.3	177.9	185.8	199.4	211.7	230.5	261.7
1 Rice	2.45	134.3	146.2	171.3	167.5	167.0	166.0	168.8	168.2	174.5	179.6	191.7	213.0	243.7
2 Wheat	1.38	138.1	151.8	174.7	176.6	175.3	175.7	181.4	184.1	191.5	216.5	225.7	239.6	264.7
3 Jowar	0.22	172.3	191.1	240.6	199.7	182.4	218.7	218.8	233.4	244.5	272.0	309.4	331.7	379.6
4 Bajra	0.11	143.4	156.6	201.2	184.0	151.3	190.3	178.6	183.0	210.8	227.6	235.7	251.7	327.1
5 Maize	0.19	148.5	154.4	193.6	178.9	171.5	189.5	181.2	187.9	205.0	224.9	235.7	256.0	291.8
6 Barley	0.03	166.3	151.7	199.2	174.3	160.2	193.8	179.5	188.6	205.3	220.8	228.8	243.6	240.5
7 Ragi	0.03	138.4	152.4	178.7	182.1	158.0	174.3	197.0	184.5	186.8	205.6	227.0	247.7	325.3
(b) Pulses	0.60	145.9	160.1	166.1	179.6	189.2	180.6	176.6	174.4	194.9	254.2	243.1	259.8	334.3
8 Gram	0.22	124.6	110.9	115.4	139.2	170.3	149.7	142.5	137.1	157.0	208.7	189.9	209.3	206.0
9 Arhar	0.13	136.2	186.2	176.3	150.3	142.6	157.5	172.8	179.3	170.8	182.0	207.4	228.5	250.2
10 Moong	0.11	164.7	181.2	180.6	186.9	205.6	208.0	195.9	187.4	219.2	303.0	267.3	286.7	420.2
11 Masur	0.04	176.6	202.6	216.0	206.8	203.9	214.1	233.4	234.7	242.8	254.0	319.0	394.9	467.2
12 Urad	0.10	175.3	197.3	234.0	295.7	273.9	239.8	217.4	216.3	270.4	403.8	336.8	338.5	459.5
(III) Sugar, Khandsari & Gur	3.93	134.4	153.5	156.0	153.2	146.1	134.6	139.3	163.3	178.8	179.8	155.2	168.7	242.4
13 Sugar	3.62	133.8	135.4	137.4	142.6	135.4	123.5	124.4	148.1	164.0	164.9	142.7	160.4	233.2
14 Khandsari	0.17	133.5	144.7	137.3	137.3	145.3	133.2	130.3	164.1	197.8	203.5	169.0	199.2	274.6
15 Gur	0.06	126.1	130.3	129.9	129.1	137.8	128.2	122.0	172.9	192.5	185.3	170.3	205.1	282.2
Food Articles	15.40	141.4	159.4	165.5	170.5	176.1	179.2	181.5	186.3	195.3	210.5	222.0	239.8	274.9
Non-Food Articles	6.14	137.5	151.8	143.0	146.5	152.9	165.4	186.3	187.6	179.1	188.2	211.9	235.8	244.6

(P) Provisional

Sorce: Office of the Economic Adviser, Ministry of Commerce & Industry.

Table 4.3: Index Numbers of Wholesale Prices in India—by Groups and Sub-Groups

(Base: 2004-05=100)

Commodities / Major Groups / Groups / Sub-Groups	Weight	2005-06	2008-09	2009-10	2010						2011
		April-March			Jan.	Aug.	Sep.	Oct.	Nov.	Dec. (P)	Jan. (P)
1	2	3	4	5	6	7	8	9	10	11	12
ALL COMMODITIES	100.000	104.4	125.9	130.4	134.8	140.7	141.5	142.4	143.1	144.1	145.9
I. PRIMARY ARTICLES	20.118	104.3	137.5	154.9	164.9	177.3	180.8	183.4	185.3	188.9	193.4
(A) Food articles	14.337	105.4	134.8	155.4	164.9	176.7	179.9	180.9	181.4	186.9	190.7
(a) Food Grains Cereals+Pulses)	4.090	107.3	145.3	166.4	179.0	174.4	174.0	173.4	174.4	172.7	175.0
a1. Cereals	3.373	106.0	143.1	161.2	170.5	168.7	169.3	169.0	171.7	169.2	171.6
a2. Pulses	0.717	113.3	155.8	190.8	219.1	201.7	196.5	194.1	187.2	189.0	191.1
b. Fruits & Vegetables	3.843	108.0	134.9	147.8	147.6	161.8	169.3	175.1	174.2	191.4	205.0
b1. Vegetables	1.736	113.7	141.9	161.8	156.8	176.2	189.5	193.9	189.2	224.9	258.5
b2. Fruits	2.107	103.3	129.1	136.2	139.9	149.9	152.7	159.7	161.8	163.8	160.9
(c) Milk	3.238	101.0	123.2	146.4	157.6	176.5	177.1	177.2	177.9	178.5	177.2
(d) Eggs, Meat & Fish	2.414	106.3	125.4	151.5	167.0	190.1	196.1	192.2	192.9	195.9	192.2
(e) Condiments & Spices	0.569	94.5	151.2	182.7	206.7	237.1	241.4	245.5	250.3	270.6	278.1
(f) Other Food Articles	0.183	107.8	175.0	196.2	186.0	178.8	184.0	184.9	187.9	184.7	186.9
(B) Non-Food Articles	4.258	96.7	129.2	136.2	143.6	153.8	160.6	166.1	170.8	171.6	177.9
(a) Fibres	0.877	96.4	137.9	140.0	149.9	157.4	183.9	193.5	205.4	201.2	221.3
(b) Oil Seeds	1.781	90.4	131.2	135.0	140.0	138.4	139.7	140.1	138.6	140.9	142.2
(c) Other Non-Food Articles	1.386	103.9	117.5	128.7	138.0	170.6	171.0	175.7	179.6	180.1	184.8
(d) Flowers	0.213	103.8	152.3	179.2	183.2	158.3	170.9	209.1	240.2	250.2	252.4
(C) Minerals	1.524	115.2	186.5	202.9	223.9	248.4	245.3	255.0	263.2	255.5	262.6
(a) Metallic Minerals	0.489	127.9	266.2	258.3	301.8	371.3	360.4	381.5	394.4	382.6	391.5
b) Other Minerals	0.135	104.8	144.2	146.0	147.4	145.2	154.1	157.6	162.8	158.0	162.5
(c) Crude Petroleum	0.900	109.8	149.7	181.4	193.0	197.1	196.4	200.9	207.1	201.1	207.5
II. FUEL & POWER	14.910	113.6	135.0	132.1	135.8	148.0	147.6	148.1	148.6	150.1	151.3
(a) Coal	2.094	117.6	151.3	156.5	163.0	163.0	163.0	163.0	163.0	163.0	163.0
(b) Mineral Oils	9.364	116.7	141.8	135.8	139.7	157.2	156.6	157.3	158.1	160.5	163.0
(c) Electricity	3.452	102.6	106.4	107.4	108.6	114.0	114.0	114.0	114.0	114.0	112.5

Source: RBI Bulletin

Table 4.4: Growth Rate of Wholesale Price Index of Foodgrains

(Base year-1993-94=100)

Commodity	Weight	1998-99	1999-2000	2000-2001	2001-2002	2002-2003	2003-2004	2004-2005	2005-2006	2006-2007	2007-2008	2008-2009	2009-2010p
1	2	3	4	5	6	7	8	9	10	11	12	13	14
(I) ALL COMMODITIES	100.00	5.9	3.3	7.2	3.6	3.4	5.5	6.5	4.4	5.4	4.6	8.4	3.8
(a) Primary Articles	22.03	12.1	1.2	2.8	3.6	3.3	4.3	3.6	2.9	7.8	7.5	10.2	10.6
(b) Fuel, Power & Lubricants	14.23	3.3	9.1	28.5	8.9	5.5	6.4	10.1	9.5	5.6	1.0	7.5	-2.4
(c) Manufactured Products	63.75	4.4	2.7	3.3	1.8	2.6	5.7	6.3	3.1	4.4	4.9	8.1	3.2
(II) FOODGRAINS	5.01	9.1	16.1	-1.5	-0.8	1.1	1.1	0.7	5.4	10.2	4.6	8.6	15.5
(a) Cereals	4.41	9.0	17.8	-2.7	-1.7	2.0	1.6	0.9	4.4	7.3	6.2	8.9	13.5
1 Rice	2.45	8.9	17.2	-2.2	-0.3	-0.6	1.7	-0.4	3.7	2.9	6.7	11.1	14.4
2 Wheat	1.38	9.9	15.1	1.1	-0.7	0.2	3.2	1.5	4.0	13.1	4.2	6.2	10.5
3 Jowar	0.22	10.9	25.9	-17.0	-8.7	19.9	0.0	6.7	4.8	11.2	13.8	7.2	14.4
4 Bajra	0.11	9.2	28.5	-8.5	-17.8	25.8	-6.1	2.5	15.2	8.0	3.6	6.8	30.0
5 Maize	0.19	4.0	25.4	-7.6	-4.1	10.5	-4.4	3.7	9.1	9.7	4.8	8.6	14.0
6 Barley	0.03	-8.8	31.3	-12.5	-8.1	21.0	-7.4	5.1	8.9	7.5	3.6	6.5	-1.3
7 Ragi	0.03	10.1	17.3	1.9	-13.2	10.3	13.0	-6.3	1.2	10.1	10.4	9.1	31.3
(b) PULSES	0.60	9.7	3.7	8.1	5.3	-4.5	-2.2	-1.2	11.8	30.4	-4.4	6.9	28.7
8 Gram	0.22	-11.0	4.1	20.6	22.3	-12.1	-4.8	-3.8	14.5	32.9	-9.0	10.2	-1.6
9 Arhar	0.13	36.7	-5.3	-14.7	-5.1	10.4	9.7	3.8	-4.7	6.6	14.0	10.2	9.5
10 Moong	0.11	10.0	-0.3	3.5	10.0	1.2	-5.8	-4.3	17.0	38.2	-11.8	7.3	46.6
11 Masur	0.04	14.7	6.6	-4.3	-1.4	5.0	9.0	0.6	3.5	4.6	25.6	23.8	18.3
12 Urad	0.10	12.5	18.6	26.4	-7.4	-12.4	-9.3	-0.5	25.0	49.3	-16.6	0.5	35.7
(III) SUGAR, KHANDSARI & GUR	3.93	14.2	1.6	-1.8	-4.6	-7.9	3.5	17.2	9.5	0.6	-13.7	8.7	43.7
13 Sugar	3.62	1.2	1.5	3.8	-5.0	-8.8	0.7	19.1	10.7	0.5	-13.5	12.4	45.4
14 Khandsari	0.17	8.4	-5.1	0.0	5.8	-8.3	-2.2	25.9	20.5	2.9	-17.0	17.9	37.9
15 Gur	0.06	3.3	-0.3	-0.6	6.7	-7.0	-4.8	41.7	11.3	-3.7	-8.1	20.4	37.6
Food Articles	15.40	12.7	3.8	3.0	3.3	1.8	1.3	2.6	4.8	7.8	5.5	8.0	14.6
Non-Food Articles	6.14	10.4	-5.8	2.4	4.4	8.2	12.6	0.7	-4.5	5.1	12.6	11.3	3.7

(P) Provisional

Sorce: Office of the Economic Adviser, Ministry of Commerce & Industry.

In order to have a clear and complete picture of food inflation in India over the years, it is necessary to have look at the WPI numbers of commercial crops, as they provide us with trends on oilseeds, edible oils, fruits, vegetable and condiments and spices. Table 4.5 shows that the index number for oilseeds, which was 128.3 in 1997-98, went up to 255.1 in 2009-10, an increase of almost hundred per cent. Groundnut seeds, rapeseed/mustard seed, cotton seed, copra, gingelly seed, niger seed, safflower seed/kardi seed, sunflower and soyabean are included in the oilseeds and their index numbers increased steadily over the years. Similarly, edible oils including gingelly oil, rapeseed oil/mustard oil, groundnut oil,cottonseed oil, sunflower oil and soyabean oil showed an increase. Condiments and spices, including black pepper, dry chillies, turmeric too registered an increase during the years 1997-98 to 2009-10. The trend is continued in 2010-11.

Table 4.6 shows more clearly the increase in prices of commercial crops. Oilseeds showed an increase in index numbers for the entire period from 1997-98 to 2009-10 except in the years 1999-2000, 2000-01 and 2005-06. Edible oils showed a decline in 1999-2000, 2000-01, 2004-05, 2005-06, and 2009-10, but went higher during all the remaining years. Index for vegetables went higher. Onion and tomato registered a high growth of 59.4 and 31.8 per cent respectively. In condiments and spices, turmeric showed a growth of 118.8 per cent during 2009-10.

Table 4.7 provides monthly world food price indices (deflated, using the World Bank Manufacturers Unit Value Index) of food in general, meat, dairy, cereals, oils, and sugar, from Jan. 1990 to Dec. 2010. The food price index stood at 110.4 points in Jan. 1990, which rose to 183.4 points in Dec. 2010. Meat price index, which was 118.3 points, remained more or less stable at 121.4 points during the said period. Dairy price index went from 93.2 points to 178.0 points, cereal price index from 106.6 points to 202.9 points, edible oils price index from 72.6 points to 224.6 points, and sugar price index from 210.7 points to 340.3 points. Table 4.7 also tells us that food inflation is a worldwide phenomenon. Except for meat

Table 4.5: Trends in Wholesale Price Index of Commercial Crops

(Base Year: 1993-94 = 100)

Commodity	Weight	1997-98	1998-99	1999-2000	2000-2001	2001-2002	2002-2003	2003-2004	2004-2005	2005-2006	2006-2007	2007-2008	2008-2009	2009-2010p
1	2	3	4	5	6	7	8	9	10	11	12	13	14	15
Oilseeds	2.67	128.3	148.5	133.4	129.3	137.6	160.2	177.8	180.8	167.1	175.7	217.7	245.9	255.1
Groundnut Seed	1.03	133.9	150.8	139.6	139.4	143.4	169.3	180.6	182.0	171.9	190.0	239.4	249.2	263.1
Rape/Mustard Seed	0.58	116.9	163.6	138.7	118.0	126.7	143.3	184.3	172.3	164.7	172.1	203.7	251.8	242.8
Cotton Seed	0.05	135.9	159.8	153.6	159.2	159.1	156.2	181.6	166.8	154.8	167.8	181.4	194.3	204.4
Copra	0.03	142.6	129.4	141.5	95.1	89.6	130.5	163.3	193.5	159.8	138.7	128.0	159.2	136.6
Gingelly Seed	0.13	115.4	157.2	154.4	132.9	134.5	157.8	169.5	177.3	169.3	187.2	205.2	266.5	333.8
Niger Seed	0.03	124.3	145.0	177.6	183.0	156.8	189.6	223.4	214.1	184.1	219.6	390.0	488.4	364.1
Safflower/Kardi	0.06	108.0	142.8	129.7	112.6	128.9	150.5	188.8	171.4	146.6	143.8	165.9	191.3	193.8
Sunflower	0.20	128.2	144.5	117.4	118.1	164.6	192.5	194.3	197.8	188.7	197 7	253.3	252.6	242.4
Soyabean	0.45	138.8	124.3	107.5	121.1	130.0	153.4	158.4	187.8	157.5	144.9	186.9	230.0	255.6
Edible Oils	2.76	113.5	139.1	122.1	103.3	112.9	138.0	157.9	156.4	146.0	154.6	175.1	188.1	177.3
Gingelly Oil	0.06	129.0	157.8	149.6	122.8	138.2	170.9	193.8	193.7	174.7	185.5	224.7	283.3	290.4
Rapeseed/Mustard Oil	0.49	115.5	179.6	140.1	112.1	121.1	147.3	193.9	177.1	159.8	165.7	194.0	232.5	209.1
Coconut Oil	0.17	140.8	131.1	142.5	98.7	95.0	121.6	156.2	178.8	150.7	141.7	139.2	167.3	151.2
Groundnut Oil	0.17	123.6	150.2	137.6	129.1	135.8	166.6	181.2	173.8	168.2	189.8	231.8	227.6	221.7
Cotton Seed Oil	0.28	101.7	128.8	114.4	96.3	111.8	126.5	126.6	127.5	112.4	124.8	159.8	161.7	146.5
Sunflower Oil	0.13	120.9	147.6	118.0	106.7	136.1	157.1	161.6	163.0	157.6	166.7	189.7	221.4	219.3
Soyabean Oil	0.18	100.5	134.8	113.0	86.7	86.9	122.7	135.8	138.1	137.4	132.4	142.9	153.4	147.7
Fruits & Vegetables	2.92	142.8	185.4	154.5	160.0	188.9	190.20	195.60	204.20	218.90	228.2	236.2	255.5	286.2
Fruits	1.46	146.3	169.3	166.8	180.7	206.1	217.50	231.10	237.30	246.60	258.3	248.4	278.2	295.4
Banana	0.28	149.4	147.3	130.2	134.7	154.0	166.60	178.80	190.30	213.20	214.4	227.3	261.5	267.5
Apple	0.44	156.2	188.7	251.4	391.6	574.1	542.1	539.70	493.00	470.60	570.5	521.8	507.3	590.0
Orange	0.05	289.3	535.9	505.7	513.5	530.9	535.70	555.30	573.20	711.40	739.9	504.9	831.1	893.2
Vegetables	1.46	139.5	201.4	142.1	139.4	171.7	162.90	160.10	171.10	191.30	198.1	224.0	232.9	276.9
Potato	0.26	84.4	226.2	93.9	84.6	198.5	190.00	111.40	169.80	199.60	235.0	257.1	215.6	343.6
Onion	0.09	136.7	261.8	132.1	107.1	123.9	130.40	169.80	137.00	169.70	160.8	233.3	232.2	282.8
Condiment & Spices	0.66	176.9	220.2	226.4	202.5	188.1	194.00	205.00	188.10	176.60	228.2	239.6	267.7	320.2
Black pepper	0.02	421.1	511.2	525.9	501.4	246.6	246.20	220.40	192.10	185.60	260.3	374.2	375.4	364.9
Chillies (Dry)	0.19	231.3	342.8	305.8	254.4	249.9	253.90	294.30	225.90	213.40	345.1	347.2	422.5	464.5
Turmeric	0.08	186.0	234.3	191.8	134.6	119.4	181.20	230.40	224.10	201.70	190.4	174.7	205.8	450.2
Raw Cotton	1.36	155.4	166.9	147.3	157.3	148.7	142.1	180.60	165.60	144.30	151.7	178.1	220.2	217.7
Raw Jute	0.11	101.8	107.9	112.9	149.8	182.5	153.60	137.10	159.90	198.80	203.7	190.6	206.5	242.9

(P) Provisional

Sorce: Office of the Economic Adviser, Ministry of Commerce & Industry.

Table 4.6: Growth Rate of Wholesale Price Index of Commercial Crops

(Base Year: 1993-94 = 100)

Commodity	Weight	1998-99	1999-2000	2000-2001	2001-2002	2002-2003	2003-2004	2004-2005	2005-2006	2006-2007	2007-2008	2008-2009	2009-2010p
1	2	3	4	5	6	7	8	9	10	11	12	13	14
Oilseeds	2.67	15.7	-10.2	-3.1	6.4	16.4	11.0	1.7	-7.6	5.1	23.9	13.0	3.7
Groundnut Seed	1.03	12.6	-7.4	-0.1	2.9	18.1	6.7	0.8	-5.5	10.5	26.0	4.1	5.6
Rape/Mustard Seed	0.58	39.9	-15.2	-14.9	7.4	13.1	28.6	-6.5	-4.4	4.5	18.4	23.6	-3.6
Cotton Seed	0.05	17.6	-3.9	3.6	-0.1	-1.8	16.3	-8.1	-7.2	8.4	8.1	7.1	5.2
Copra	0.03	-9.3	9.4	-32.8	-5.8	45.6	25.1	18.5	-17.4	-13.2	-7.7	24.4	-14.2
Gingelly Seed	0.13	36.2	-1.8	-13.9	1.2	17.3	7.4	4.6	-4.5	10.6	9.6	29.9	25.3
Niger Seed	0.03	16.7	22.5	3.0	-14.3	20.9	17.8	-4.2	-14.0	19.3	77.6	25.2	-25.5
Safflower/Kardi	0.06	32.2	-9.2	-13.2	14.5	16.8	25.4	-9.2	-14.5	-1.9	15.4	15.3	1.3
Sunflower	0.20	12.7	-18.8	0.6	39.4	17.0	0.9	1.8	-4.6	4.8	28.1	-0.3	-4.0
Soyabean	0.45	-10.4	-13.5	12.7	7.3	18.0	3.3	18.6	-16.1	-8.0	29.0	23.1	11.1
Edible Oils	2.76	22.6	-12.2	-15.4	9.3	22.2	14.4	-0.9	-6.6	5.9	13.3	7.4	-5.7
Gingelly Oil	0.06	22.3	-5.2	-17.9	12.5	23.7	13.4	-0.1	-9.8	6.2	21.1	26.1	2.5
Rapeseed/Mustard Oil	0.49	55.5	-22.0	-20.0	8.0	21.6	31.6	-8.7	-9.8	3.7	17.1	19.8	-10.1
Coconut Oil	0.17	-6.9	8.7	-30.7	-3.7	28.0	28.5	14.5	-15.7	-6.0	-1.8	20.2	-9.6
Groundnut Oil	0.17	21.5	-8.4	-6.2	5.2	22.7	8.8	-4.1	-3.2	12.8	22.1	-1.8	-2.6
Cotton Seed Oil	0.28	26.6	-11.2	-15.8	16.1	13.1	0.1	0.7	-11.8	11.0	28.0	1.2	-9.4
Sunflower Oil	0.13	22.1	-20.1	-9.6	27.6	15.4	2.9	0.9	-3.3	5.8	13.8	16.7	-0.9
Soyabean Oil	0.18	34.1	-16.2	-23.3	0.2	41.2	10.7	1.7	-0.5	-3.6	7.9	7.3	-3.7
Fruits & Vegetables	2.92	29.8	-16.7	3.6	18.1	0.7	2.8	4.4	7.2	4.2	3.5	8.2	12.0
Fruits	1.46	15.7	-1.5	8.3	14.1	5.5	6.3	2.7	3.9	4.7	-3.8	12.0	6.2
Banana	0.28	-1.4	-11.6	3.5	14.3	8.2	7.3	6.4	12.0	0.6	6.0	15.0	2.3
Apple	0.44	20.8	33.2	55.8	46.6	-5.6	-0.4	-8.7	-4.5	21.2	-8.5	-2.8	16.3
Orange	0.05	85.2	-5.6	1.5	3.4	0.9	3.7	3.2	24.1	4.0	-31.8	64.6	7.5
Vegetables	1.46	44.4	-29.4	-1.9	23.2	-5.1	-1.7	6.9	11.8	3.6	13.1	4.0	18.9
Potato	0.26	168.0	-58.5	-9.9	134.6	-4.3	-41.4	52.4	17.6	17.7	9.4	-16.1	59.4
Onion	0.09	91.5	-49.5	-18.9	15.7	5.2	30.2	-19.3	23.9	-5.2	45.0	-0.5	21.8
Condiment & Spices	0.66	24.5	2.8	-10.6	-7.1	3.1	5.7	-8.2	-6.1	29.2	5.0	11.7	19.6
Black pepper	0.02	21.4	2.9	-4.7	-50.8	-0.2	-10.5	-12.8	-3.4	40.2	43.8	0.3	-2.8
Chillies (Dry)	0.19	48.2	-10.8	-16.8	-1.8	1.6	15.9	-23.2	-5.5	61.7	0.6	21.7	9.9
Turmeric	0.08	26.0	-18.1	-29.8	-11.3	51.8	27.2	-2.7	-10.0	-5.6	-8.2	17.8	118.8
Raw Cotton	1.36	7.4	-11.7	6.8	-5.5	-4.4	27.1	-8.3	-12.9	5.1	17.4	23.6	-1.1
Raw Jute	0.11	6.0	4.6	32.7	21.8	-15.8	-10.7	16.6	24.3	2.5	-6.4	8.3	17.6

(P) Provisional

Sorce: Office of the Economic Adviser, Ministry of Commerce & Industry.

price index, which showed a decline from the levels of 1990, all other price indices showed an increase. While, the prices of

Table 4.7: Monthly Real Food Price Indices (2002-2004=100)

Date	Food Price Index	Meat Price Index	Dairy Price Index	Cereals Price Index	Oils Price Index	Sugar Price Index
1/1990	110.4	118.3	93.2	106.6	72.6	201.7
2/1990	111.7	123.3	90.9	104.3	72.6	208.1
3/1990	108.9	122.7	72.8	102.7	74.3	218.2
4/1990	113.7	130.0	84.4	105.6	71.8	216.5
5/1990	112.4	134.6	69.1	105.5	74.0	207.4
6/1990	110.0	135.3	69.1	103.2	71.4	184.2
7/1990	107.1	134.6	69.1	97.2	71.2	170.3
8/1990	105.0	135.7	65.2	93.4	73.8	155.3
9/1990	105.2	139.5	67.4	87.8	73.0	157.2
10/1990	104.3	138.2	68.8	88.9	74.6	139.5
11/1990	103.5	133.9	69.7	88.1	78.3	143.0
12/1990	104.3	131.1	79.1	88.9	80.5	138.3
1/1991	103.0	130.8	80.9	88.6	78.3	122.5
2/1991	103.8	133.8	80.3	90.2	76.4	118.5
3/1991	102.8	127.6	78.5	93.1	76.8	127.2
4/1991	100.1	123.7	73.7	94.6	74.7	118.5
5/1991	97.5	120.8	72.5	93.5	73.7	105.5
6/1991	100.3	123.7	74.4	92.6	74.0	128.1
7/1991	99.9	121.8	69.1	91.7	76.1	143.5
8/1991	99.2	117.3	71.4	95.9	77.8	131.7
9/1991	101.2	119.8	77.8	96.8	77.5	129.3
10/1991	103.0	118.5	83.8	100.0	81.6	127.0
11/1991	103.3	118.5	87.2	100.4	82.0	120.5
12/1991	104.7	118.9	87.2	103.5	82.7	125.3
1/1992	101.8	115.7	87.0	101.7	80.2	111.6
2/1992	101.8	115.3	87.0	105.0	78.4	105.1
3/1992	103.0	117.3	86.2	104.7	81.2	110.2
4/1992	100.9	111.5	86.2	99.9	80.8	126.8
5/1992	101.2	111.0	89.7	98.7	81.3	128.6
6/1992	103.3	112.7	94.5	98.0	82.5	138.9
7/1992	101.7	113.3	95.3	93.5	78.2	138.2
8/1992	99.2	112.6	93.3	89.0	76.4	131.8
9/1992	100.8	114.1	96.0	92.3	78.3	124.8
10/1992	98.8	112.6	90.6	92.2	78.4	116.8
11/1992	100.0	115.5	88.5	93.4	80.8	114.9
12/1992	97.7	112.0	87.6	92.2	79.4	109.3
1/1993	98.6	114.3	86.8	92.6	80.0	109.7
2/1993	98.8	114.6	87.9	91.3	79.7	114.0
3/1993	100.0	113.4	86.8	91.2	78.5	141.4
4/1993	100.1	113.8	85.4	90.4	78.1	148.4
5/1993	100.6	116.5	84.3	87.5	77.3	157.5

(Contd...)

Date	Food Price Index	Meat Price Index	Dairy Price Index	Cereals Price Index	Oils Price Index	Sugar Price Index
6/1993	97.8	115.8	84.3	83.3	76.8	138.3
7/1993	98.5	116.1	81.1	88.2	80.4	128.9
8/1993	96.6	112.3	78.2	89.6	79.3	124.3
9/1993	96.5	111.6	73.7	92.3	79.0	127.0
10/1993	97.8	112.5	67.2	97.7	78.4	137.0
11/1993	99.4	108.1	67.6	106.2	84.6	134.7
12/1993	101.9	106.9	68.6	109.3	95.6	140.0
1/1994	99.4	104.0	71.9	105.0	93.1	132.4
2/1994	98.9	105.1	71.8	102.6	88.4	139.0
3/1994	98.9	105.1	72.6	98.3	89.5	150.9
4/1994	97.6	107.1	66.5	95.8	92.1	141.5
5/1994	99.5	110.1	66.5	94.5	97.1	148.8
6/1994	98.6	106.0	70.6	92.0	97.7	154.9
7/1994	97.1	108.0	71.3	85.6	95.8	151.3
8/1994	99.9	109.6	72.8	87.5	103.8	155.5
9/1994	104.1	110.1	78.4	91.9	114.0	161.8
10/1994	105.0	109.8	81.8	93.9	111.8	163.8
11/1994	107.9	109.8	83.5	93.0	124.5	179.1
12/1994	107.4	102.8	86.5	95.4	125.1	188.5
1/1995	100.7	94.4	88.1	90.4	111.0	179.1
2/1995	100.8	95.1	90.8	89.7	110.2	174.8
3/1995	103.0	100.2	91.7	89.2	111.9	177.0
4/1995	101.7	101.7	90.9	90.0	103.9	166.2
5/1995	101.3	98.8	91.1	93.7	102.1	164.0
6/1995	102.6	94.6	91.1	99.8	106.7	170.1
7/1995	107.4	99.6	96.4	106.8	111.1	164.9
8/1995	105.6	99.5	96.4	104.6	106.8	157.5
9/1995	105.3	99.7	96.4	109.5	102.9	141.8
10/1995	107.4	98.1	97.4	115.9	107.5	143.7
11/1995	108.0	99.7	97.4	116.1	106.5	145.4
12/1995	106.9	95.4	97.0	119.0	101.9	149.4
1/1996	112.7	102.4	101.9	126.0	101.0	159.9
2/1996	113.7	103.3	101.6	129.3	97.9	163.5
3/1996	115.8	108.5	100.3	131.5	96.9	164.8
4/1996	116.4	100.0	100.1	144.0	104.5	152.9
5/1996	118.2	102.4	97.6	150.8	104.9	145.4
6/1996	115.3	100.8	97.8	142.6	99.1	155.3
7/1996	113.2	98.0	98.1	137.7	95.8	163.5
8/1996	113.1	103.5	97.3	130.1	99.6	157.9
9/1996	108.7	104.1	96.8	113.6	102.6	152.1
10/1996	105.1	101.6	97.6	107.7	98.6	141.9
11/1996	103.4	102.6	95.6	102.5	99.5	136.8
12/1996	104.1	103.9	95.9	102.9	99.9	137.1
1/1997	111.1	108.7	103.3	110.8	108.8	146.7
2/1997	112.1	110.9	102.2	111.6	109.6	148.3
3/1997	114.7	115.7	101.9	115.0	107.7	152.4

(Contd...)

Date	Food Price Index	Meat Price Index	Dairy Price Index	Cereals Price Index	Oils Price Index	Sugar Price Index
4/1997	112.5	109.1	100.5	115.1	108.2	155.0
5/1997	111.7	109.5	100.8	111.7	108.9	152.8
6/1997	109.6	108.9	100.2	105.7	106.0	156.8
7/1997	105.6	103.6	99.2	101.3	101.4	153.9
8/1997	108.1	105.4	99.0	106.7	101.2	160.5
9/1997	106.5	100.2	100.9	105.9	105.1	155.4
10/1997	108.2	99.2	103.6	107.1	113.0	156.5
11/1997	109.4	99.9	104.0	105.1	119.2	164.8
12/1997	107.7	96.1	104.2	104.0	116.4	169.2
1/1998	111.6	100.7	108.1	106.6	125.2	164.7
2/1998	109.2	96.1	106.1	106.6	127.9	152.9
3/1998	108.8	96.9	103.0	107.3	131.6	140.3
4/1998	108.2	98.2	102.7	103.4	133.6	138.2
5/1998	106.3	93.2	100.7	102.4	139.9	131.6
6/1998	104.5	97.4	99.1	100.6	129.8	115.5
7/1998	101.8	90.3	99.0	97.9	130.0	123.2
8/1998	99.6	89.2	99.2	92.1	128.8	120.9
9/1998	98.7	91.2	96.4	91.9	130.7	103.1
10/1998	100.5	92.2	93.4	98.4	130.7	106.4
11/1998	100.9	90.7	93.4	99.2	130.8	114.9
12/1998	100.1	91.4	93.5	97.0	127.3	115.2
1/1999	99.8	92.4	93.8	97.9	120.3	116.0
2/1999	94.8	91.0	92.6	94.2	106.7	97.6
3/1999	93.6	93.9	91.5	94.5	97.3	86.1
4/1999	91.8	93.0	86.5	92.3	101.4	77.5
5/1999	91.0	92.9	85.6	90.8	97.6	82.3
6/1999	90.2	93.1	85.3	92.0	87.3	86.3
7/1999	87.6	94.6	83.8	88.6	78.6	77.0
8/1999	90.0	96.2	83.8	91.1	84.2	82.3
9/1999	92.2	99.1	84.5	90.2	86.7	95.4
10/1999	91.4	98.8	84.7	87.7	85.2	96.9
11/1999	91.0	99.8	85.4	87.2	82.6	93.0
12/1999	89.1	97.4	87.0	85.4	80.0	86.0
1/2000	90.1	95.6	91.5	89.7	79.8	82.0
2/2000	90.2	97.4	91.9	90.8	76.0	77.3
3/2000	90.7	100.2	91.2	89.3	77.5	75.1
4/2000	91.4	98.8	91.6	88.7	79.6	88.0
5/2000	92.1	100.6	92.4	88.9	72.1	101.0
6/2000	92.5	99.5	96.7	84.9	69.4	122.3
7/2000	92.7	97.9	100.1	80.9	69.0	140.8
8/2000	92.7	96.5	100.8	80.1	67.3	152.6
9/2000	91.8	93.5	103.2	83.2	62.5	146.6
10/2000	93.6	92.9	105.9	87.4	60.1	157.1
11/2000	93.2	91.9	106.7	88.8	62.1	145.1
12/2000	95.6	95.4	107.5	92.1	62.9	146.5
1/2001	97.0	93.7	110.2	94.8	63.6	155.5

(Contd...)

Date	Food Price Index	Meat Price Index	Dairy Price Index	Cereals Price Index	Oils Price Index	Sugar Price Index
2/2001	96.4	96.0	109.9	93.1	61.3	148.7
3/2001	96.4	96.8	111.1	92.0	64.6	139.7
4/2001	94.7	95.5	111.3	89.5	64.2	131.7
5/2001	97.2	98.8	115.9	89.4	61.7	144.3
6/2001	96.7	98.0	116.6	88.7	65.6	136.2
7/2001	99.4	97.3	117.3	92.4	80.0	132.4
8/2001	100.4	101.4	116.3	92.0	84.5	122.2
9/2001	100.0	105.5	115.7	91.1	77.4	115.1
10/2001	98.4	104.6	117.5	90.5	73.6	102.3
11/2001	99.5	102.8	113.9	91.9	80.4	115.6
12/2001	99.3	102.9	107.7	92.3	84.1	117.9
1/2002	97.5	99.8	101.9	93.6	83.0	118.7
2/2002	95.5	100.8	101.8	91.7	80.4	99.8
3/2002	95.9	104.0	98.0	90.8	80.0	102.1
4/2002	92.7	96.5	94.7	88.7	82.7	105.0
5/2002	91.1	94.9	86.8	90.9	86.9	92.6
6/2002	91.7	94.4	82.0	93.8	94.4	87.7
7/2002	93.8	94.8	78.1	100.5	95.4	97.4
8/2002	96.6	95.6	77.0	107.8	100.9	96.0
9/2002	100.3	96.0	79.4	119.2	96.7	106.1
10/2002	101.2	95.0	81.5	118.3	100.3	114.5
11/2002	103.5	96.8	86.5	115.5	109.1	119.4
12/2002	103.2	96.4	92.9	108.9	112.2	121.2
1/2003	96.9	93.1	89.3	98.5	102.0	116.2
2/2003	98.2	94.3	92.6	98.4	99.0	127.7
3/2003	97.0	96.2	93.8	95.8	95.0	116.8
4/2003	94.8	92.3	91.9	95.5	95.5	109.9
5/2003	95.5	93.6	91.7	97.4	97.8	101.7
6/2003	95.1	94.3	91.6	95.7	99.6	95.3
7/2003	94.3	95.4	92.7	92.7	95.2	97.0
8/2003	96.7	99.1	93.6	97.6	92.7	96.9
9/2003	98.5	103.8	96.4	97.5	96.9	84.9
10/2003	101.8	105.6	100.6	98.4	109.2	84.5
11/2003	104.6	107.5	102.4	103.6	111.4	86.3
12/2003	106.5	108.5	104.5	105.3	115.1	89.2
1/2004	100.9	103.5	99.8	101.0	107.9	77.0
2/2004	102.5	100.9	105.7	103.4	113.6	77.6
3/2004	105.7	104.3	107.3	107.3	114.8	85.7
4/2004	105.2	99.6	108.2	110.0	115.2	87.3
5/2004	104.2	99.6	111.3	107.9	110.2	84.1
6/2004	105.5	106.2	116.2	104.4	100.0	92.0
7/2004	103.6	103.5	119.2	96.3	99.0	105.0
8/2004	103.3	104.6	119.5	94.0	99.8	100.5
9/2004	104.2	105.6	120.5	95.0	100.4	102.0
10/2004	104.5	105.2	121.2	94.1	98.9	112.2
11/2004	105.6	106.7	123.2	95.4	100.3	108.3

(Contd...)

Date	Food Price Index	Meat Price Index	Dairy Price Index	Cereals Price Index	Oils Price Index	Sugar Price Index
12/2004	105.8	106.3	124.3	96.3	98.8	109.5
1/2005	106.8	108.3	124.9	97.3	95.0	115.7
2/2005	106.4	107.9	125.6	95.8	93.4	120.6
3/2005	108.8	110.3	126.2	98.2	100.5	117.9
4/2005	105.6	106.3	124.9	94.1	98.5	114.0
5/2005	105.7	107.8	125.6	93.2	97.1	113.9
6/2005	106.9	108.3	125.2	95.1	97.8	120.1
7/2005	106.4	104.2	126.4	96.2	97.1	127.9
8/2005	105.7	102.3	128.4	95.2	94.2	131.8
9/2005	107.8	104.0	129.1	97.9	96.0	136.8
10/2005	109.4	103.1	128.7	100.1	100.3	147.6
11/2005	107.9	101.1	127.9	97.8	98.2	151.0
12/2005	109.6	101.0	126.1	100.0	95.2	177.1
1/2006	109.3	98.5	119.9	99.2	93.6	205.7
2/2006	112.6	98.7	120.1	102.6	95.2	234.4
3/2006	110.3	95.9	117.9	101.2	95.3	225.2
4/2006	110.9	96.2	115.5	103.1	96.9	228.4
5/2006	113.0	99.9	115.0	107.0	99.7	219.7
6/2006	110.6	97.6	114.7	106.4	99.5	201.2
7/2006	113.0	97.9	115.0	110.4	103.4	209.6
8/2006	110.8	99.0	113.4	108.9	107.3	175.7
9/2006	110.3	99.0	113.5	113.1	104.4	157.8
10/2006	113.4	98.3	115.9	124.7	106.0	152.0
11/2006	118.1	98.7	121.8	132.9	114.6	153.9
12/2006	120.3	98.8	130.9	132.5	121.1	151.1
1/2007	115.1	95.3	128.6	126.4	115.0	136.6
2/2007	117.3	95.4	134.6	131.4	116.1	131.9
3/2007	118.3	96.0	140.1	130.3	118.2	130.2
4/2007	120.3	94.9	154.5	127.0	129.0	121.3
5/2007	123.3	96.5	159.3	128.7	139.0	117.6
6/2007	130.8	97.9	183.8	136.4	145.9	115.9
7/2007	136.1	98.2	205.8	136.4	150.7	126.9
8/2007	141.8	101.4	216.0	145.6	155.3	122.3
9/2007	149.2	102.0	221.9	164.9	162.4	121.7
10/2007	152.4	100.3	226.0	170.4	172.3	124.8
11/2007	158.1	103.3	236.2	172.7	188.3	126.0
12/2007	162.7	101.3	234.1	189.7	191.7	133.6
1/2008	159.0	97.0	210.7	190.6	199.1	140.1
2/2008	171.9	98.1	207.7	223.7	218.5	158.0
3/2008	174.0	101.8	204.9	223.8	228.6	154.3
4/2008	171.7	101.2	199.2	226.0	220.5	146.9
5/2008	172.4	108.5	197.7	220.0	223.7	141.1
6/2008	176.0	110.3	198.3	225.5	232.9	141.8
7/2008	171.5	110.1	196.8	211.5	218.2	166.4
8/2008	162.0	112.0	187.2	197.3	182.6	170.8
9/2008	152.6	113.2	167.5	186.1	164.7	158.2

(Contd...)

Date	Food Price Index	Meat Price Index	Dairy Price Index	Cereals Price Index	Oils Price Index	Sugar Price Index
10/2008	134.7	111.4	152.4	156.9	125.9	139.1
11/2008	124.0	104.6	131.5	146.9	110.0	141.5
12/2008	118.1	100.4	117.0	143.6	104.1	137.4
1/2009	123.5	102.3	105.1	158.8	114.9	152.7
2/2009	119.6	98.2	98.3	152.5	112.7	161.5
3/2009	120.2	98.5	101.2	152.9	110.8	163.5
4/2009	122.8	98.5	101.0	154.0	126.5	166.6
5/2009	131.0	101.9	106.4	159.6	143.5	196.0
6/2009	130.0	101.2	105.6	159.4	137.2	200.5
7/2009	126.6	102.7	108.3	143.7	123.6	224.9
8/2009	130.9	102.6	111.2	139.4	134.5	273.8
9/2009	131.5	101.8	123.9	135.7	128.7	281.2
10/2009	134.8	100.6	135.5	142.9	130.5	276.4
11/2009	145.0	103.2	179.0	147.0	139.1	271.7
12/2009	148.2	103.3	185.5	147.2	145.6	287.2
1/2010	148.6	105.6	172.5	145.4	144.2	320.8
2/2010	145.3	107.0	163.4	140.3	144.5	308.2
3/2010	139.0	109.9	160.1	134.7	149.3	226.2
4/2010	140.6	115.4	174.5	132.2	148.2	199.4
5/2010	140.4	117.0	178.7	132.5	145.5	184.3
6/2010	138.9	116.6	173.5	129.1	143.8	192.1
7/2010	142.4	114.9	169.0	139.5	149.0	211.3
8/2010	151.0	117.9	164.8	158.2	164.3	224.4
9/2010	160.7	116.8	169.4	177.9	168.8	271.7
10/2010	174.8	134.4	173.1	187.9	187.9	298.3
11/2010	181.3	136.5	177.5	190.8	207.8	318.9
12/2010	190.2	140.8	178.0	203.1	244.6	340.3
1/2011	202.9	145.7	194.6	215.4	244.3	369.6
2/2011	208.3	147.7	202.4	227.5	245.7	367.9
3/2011	202.2	148.3	206.1	221.6	228.6	327.5

Source: Food and Agricultural Organisation, World Food Reports

edible oils more than doubled during the period, those of sugar also went up substantially. Same has been the case with India which experienced high inflation, particularly during the last three to four years.

Food inflation generally is directly related to a number of factors. High food inflation is said to be the result of rapid financialisation of food market, unchecked flow of speculative capital into the derivatives market for major food crops, primitive ways of farming in large parts of the country, vagaries of weather adversely impacting agriculture production, poor storage facilities, bottlenecks like hoarding, black marketing, etc. faulty public distribution system, rising demand due to increasing population, improvement in the earnings of people, among other things. The most significant cause of rising prices of food articles, however is the low agriculture production vis-à-vis demand.

Table 4.8 gives a clear picture of yield of major crops in India, viz. rice, wheat, jowar, bajra, maize, ragi, millets, barley, coarse cereals and pulses. It can be observed that the the yield per hectare has not shown any significant increase, has remained static, or in some cases has actually gone down. The per hectare yield of rice, which was 1986 kg in 1999-2000 reached 2130 kg in 2009-10, an increase of just six per cent in 10 years. The yield of wheat went only to 2830 kg/ha in 2009-10 from 2778 kg/ha in 1999-2000, an increase of less than two per cent in 10 years. Jowar went from 847 kg/ha to 911kg/ha, while the yield of bajra increased from 650 kg/ha to 728 kg/ha during the said period. Similarly, the yield of maize went from 1792 kg/ha to 2002 kg/ha; that of ragi from 1401 kg/ha to 1510 kg/ha; that of barley from 1997 kg/ha to 2089 kg/ha; that of coarse cereal from 1034 kg/ha to 1222 kg/per ha; and that of cereals from 1926 kg/ha to 2183 kg/ha. The yield of millets actually went down from 438 kg/ha in 1999-2000 to 435 kg/ha in 2009-10. Similarly, the yield of pulses went down from 635 kg/ha to 625 kg/ha during the said period. It can be seen from Table 4.8 that there have been variations in the per hectare yield of foodgrain, but it has remained more or less the same. The figures reflect poorly on Indian agriculture insofar as the production is concerned. Many reasons can be attributed to this poor yield such as primitive ways of farming in many parts of the country, poverty of farmers in general due to which they are unable to buy inputs like high-yielding varieties of seeds, fertilizers, pesticides, insecticides, etc., non-availability of proper irrigation, poor storage and marketing facilities, and most importantly, vagaries of weather in the shape of insufficient or untimely rain, droughts, floods, etc. All these factors translate into the fact that agriculture production per hectare in India is low and there is always pressure on the supply to meet the ever-increasing demand, leading to high food inflation.

Table 4.8: All-India Estimates of Yield of Major Crops

Crops	Season	Yield (kg/Hectare)										
		1999-2000	2000-01	2001-02	2002-03	2003-04	2004-05	2005-06	2006-07	2007-08	2008-09	2009-10*
1	2	3	4	5	6	7	8	9	10	11	12	13
Rice	Autumn	1534	1404	1532	1202	1385	1327	1349	1526	1396	1582	
	Winter	1736	1726	1938	1595	1868	1756	1795	2000	1891	1967	
	Kharif	2049	1882	2074	1766	2174	2039	2199	2086	2278	2192	
	Total Kharif	1892	1788	1982	1658	2004	1883	1990	2024	2095	2081	2025
	Rabi/Summer	2897	3042	2992	2783	2947	3077	3127	3130	3147	3009	3032
	Total	1986	1901	2079	1744	2078	1984	2102	2131	2202	2178	2130
Wheat	Rabi	2778	2708	2762	2610	2713	2602	2619	2708	2802	2907	2830
Jowar	Kharif	998	938	945	995	1085	987	1082	992	1176	1055	879
	Rabi	713	594	625	552	377	641	726	727	894	904	935
	Total	847	764	771	754	716	797	880	844	1021	962	911
Bajra	Kharif	650	688	869	610	1141	859	802	886	1042	1015	728
Maize	Kharif	1695	1707	1896	1552	1932	1740	1799	1660	2122	2048	1705
	Rabi/Summer	2594	2921	2952	2851	2987	3224	3076	3793	3854	4387	3629
	Total	1792	1822	2000	1681	2041	1907	1938	1912	2335	2414	2002
Ragi	Kharif	1401	1553	1442	930	1180	1567	1534	1226	1552	1477	1510
Small Millets	Kharif	438	412	440	383	473	434	443	475	530	491	435
Barley	Rabi	1997	1840	2160	2006	1975	1958	1938	2055	1985	2394	2089
Coarse Cereals	Kharif	1032	1042	1167	972	1314	1168	1178	1144	1410	1371	1110
	Rabi	1040	973	1005	947	858	1102	1152	1316	1510	1735	1594
	Total	1034	1027	1131	966	1221	1153	1172	1182	1431	1459	1222
Cereals	Kharif	1587	1512	1688	1417	1739	1618	1693	1706	1846	1841	
	Rabi	2483	2438	2476	2319	2413	2382	2427	2526	2645	2721	
	Total	1926	1844	1980	1753	1983	1903	1968	2022	2151	2183	

1	2	3	4	5	6	7	8	9	10	11	12	13
Tur (Arhar)	Kharif	786	618	679	651	670	667	765	650	826	671	723
Pulses Other Than Tur	Kharif	333	313	349	298	466	304	300	349	429	377	204
Gram	Rabi	833	744	853	717	811	815	808	845	762	895	895
Pulses Other Than Gram	Rabi	673	615	628	590	640	622	610	611	567	642	702
Pulses	Kharif	492	417	451	417	528	417	456	449	557	478	408
	Rabi	760	684	756	661	742	735	727	751	688	804	604
	Total	635	544	607	543	635	577	598	612	625	659	625
Foodgrains	Kharif	1441	1357	1510	1272	1551	1430	1511	1522	1644	1654	1498
	Rabi	2091	2067	2076	1933	2004	1988	2020	2091	2174	2263	2197
	Total	1704	1626	1734	1535	1727	1652	1715	1756	1860	1909	1798

*4th Advance Estimates released as on 19.07.2010.

Source: Directorate of Economics and Statistics, Department of Agriculture and Cooperation.

Table 4.9 provides year-wise figures of area, production and yield of kharif and rabi in India from 1966-67 to 2009-10. In case of kharif the production went up from about 49 MT in 1966-67 to around 101 MT in 1989-90, due to Green Revolution marked by extensive use of fertilizers and adopting other modern methods of agriculture. But sine then the production has risen only to around 115 MT in 2009-10. Similarly, production in rabi season, which increased three-fold from 1966-67 to 1992-93, has not risen as sharply thereafter. It can also be observed from Table 4.9 that the per hectare yield improved in the seventies and the eighties, but has remained nearly static in the nineties and after the turn of the century. It is rightly said that we need a Second Green Revolution to increase our agriculture production.

Table 4.9 also provides important data on the area under agriculture production in India. In 1966-67, the total area under cultivation in the country kharif season, growing rice, maize, millets, sugarcane, etc. was 78.21 million hectares (mha) which has now reduced to just 69.05 mha as of Sept. 2010. The area under cultivation in rabi season, growing wheat, barley, oilseeds, pulses, etc., which was 37.09 mha in 1966-67 stood at 52.04 mha in 2009-10. Overall, the total area under cultivation in India, which was 115.30 mha in 1966-67, was 121.37 mha in 2009-10. This tells us that there has been no effort worth the name for reclamation of large tracts of land which lie waste in various parts of the country. Estimates of the National Wasteland Development Board (NWDB) reveal that 63.05 mha of land in India is wasteland. It constitutes 20 per cent of the total geographical area of the country. It includes 14 mha of degraded forests which are dying and serving no real purpose. This waste means less agriculture production as there is more pressure on existing land being used for cultivation, which is losing its fertility due to regular cropping. It would however be wrong to say that no idle land has been made fit for cultivation and brought under the plough during this period.

According to Speck SpecialTech Ltd., a geographical company that offers comprehensive GIS solutions, the

Table 4.9: Season-wise Area, Production and Yield of Foodgrains

A - Area in Million Hectares
P - Production in Million Tonnes
Y - Yield in kg./Hectare.

Year	Kharif			Rabi			Total		
	A	P	Y	A	P	Y	A	P	Y
1	2	3	4	5	6	7	8	9	10
1966-67	78.21	48.89	625	37.09	25.34	683	115.30	74.23	644
1967-68	81.49	60.76	746	39.93	34.29	859	121.42	95.05	783
1968-69	80.40	59.57	741	40.03	34.44	860	120.43	94.01	781
1969-70	82.30	62.35	758	41.27	37.15	900	123.57	99.50	805
1970-71	82.36	68.92	837	41.96	39.50	941	124.32	108.42	872
1971-72	79.22	62.99	795	43.40	42.18	972	122.62	105.17	858
1972-73	78.34	58.64	749	40.94	38.39	938	119.28	97.03	813
1973-74	84.12	67.84	806	42.42	36.83	868	126.54	104.67	827
1974-75	79.74	59.10	741	41.34	40.73	985	121.08	99.83	824
1975-76	83.15	73.89	889	45.03	47.14	1047	128.18	121.03	944
1976-77	81.18	66.53	820	43.18	44.64	1034	124.36	111.17	894
1977-78	82.88	77.72	938	44.64	48.69	1091	127.52	126.41	991
1978-79	82.85	78.08	942	46.16	53.82	1166	129.01	131.90	1022
1979-80	80.79	63.25	783	44.42	46.45	1046	125.21	109.70	876
1980-81	83.21	77.65	933	43.46	51.94	1195	126.67	129.59	1023
1981-82	83.93	79.38	946	45.21	53.92	1193	129.14	133.30	1032
1982-83	79.08	69.90	884	46.02	59.62	1296	125.10	129.52	1035
1983-84	84.14	89.23	1060	47.02	63.14	1343	131.16	152.37	1162
1984-85	81.18	84.52	1041	45.49	61.02	1341	126.67	145.54	1149
1985-86	81.80	85.25	1042	46.22	65.19	1410	128.02	150.44	1175
1986-87	81.46	80.20	985	45.74	63.22	1382	127.20	143.42	1128
1987-88	74.89	74.56	996	44.80	65.79	1469	119.69	140.35	1173
1988-89	82.03	95.64	1166	45.64	74.28	1628	127.67	169.92	1331
1989-90	81.40	100.99	1241	45.37	70.05	1544	126.77	171.04	1349
1990-91	80.78	99.44	1231	47.06	76.95	1635	127.84	176.39	1380
1991-92	78.02	91.59	1174	43.85	76.79	1751	121.87	168.38	1382
1992-93	77.92	101.47	1302	45.23	78.01	1725	123.15	179.48	1457
1993-94	75.81	100.40	1324	46.94	83.86	1787	122.75	184.26	1501
1994-95	75.19	101.09	1344	48.67	90.41	1858	123.86	191.50	1546
1995-96	73.60	95.12	1292	47.42	85.30	1799	121.02	180.42	1491
1996-97	75.34	103.92	1379	48.24	95.52	1980	123.58	199.44	1614
1997-98	74.15	101.58	1370	49.70	90.68	1825	123.85	192.26	1552
1998-99	73.99	102.91	1391	51.18	100.69	1967	125.17	203.60	1627
1999-00	73.24	105.51	1441	49.87	104.29	2091	123.11	209.80	1704
2000-01	75.22	102.09	1357	45.83	94.73	2067	121.05	196.81	1626
2001-02	74.23	112.07	1510	48.55	100.78	2076	122.78	212.85	1734
2002-03	68.56	87.22	1272	45.30	87.55	1933	113.86	174.77	1535
2003-04	75.44	117.00	1551	48.01	96.19	2004	123.45	213.19	1727
2004-05	72.26	103.31	1430	47.82	95.05	2004	120.08	198.36	1652
2005-06	72.72	109.87	1511	48.88	98.73	2020	121.60	208.60	1715
2006-07	72.67	110.58	1522	51.04	106.71	2091	123.71	217.28	1756
2007-08	73.56	120.96	1644	50.51	109.82	2174	124.07	230.78	1860
2008-09	71.43	118.14	1654	51.40	116.33	2263	122.83	234.47	1909
2009-10*	69.33	103.84	1498	52.04	114.36	2197	121.37	218.20	1798
2010-11**	69.05	114.63	1660	-	-	-	-	-	-

* Fourth Advance Estimates as released on 19.07.2010.

** First Advance Estimates as released on 23.09.2010.

Source: Directorate of Economics and Statistics, Department of Agriculture and Cooperation.

Government of India has realized the enormous significance of developing wastelands into sustainable and productive assets and launched the Integrated Wastelands Development Program (IWDP) in 1989-90. It launched in January 2003, "Hariyali", the new initiative to operationalize village-wise watershed development programs, under which IWDP shall be concurrently implemented. Today, policymakers and planners consider watershed-wise wasteland development as a national program that truly constitutes an efficient model for integrated rural development.[1] These efforts are appreciable, but the fact of the matter is that so far only around 10 to 15 per cent of total wasteland has been reclaimed, which is negligible considering the total area of wasteland in the country.

Another factor which needs to be considered is that rapid urbanization in countries like India is harming the cause of agriculture in various ways. A large number of people are moving from villages to cities every year for better opportunities and facilities. As cities are expanding, tracts of nearby land, including agriculture land are being acquired to build housing colonies. As industry in India is developing fast, large pieces of land have been acquired to set up large industries. Under Special Economic Zone (SEZ) scheme, thousands of acres of land, including agriculture land were acquired in various states. In some cases, such acquisition was against the wishes of landowners, many of whom were farmers, but under the provisions of Land Acquisition Act which empowers the government to acquire any land for industry. There were violent incidents at some places like Singur in West Bengal where people were not prepared to sell their land.

But the sad story of agriculture continues as more and more land continues to be taken for setting up large industries, making housing colonies or for other projects of development. Industrial development is not something bad, but it should not be done at the cost of agriculture and environment. Unfortunately, in India, industry is being developed with utter disregard for agriculture and environment. Experts like Dr. Swaminathan have been suggesting all along that only those land should be acquired for industry which is not fit for farming. Farmers must not be asked to sell their land to set up industry. But these suggestions are being ignored, the result being availability of less areas of land for agriculture and low food production, and hence high food inflation.

Table 4.10 provides consolidated year-wise data on area, production and yield of agriculture in India since 1950-51. Again it can be observed that the progress is quite acceptable upto 1980s after which it has stagnated. In addition, Table 4.10 provides important information regarding the area under irrigation as a percentage to total area under cultivation, year-wise, from 1950-51 to 2007-08. It can be observed that in 1950-51, only 18.1 per cent of the total cultivable land in India was under irrigation. In 1960-61, i.e. in 10 years, the percentage reached only 19.01. In other words, the progress was dismal. India's agriculture remained totally dependent on rain for irrigation. In 1970-71, the irrigated area was only 24.1 per cent of the total cultivable land in India, which reached 29.7 per cent in 1980-81. In the 1980s and the 1990s there were efforts to improve irrigation facilities by providing more connectivity to canals in the states of UP, MP, Bihar, Maharashtra and Karnataka. A program called Minor Irrigation Program was launched throughout the country whereby farmers could avail loans from the banks on low rate of interest to buy pump sets, etc. The percentage of irrigated land thus improved to 35.1 in 1990-91 and further to 43.4 in 2000-01. At present about 47 per cent of total cultivated land in India is irrigated, which means that more than half the land still has no access to proper irrigation facilities. This is one of the reasons of our low agriculture production and higher prices of food.

Table 4.11 shows the production and yield of foodgrain and all-India percentage of major producing states. Punjab, occupying 6.46 mha produced 26.86 MT of foodgrain in 2007-08, which increased to 27.33 MT in 2008-09. In comparison, Rajasthan and Maharashtra occupying 13.21 mha and 11.42 mha respectively, produced only 16.68 MT and 11.43 MT respectively in 2008-09. This shows that the production in most states is very low. A comparison of foodgrain production and yield in 2007-08 and 2008-09 tells

Table 4.10: All-India Area, Production and Yield of Foodgrains Alongwith Coverage Under Irrigation

Area - Million Hectares
Production - Million Tonnes
Yield - kg./Hectare

Year	Area	Production	Yield	Area Under Irrigation(%)
1	2	3	4	5
1950-51	97.32	50.82	522	18.1
1951-52	96.96	51.99	536	18.4
1952-53	102.09	59.20	580	18.1
1953-54	109.07	69.82	640	18.1
1954-55	107.86	68.03	631	18.4
1955-56	110.56	66.85	605	18.5
1956-57	111.14	69.86	629	18.2
1957-58	109.48	64.31	587	19.3
1958-59	114.76	77.14	672	18.7
1959-60	115.82	76.67	662	18.8
1960-61	115.58	82.02	710	19.1
1961-62	117.23	82.71	706	19.1
1962-63	117.84	80.15	680	19.8
1963-64	117.42	80.64	687	19.8
1964-65	118.11	89.36	757	20.2
1965-66	115.10	72.35	629	20.9
1966-67	115.30	74.23	644	22.2
1967-68	121.42	95.05	783	21.6
1968-69	120.43	94.01	781	23.6
1969-70	123.57	99.50	805	23.7
1970-71	124.32	108.42	872	24.1
1971-72	122.62	105.17	858	24.5
1972-73	119.28	97.03	813	25.4
1973-74	126.54	104.67	827	24.5
1974-75	121.08	99.83	824	26.5
1975-76	128.18	121.03	944	26.5
1976-77	124.36	111.17	894	27.4
1977-78	127.52	126.41	991	27.7
1978-79	129.01	131.90	1022	28.8
1979-80	125.21	109.70	876	30.3
1980-81	126.67	129.59	1023	29.7
1981-82	129.14	133.30	1032	29.6
1982-83	125.10	129.52	1035	30.8
1983-84	131.16	152.37	1162	30.9
1984-85	126.67	145.54	1149	31.9
1985-86	128.02	150.44	1175	31.4
1986-87	127.20	143.42	1128	32.6
1987-88	119.69	140.35	1173	33.5
1988-89	127.67	169.92	1331	34.4

(*Contd...*)

1	2	3	4	5
1989-90	126.77	171.04	1349	35.0
1990-91	127.84	176.39	1380	35.1
1991-92	121.87	168.38	1382	37.4
1992-93	123.15	179.48	1457	37.4
1993-94	122.75	184.26	1501	38.7
1994-95	123.86	191.50	1546	39.6
1995-96	121.01	180.42	1491	40.1
1996-97	123.58	199.44	1614	40.0
1997-98	123.85	192.26	1552	40.8
1998-99	125.17	203.61	1627	42.4
1999-00	123.10	209.80	1704	43.9
2000-01	121.05	196.81	1626	43.4
2001-02	122.78	212.85	1734	43.0
2002-03	113.86	174.77	1535	42.8
2003-04	123.45	213.19	1727	42.2
2004-05	120.00	198.36	1652	44.2
2005-06	121.60	208.60	1715	45.5
2006-07	123.71	217.28	1756	46.3
2007-08	124.07	230.78	1860	46.8
2008-09	122.83	234.47	1909	NA
2009-10*	121.37	218.20	1798	NA
2010-11**	69.05	114.63	1660	NA

* Fourth Advance Estimates as released on 19.07.2010.

** First Advance Estimates as released on 23.09.2010.

Note: The yield rates given above have been worked out on the basis of production and area figures taken in '000 units.

Source: Directorate of Economics and Statistics, Department of Agriculture and Cooperation.

us that there is little improvement and that the figures are almost static. This reflects poorly on Indian agriculture. If this trend continues, the prices of food will continue to be high as demand will increase with increase in population.

Rice is a major cereal in India. A large population of the country consume rice daily as food. Table 4.12 shows year-wise production and yield of rice in India from 1950-51, to 2009-10. It also shows area under rice production and percentage of area under irrigation. The area in which rice is grown has not increased much over the years. In 1950-51, it was 30.81 mha and in 2009-10 it increased to 41.85 mha. This indicates that little improvement has been made in reclaiming the waste land in India. Rice production has risen from 20.56 MT in 1950-51 to 84.98 MT in 2000-01 and 89.13 MT in 2009-10. But during the last ten years or so, the production

Table 4.11: Area, Production and Yield of Foodgrains During 2007-08 and 2008-09 in Major Producing States Alongwith Coverage Under Irrigation

Area - Million Hectares
Production - Million Tonnes
Yield - kg./Hectare

State	2008-09 Area	% to All - India	Production	% to All - India	Yield	2007-08 Area	% to All - India	Production	% to All - India	Yield	Area Under Irrigation(%) 2007-08*
1	2	3	4	5	6	7	8	9	10	11	12
Uttar Pradesh	19.76	16.08	46.73	19.93	2365	19.08	15.38	42.09	18.24	2206	74.9
Punjab	6.46	5.26	27.33	11.66	4231	6.30	5.08	26.82	11.62	4255	98.0
Andhra Pradesh	7.44	6.06	20.42	8.71	2744	7.39	5.96	19.30	8.36	2613	58.1
Rajasthan	13.21	10.75	16.68	7.11	1263	13.61	10.97	16.06	6.96	1180	28.0
West Bengal	6.54	5.32	16.30	6.95	2493	6.36	5.13	16.05	6.95	2525	48.4
Haryana	4.61	3.75	15.61	6.66	3388	4.48	3.61	15.31	6.63	3420	88.5
Madhya Pradesh	11.91	9.70	13.91	5.93	1168	11.29	9.10	12.07	5.23	1069	44.4
Bihar	6.92	5.63	12.22	5.21	1766	7.03	5.67	10.86	4.71	1546	63.1
Maharashtra	11.42	9.29	11.43	4.87	1001	13.21	10.65	15.19	6.58	1150	17.5
Karnataka	7.46	6.07	11.28	4.81	1511	7.87	6.34	12.19	5.28	1548	25.8
Orissa	5.43	4.42	7.40	3.16	1363	5.49	4.42	8.14	3.53	1484	35.1
Tamil Nadu	3.19	2.60	7.10	3.03	2225	3.10	2.50	6.58	2.85	2125	58.4
Gujarat	4.06	3.31	6.48	2.76	1595	4.48	3.61	8.21	3.56	1831	42.2
Chhattisgarh	4.96	4.04	5.17	2.20	1041	5.08	4.09	6.29	2.73	1238	26.9
Jharkhand	2.43	1.98	4.19	1.79	1720	2.44	1.97	4.16	1.80	1709	8.0
Assam	2.67	2.17	4.14	1.77	1551	2.52	2.03	3.47	1.50	1378	3.4
Uttarakhand	1.03	0.84	1.77	0.75	1715	1.01	0.81	1.80	0.78	1785	40.2
Others	3.33	2.71	6.31	2.69	@	3.33	2.68	6.19	2.68	@	-
All India	**122.83**	**100.00**	**234.47**	**100.00**	**1909**	**124.07**	**100.00**	**230.78**	**100.00**	**1860**	**46.8**

@ - Since area/production is low in individual states, yield rate is not worked out.

Note: States have been arranged in descending order of percentage share of production during 2007-08.

* Provisional

Source: Directorate of Economics and Statistics, Department of Agriculture and Cooperation.

Table 4.12: All-India Area, Production and Yield of Rice Alongwith Coverage Under Irrigation

Area - Million Hectares
Production - Million Tonnes
Yield - kg./Hectare

Year	Area	Production	Yield	Area Under Irrigation(%)
1	2	3	4	5
1950-51	30.81	20.58	668	31.7
1951-52	29.83	21.30	714	31.7
1952-53	29.97	22.90	764	32.3
1953-54	31.29	28.21	902	33.6
1954-55	30.77	25.22	820	34.4
1955-56	31.52	27.56	874	34.9
1956-57	32.28	29.04	900	35.4
1957-58	32.30	25.53	790	36.4
1958-59	33.17	30.85	930	36.3
1959-60	33.82	31.68	937	35.8
1960-61	34.13	34.58	1013	36.8
1961-62	34.69	35.66	1028	37.5
1962-63	35.69	33.21	931	37.4
1963-64	35.81	37.00	1033	37.1
1964-65	36.46	39.31	1078	37.3
1965-66	35.47	30.59	862	36.5
1966-67	35.25	30.44	863	37.9
1967-68	36.44	37.61	1032	38.6
1968-69	36.97	39.76	1076	38.4
1969-70	37.68	40.43	1073	38.2
1970-71	37.59	42.22	1123	38.4
1971-72	37.76	43.07	1141	37.2
1972-73	36.69	39.24	1070	39.1
1973-74	38.29	44.05	1151	38.4
1974-75	37.89	39.58	1045	38.8
1975-76	39.48	48.74	1235	38.7
1976-77	38.51	41.92	1089	38.4
1977-78	40.28	52.67	1308	40.2
1978-79	40.48	53.77	1328	41.6
1979-80	39.42	42.33	1074	42.8
1980-81	40.15	53.63	1336	40.7
1981-82	40.71	53.25	1308	41.5
1982-83	38.26	47.12	1231	42.0
1983-84	41.24	60.10	1457	42.7
1984-85	41.16	58.34	1417	43.7
1985-86	41.14	63.83	1552	42.9
1986-87	41.17	60.56	1471	44.1

(Contd...)

1	2	3	4	5
1987-88	38.81	56.86	1465	43.6
1988-89	41.73	70.49	1689	45.8
1989-90	42.17	73.57	1745	46.1
1990-91	42.69	74.29	1740	45.5
1991-92	42.65	74.68	1751	47.3
1992-93	41.78	72.86	1744	48.0
1993-94	42.54	80.30	1888	48.6
1994-95	42.81	81.81	1911	49.8
1995-96	42.84	76.98	1797	49.9
1996-97	43.43	81.74	1882	51.0
1997-98	43.45	82.53	1900	50.8
1998-99	44.80	86.08	1921	52.3
1999-00	45.16	89.68	1986	53.9
2000-01	44.71	84.98	1901	53.6
2001-02	44.90	93.34	2079	53.2
2002-03	41.18	71.82	1744	50.2
2003-04	42.59	88.53	2077	52.6
2004-05	41.91	83.13	1984	54.7
2005-06	43.66	91.79	2102	56.0
2006-07	43.81	93.36	2131	56.7
2007-08	43.91	96.69	2202	56.9
2008-09	45.54	99.18	2178	NA
2009-10*	41.85	89.13	2130	NA
2010-11**	36.95	80.41	2177	NA

* Fourth Advance Estimates as released on 19.07.2010.

** First Advance Estimates as released on 23.09.2010.

Note: The yield rates given above have been worked out on the basis of production and area figures taken in '000 units.

Source: Directorate of Economics and Statistics, Department of Agriculture and Cooperation.

has remained static. All these factors are sesponsible for stiff prices of rice during the last many years.

Table 4.13 shows that West Bengal, AP, UP and Punjab are the major rice-producing states in India. They produced 14.72 MT, 13.32 MT, 11.78 MT and 10.49 MT of rice respectively in 2007-08. The production increased to 15.04 MT, 14.24 MT, 13.10 MT and 11.00 MT respectively in 2008-09. Orissa and Bihar also produced 6.81 MT and 5.59 MT of rice respectively in 2008-09. Tamil Nadu produced 5.18 MT. In many areas in other states the conditions are not suitable for growing rice and thus their contribution was comparatively less. Punjab has the highest per hectare yield as it has 99.4 per

Table 4.13: Area, Production and Yield of Rice during 2007-08 and 2008-09 in Major Producing States Alongwith Coverage Under Irrigation

Area - Million Hectares
Production - Million Tonnes
Yield - kg./Hectare

State	2008-09 Area	% to All - India	Production	% to All - India	Yield	2007-08 Area	% to All - India	Production	% to All - India	Yield	Area Under Irrigation(%) 2007-08*
1	2	3	4	5	6	7	8	9	10	11	12
West Bengal	5.94	13.03	15.04	15.16	2533	5.72	13.03	14.72	15.22	2573	48.4
Andhra Pradesh	4.39	9.63	14.24	14.36	3246	3.98	9.06	13.32	13.78	3344	96.6
Uttar Pradesh	6.03	13.25	13.10	13.20	2171	5.71	13.00	11.78	12.18	2063	77.2
Punjab	2.74	6.01	11.00	11.09	4022	2.61	5.94	10.49	10.85	4019	99.4
Orissa	4.45	9.78	6.81	6.87	1529	4.45	10.13	7.54	7.80	1694	46.4
Bihar	3.50	7.68	5.59	5.64	1599	3.57	8.13	4.42	4.57	1237	57.0
Tamil Nadu	1.93	4.24	5.18	5.23	2683	1.79	4.08	5.04	5.21	2817	92.7
Chattisgarh	3.73	8.20	4.39	4.43	1176	3.75	8.54	5.43	5.62	1446	32.9
Assam	2.48	5.46	4.01	4.04	1614	2.32	5.28	3.32	3.43	1428	3.7
Karnataka	1.51	3.32	3.80	3.83	2511	1.42	3.23	3.72	3.85	2625	73.7
Jharkhand	1.68	3.70	3.42	3.45	2031	1.65	3.76	3.34	3.45	2018	5.6
Haryana	1.21	2.66	3.30	3.33	2726	1.08	2.46	3.61	3.73	3361	99.9
Maharashtra	1.52	3.34	2.28	2.30	1501	1.57	3.58	3.00	3.10	1903	26.4
Madhya Pradesh	1.68	3.69	1.56	1.57	927	1.56	3.55	1.46	1.51	938	15.4
Gujarat	0.75	1.64	1.30	1.31	1744	0.76	1.73	1.47	1.52	1942	57.4
Kerala	0.23	0.51	0.59	0.60	2519	0.23	0.52	0.53	0.55	2310	67.4
Others	1.75	3.85	3.56	3.59	@	1.74	3.96	3.50	3.62	@	-
All India	**45.54**	**100.00**	**99.18**	**100.00**	**2178**	**43.91**	**100.00**	**96.69**	**100.00**	**2202**	**56.9**

@ - Since area/production is low in individual states, yield rate is not worked out.

Note: States have been arranged in descending order of percentage share of production during 2008-09.

* Provisional

Source: Directorate of Economics and Statistics, Department of Agriculture and Cooperation.

Table 4.14: Growth Rates of Production of Principal Crops in India from 1994-95 to 2009-10
(Base: T.E.1993-94 = 100)

(Per cent)

Crop	1994-95	1995-96	1996-97	1997-98	1998-99	1999-2000	2000-01	2001-02	2002-03	2003-04	2004-05	2005-06	2006-07	2007-08	2008-09	2009-10	Average Growth During 1994-95 to 2009-10*
1	2	3	4	5	6	7	8	9	10	11	12	13	14	15	16	17	18
Rice	1.85	-5.91	6.16	1.02	4.29	4.19	-5.25	9.84	-23.06	23.26	-6.09	10.42	1.70	3.58	2.57	-10.14	1.15
Wheat	9.91	-5.60	11.69	-4.32	7.45	7.13	-8.76	4.43	-9.63	9.73	-4.88	1.05	9.30	3.65	2.68	0.04	2.12
Jowar	-22.75	4.04	17.26	-31.18	11.79	3.20	-13.30	0.36	-7.20	-4.72	8.43	5.32	-6.28	10.84	-8.58	-3.70	-2.28
Bajra	43.92	-24.83	46.10	-2.83	-9.01	-16.87	16.90	22.56	-43.04	156.61	-34.50	-3.12	9.63	18.36	-10.86	-26.89	8.88
Maize	-7.44	7.26	12.99	0.42	3.06	3.25	4.64	9.27	-15.26	34.37	-5.42	3.80	2.63	25.56	4.09	-15.45	4.24
Ragi	-9.81	6.81	-6.17	-11.07	24.98	-12.22	19.31	-13.07	-44.59	49.40	23.74	-3.24	-38.66	49.09	-5.22	-3.68	1.60
Small millets	-13.00	-2.34	-6.51	-11.48	4.02	-7.84	-5.06	-1.74	-20.36	22.75	-15.29	-1.26	1.70	14.82	-19.23	-20.89	-5.11
Barley	31.46	-12.49	-3.19	14.85	-8.43	-5.90	-1.13	-0.43	-1.20	-7.80	-6.97	1.12	8.79	-9.93	41.22	-23.23	1.05
Coarse Cereals	-2.71	-3.44	17.80	-10.50	2.58	-3.38	2.48	7.68	-21.91	44.93	-11.64	1.75	0.03	20.13	-1.75	-15.65	1.65
Total Cereals	3.68	-5.51	9.37	-2.29	5.10	4.24	-5.57	7.83	-18.71	21.04	-6.48	6.27	3.82	6.37	1.80	-7.41	1.47
Gram	29.23	-22.62	11.76	10.20	10.90	-24.74	-24.67	41.96	-22.59	34.95	-4.34	1.94	13.60	-9.24	22.82	4.09	4.58
Tur	-20.39	7.80	14.98	-30.37	46.41	-0.52	-16.61	0.58	-3.27	7.80	-0.40	16.66	-15.48	32.92	-26.35	12.66	1.65
Other Pulses	1.67	-12.70	25.58	-14.65	8.03	3.85	-11.28	13.30	65.13	45.27	-22.22	-5.02	9.97	6.98	-11.72	-10.38	5.74
Total Pulses	8.93	-14.60	16.91	-6.57	15.18	-11.54	-18.20	22.02	12.34	33.10	-10.74	2.28	6.29	3.97	-1.32	0.22	3.64
Total Foodgrains	4.37	-6.81	10.43	-2.89	6.44	1.95	-7.16	9.41	-14.86	22.57	-7.06	5.75	4.13	6.21	1.60	-6.94	1.70

(Contd...)

1	2	3	4	5	6	7	8	9	10	11	12	13	14	15	16	17	18
Groundnut	2.96	-5.97	14.03	-14.75	21.83	-41.46	21.87	9.66	-41.36	97.91	-16.64	17.99	-39.16	88.80	-21.94	-23.14	4.41
Sesamum	4.02	-9.39	20.61	-11.32	-7.18	-8.99	7.90	34.76	-36.76	77.23	-13.81	-4.90	-3.54	22.40	-15.40	2.59	**3.64**
Rapeseed & Mustard	6.03	4.19	11.00	-29.33	20.43	2.20	-27.66	21.39	-23.67	62.16	20.69	7.09	-8.53	-21.57	23.43	-10.94	**3.56**
Sunflower	-9.66	3.25	-0.61	-29.17	6.64	-26.51	-6.81	5.12	28.42	6.62	27.55	21.26	-14.70	19.19	-20.85	-22.28	**-0.78**
Soyabean	-17.16	29.60	5.49	20.22	10.52	-0.86	-25.50	13.02	-21.94	67.98	-12.06	20.32	6.98	23.92	-9.69	1.42	**7.02**
Nine Oilseeds	-0.22	2.62	10.49	-14.11	16.10	-16.92	-10.09	12.28	-28.53	69.84	-2.48	14.24	-14.27	22.50	-6.84	-10.07	**2.78**
Total Oilseeds	1.88	2.00	8.96	-12.99	14.07	-15.54	-7.99	9.98	-23.25	53.74	-0.59	14.34	-9.56	11.45	-14.74	6.15	2.37
Cotton (lint)	10.68	8.22	10.65	-23.73	13.23	-6.17	-17.40	4.97	-12.74	59.20	19.66	12.60	22.34	14.37	-13.94	7.44	**6.84**
Jute	8.65	-4.04	29.84	-0.05	-11.28	6.70	-1.18	13.60	-2.93	-0.22	-8.31	6.07	3.49	-0.94	-5.73	11.06	**2.80**
Mesta	0.99	4.88	3.31	-9.61	-7.82	15.95	9.69	-11.69	-8.47	-8.03	-5.24	-0.33	9.86	3.61	-26.20	-19.17	**-3.02**
Jute & Mesta	8.04	-3.31	27.49	-0.71	-11.23	7.31	-0.40	11.61	-3.28	-0.67	-8.15	5.71	3.82	-0.55	-7.54	8.93	**2.32**
Total Fibres	10.37	7.14	11.94	-21.63	10.37	-4.91	-15.62	5.76	-11.49	50.61	-8.00	5.39	4.12	9.40	-12.01	7.91	3.08
Sugarcane	19.94	2.07	-1.27	0.68	3.28	3.67	-1.13	0.42	-3.31	-18.62	1.38	18.59	26.44	-2.06	-18.14	0.00	**2.00**
Potato	0.00	8.26	28.53	-27.13	33.79	4.67	-9.00	6.38	-3.19	-0.90	2.48	1.16	-7.21	28.36	20.79	-35.38	**3.23**
Tobacco	7.07	-9.00	15.49	3.24	15.63	-29.19	-34.22	58.25	-9.86	9.94	-0.15	0.56	-5.94	-5.03	25.95	0.00	**2.67**
Non-Foodgrains	7.32	2.69	6.80	-7.60	9.39	-6.15	-4.53	5.41	-11.09	19.15	1.60	16.05	19.45	1.83	-10.76	-6.57	2.69
All Principal Crops	5.77	-2.54	8.68	-5.08	7.85	-1.79	-6.00	7.62	-13.20	21.00	-1.63	12.16	14.33	3.17	-6.88	-6.69	2.30

*Based on fourth advance estimates released on 19.07.2010.

Source: Directorate of Economics and Statistics, Department of Agriculture and Cooperation.

cent of land under irrigation. Rice is one of the crops that need high irrigation. If the facilities are improved, the rice production can be increased, but as of now the production is not sufficient vis-à-vis supply, resulting in high food inflation.

Table 4.14 provides important data on percentage growth of production of principle crops like rice, wheat, jcwar, bajra, maize, ragi, millets, barley, coarse cereals and pulses in India. In all these crops there is a pattern of increases in some years and decreases in others. Some years have been particularly bad for agriculture when most of the crops showed a negative growth. In 1997-98, for example, only rice, maize, and gram showed a positive growth, while all other crops registered a negative growth. In 2002-03, rice, wheat, jowar, bajra, maize, ragi, millets, coarse cereals and many pulses showed a decrease. Total foodgrain showed a negative growth of 14.86 per cent over the previous year. The year 2009-10 again saw the average growth going negative for most of the crops. This is a clear indication that India agriculture remains at the mercy of weather. If the monsoon is weak or excessively strong there are droughts or floods, adversely impacting food production. We need a large infrastructure to provide irrigation to dry lands as also to prevent floods from doing widespread damage, i.e by taking timely precautions, and diverting rain water to different areas through canals and streams, harnessing rain water, making more ponds, tanks, and desilting major water sources like rivers, lakes, etc. If these measures are not taken, floods and droughts will continue to play havoc with our agriculture and food inflation will remain high.

Table 4.15 provides a comparison of area under agriculture, production and yield between the world, and some major producing countries including India. This comparison is for major crops like paddy, wheat, maize, groundnut and sugarcane. India grew paddy on 44,000 thousand ha and produced 1,48,260 MT of rice. In comparison, China used only 29,493 thousand ha of land, but produced much higher quantity of rice, i.e. 1,93,354 MT. India's per hectare yield is lowest among the reported countries except Thailand. India produces only 3,370 kg/ha of rice as against the world average

Table 4.15: Area, Production and Yield of Principal Crops in Various Countries in 2008

Area ('000 Hectares)
Production ('000 Tonnes)
Yield (kg./Hectare)

Country	Area	Production	Yield
1	2	3	4
1. Paddy			
World	158955	685013	4309
Bangladesh	11741	46905	3995
Brazil	2862	12100	4229
China	29493	193354	6556
Egypt	745	7253	9731
India	44000	148260	3370
Indonesia	12309	60251	4895
Japan	1700	11029	6488
Myanmar	8200	30500	3720
Pakistan	2963	10428	3520
Philippines	4460	16816	3770
Russian Federation	160	738	4603
Thailand	10248	30467	2973
U.S.A.	1204	9240	7672
Vietnam	7414	38725	5223
2. Wheat			
World	223564	689946	3086
Argentina	4284	8428	1967
Bangladesh	388	844	2175
Canada	10032	28611	2852
China	23617	112463	4762
Egypt	1227	7977	6501
France	5492	39002	7101
India	28039	78570	2802
Iran	4750	10000	2105
Italy	2289	8855	3869
Pakistan	8550	20959	2451
Romania	2098	7181	3422
Russian Federation	26070	63765	2446
Spain	2067	6714	3248
Syria	1668	4041	2423
Turkey	7583	17782	2345
U.K.	2080	17227	8281
U.S.A.	22542	68026	3018
Ukraine	7054	25885	3670
Australia	13552	21397	1579
3. Maize			
World	161017	822713	5109
Argentina	3412	22017	6452
Brazil	14445	59018	4086
Canada	1169	10592	9062
China	29883	166035	5556
France	1702	15819	9294

(Contd...)

1	2	3	4
Egypt	820	6544	7977
Hungry	1200	8963	7472
India	8300	19290	2324
Indonesia	4003	16324	4078
Italy	1053	9491	9010
Mexico	7354	24320	3307
Pakistan	1118	4036	3611
Philippines	2661	6928	2604
Romania	2432	7849	3227
Russian Fed	1732	6682	3859
Turkey	594	4274	7198
U.S.A.	31826	307384	9658
4. Groundnut (in shell)			
World	24590	38201	1554
Argentina	227	625	2750
Brazil	113	297	2623
China	4623	14341	3102
India	6850	7338	1071
Indonesia	636	774	1216
Japan	8	19	2262
Myanmar	650	1000	1538
Nigeria	2300	3900	1696
Senegal	670	647	966
Sudan	954	716	751
Thailand	65	114	1754
U.S.A.	610	2335	3829
Uganda	244	173	709
Vietnam	256	534	2085
5. Sugarcane			
World	24375	1743093	71510
Argentina	355	29950	84366
Australia	390	33973	87110
Bangladesh	130	4984	38475
Brazil	8141	648921	79709
China	1709	124918	73114
Colombia	383	38500	100420
Cuba	380	15700	41283
Egypt	136	16470	121136
Guatemala	287	25437	88630
India	5055	348188	68877
Indonesia	416	26000	62563
Mauritius	62	4533	73100
Mexico	669	51107	76367
Thailand	1054	73502	69707
Pakistan	1241	63920	51494
Philippines	398	26601	66839
U.S.A.	374	27603	73765

Source: FAO, Regional Office for Asia and the Pacific, Bangkok.

of 4,309/ha. Egypt has the highest yield at 9,731 kg/ha, which is nearly three times that of ours. The USA, Brazil and Japan also have high yields of 7,672 kg/ha, 6,556 kg/ha and 6,488 kg/ha respectively.

India produces 78,570 thousand tonnes of wheat from 28,039 thousand ha of land, while China uses only 23,617 thousand ha of land and produces much high quantity of wheat, i.e. 1,12,463 thousand tonnes. Our per hectare yield of wheat is among the lowest in the world. We produce only 2,802 kg/ha against the world average of 3,086 kg/ha. The UK and France have much higher yield at 8,281 kg/ha and 7,101 kg/ha respectively.

In case of maize, India's production and yield are very low. Our yield is only 2,324 kg/ha which is less than half the world average of 5,109 kg/ha. The US, France, Canada and Italy have very high yield at 9,658 kg/ha, 9,284 kg/ha, 9,06kg/ha and 9,010 kg/ha respectively. Egypt, Hungry and Turkey have three times the per hectare yield of that in India.

Groundnut is a major source of oil. The seeds are also consumed by a large number of people in various ways. Our groundnut is the lowest among the reporting countries except Senegal, Sudan and Uganda. We produce groundnut with a yield of 1,071 kg/ha as gainst the world average of 1,554 kg/ha. The yield in the US is nearly four times as much as ours, while the yield in China is about three times that of ours.

We are doing slightly better in sugarcane production than in other crops, but here too, our yield at 68,877 kg/ha is less than the world average of 71,510 kg/ha. In comparison, Egypt and Colombia produce sugarcane at 1,21,136 kg/ha and 1,00,420 kg/ha respectively. Egypt, Australia, Argentina and Brazil also have a much higher yield than India.

The foregoing facts reveal that although India has large areas for growing various type of crops, its production and yield are low. Its per hectare yield is among the lowest in the world. This can be attributed to several facts, the most important of which are that the farming methods of majority of its farmers are primitive and that its agriculture is largely dependent on rainfall for irrigation. The countries like the US, Egypt, France and others with a high yield, have adopted modern methods of farming. If we have to solve our food problem, we must modernize our agriculture, otherwise high food inflation will continue to afflict the people as it has been doing for the last few years.

Table 4.16 presents some interesting facts about Indian agriculture and underscores the truth that India is one of the largest food produces in the world. In terms of total area it is the seventh largest country in the world. It is the second largest after the US for arable land, i.e. land suitable for growing crops. In cereals production, India is behind only the US and China, while for wheat and rice production it stands second in the world after China. It is number one producer of pulses in the world. In terms of production of fruits and vegetables including onions and potatoes it is the second largest producer in the world after China. It is also the second largest producer of sugarcane after Brazil. It is third in tea and seventh in coffee production. India is the largest producer of milk, third largest producer of eggs after China and the US, and the fifth largest producer of meat in the world after China, the US, Brazil and Germany.

The above facts lead us to the questions: If India is one of the largest produces of food in the world, then why is the food in limited supply and why are the prices so high? Why is India placed so poorly in the World Hunger Index, behind even countries like Bangladesh? Why the large masses in India are poor have no food security?

Many people have blamed the government policies and the faulty public distribution system (PDS) for high food inflation. The paradox of the food economy in India is that while more than 500 million people are undernourished and many more are vulnerable to food insecurity, over 20 million tonnes of foodgrains are being held in the government godowns. It is believed that these stocks are enough to provide half an individual's annual cereal requirement, to more than 500 million people. Instead of releasing these stocks to ease out high prices, the government's policy is to cut back the PDS

Table 4.16: India's Position in World Agriculture in 2008

Item	India	World	% Share	India's Position Rank	Next to
1	2	3	4	5	6
1. Area (Million Hectares)					
Total Area	329	13442	2.4	Seventh	Russian Federation, Canada, USA, China, Brazil, Australia
Land Area	297	13009	2.3	Seventh	Russian Federation, China, USA, Canada, Brazil, Australia
Arable Land	159	1411	11.2	Second	USA
2. Population* (Million)					
Total	1181	6750	17.5	Second	China
Agriculture	583	2617	22.3	Second	China
3. Economically Active Population* (Million)					
Total	472	3178	14.8	Second	China
Agriculture	262	1295	20.2	Second	China
4. Crop Production (Million Tonnes)					
(A) : Total Cereals	267	2525	10.6	Third	China, USA
Wheat	79	690	11.4	Second	China
Rice (Paddy)	148	685	21.6	Second	China
Total Pulses	15	61	25.1	First	
(B) : Oilseeds					
Groundnut (in shell)	7	38	19.2	Second	China
Rapeseed	6	58	10.1	Third	Canada, China
5. Fruits & Vegetables (Million Tonnes)					
(A) : Vegetables & Melons	79	916	8.6	Second	China
(B) : Fruits excluding Melons	63	572	10.9	Second	China
(C) : Potatoes	34	314	11.0	Second	China
(D) : Onion (Dry)	8	67	12.2	Second	China
6. Commercial Crops (Million Tonnes)					
(A) : Sugarcane	348	1743	20.0	Second	Brazil
(B) : Tea	0.81	4.74	17.0	Third	China, Turkey
(C) : Coffee (green)	0.26	8.24	3.2	Seventh	Brazil, Vietnam, Colombia, Indonesia, Ethiopia, Mexico
(D) : Jute & Jute like Fibres	2.02	3.20	63.3	First	
(E) : Cotton(lint)	3.77	22.85	16.5	Second	China
(F) : Tobacco Leaves	0.52	6.88	7.6	Third	China, Brazil
7. Livestock (Million Heads)					
(A) : Cattle	175	1347	13.0	Second	Brazil
(B) : Buffaloes	99	181	54.6	First	

(*Contd...*)

1	2	3	4	5	6
(C) : Camels	0.63	24.73	2.6	Tenth	Somalia, Sudan, Ethiopia, Niger, Mauritania, Kenya, Mali, Pakistan, Chad
(D) : Sheep	65	1078	6	Third	China, Australia
(E) : Goats	126	862	14.6	Second	China
(F) : Chicken	621	18398	3.4	Fifth	China, USA, Indonesia, Brazil
8. Animal Products					
(A) : Total Milk ('000 MT)	109000	693707	15.7	First	
(B) : Eggs Total ('000 MT)	2740	65586	4.2	Third	China, USA
(C) : Total Meat ('000 MT)	6796	279953	2.4	Fifth	China, USA Brazil, Germany
9. Implements (Thousands numbers)**					
Agricultural Tractors-in-use	3149	29320	10.7	Second	USA

* Estimated and projected figure for 2008

** Figures relate to 2007

Source: FAO, Regional Office for Asia and the Pacific, Bangkok.

further. Rather than using the abundance of grain as an opportunity to raise consumption among the people, the government seems interested in selling its stocks in foreign markets at subsidised prices.

The government has accepted in the Parliament that there have been problems in distribution of foodgrains under the public distribution system (PDS) and the situation was still serious though there has been some improvement. "There are some problems in distribution of foodgrains under the PDS. A committee appointed by the government and another by the Supreme Court observed flaws in the system. I have conducted many reviews and though there is some improvement, the situation is still serious", Agriculture Minister Sharad Pawar said in the Rajya Sabha.

Replying to supplementaries during Question Hour, he expressed dissatisfaction over efforts made by states to curb distribution of bogus ration cards. "I have requested state governments to run campaigns to eliminate bogus ration cards. Work is on but I am not satisfied with the progress. Though as per the Planning Commission, there are 6.5 crore BPL families, states have allotted 10 crore ration cards to them", he stated. To another supplementary, Pawar said his ministry was having discussions with stakeholders on the parameters of the proposed National Food Security Act. "Under the proposed law, every BPL family will get 25 kg of foodgrains per month", he elaborated adding that the ministry was getting a lot of suggestions from several states on the proposed measure.

Table 4.17 provides information about the minimum support price (MSP) of kharif crops, rabi crops and other crops from 2004-05 to 2010-11. It can be observed that the MSP of major kharif crops, viz. paddy and maize was increased from ₹ 560 and ₹ 525 per quintal in 2004-05 to ₹ 1,000 and ₹ 880 per quintal respectively in 2010-11. The MSP of some pulses like arhar, moong and urad went from ₹ 1,390, 1,410 and 1,410 per quintal respectively to ₹ 3,000, 3,170 and 2,900 per quintal respectively in the said period.

In case of rabi crops, the MSP of wheat saw an increase from ₹ 640 per quintal in 2004-05 to ₹ 1,100 per quintal in 2009-10. In other crops, the MSP of copra and sugarcane was increased from ₹ 3,500 and ₹ 75 per quintal to ₹ 4,400 and ₹ 139 per quintal respectively. Thus, the MSPs of all major crops were doubled in a period of five years. This explains the high food inflation in the last few years. It is pertinent to mention here that the increase in the MSP was necessary keeping in view the increasing input costs of farming. Higher MSP has benefitted the farmers and has pushed the prices further because of higher purchasing power of the farmers, which translates itself into more demand for goods including food articles.

It is a well-known fact that high food inflation affects the poor the most as most of their income is spent on purchasing foodgrains, pulses, vegetables, etc. In order that the poor masses may be able to afford foodgrain, the government has provided for a system of food safety network through which people below poverty line (BPL) can get foodgrain at a much cheaper rate. Table 4.18 shows the central issue prices for wheat and rice from 1997 to 2008, for people above poverty line (ABL) and those below poverty line. It can be observed

Table 4.17: Minimum Support Prices of Various Agricultural Commodities (According to Crop year) As on 10.06.2010

(₹ per quintl)

Sl. No	Commodity	Variety	2004-05	2005-06	2006-07	2007-08	2008-09	2009-10	2010-11
1	2	3	4	5	6	7	8	9	10
	Kharif Crops								
1.	Paddy	Common560	570	580^645$$/850~		850$	950&	1000	
		Grade 'A'	590	600	610^	675$$/880~	880$	980	1030
2.	Jowar	Hybrid	515	525	540	600	840	840	880
		Maldandi	-	-	555	620	860	860	900
3.	Bajra		515	525	540	600	840	840	880
4.	Maize		525	540	540	620	840	840	880
5.	Ragi		515	525	540	600	915	915	965
6.	Arhar(Tur)		1390	1400	1410	1550^^	2000	2300	3000!!
7.	Moong		1410	1520	1520	1700^^	2520	2760	3170!!
8.	Urad		1410	1520	1520	1700^^	2520	2520	2900!!
9.	Cotton	F-414/H-777/J34	1760	1760	1770	1800	2500a	2500a	2500a
		H-4	1960	1980	1990	2030	3000aa	3000aa	3000aa
10.	Groundnut In Shell		1500	1520	1520	1550	2100	2100	2300
11.	Sunflower Seed		1340	1500	1500	1510	2215	2215	2350
12.	SOYABEEN	BLACK	900	900	900	910	1350	1350	1400
	YELLOW		1000	1010	1020	1050	1390	1390	1440
13.	Sesamum		1500	1550	1560	1580	2750	2850	2900
14.	Nigerseed		1180	1200	1220	1240	2405	2405	2450
	Rabi Crops								
15.	Wheat		640	650$	750$$	1000	1080	1100	
16.	Barley		540	550	565	650	680	750	
17.	Gram		1425	1435	1445	1600	1730	1760	
18.	Masur (Lentil)		1525	1535	1545	1700	1870	1870	
19.	Rapeseed/Mustard		1700	1715	1715	1800	1830	1830	
20.	Safflower		1550	1565	1565	1650	1650	1680	
21.	Toria		1665	1680	1680	1735	1735	1735	
	Other Crops								
22.	Copra	Milling	3500	3570	3590	3620	3660	4450	4450
	(Calender Year)	Ball	3750	3820	3840	3870	3910	4700	4700
23.	De-Husked Coconut		-	-	-	-	988	1200	1200
24.	Jute		890	910	1000	1055	1250	1375	1575
25.	Sugarcane@		74.50	79.50	80.25	81.18	81.18	129.84[]	139.12[]*
26.	Tobacco(Vfc)	Black Soil(F2 Gr)	32.00	32.00	32.00	32.00	-		
	(₹ per kg.)	Light Soil (L2 Gr)	34.00	34.00	34.00	34.00	-		

$ An additional incentive bonus of ₹ 50 per quintal was payable over the Minimum Support Price(MSP).

$$ An additional incentive bonus of ₹ 100 per quintal is payable over the Minimum Support Price(MSP).

^ An additional incentive bonus of ₹ 40 per quintal is payable on procurement between 1.10.2006 to 31.03.2007.

In case of Bihar and Kerala additional incentive bonus extended upto 31.5.2007 and in case of Andhra Pradesh, Chhatisgarh, Orissa, Tamil Nadu and West Bengal additional incentive bonus extended upto 30.9.2007.

* At 9.5 per cent recovery, subject to a premium of ₹ 1.46 for every 0.1 per cent increase in the recovrey above 9.5 per cent.

** A bonus of ₹ 40 per quintal is payble over & above the MSP.

~ From 12.06.2008

a Staple length (mm) of 24.5 - 25.5 and micronaire value of 4.3 - 5.1

aa Staple length (mm) of 29.5 - 30.5 and micronaire value of 3.5 - 4.3

& An additional incentive bonus of ₹ 50 per quintal is payable over the Minimum Support Price(MSP).

[] Fair and remunerative price.

!! Additional incenntive at the rate of ₹ 5 per kg of tur, urad and monge sold to procuremant agencies is payble during the harvest/arrival period of two months.

Source: Directorate of Economics and Statistics, Department of Agriculture and Cooperation.

that the changes made in the issue prices for BPL families over the years are quite small so that these people may get foodgrain as per their requirement from their meager means.

Table 4.19 gives the marketed surplus ratio for foodgrains, pulses, oilseeds, commercial crops and vegetables in major producing states in the years 2005-06, 2006-07 and 2007-08. The data tells us the quantity of rice, wheat, maize, pulses, oilseeds, sugarcane, vegetables, etc. marketed out of produced during the said years. It can be observed that the ratio of marketed foodgrains to surplus is increasing because the input costs of farmers are increasing and they have marketed more out of their produce to recover the costs. This may boost supply, but it also means that the farmers have less for their own consumption and may have to buy from the market if

Table 4.18: Central Issue Prices of Rice, Wheat and Coarse Grains

(₹ per Quintal)

Period	APL		BPL
	Common	Grade "A"	Common/Grade"A"
1	2	3	4
RICE			
01.12.1997 to 28.01.1999	550@	700	350
29.01.1999 to 31.3.2000	700@	905	350
01.04.2000 to 24.7.2000	1135@	1180	590
25.07.2000 to 11.07.2001	1087@	1130	565
12.07.2001 to 31.03.2002	795@	830	565
01.04.2002 to 30.06.2002	695@	730	565
01.07.2002 to 18.02.2008	795@	830	565
WHEAT			
01.06.1997 to 28.01.1999	450		250
29.01.1999 to 31.03.1999	650		250
01.04.1999 to 31.03.2000	682		250
01.04.2000 to 24.07.2000	900		450
25.07.2000 to 11.07.2001	830		415
12.07.2001 to 31.03.2002	610		415
01.04.2002 to 30.06.2002	510		415
01.07.2002 to 18.02.2008	610		415
COARSE GRAINS	APL	BPL	AAY
16.11.2005	70% of Economic cost	50% of Economic cost	₹ 2.00 per kg.
03.10.2008	₹ 4.00 per kg.	₹ 3.00 per kg.	₹ 1.50 per kg.

@ Applicable only to J&K, H.P, North Eastern States, Sikkim and Uttarakhand

Note: Central issue price for AAY household fixed @ ₹ 3 per kg. For rice and ₹ 2 per kg for wheat since its inception in December 2000 and it has not been revised.

Source: Department of Food & Public Distribution.

Table 4.19: Marketed Surplus Ratio (MSR) of Important Agricultural Commodities in Various States (Based on Comprehensive Scheme for Studying Cost of Cultivation of Principal Crops in India)

Group of Crops	Crops	State	MSR		
			2005-06	2006-07	2007-08
1	2	3	4	5	6
I. Foodgrains: Cereals	1. Rice	Andhra Pradesh	79.99	84.46	91.99
		Assam	65.64	34.55	25.96
		Bihar	68.04	79.28	80.03
		Haryana	96.82	99.05	95.18
		Karnataka	94.35	94.59	85.47
		Kerala	63.20	73.55	72.98
		Madhya Pradesh	69.11	63.04	78.98
		Orissa	59.08	67.91	66.18
		Punjab	98.12	98.66	98.06
		Tamil Nadu	74.54	80.03	83.80
		Uttar Pradesh	38.93	79.62	36.30
		West Bengal	48.51	68.40	64.45
	All-India		71.25	79.17	72.64
	2. Wheat	Bihar	59.27	66.55	73.58
		Gujarat	91.50	85.74	66.99
		Haryana	66.24	72.46	81.53
		Himachal Pradesh	48.03	51.82	49.88
		Madhya Pradesh	54.76	65.57	75.95
		Punjab	76.46	81.33	90.58
		Rajasthan	49.25	62.61	64.38
		Uttar Pradesh	35.00	53.63	29.90
	All-India		54.90	66.09	61.87
	3. Maize	Andhra Pradesh	95.15	97.59	100.00
		Bihar	86.00	77.51	90.48
		Himachal Pradesh	44.19	57.17	52.85
		Karnataka	96.85	96.54	98.79
		Madhya Pradesh	51.67	30.87	52.45
		Rajasthan	55.30	58.24	67.34
		Uttar Pradesh	61.99	64.59	54.59
	All-India		80.01	78.56	82.87
	4. Jowar	Andhra Pradesh	44.20	72.24	57.59
		Karnataka	41.19	55.33	58.84
		Madhya Pradesh	31.88	55.85	75.87
		Maharashtra	50.87	62.75	61.03
		Rajasthan	50.39	59.39	60.91
	All-India		46.25	61.02	61.46
	5. Bajra	Gujarat	71.43	76.82	79.99
		Haryana	82.50	82.60	81.49
		Maharashtra	63.04	68.83	63.76
		Rajasthan	44.77	62.43	44.21
		Uttar Pradesh	76.90	89.07	80.67
	All-India		61.44	72.21	61.78
	6. Barley	Rajasthan	-	70.06	72.43
		Uttar Pradesh	25.67	41.68	71.08
	All-India		11.72	58.85	71.92

(Contd...)

1	2	3	4	5	6
	7. Ragi	Andhra Pradesh	63.28	-	-
		Karnataka	47.54	27.58	22.17
	All-India		48.23	27.58	22.17
II. Pulses	8. Arhar	Karnataka	90.93	98.13	93.98
		Madhya Pradesh	66.33	90.17	60.81
		Maharashtera	80.90	87.73	75.06
		Orissa	67.28	67.15	63.78
		Uttar Pradesh	43.00	60.21	88.24
	All-India		73.29	83.61	79.16
	9. Gram	Bihar	50.82	78.79	70.61
		Madhya Pradesh	83.26	83.65	97.28
		Rajasthan	77.78	62.43	77.09
		Uttar Pradesh	40.42	68.76	85.48
	All-India		74.06	76.81	90.81
	10. Urad	Andhra Pradesh	82.97	15.49	74.07
		Madhya Pradesh	75.70	77.93	70.92
		Maharashtra	94.08	89.06	93.46
		Orissa	63.05	78.75	71.60
		Rajasthan	41.25	71.66	68.87
		Tamil Nadu	95.14	80.65	91.17
		Uttar Pradesh	52.66	76.40	70.35
	All-India		75.55	78.40	80.06
	11. Moong	Andhra Pradesh	93.06	53.99	93.39
		Maharashtra	77.78	86.80	90.63
		Orissa	48.99	63.42	60.95
		Rajasthan	72.47	83.76	77.17
	All-India		77.69	80.26	84.37
	12. Lentil	Bihar	58.55	78.75	72.95
		Madhya Pradesh	91.90	99.03	94.89
		Uttar Pradesh	55.70	67.02	84.96
	All-India		68.73	79.03	85.66
III. Oilseeds	13. Groundnut	Andhra Pradesh	84.04	94.13	88.60
		Gujarat	90.13	94.82	90.08
		Karnataka	65.77	85.35	82.56
		Maharashtra	61.06	75.09	71.95
		Tamil Nadu	96.61	94.02	95.72
	All-India		85.88	91.60	88.61
	14. Rapeseed & Mustard	Gujarat	100.00	95.67	98.78
		Haryana	93.48	87.64	96.10
		Madhya Pradesh	68.01	71.60	99.02
		Rajasthan	88.43	93.85	98.65
		Uttar Pradesh	41.92	73.68	88.53
		West Bengal	51.87	76.45	82.08
	All-India		80.20	87.72	95.44
	15. Soyabean	Madhya Pradesh	90.45	95.15	96.44
		Maharashtra	100.00	96.85	96.21
	All-India		93.89	95.79	96.34
	16. Sunflower	Andhra Pradesh	-	-	100.00
		Karnataka	100.00	99.09	97.72
		Maharashtra	99.60	90.57	85.02
	All-India		76.86	97.18	96.44

(Contd...)

1	2	3	4	5	6
	17. Sesamum	Gujarat	100.00	97.54	96.60
		Madhya Pradesh	70.54	98.94	88.15
		Orissa	51.93	71.05	85.25
		Rajasthan	82.02	82.98	72.74
	All-India		87.48	91.28	85.98
	18. Safflower	Karnataka	98.22	46.67	100.00
		Maharashtra	-	-	-
	All-India		98.22	46.67	100.00
	19. Nigerseed	Madhya Pradesh	100.00	82.14	95.12
		Orissa	87.86	67.86	98.54
	All-India		92.52	73.58	97.13
IV. Other Commercial Crops	20. Sugarcane	Andhra Pradesh	98.06	-	-
		Haryana	100.00	-	-
		Karnataka	100.00	100.00	100.00
		Uttar Pradesh	100.00	-	-
	All-India		99.85	100.00	100.00
	21. Cotton	Gujarat	100.00	97.73	97.77
		Haryana	80.44	85.41	85.59
		Karnataka	100.00	100.00	100.00
		Madhya Pradesh	98.38	100.00	100.00
		Rajasthan	100.00	97.57	96.33
	All-India		96.91	96.23	96.15
	22. Jute	West Bengal	76.80	97.35	83.01
	All-India		76.80	97.35	84.78
V. Vegetables	23. Onion	Karnataka	99.46	99.62	99.46
	All-India		99.46	99.62	42.13
	24. Potato	Bihar	88.86	92.83	96.45
		Uttar Pradesh	73.09	73.97	91.80
		West Bengal	94.10	89.86	28.86
	All-India		82.52	80.19	63.98

Note: All India figures are weighted average of states listed above.
- Not Reported
Source: Directorate of Economics and Statistics, Department of Agriculture and Cooperation.

their own surplus falls short after some time, thus increasing demand.

Table 4.20 provides year-wise information, from 1951 to 2009, about the per capita availability of rice, wheat, gram, pulses and foodgrains in total, per day in India. The per capita availability of rice which was around 160 gm per day in 1951 went to over 200 gm by 2000 but came down to around 190 gm in 2009. The per capita availability of wheat which was 66 gm per day in 1951 increased to 180 gm in 2003, but decreased to 155 gm in 2009. The per capita availability of foodgarin was 395 gm per day in 1951. It went to 494 gm in 2002, but came down to 444 gm 2009.

Apart from foodgrains, other articles of consumption include edible oils, sugar, tea, coffee, etc. Table 4.21 provides year-wise information from 1960-61 to 2008-09 on per capita availability of certain important articles of consumption. The per capita availability of edible oils and sugar was 3.2 kg and 4.8 kg respectively in 1960-61. It went up to 6.1 kg and 12.5 kg respectively in 1993-94 and further to 12.1 kg and 18.8 kg respectively in 2008-09.

The increase in per capita availability of foodgrain from 1951 to around 2000 as shown in Tables 4.20 and 4.21 can be attributed to the increase in agriculture production due to Green Revolution. When the intensity of Green Revolution decreased, after the 1990s, the per capita availability of foodgrain declined. The decrease in per capita availability of foodgrains has also been due to the fact that the population of the country is increasing at a rapid rate. As per data released on Census 2011, India's population has increased to 121 crore which is quite alarming. Thus, if we need to increase our supply and keep the demand in check, we have to boost our agriculture by modernizing it, and bring the rate of increase of population to zero.

Table 4.22 gives a comparison of expenditure on cereals and non-cereals in rural areas and urban areas. In rural areas, the percentage of monthly per capita expenditure on cereals is more than that in urban areas. In case of non-cereals, the urban people spend more than those living in rural areas. The spending on cereals is however decreasing in percentage terms in both rural as well as urban areas. This may mean that there is a change in food habits in India. More and more people are shifting to non-cereals, including processed food, eggs, meat, fruit, milk, etc. Thus has also put pressure on the supply of these food items and increased their prices.

Table 4.23 shows the actual growth of India's GDP at factor cost at 2004-05 prices. It can be observed that the GDP grew at 9.5 per cent, 9.6 per cent and 9.3 per cent in the years 2005-06, 2006-07 and 2007-08 respectively. In comparison, agriculture grew at 5.1 per cent, 4.2 per cent and 5.8 per cent

Table 4.20: Per Capita Net Availability of Foodgrains (Per Day) in India

(Grams per day)

(AS on 20.07.2010)

Years	Rice	Wheat	Other cereals	Cereals	Gram	Pulses	Food-grains
1	2	3	4	5	6	7	8
1951	158.9	65.7	109.6	334.2	22.5	60.7	394.9
1956	187.7	61.5	111.2	360.4	29.0	70.3	430.7
1961	201.1	79.1	119.5	399.7	30.2	69.0	468.7
1966	161.9	95.4	102.6	359.9	18.3	48.2	408.1
1971	192.6	103.6	121.4	417.6	20.0	51.2	468.8
1976	187.2	79.5	107.4	373.8	20.2	50.5	424.3
1981	197.8	129.6	89.9	417.3	13.4	37.5	454.8
1985	188.8	138.6	87.9	415.3	12.9	38.1	453.4
1990	212.1	132.6	86.8	431.5	10.7	41.1	472.6
1991	221.7	166.8	80.0	468.5	13.4	41.6	510.1
1992	217.0	158.6	58.9	434.5	10.1	34.3	468.8
1993	201.1	140.2	86.6	427.9	10.7	36.2	464.1
1994	207.4	159.5	67.1	434.0	11.8	37.2	471.2
1995	220.0	172.7	64.9	457.6	14.9	37.8	495.5
1996	204.4	176.0	62.0	442.5	11.3	32.7	475.2
1997	214.0	179.1	72.9	466.0	12.4	37.1	503.1
1998	200.3	151.5	62.4	414.2	13.4	32.8	447.0
1999	203.4	162.3	63.4	429.2	14.6	36.5	465.7
2000	203.7	160.0	59.0	422.7	10.8	31.8	454.4
2001	190.5	135.8	56.2	386.2	8.0	30.0	416.2
2002	228.7	166.6	63.4	458.7	10.7	35.4	494.1
2003	181.4	180.4	46.7	408.5	8.5	29.1	437.6
2004	195.4	162.2	69.3	426.9	11.2	35.8	462.7
2005	177.3	154.3	59.4	390.9	10.6	31.5	422.4
2006	198.0	154.3	60.5	412.8	10.7	32.5	445.3
2007	194.0	157.8	55.5	407.4	11.9	35.5	442.8
2008	175.4	145.1	54.1	394.2	10.6	41.8	436.0
2009	188.4	154.7	63.9	407.0	12.9	37.0	444.0

Notes:
1. The net availability of foodgrains is estimated to be Gross Production (-) seed, feed & wastage, (-) exports (+) imports, (+/-) change in stocks.
2. The net availability of foodgrains divided by the population estimates for a particular year indicate per capita availability 'of foodgrains in terms of kg/year. Net availability, thus worked out further divided by the number of days in a year i.e., '365 days gives us net availability of foodgrains in terms of grams / day.
3. Figures in respect of per capita net availability given above are not strictly representative of actual level of consumption 'in the country especially as they do not take in to account any change in stocks in possession of traders, producers' and consumers.
4. For calculation of per capita net availability the figures of net imports from 1981 to 1994 are based on imports and exports on Government of India account only. Net imports from 1995 ownwards are the total exports and imports (on Government as well as private accounts).
5. Cereals includes rice,wheat and other cereals.
6. Pulses includes all kharif and rabi pulses.
7. Foodgrains includes rice, wheat,other cereals and all pulses.

Source: Directorate of Economics and Statistics, Department of Agriculture and Cooperation.

Table 4.21: Per Capita Availability of Certain Important Articles of Consumption

Year	Edible Oils (a) (kgs.)	Vanaspati e (kgs.)	Sugar (Nov-Oct) f (kgs.) d	Cloth (meters)			Tea c (gms)	Coffee c (gms)
				Cotton b	Man-made	Total		
1	2	3	4	5	6	7	8	9
1960-61	3.2	0.8	4.8	13.8	1.2	15.0	296.0	80.0
1965-66	2.7	0.8	5.7	14.7	1.7	16.4	346.0	72.0
1971-72	3.0	1.1	6.8	12.4	2.2	14.6	426.0	65.0
1972-73	2.4	1.0	6.2	13.2	2.0	15.2	458.0	69.0
1973-74	3.4	0.8	6.1	12.0	1.9	13.9	492.0	64.0
1974-75	3.3	0.6	5.8	12.9	1.7	14.6	471.0	62.0
1975-76	3.5	0.8	6.1	12.6	2.0	14.6	446.0	62.0
1976-77	3.2	0.9	6.0	11.4	2.4	13.8	450.0	71.0
1977-78	3.8	0.9	7.2	9.5	4.0	13.5	516.0	73.0
1978-79	3.8	1.0	9.6	10.2	4.8	15.0	599.0	77.0
1979-80	3.7	1.0	7.8	10.1	4.6	14.7	521.0	73.0
1980-81	3.8	1.2	7.3	12.9	4.4	17.3	511.0	74.0
1981-82	5.1	1.3	8.2	12.2	4.9	17.1	466.0	79.0
1982-83	4.5	1.3	9.0	11.8	4.3	16.1	525.0	82.0
1983-84	5.8	1.2	10.5	12.6	4.7	17.3	519.0	78.0
1984-85	5.5	1.3	10.7	12.6	4.6	17.2	576.0	72.0
1985-86	5.0	1.3	11.1	15.4	6.1	21.5	589.0	71.0
1986-87	5.0	1.2	11.4	15.2	6.6	21.8	545.0	76.0
1987-88	5.8	1.2	11.7	14.0	7.0	21.0	592.0	72.0
1988-89	5.3	1.2	12.1	15.0	8.0	23.0	612.0	79.0
1989-90	5.3	1.1	12.3	14.6	8.1	22.7	571.0	65.0
1990-91	5.5	1.0	12.7	15.1	9.0	24.1	612.0	59.0
1991-92	5.4	1.0	13.0	13.7	9.2	22.9	655.0	64.0
1992-93	5.8	1.0	13.7	15.6	8.9	24.5	649.0	60.0
1993-94	6.1	1.0	12.5	15.9	10.3	26.2	667.0	56.0
1994-95	6.3	1.0	13.2	15.2	10.8	26.0	664.0	55.0
1995-96	7.0	1.0	14.1	16.3	11.7	28.0	646.0	55.0
1996-97	8.0	1.0	14.6	16.2	13.1	29.3	657.0	58.0
1997-98	6.2	1.0	14.5	15.9	15.0	30.9	635.0	58.0
1998-99	8.5	1.3	14.9	13.1	15.1	28.2	684.0	65.0
1999-00	9.0	1.4	15.6	14.2	16.4	30.6	642.0	55.0
2000-01	8.2	1.3	15.8	14.2	16.5	30.7	631.0	58.0
2001-02	8.8	1.4	16.0	14.8	17.2	32.0	650.0	67.0
2002-03	7.2	1.4	16.3	14.4	17.0	31.4	623.0	67.0
2003-04	9.5	1.2	16.1	13.4	17.6	31.0	662.0	70.0
2004-05	10.2	1.2	15.5	14.1	19.4	33.5	663.0	75.0
2005-06	10.6	1.1	16.3	16.4	19.7	36.1	687.0	80.0
2006-07	11.1	1.1	16.8	18.0	21.6	39.6	687.0	85.0
2007-08	11.4	1.2	17.8	19.0	22.8	41.9	na	na
2008-09 P	12.1	1.3	18.8	17.9	21.1	39.0	na	na

(P) Provisional na- Not Available

Note: The of cloth prior to 1980-81 is calendar year wise, in meters up to 1984-85 and square meter from 1985-86 onwards.

a: Includes Groundnut Oil, Sesamum Oil, Rapeseed Oil, Coconut Oil, Nigerseed Oil, Soyabean Oil and Sunflower oil but excludes oil used for manufacture of vanaspati.

b: Figures for blended/mixed fabrics were not separately available prior to 1969. These have been included under man made fibre fabrics after 1969.

c: Figures upto 1971-72 relate to coffee season and thereafter on calendar year basis. The figures for 1972-73 correspond to 1973 and so on.

d: Relates to actual releases for domestic consumption.

e: Relates to calendar year.

f: From 1967-68 onwards sugar season is from October-September.

Source: *Economic Survey 2009-10*

Table 4.22: Share of Monthly Per Capita Expenditure on Cereals and Non-Cereals in Total Food Items

(Per Cent)

Year	Rural Areas		Urban Areas	
	Cereals	Non-Cereals	Cereals	Non-Cereals
1	2	3	4	5
1987-88	40.99	59.01	26.46	73.54
1993-94	38.30	61.70	25.69	74.31
1999-2000	37.31	62.69	25.70	74.30
2000-01	35.58	64.42	25.13	74.87
2001-02	34.55	65.45	24.30	75.70
2002 (July-Dec.)	33.10	66.90	23.42	76.58
2003 (Jan-Dec.)	33.41	66.59	23.76	76.24
2004 (Jan-June)	33.55	66.45	23.92	76.08
2004-05 (July-June)	32.72	67.28	23.65	76.35
2005-06 (July-June)	31.91	68.09	23.47	76.53
2006-07 (July-June)	31.59	68.41	22.97	77.03

Source: National Sample Survey Organisation (63rd round)

Table 4.23: Growth in GDP at Factor Cost at 2004-2005 Prices (Per Cent)

	2005-06	2006-07	2007-08	2008-09PE	2009-10QE	2010-11AE
Agriculture, Forestry & Fishing	5.1	4.2	5.8	-0.1	0.4	5.4
Mining & Quarrying	1.3	7.5	3.7	1.3	6.9	6.2
Manufacturing	10.1	14.3	10.3	4.2	8.8	8.8
Electricity, Gas & Water Supply	7.1	9.3	8.3	4.9	6.4	5.1
Construction	12.8	10.3	10.7	5.4	7.0	8.0
Trade, Hotels, Transport & Communication	12.1	11.7	10.7	7.6	9.7	11.0
Financing, Insurance, Real Estate & Business Services	12.7	14.0	11.9	12.5	9.2	10.6
Community, Social & Personal Services	7.0	2.9	6.9	12.7	11.8	5.7
GDP at Factor Cost	9.5	9.6	9.3	6.8	8.0	8.6

Source: CSO

during these years respectively. In 2008-09, India's GDP grew only at 6.8 per cent because of global economic slowdown. Agriculture had a negative growth of –0.1 per cent in 2008-09 and a poor growth of 0.4 per cent in 2009-10 although the GDP growth picked up at 8.0 per cent in 2009-10. Thus, agriculture has been our weak link in the overall GDP growth. Our GDP growth has been quite robust all these years but inflation, including food inflation has persisted. This shows that there is little or no connection between GDP growth and inflation, particularly food inflation which depends on availability of food vis-à-vis demand.

Table 4.24: Public and Private Investment in Agriculture and Allied Sectors

(at 2004-05 prices)

Year	Investment in Agriculture & Allied sectors (₹ crore)			Share in Investment (per cent)	
	Total	Public	Private	Public	Private
2004-05	78848	16183	62665	20.5	79.5
2005-06	93121	19909	73211	21.4	78.6
2006-07	94400	22978	71422	24.3	75.7
2007-08	110006	23039	86967	20.9	79.1
2008-09	138597	24452	114145	17.6	82.4

Source: Central Statistical Organisation

Note: CSO has changed the base year from the year 1999-2000 to 2004-05

India's agriculture has suffered from various shortcomings like primitive ways of farming, poor irrigation, low use of fertilizers, pesticides, etc. There has also been shortage of capital and investment in agriculture. Table 4.24 provides information on public and private investment in agriculture in India from 2004-05 to 2008-09. It can be observed that public investment has risen from ₹ 16,183 crore in the year 2004-05 to ₹ 24,452 in the year 2008-09. Considering the magnitude of India's agriculture, this investment is very small, and taking into account the fact that the input costs have risen sharply, this increase is meager. As a percentage of total investment in agriculture, that by the government has actually gone down from 20.5 per cent in 2004-05 to 17.6 per cent in 2008-09. Although private investment in agriculture in India has increased, it is not at all sufficient. This is also one of the reasons of our poor production, low yield and high price of food.

Table 4.25: Area under Oil Palm

(Target and achievement in hectares)

Year	Target	Achievement
2006-07	12,000	18,176
2007-08	29,580	21,330
2008-09	31,500	26,178

Source: Department of Agriculture and Cooperation, Ministry of Agriculture

The prices of edible oils have increased sharply during recent times due to increasing demand. Copra, groundnut, cotton seed, mustard, sesame, sunflower, oil palm, etc. are the main sources of edible oils. In case of oil palm which gives cheaper edible oil, the government has set a year-wise target of area coverage through the Oil Palm Development Programme. The progress in this regard from 2006-07 to 2008-09 is shown in Table 4.25. Except for the year 2006-07, the targets have not been met.

As has been stated earlier, Indian agriculture has not been modernized. Not many farmers are not using high quality inputs like high-yielding seeds, fertilizers, pesticides, insecticides, etc. Most of our farmers are poor and hence cannot afford these inputs, the prices of which have increased further during the last few years. In order to help the poor farmers, the government is distributing seed mini-kits to farmers under the Seed Mini-kit Distribution Program. Table 4.26 provides information about the number of seed mini-kits for oilseeds and pulses distributed during summer and kharif seasons 2008, rabi and summer seasons 2008-09, and kharif and rabi seasons 2009-10. This program will make a small impact considering the large number of poor farmers in India. In order that production and yield may increase substantially, the number of seed mini-kits has to be increased manifold. These kits will also have to be distributed each season and for more crops to increase our agriculture production and improve our per hectare yield.

Table 4.26: Year and Season-wise Allocation of Seed Mini-kits During the Last Two Years

(Number of seed minikits)

Season	Oilseeds	Pulses	Total
Summer 2008	29,985	2,36,425	2,66,410
Kharif 2008	4,64,366	3,55,787	8,20,153
Rabi 2008-09	7,13,943	5,45,000	12,58,943
Summer 2008-09	29,625	2,75,750	3,05,375
Kharif 2009-10	3,82,512	5,04,289	8,86,801
Rabi 2009-10	12,32,210	14,12,772	26,44,982

Source: Department of Agriculture and Cooperation, Ministry of Agriculture

With regular cropping year after year, the soil becomes deficient in certain minerals, etc. which if not replenished gives low yield. Some soils are by nature deficient in certain minerals. That is why there is need to use fertilizers like urea, nitrogen, phosphate, potash, etc. the farmers in India being largely poor, they are unable to afford various type of fertilizers. Table 4.27 provides year-wise data on the use of fertilizers from 2000-01 to 2008-09. It is observed that urea is used more than any other type of fertilizers and its use has increased by about 40 per cent during this period. Nitrogen, phosphate and potash are now increasingly being used besides Di-Ammonium Phosphate (DAP) and Muriate of Potash (MOP). Agriculture yield has improved as a result, but since the demand for food is increasing due to increase in population, there is need to use more and more fertilizers so that the availability of foodgrain and other food items increase and prices remain under control.

Various types of fertilizers are produced in India. Table 4.28 provides data on production, imports and consumption of nitrogenous, phosphatic and potassic fertilizers in India for 1970-71, 1980-81 and 1990-91 to 2010-11. It can be seen that the production has increased phenomenally from 1970-71 in all the said types of fertilizers. The import of such fertilizers has also increased many times over. This increase in production, and if need be, imports and consumption need to be sustained and further improved if we are to maintain food security.

Fertilizers are necessary for increasing agriculture production and per hectare yield which are among the lowest in the world. The majority of our farmers being poor and unable to afford various types of fertilizers required to raise healthy crops. It is

Table 4.27: Use of Fertilizers

(lakh tonnes)

Year	Urea	DAP	MOP	Complex	Nitrogen (N)	Phosphate (P)	Potash (K)	Total (N+P+K)
2000-01	191.86	58.84	18.29	47.80	109.20	42.15	15.67	167.02
2001-02	199.17	61.81	19.93	49.63	113.10	43.82	16.67	173.60
2002-03	184.93	54.73	19.12	48.10	104.74	40.19	16.01	160.94
2003-04	197.67	56.24	18.41	47.57	110.77	41.24	15.98	167.99
2004-05	206.65	62.56	24.06	56.80	117.13	46.24	20.61	183.98
2005-06	222.97	67.64	27.31	66.94	127.23	52.04	24.13	203.40
2006-07	243.37	73.81	25.86	67.99	137.73	55.43	23.35	216.51
2007-08	259.63	74.97	28.81	65.70	144.19	55.15	26.36	225.70
2008-09	266.49	92.31	40.77	68.05	150.90	65.06	33.13	249.09

Source: Department of Agriculture and Cooperation, Ministry of Agriculture

Table 4.28: Production, Imports and Consumption of Fertilizers

(Thousand tonnes of nutrients)

	1970-71	1980-81	1990-91	2000-01	2004-05	2005-06	2006-07	2007-08	2008-09	2009-10	2010-11a
1	2	3	4	5	6	7	8	9	10	11	12
A Nitrogenous fertilizers											
Production	830	2164	6993	11004	11338	11354	11578	10900	10870	11900	12175
Imports	477	1510	414	154	411	1385	2689	3677	3844	3447	3448
Consumption	1487	3678	7997	10920	11714	12723	13773	14419	15090	15580	NA
B Phosphatic fertilizers											
Production	229	842	2052	3748	4067	4221	4517	3807	3464	4321	4532
Imports	32	452	1311	396	296	1122	1322	1391	2927	2756	3515
Consumption	462	1214	3221	4215	4624	5204	5543	5515	6506	7274	NA
C Potassic fertilizers											
Imports	120	797	1328	1541	2045	2747	2069	2653	3380	2945	3022
Consumption	228	624	1328	1567	2060	2413	2335	2636	3313	3632	NA
D All fertilizers (NPK)											
Production	1059	3006	9045	14752	15405	15575	16095	14707	14334	16221	16707
Imports	629	2759	2758	2090	2752	5254	6080	7721	10151	9148	9985
Consumption	2177	5516	12546	19702	18398	20340	21651	22570	24909	26486	NA

Source: Ministry of Chemicals & Fertilizers, Department of Fertilizers

a Estimated (Production figures are considered actual for April-November 2010 and estimated for Dec. 2010-March 2011

Note: Import figures are from April-November 2010; Figures may not add up to total

The entire demand of Potassic fertilizers is met through import.

therefore necessary that the prices thereof be kept low. Urea is the only fertilizer which is under statutory price control. The maximum retail price (MRP) is fixed by the government for phosphatic and potassic fertilizers under the concession scheme to ensure their availability to farmers under a reasonable price. The government has rationalized the MRPs of complex fertilizers based on the nutrient content of nitrogen, phosphate and potash in the MRP of straight fertilizers like urea, DAP and MOP, w.e.f. June 2008.

Nutrient-based Fertilizer Subsidy

The Government of India has been providing fertilizer subsidy to farmers all along although there have been suggestions to discontinue it. The government also constituted a Group of Ministers to examine the nutrient-based subsidy policy and measures for the rationalization of fertilizer subsidy disbursement, and to make recommendations keeping in view the objectives of strengthening the balanced use of fertilizers and efficient nutrient management for sustainable agriculture; avoiding indiscriminate use of fertilizers which may lead to

Table 4.29: Monthly Break-up of WPI Food Inflation

(Per Cent)

	All Commodities		(A) Food Articles		(B) Food Products		(A+B) Food Combined	
Wt%	100		14.34		9.97		24.31	
Period	2009-10	2010-11	2009-10	2010-11	2009-10	2010-11	2009-10	2010-11
Apr.	0.89	11.00	8.69	20.49	8.86	9.09	8.76	16.09
May	1.21	10.60	8.91	21.37	10.12	7.09	9.37	15.85
Jun.	-0.71	10.28	11.28	20.97	9.05	6.13	10.42	15.30
Jul.	-0.62	10.02	12.74	18.48	8.46	7.34	11.10	14.31
Aug.	0.31	8.32	14.36	14.96	10.73	4.58	12.97	11.06
Sep.	1.09	8.93	13.92	16.29	12.08	3.62	13.21	11.49
Oct.	1.48	9.12	12.47	14.64	12.97	3.75	12.66	10.56
Nov.	4.50	7.48P	16.73	9.41P	17.94	0.57P	17.17	6.11P
Dec.	6.92	8.43P	20.76	13.55P	19.30	0.35P	20.21	8.59P
Jan.	8.53		20.19		19.16		19.80	
Feb.	9.68		21.85		17.68		20.22	
Mar.	10.23		20.65		15.11		18.50	

Source: The Office of the Economic Adviser, Ministry of Commerce and Industry.

Note: P—Provisional.

high subsidy burden; giving incentives for more people to invest in the fertilizer industry; and ensuring higher agriculture production.

Table 4.29 gives the monthly break-up of WPI food inflation from Apr. 2009 to Dec. 2010 for commodities, food articles, food products and all of these combined. It can be observed that the WPI for food articles remained high for almost the entire reporting period. The price of food products remained under pressure from Aug. 2009 and spurted from Nov. 2009 onwards. In case of food combined, the prices remained high from Jun. 2009 onwards and remained very high from Nov. 2009 to most of 2010.

It has already been stated that high inflation is being experienced not only in India but also worldwide. Table 4.30 provides a comparison between global and domestic inflationary trends for Dec. 2009, Mar. 2010 and Dec. 2010. It can be seen that there was little change in domestic and global inflation in case of agriculture for Dec. 2009 and Dec. 2010. An important point to be noted is that the prices of fertilizers went down sharply globally but that did not happen in India.

Table 4.30: Domestic and Global Y-o-Y Inflation Trend (Per Cent)

(Base: 2004-05=100)

Commodity	Domestic Dec-09	Global Dec-09	Domestic Mar-10	Global Mar-10	Domestic Dec-10	Global Dec-10
Agriculture	18.5	28.5	20.6	17.8	15.3	27.8
Beverages	6.5	27.8	8.2	23.0	5.3	32.4
Energy	4.6	55.4	13.8	60.1	11.2	19.7
Fats & Oils	-0.7	34.6	3.3	18.2	5.0	35.4
Fertilizers	7.0	-41.7	6.2	-27.1	5.5	39.6
Food	20.2	23.8	18.5	8.5	8.6	25.3
Grains	19.5	5.0	13.2	-10.3	-2.6	25.3
Metal & Minerals	-7.1	42.8	3.4	41.4	12.4	38.6
Non-fuel	7.4	27.8	9.6	23.0	7.9	32.4
Raw Materials	11.1	36.5	26.1	44.0	24.1	45.8
Timber	-1.3	-9.2	8.8	-5.6	50.3	13.4
Other Raw materials	18.3	88.4	44.2	91.1	33.6	63.5
Other Food	16.3	30.7	7.0	16.9	-0.5	10.2

Sources: Pink sheet of the World Bank and the Office of the Economic Adviser, Ministry of Commerce and Industry.

Food vs Fuel

Fuel in its various forms to run industries, move cars, buses and trains, light offices and households, etc. is more in demand than anything else in the world. As the stocks of oil and other sources of energy like coal are dwindling and the prices thereof are skyrocketing, there are frantic efforts to develop alternative forms of power, energy, primarily fuel. What has come out of years of research is fuel prepared from some specific plant variety, and is known as bio-fuel. Several countries including India are trying to prepare bio-fuel in large quantities to meet their demands and at the same time avoid the costly import of petroleum. As large tracts of farmland are being used to raise crops for bio-fuels, the production is well and truly being considered detrimental to food supply and thus, cause high food inflation.

Jatropha curcus is a drought-resistant perennial, growing well in marginal/poor soil. It grows relatively quickly and lives, producing seeds for 50 years. It is called the wonder plant as it produces seeds with an oil content of 37 per cent. The oil can be combusted as fuel without being refined. It burns with clear smoke-free flame, and has been tested successfully as fuel for simple diesel engine. The by-products are press cake, a good organic fertilizer, oil contains also insecticide.[5] Seeing the qualities of jatropha, people are increasingly taking to raising this crop.

Apart from jatropha, some farm commodities like maize, sugar cane and some vegetable oils can also be used to make bio-fuels. For example, since 2006, land that was also formerly used to grow other crops in the US is now used to grow maize for bio-fuels, and a larger share of maize is used for ethanol production, which reached 25 per cent in 2007. This development has not gone well with some experts. According to Lester R. Brown, since converting the entire grain harvest of the US would only produce 16 per cent of its auto fuel needs, some experts believe that placing energy markets in competition with food markets for scarce arable land will inevitably result in higher food prices.[6] With global demand for bio-fuels on the increase due to the oil price increase taking place frequently, particularly since 2003, there is a desire to reduce dependency on petroleum fuel. Other arguments given in favour of bio-fuel are that it reduces greenhouse gas (GHG) emissions from transportation and that large wasteland will be put to economic use. It may be mentioned here that although the US has taken a lead role in preparing bio-fuels, many other countries including India are also making it. This has not only adversely affected the food security at the domestic level but also at international level, because less quantities of maize, sugar and vegetable oils, which are used to make bio-fuels, will be available for international trade. Countries like America, which have surplus maize, etc. can afford to use it for making bio-fuels, but they must also think about world food security at large and about the countries which depend on import of maize from other countries like the US. Another important point to be noted is that America is a very large country and has large tracts of non-farmland which it can use for raising jatropha crops. But there are many countries which area-wise are quite small. They can ill afford to raise crops for bio-fuel. Nor do they have much wasteland for jatropha crops. They must instead reclaim their wasteland if any to grow foodgrain.

A World Bank policy research working paper published on July 2008 stated that the increase in food commodities prices was led by grains, with sharp price increases in 2005 despite record crops worldwide. From January 2005 until June 2008, the prices of maize almost tripled, those of wheat increased 127 per cent, and of rice went up a whopping 170 per cent. The increase in grain prices was followed by increases in fats and oil prices in mid-2006. The study also found that sugar cane production increased even more rapidly. The World Bank paper concluded that bio-fuels produced from grains have raised food prices in combination with other related factors between 70 to 75 per cent, but ethanol produced from sugar cane has not contributed significantly to the recent increase in food commodities prices.

An economic assessment report published by the OECD in July 2008 found that "...the impact of current bio-fuel policies on world crop prices, largely through increased demand for cereals and vegetable oils, is significant but should not be overestimated. Current bio-fuel support measures alone are estimated to increase average wheat prices by about 5 per cent, maize by around 7 per cent and vegetable oil by about 19 per cent over the next 10 years."[7] Corn is used to make ethanol and prices went up by a factor of three in less than three years.[8] Wheat is up by almost a factor of three in three years, while soybeans are up by a factor of two in two years (all measured in US dollars).

Since corn is widely used as feed for livestock, higher corn prices lead to higher prices in animal source food. Vegetable oil is used to make bio-diesel and has nearly doubled in price in the last few years. It is a known fact that the price is roughly tracking crude oil prices. The 2007-08 world food price crisis is blamed partly on the increased demand for bio-fuels. During the same period, the prices of rice went up by a factor of three even though rice is not directly used in bio-fuels.[9]

The findings of World Bank report were supported by the Union of Concerned Scientists in one of their newsletters in which they remarked that the World Bank analysis "contradicts U.S. Secretary of Agriculture Ed Schaffer's assertion that bio-fuels account for only a small percentage of rising food prices".

According to Donald Michell, a World Bank policy research working paper released in July 2008[10] concluded that "...large increases in bio-fuels production in the United States and Europe are the main reason behind the steep rise in global food prices. It also stated that "Brazil's sugar-based ethanol did not push food prices appreciably higher".[11] However, a subsequent study conducted by World Bank in 2010 stated that their previous study may have overestimated the contribution of bio-fuel production, as "the effect of bio-fuels on food prices has not been as large as originally thought, but that the use of commodities by financial investors (the so-called "financialisation of commodities") may have been partly responsible for the 2007-08 spike".[12] An independent study by Organisation for Economic Co-operation and Development (OECD) also found that the impact of bio-fuels on food prices are much smaller.

These contradictory reports notwithstanding, the fact cannot be denied that there has been some impact of bio-fuel production on food availability. Moreover, there is all likelihood that as the petroleum resources worldwide dwindle further and the production of petroleum products decreases, more nations will go for bio-fuel production and in greater quantities to meet their energy demands. It is therefore necessary to make elaborate plans whereby a balance is created between bio-fuel production and food availability.

It has been argued that increase in food prices should not be entirely blamed on bio-fuels as energy costs are a significant cost for farming inputs including fertilizers, pesticides, etc. and food distribution because of rise in transportation costs. Some experts have mentioned that the China factor as one of the causes of global food price rise. According to them, China and other countries have had significant increases in their imports as their economies have grown. It has also been stated that part of the food price increase for international food commodities measured in US dollars is due to the dollar being devalued. Protectionism is also said to be yet another important contributor to price increases.

Government Regulations of Bio-fuel and Food

The governments of countries like France, Germany, the USA and the UK have supported bio-fuels with tax breaks and subsidies. Such policies have the unintended consequence of diverting resources from food production and leading to surging food prices by causing distortions of supply and demand.[13]

In some countries, fuel for agricultural use does not have fuel taxes as farmers get duty-free petrol or diesel fuel. Similarly, bio-fuels often have subsidies and low/no retail fuel taxes. Bio-fuels compete with retail gasoline and diesel prices which have substantial taxes included. The net result is that it is possible for a farmer to use more than a gallon of fuel to make a gallon of bio-fuel and still make a profit. Some argue that this is a bad distortion of the market.[14] Some economists have studied how much energy goes into making ethanol from corn and how that compares to the energy in the ethanol. Most of them are of the opinion that the distortions caused by such government policies as explained above can make things happen that would not make sense in a free market.

Oil Price Increases

As stated earlier, the oil prices are linked with bio-fuel. An increase in the price of oil results in an increased demand for bio-fuels. And this has actually happened since 2003 when the oil prices have seen many hikes. Since transforming vegetable oil into bio-diesel is neither very difficult, nor costly, there is a scope of arbitrage if vegetable oil is much cheaper than diesel. As diesel is also made from crude oil, vegetable oil prices are partially linked to crude oil prices. Farmers are lured to switch to growing vegetable oil crops if those are more profitable than food crops. So all food prices are linked to vegetable oil prices, and in turn to crude oil prices. Demand for oil is outstripping the supply of oil and oil depletion is expected to cause crude oil prices to go up over the next 50 years. Record oil prices are inflating food prices worldwide.

In Germany and Canada, it is now much cheaper to heat a house by burning grain than by using fuel derived from crude oil.[15] With oil hovering around US$ 100/barrel a savings of a factor of three on heating costs is possible. When crude oil was at $25/barrel there was no economic incentive to switch to a grain-fed heater. Many experts are of the opinion that the problem may not be easy to solve because there is a potential clash between bio-fuels and food as they also use significant agricultural resources such as water.

A recent UN report on bio-fuel has also raised the issues regarding food security and bio-fuel production. Jean Ziegler, the former UN Special Rapporteur on food, concluded that while the arguments for bio-fuels in terms of energy efficiency and climate change are legitimate, the effects for the world's hungry of transforming wheat and maize crops into bio-fuel are "absolutely catastrophic", and terms such use of arable land a "crime against humanity". Ziegler also called for a 5-year moratorium on bio-fuel production.[16] His proposal was however rejected by the UN General Secretary Ban Ki-moon, who called for a comprehensive review of the policies on bio-fuels, and said that "just criticising bio-fuel may not be a good solution".[17]

It has also been argued that there are food surpluses in many developed countries. In UK, for example, there was a wheat surplus of around two million tonnes in 2005. However, this surplus could produce sufficient bio-ethanol to replace only around 2.5 per cent of the country's petroleum consumption, without requiring any increase in wheat cultivation or reduction in food supply or exports. Thus, above a few per cent, there would be direct competition between first generation bio-fuel production and food production. For instance, if the UK wanted to replace 5 per cent of its fuel with bio-fuel, it would have to shift large quantities of wheat from food stock for preparing bio-ethanol. This is one of the reasons why the second generation bio-fules, i.e bio-fuels made from lignocellulosic crops are increasingly important.

Non-food Crops for Bio-fuel

It has been proposed that only non-food crops be used for bio-fuel, which will avoid direct competition for commodities like corn and vegetable oil. However, as long as farmers can make more money by switching to bio-fuels they will continue to do so. And the law of demand and supply is simple: If fewer farmers are producing food the price of food will rise.

Second generation bio-fuels use lignocellulosic raw material like forest residues, also called brown waste and black liquor from Kraft process or sulfite process pulp mills. Third generation bio-fuels, which are bio-fuels prepared from algae, use non-edible raw material sources that can be used for bio-diesel and bio-ethanol.

Remedies

A lot of research and development efforts are currently being put into the production of second generation bio-fuels from non-food crops, crop residues and waste like biomass. It is belived and rightly so that second generation bio-fuels could hence potentially combine farming for food and fuel. Several studies have shown that bio-fuel production can be significantly increased without increased acreage.

The world is at a stage where it has to find alterative sources of energy without further loss of time. One such alternative is harnessing nuclear energy for peaceful purposes. The Indo-US Nuclear Deal 2008 can therefore be termed as a great step in this direction.

Measures to Contain Inflation, Particularly Food Inflation

The government has taken monetary, fiscal and administrative measures to contain inflation, particularly food inflation. The Reserve Bank of India has been reviewing the monetary policy from time to time and has taken suitable measures to moderate demand to levels consistent with the capacity of the economy to maintain its growth without provoking price rise. It has already raised its key policy rates several times in the past two years and has narrowed the liquidity adjustment facility (LAF) corridor to reduce volatility of rates. The economy has witnessed aggressive tightening since March 2010. As per the announcement of the RBI on 25 January 2011, the repo rate and reverse repo rate are 6.5 per cent and 5.5 per cent respectively.

In order to ensure a regular supply of food, the government has reduced import duties to zero on rice, wheat, pulses, edible oils (crude), butter, and ghee, and to 7.5 per cent on refined and hydrogenated oils and vegetable oils. Sugar prices have skyrocketed during the last few years. Thus, the import of raw sugar has been allowed at zero duty under open general licence (OGL).

Besides above, many administrative measures have been taken. Levy obligation in respect of all imported raw sugar and white sugar has been removed. The government also put a ban on export of non-basmati rice, edible oils (except coconut oil and forest based oil) and pulses (except white chana). Minimum export price (MEP) was used to regulate exports of onion (at US$ 1200 per tonne for December 2010) and basmati rice (at US$ 900 per MT) as prices of these commodities went up. The Forward Market Commission suspended the futures trading of rice and pulses like tur and urad. The stock limit orders were extended in the case of pulses, paddy, and rice up to 30 September 2011 and edible oil and edible oilseeds up to 31 March 2011. Export of onion (all varieties) was not permitted with effect from 22 December 2010 until the prices eased out. Besides, full exemption from basic custom duty, special additional duty and education cess was provided to onions and shallots with effect from 21 December 2010. National Agricultural and Cooperative Marketing Federation (NAFED) and National Cooperative Consumers Federation (NCCF) were asked to undertake the sale of onions at lower prices from their retail outlets at various locations, with suitable budgetary support to be provided for this purpose.

Some other administrative steps were initiated to have a long-term effect of keeping food prices under check. It was decided to prepare and bring a scheme to support the State Governments in the setting up of farmers' markets and mobile bazaars and improve the functioning of civil supplies corporations and cooperatives. It was felt that the existing PDS was weak and needed to be strengthened through computerization and other steps, including opening more procurement windows across the country. It was also decided to ask the State Governments to review the Agriculture Produce Marketing Committee (APMC) Act and, in particular, consider exempting horticultural products from their purview thereby mitigating marketing and distribution bottlenecks in this crucial sector. In order to ensure that the farmers feel encouraged to bring their produce directly to the grain market, and there is a smooth movement of essential commodities, it was decided that the State Governments will be asked to consider waiving mandi tax, octroi, and other local levies. This will also reduce the burden of commission agent charges on the farmers.

Supply chains and cold storages play an important role in the availability of various type of food articles. Therefore, the government decided to bring policy changes whereby investment in supply chains, including provisions for cold storages will be encourage with sops, etc. These supply chains will be synchronized with organized retail chains for quicker and more efficient distribution of farm products, minimizing wastage. The Department of Food and Public Distribution, Ministry of Food Processing Industries, and the Planning Commission will jointly work out schemes for this purpose.

The government has set up an Inter-Ministerial Group (IMG) under the Chief Economic Adviser, Ministry of Finance, which will review the overall inflation situation, with particular reference to primary food articles. The Group will assess among other things, production/rainfall trends and build an institutional machinery to read warning signals, study international trends, recommend action on the fiscal, monetary, production, marketing, distribution, and infrastructure fronts to prevent price spikes, and suggest measures to strengthen collection and analysis of data and forecasting.[18]

The price situation in different states will also be reviewed by the Committee of Secretaries under the Cabinet Secretary, which will advise the concerned departments of the Central Government to maintain close coordination with state agencies to get direct feedback with a view to taking suitable remedial measures on a fast track.[19]

FAO's Initiative on Soring Food Prices

The Food and Agriculture Organization (FAO) has assessed the food price situation worldwide and stated that food prices are likely to remain high in future, though they may eventually drop to less extreme levels: "...by 2017, when compared to the average of the observed prices during the period 2005-07, the real price of wheat (deflated by the MUV) is expected to have increased by 2 per cent; rice by 1 per cent; oilseeds by 33 per cent; vegetable oils by 51 per cent, and sugar by 11 per cent."[20] Seeing the trend in India in 2010-11, it can be stated that the prices have risen even more sharply than FAO predicted and that they are likely to remain high despite government's assurances to the contrary.

According to FAO, since different countries have different situations, the response to high food prices should also vary accordingly, and there can be no universal policy or action to address the situation. *FAO's Guide for Policy and Programmatic*

Actions at Country Level to Address High Food Prices aims at helping those involved in developing action plans to address the current issue of high food prices. It, inter alia, looks at availability instruments that could be used to mitigate the problem of high food inflation.

It is believed that the situation of high food prices usually adversely impacts the trust between the stakeholders like producers, traders, the government and the consumers at large. The government is under pressure to deal with the situation urgently. The quick "policy fixes do not necessarily result in the desired outcomes because they are taken without proper consultation of stakeholders or a sufficient analysis of the consequences that decisions taken will have on the economy."[21] Thus, according to FAO, it is imperative that a broad national consultation be organized. The key stakeholders to be involved include the concerned government ministries, local governments, development partners, representatives from private sector including traders, processors, importers, farmer and consumer organizations, representatives from various political parties, and experts including academics.

The meetings of stakeholders provide an opportunity "to review available options and to assess their possible implications". The key results sought in such meetings include (i) at least a broad consensus on the overall objective of agreed action plan; (ii) agreement on the commitment to implement the decided action plan; (iii) making smaller committees or task forces to pilot actions to curb high food inflation; (iv) identification of pertinent issues like fertilizer policy, safety nets like food subsidy, etc. It must however be noted that some rapid analysis is necessary to give evidence that appropriate actions are necessary. Such analysis should focus on food availability, key food items' prices, food and nutrition security, coverage and reach of safety nets, legal entitlements, food aid flows, current policies and their effect on food prices, availability of agriculture inputs and their price movements, capacity to transport and distribute food, major determinants of food prices, price differences of same commodity at different places, difference between the price at the farm gate and in the market, the system of information flow on the markets. It is only after proper analyses have been made on all of these factors that informed suggestions can be made regarding some policy action. Anti-inflationary measures can be broadly divided into different forms.

Macroeconomic Policy Measures

According to FAO, in low-income countries, i.e. with less than US$ 1,000 per person per annum, food is a key expenditure for the large section of population. For the poorest among the people such as those living below the poverty line and other weaker sections in case of India, food expenditure constitutes over 60 per cent of their consumption expenditure. Thus, any measure impinging on food consumption will have an effect on government budget. For example, food subsidies will increase government expenditure, and reducing taxes and tariffs will bring down government revenue. These budgetary implications may requite the government to cut other spending so that the fiscal position may not worsen. This may affect economic stability. Therefore, while cutting down expenditure, care must be taken to avoid decreasing expenditure on essential programs like education, infrastructure, etc. which have long-term positive effects on food security and alleviation of poverty.

While mobilizing budgetary resources, a decision has to be taken whether to reallocate resources to channels that will reduce food inflation, which will affect the sectors from which the resources are partly shifted, or to allow the budgetary deficit to increase. But there is a level beyond which the budgetary deficit must not be allowed to go, because the consequences of large deficit, like debt accumulation, trade deficit, economic instability, loss of value of currency are quite serious. Therefore, it is better to go for diversion of resources, if required.

Trade-related Measures

According to FAO, changes in trade policies are the most common measures taken by the countries facing high food inflation as a means of trying to protect the domestic market from the increasing prices in the international markets. Export bans or limitations on the quantity of export are put in countries which export foodgrain, while in the importing countries, the usual measure is to cut import taxes to facilitate more imports and thus boost supply, bringing down prices. Reduction in import taxes on agriculture inputs is desirable in countries like India where there is a shortage of quality inputs, the yield is low and farming is yet to be modernized in large parts. Another trade-related measure is the reduction of duty, though it may have an indirect effect, i.e. reduction in the duty of one good bringing down the price of another good. For example, reducing the duty on petroleum, brings down the price of food products as petroleum is used as an input in food production. Reducing taxes on imports also reduces the protection of local producers, and they will not be able to increase the prices.[22]

Giving tax breaks to importers of food is another trade-related measure to improve the availability of food in the short run, for example exempting the final goods from value added tax (VAT). Imports can also be stimulated by giving financial support in the form of loan guarantee or interest subsidy. It would encourage import which otherwise may not have been made or it may increase the volume of import.

In many countries including India, the customs procedures and other formalities are quite complicated, which not only causes delays but also increases transaction costs. Simplifying these procedures would help reduce trade costs and stimulate imports of final consumption goods as well as intermediate goods used as inputs in agriculture. In order to speed up imports of essential or strategic food items, a one-stop shop approach should be adopted.

In conditions of high food inflation, many countries which produce surplus food usually put restrictions on exports, and sometimes even put a ban on food exports. According to FAO, such interventions have exacerbated the global food market situation and may complicate the efficacy of all trade-related measures:

> If surplus food-producing countries restrict exports, the global market becomes smaller and more volatile. In

> this case actions such as reducing import taxes, providing tax breaks for importers or enacting other financial support initiatives may have only a very limited effect in securing greater imports or making more food available to local populations.[23]

However, export bans and limitations are resorted to with the aim of keeping supplies of food within the country and thus helping the consumers both in terms of availability of food and reasonable prices. These measures also push down producer prices creating disincentives to expand production.

Measures for Consumers

Various measures in favour of consumers can be put in place to deal with food inflation. Such measures can be broadly divided into tax policies; market management policies; safety nets for poor sections; and measures relating to disposable income.

Tax policies can be changed whereby VAT is either reduced or removed on certain food products so that the price thereof gets reduced to the extent of reduction or exemption of the tax. But since it will also reduce the revenue for the state, the government will have to cut down on expenditure also, to keep the budget deficit under control. Reduction in road taxes and other taxes on transporters, including those by the State Government also helps in removing the price differentials in different regions. "Depending on the structure of the market, the benefit of this reduction will be shared differently among the producers/importers, consumers and the intermediaries. Whatever benefit will go to the producers will be through an increase in the price they are paid for their produce. This will encourage them to produce more in the next season."[24]

The problem with reducing transportation taxes, etc., according to FAO, is that it will reduce the government's revenue leaving less amount with it for spending on various activities of development. Another problem is that at times, when the competition is low, the producers may not pass the benefit of reduction in taxes, duties, etc. to the consumers. There is an implementation problem as well, because exempting certain food items from transportation taxes makes it difficult to identify and segregate those items especially when they are being transported with other items which carry usual taxes.

FAO's *Guide for Policy and Programmatic Actions at Country Level to Address High Food Prices* points out that high food prices in many countries have been accompanied by a low supply of food in the markets. This may be due to poor harvests during the preceding season, or because of the tendency of farmers and traders to keep stocks with the aim of selling them at higher prices later. The government can deal with this situation by importing the food items which are in short supply or by putting the reserves available in the godowns, etc. Using the first or the second approach or both the approaches combined will depend on the situation and opportunities available. According to FAO, "Low-income food deficit developing countries will need budget and balance of payment support to face increasing food support bills as well as higher energy costs. Besides, the important role of compensatory finance arrangements such as those that can be provided by the International Monetary Fund (IMF) and facilities offered by the World Bank."[25]

With these measures, the prices can be kept in check. When the prices ease out because of boost in supply due to imports, the operators may also want to bring out the hoarded stocks lest the prices fall further, which actually happens in such situations. With increased supply, more food is available for distribution among the poor at subsidized rates as per government's safety net programs. One drawback of importing food with IMF aid, etc. is that if more and more countries go for it, the food prices in the international market will increase.

Food aid in kind is also provided with the help of international organizations. Such aid can prove critical and play a life-saving role in poor countries where populations are highly vulnerable, face food hardship and a serious lack of access. However, as pointed out by FAO, in providing food aid in large quantities, as with the World Food Program (WFP), the cost is very high: "USD 1 value of food delivered costs USD 2 by the time it reaches the beneficiaries". This approach is thus recommended in dire situations, and where other measures like importing through normal channels, etc. are likely to take a long time and there is an acute shortage of food.

As stated earlier, hoarding of essential food items in large quantities by speculators/suppliers, which creates an artificial shortage of those items, and black marketing, etc. are illegal activities. One of the measures to stop such activities is to deal strictly with hoarders, etc. so that it works as a deterrent. Keeping a regular watch on suppliers, etc., raiding and searching their godowns are necessary. In conditions of acute shortage and very high prices of certain items, the government may take possession of goods stored by speculators or force them to sell in the market at normal prices. The government may also bring out those food items as are short in the market from its own godowns to boost supply.

Safety nets include food subsidies, food or cash transfers. The objective is to help vulnerable sections of society maintain an adequate level of food consumption when confronted with high food prices. Food items can be provided from the existing government stock or through import of essential items in case they are not locally available. Cash transfers or food vouchers are done through programs that "entail distribution of either cash or vouches that the beneficiaries can use to purchase food on the market or in dedicated shops".[26]

Safety nets not only shield the poor from high inflation but also contribute to social welfare. Exchange of food may be restricted to certain specific food items based on nutritional benefits. It thus helps in the caloric intake of people and improves their dietary quality. Some drawbacks have also been found in this measure of safety nets. If sufficient food is not available in the market, the food vouchers and cash transfers will increase the prices. It has been stated that food vouchers can become a parallel currency that may be used for purposes other than buying food. Cash transfers can be misused even more easily, making leakages to other than the intended use. Making food available at subsidized rates breeds corrupt practices like embezzlement as seen in India. However, these risks can be minimized through transparency in eligibility criteria, budget allocation and resource allocation at all levels.

Measures for Producers

It has often been found in the developing countries that high food prices are not transferred to the producers, i.e. they do not get a high price for their produce and thus they have no incentive to produce more. This happens because the prices in the producing areas are low but are high in the markets. In such conditions, an attempt to boost agriculture supply may lead to a collapse of prices in the rural areas, which may work as a disincentive for producers to engage themselves in any activity to increase production in the medium or long run. According to FAO, "It is therefore strongly suggested that any production programme implemented should absolutely be linked to marketing arrangements that secure a fair price for producers that would reflect the general increase of consumer prices." For this to be achieved it is necessary to analyse price transmission track market inefficiencies and to identify policies and programmes that could be taken to provide incentives to the producers. Some of the initiatives suggested by FAO include preparing and implementing production schemes that will promote home gardens and off-season utilization of irrigated land for growing vegetables, etc.; facilitate the procurement and distribution of farm inputs at regional level by providing credit facilities; and create proper storage, marketing and other infrastructure facilities. For poor farmers there can be production safety nets such as providing high quality seed kits, etc.

Some marketing management measures are necessary to ensure price transmission to the producers. Such measures can be both at the micro and the macro level. "At the micro level, the problem can be addressed by rapidly putting in place, as a matter of priority a national market information system (price observatory) and conducting rapid value chain analysis or development workshops to identify constraints to price transmission. At the macro level, marketing arrangements such as the creation of producer groups in the framework of support programmes and contact farming can be used."[27]

The national market information system should involve disseminating and analyzing price data for major agriculture commodities in the key markets. This will help the producers and traders in having information about the prices throughout the country, which will limit market segmentation which is the main cause of price differentials. It will also enable the farmers and small traders to better negotiate prices while selling their stocks. The value chain development workshop is a process through which stakeholders of a value can negotiate and take concerted decisions, actions and commitments to improve the functioning of particular value chain. Such workshop can be implemented in a situation of urgency without more prior detailed analysis of the value chain.

The government may also consider re-engagement in marketing. As seen in the high food inflation in the last few years, there have been several reasons for this situation such as inclement weather, poverty of farmers, alternative use of arable lands, etc. Many traders take advantage of the situation in anticipation of shortage and high prices ahead and take to the practices of hoarding, etc. This necessitates public marketing to ensure smooth food supply. However, such measure should be kept as an option during negotiations to get better collaboration from the private sector, instead of going for direct re-engagement in marketing. If necessary it may be resorted to in case of acute shortage and very high price of certain food items.

Conclusion

Food inflation has persisted in India for the last few years. High food prices are an international phenomena. But each country has its own factors responsible for supply not matching the demand. For countries largely dependent on imports of foodgrain, etc. the local prices will be determined by prices in the international market and the quantities available vis-à-vis demand. For countries like America wanting to produce alternative sources of energy from maize and vegetable oils, the prices of these items will depend on how much of these crops are used to make bio-fuels, etc. In case of India, the problem of high food prices during the last many years is due to a large number of factors including old methods of farming, poverty of farmers who cannot afford costly inputs, vagaries of weather, uncertain monsoons, poor irrigation facilities, lack of proper storage and marketing facilites, exploitation by intermediaries, poor PDS, increasing demand for food because of large population and increasing rate of popuation growth and a general rise in the income of people due to the rapid economic growth of the country.

Many of the reasons outlined above are beyond anybody's control. For example if monsoons are uncertain, they are likely to remain so. What can be done in this regard is to strengthen irrigation facilities so that our agriculture is less dependent on rainfall. We can also make arrangements like bunds and barriers to stop floods and desilt rivers, ponds, lakes, etc. to ensure larger and smoother flow of water. Efforts so far in this direction have not been satisfactory and thus, need to be strengthened.

Similarly, if the income of people is rising due to fast economic growth, it is a positive development, though it increases demand for goods and services as well as for food. This is likely to continue. The steps needed in this direction are to control the growth of population and reclaim large tracts of wasteland to grow more food. As already seen in Tables 4.9, 4.11 and 4.15 India's agriculture yield is among the lowest in the world. It needs to be improved considerably so ensure food security and to keep the food prices under control. The measures suggested by the FAO can prove very effective if we implement them after analyzing the market situation. It must be mentioned here that false assurances by the government that prices will come down soon will not turn into reality unless right policy actions suggested above are taken.

Sustained inflation is, in part, a by-product of growth, financial inclusion and low bank deposit rates. With more people putting their savings in banks and mutual funds, the scope of the RBI and government to increase money and run a fiscal deficit may go down. A deficit that earlier did not cause inflation may now do so because ordinary citizens are putting their money into circulation. In the parlance of economics, there may be a steady increase in the velocity of circulation of money. Unfortunately, there are no known formulae for how much we have to cut back on deficit and liquidity to counteract the fact of rising velocity. This will have to be achieved through trial and error and may not solve the problem of high inflation in the short run.

Notes

1. "State of the Economy and Prospects." *Economic Survey 2010-21.*
2. *Ibid.*
3. "Micro-foundations of Macroeconomic Development." *Economic Survey 2010-11.*
4. Integrated Wasteland Information System (InWIS) www.speckspecialtech.com
5. Global Authority on Nonfood Biodiesel Crops (http://www.jatrophaworld.org).
6. Lester R. Brown (2007). "Bio-fuels Blunder: Massive Diversion of U.S. Grain to Fuel Cars is Raising World Food Prices, Risking Political Stability." Testimony before U.S. Senate Committee on Environment and Public Works.
7. Directorate for Trade and Agriculture, OECD (2008).
8. Corn (C, CBOT): Monthly Price Chart" (http://futures.tradingscharts.com/printchart/CNIM).
9. "Understanding the Global Rice Crisis" (http://www.businessweek.com/globalbiz/content/apr2008/gb20080428-894449.htm).
10. Donald Mitchell (July 2008). "A Note on Rising Food Crisis" (http://www-wds.worldbank.org).
11. World Bank: "Bio-fuels—major drivers of food price rise" (http://www.alertnet.org).
12. John Baffes and Tossos Haniotis (July 2010). "Placing the 2006/08 Commodity Price Boom into Perspective" (http://www-wds.worldbank.org).
13. "The End of Cheap Food." *The Economist* (http://www.economist.com).
14. C. Ford Runge and Benjamin Senaueur. "How Bio-fuels Could Starve the Poor. Foreign Affairs" (http://www.foreignaffairs.org).
15. "Grain gaining steam as home-heating option." CBC/News. (http://www.cbc.ca/health/story/2005/10/14/grain-stove 05114.html).

16. George Monbiot (2007). "If we want to save the planet, we need a five-year freeze on bio-fuels." *The Guardian.*
17. Julian Borger (2008). "UN chief calls for a review of bio-fuels policy." *The Guardian.*
18. "Prices and Monetary Management." *Economic Survey 2010-11.*
19. *Ibid.*
20. "Introduction". *Guide for Policy and Programmatic Actions at Country Level to Address High Prices.* FAO (2011).
21. *Ibid.*
22. "Accompanying Process and Analytical Underpinning." *Guide for Policy and Programmatic Actions at Country Level to Address High Food Prices.* FAO (2011)
23. "Immediate Policy and Programmatic Actions." *Guide for Policy and Programmatic Actions at Country Level to Address High Prices.* FAO (2011).
24. *Ibid.*
25. *Ibid.*
26. *Ibid.*
27. *Ibid.*

5

Non-Food Inflation in India

Inflation has taken the centre stage in Indian economy due to the rising wholesale prices and the consumer prices being in double digits. Generally, prices of specific goods or services may go up or down relative to the prices of other goods and services reflecting changes in productivity or demand and supply conditions. But when the overall price level rises, it erodes the purchasing power of income, raises the cost of living and lowers the real value of savings. The level of inflation is critical in terms of maintaining competitiveness of domestic industry in a liberalised trading and market determined exchange rate regime. More importantly, it is the poor who are most vulnerable as they do not have any effective hedge against inflation. The issue of inflation and its measurement receive a lot of attention in India because large masses of its population are poor.

Inflation Measurement in India

India has a rich tradition of collection and dissemination of price statistics dating back to 1861 when the Index of Indian Prices was released. In India, there are five different primary measures of inflation—the Wholesale Price Index (WPI) and four measures of the Consumer Price Index (CPI). The four measures of the Consumer Price Index are the CPI for Industrial Workers (IW), Agricultural Labourers (AL), Rural Labourers (RL) and Urban Non-Manual Employees (UNME). Of these, the WPI is considered as the headline inflation measure because of its availability at high frequency. While the WPI does not cover prices of services, CPIs are meant to reflect the cost of living conditions for a homogeneous group of consumers based on retail prices. Among the four measures of CPI, the CPI-IW has a broader coverage than the others. In the organised sector, CPI-IW is used as a cost of living index. However, old base periods—for WPI (2004-05), CPI-UNME (1984-85), CPI-RL (1986-87), CPI-AL (1986-87) and CPI-IW (2001)—fail to capture the rapid structural changes in the economy.

Table 5.1: Decadal Average Inflation

Decades	WPI	CPI-IW	GDP Deflator	PFCE Deflator
1971-72 to 1980-81	10.3	8.3	8.8	8.4
1981-82 to 1990-91	7.1	9.0	8.7	8.3
1991-92 to 2000-01	7.8	8.7	8.1	8.5
2001-02 to 2008-09	5.2	5.3	4.6	4.4
Long-term Trend 1971-72 to 2008-09	7.7	8.0	7.7	7.6

Source: RBI

Implicit economy-wide inflation estimate is also provided by the Gross Domestic Product (GDP) deflator and Private Final Consumption Expenditure (PFCE) deflator from the National Accounts Statistics (NAS). GDP Deflator is a comprehensive measure of inflation, implicitly derived from national accounts data as a ratio of GDP at current prices to constant prices. While it encompasses the entire spectrum of economic activities including services, it is available on a quarterly basis with a lag of two months since 1996. The overall WPI index, on the other hand, is available on a monthly basis with a lag of fortnight since October 24, 2009. However, the prices for two sub-groups—primary article (weight in WPI: 22.03 per cent) and fuel and power, light and lubricants (weight in WPI: 14.23 per cent)—are available on a weekly basis with a lag of a fortnight. The WPI is extensively used for deflating nominal price estimates to derive real price estimates. However, over the years, the representativeness of WPI has reduced as it does not capture the price movement in the services sector which has a larger and increasing share of GDP—about 65 per cent in 2008-09.

Divergence between WPI and CPI

In recent years, the divergence between WPI and CPIs has widened in terms of their weighting pattern. First, services are not covered under WPI while they are, to different degrees, covered under CPIs. Consequently, service price inflation has a greater influence on CPIs. Second, the fuel group has a much higher weight in the WPI (14.2 per cent) than the CPIs (5.5 to 8.4 per cent). As a result, the movement in international crude prices has a greater bearing on WPI than on the CPIs. Third, food has a larger weight in CPI—ranging from 46 per cent in CPI-IW—to 69 per cent in CPI-AL, whereas it has a weight of only 27 per cent (including manufactured food items) in WPI. The CPIs are, therefore, more sensitive to changes in prices of food items.

Chart 5.1: Long-run Relationship between WPI and CPI Inflation

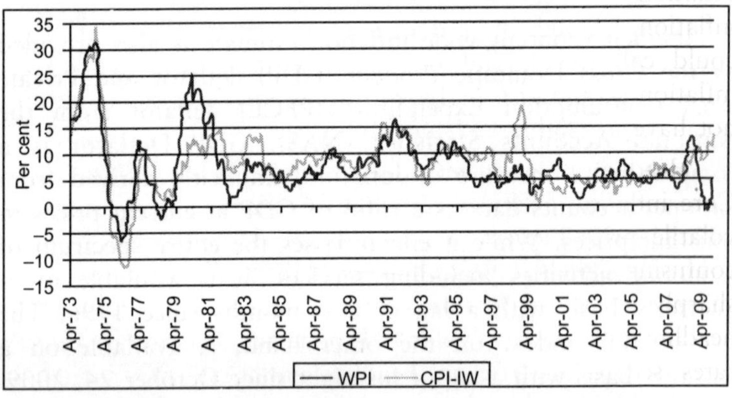

Source: RBI

The increasing divergence between WPI and CPI since early 2008 (Chart 5.2) could be attributed to the fluctuations in the price of minerals and metals, which do not form a part of the CPI group, and a significant inflation of over 8 per cent in services such as medical care, education, recreation and amusement, transport and communication and personal care, which reflected in CPI-IW.

Chart 5.2: Divergence between WPI and CPI Inflation

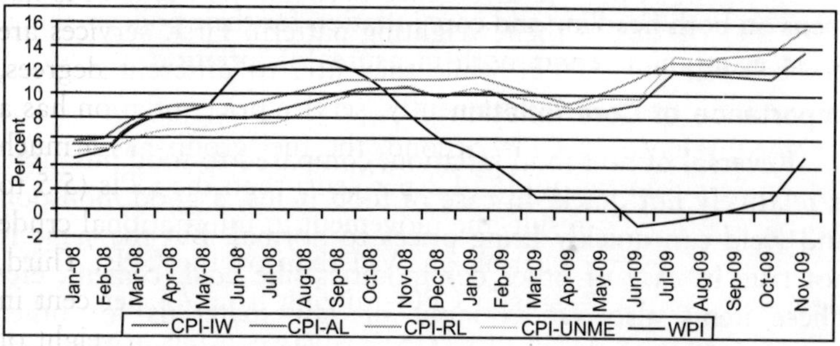

Source: RBI

Core Inflation

In its monetary policy, the Reserve Bank of India (RBI) takes into account two measures of inflation. First is headline inflation and second is non-food manufacturing products inflation. Though India does not have separate categories, we could call the second one as core inflation. Ideally, core inflation should also be based on CPI inflation but India does not have a reliable CPI measure as yet.

Headline inflation includes all the items in the WPI index. Core inflation excludes certain food and fuel items that face volatile price movements. It is because these prices provide confusing signals to policymakers as their prices could increase sharply for few weeks and then decline sharply. This makes headline inflation also volatile. If policymakers increase interest rates seeing the rise in headline inflation, they could be surprised by a sudden lower trend in coming weeks. The policy is further complicated due to the fact that monetary policy impacts economies with a lag.

Hence, core inflation has emerged as an alternative for measuring inflation. In this, volatile items like food prices and fuel items are excluded. However, some economists criticize using core inflation as a measure of inflation. As food and fuel are important items for consumption, they should not be excluded from the inflation measure. A focus on core inflation will miss the overall inflation trend. Suppose the prices of food and fuel increase for a prolonged period, this will not show in core inflation but in headline inflation. Therefore, policymakers focus on both headline and core inflation for their policymaking. Most economies report both measures of inflation.

Importance of Core Inflation

Reversal of non-food inflation, compared to food inflation, is relatively not quick. In case of food items, a good monsoon and yield can quickly bring prices to normal. But the same is not true in case of other commodities like coal, cement, etc. These items also act as input or raw materials for other manufacturing industries and hence the process even gets worse and the prices continue to increase. Thus, core inflation, once it sets in, is not easy to do away with and tends to trouble the policymakers for a comparatively longer duration. Hence, studying and keeping track of core inflation is more important and necessary than food and fuel inflation.

Calculating Core Inflation

In India, core inflation is not reported and only headline inflation is reported. However, core inflation can be computed. For this, WPI inflation is divided into three broad categories—primary articles, fuel products, and manufacturing items. The first two categories include food articles and fuel items which can be excluded. The third category also includes food products which tends to be volatile as well and moves in line with prices of primary articles. So after excluding food products from manufacturing sector, we get non-food manufactured products inflation. This can also be called as core inflation for India. The weight of manufactured products in the total WPI index is 63.8 per cent and food products is 11.5 per cent. So core inflation has items which constitute about 52 per cent of the total headline inflation.

The Chart below shows movement of core inflation since Jan. 2000. It peaked in August 2008 at 11.14 per cent leading to multiple hikes at that time. The inflation then declined thereafter because of the global financial crisis and then increased sharply to 4.2 per cent in February 2010. Since then, the RBI has raised its policy rates several times in concurrence with the continued rise in core inflation.

Chart 5.3: Movement of Core Inflation

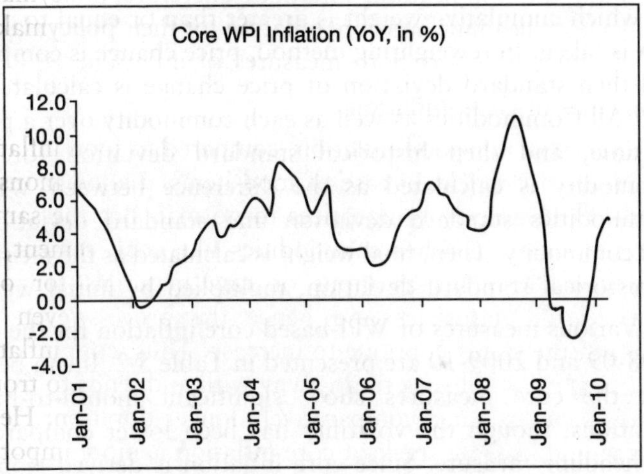

Source: RBI

Various Core Inflation Measures

Central banks show interest in core measure of inflation as it helps in some way to understand demand-side inflation pressures in the economy. The main argument here is that the central bank should effectively be responding to the movements in permanent component of the price level rather than temporary deviations. There are many variants of core inflation which try to remove the volatility of price changes by statistical means. These include truncation of commodities based on standard deviation of price changes, trimmed mean, median and other filter-based smoothing techniques.[1]

1.5 SD method excludes all those commodities in which percentage price change is more than mean plus/minus 1.5 standard deviation over mean price change. In the trimmed mean procedure, price change of each commodities are estimated, and then they are arranged in the increasing order to calculate cumulative weight of the series and then those commodities are cut for which cumulative weight is less than 8 per cent or greater than 92 per cent. In the median method, price change is computed for all the commodities, and is arranged in ascending order, and then cumulative weight of the new series is calculated and the inflation of the first commodity for which cumulative weight is greater than or equal to 50 per cent is taken. In reweighting method, price change is computed, and then standard deviation of price change is calculated for WPI-All Commodities as well as each commodity over a period of time, and then historical standard deviation for each commodity is calculated as the difference between WPI-All Commodities standard deviation and standard deviation of that commodity. Then, final weight is calculated as the reciprocal of historical standard deviation, multiplied by initial weight.

Various measures of WPI-based core inflation for the years 2008-09 and 2009-10 are presented in Table 5.2. It can be seen that the core measures show significant month-to-month variations, though the volatility has been lower compared to the headline measure. Since core inflation is derived from the headline, it reflects the weaknesses in the primary measure of inflation. A prerequisite of a good inflation measure is that it is broader in coverage and the base period is updated frequently, reflecting structural changes in the economy.

In Indian context, the core inflation is derived by exclusion of food and energy from CPI/WPI. It thus discards a substantial portion of the commodity basket. So the price movement of the remaining commodities may not be representative of the underlying inflationary trend. Although these prices have substantial effects on the overall index, they often are quickly reversed. But the reversal of volatile prices sometimes is not short-lived. Therefore, determining when to use a core inflation measure versus an overall inflation measure remains a complex issue.

Main Features of the New WPI Series

A new WPI series with 2004-05 base has been released on 14 September 2010. A representative commodity basket comprising 676 items has been selected and weighting diagram derived for the new series. The total number of price quotations has also been increased from 1918 in the old series to 5482 in the new series, indicating better representation of the prices in the wholesale markets. Sector-wise price quotations have been

Table 5.2: Various WPI-based Core Inflation Measures

Month	Headline	1.5SD	Trimmed	Median	Reweight	Excluding FPLL	Excluding FPLL and Food	Excluding Food
Jan-08	4.5	3.0	3.1	1.6	4.2	4.6	5.3	4.9
Feb-08	5.3	3.4	3.5	2.1	4.5	5.4	5.9	5.6
Mar-08	7.5	4.5	5.1	2.9	5.6	7.8	8.1	7.8
Apr-08	8.0	5.3	5.1	3.0	6.2	8.3	9.0	8.5
May-08	8.9	5.8	5.7	3.7	6.5	9.2	10.1	9.5
Jun-08	11.8	8.4	7.4	6.5	7.9	10.6	11.8	12.9
Jul-08	12.4	8.5	8.0	6.3	7.9	11.0	12.3	13.6
Aug-08	12.8	8.8	8.5	6.7	8.0	11.6	12.8	13.9
Sep-08	12.3	9.2	8.1	6.6	7.8	11.1	12.0	13.2
Oct-08	11.1	10.1	8.0	7.0	7.5	10.3	10.3	11.3
Nov-08	8.5	7.6	7.1	6.3	6.7	9.0	8.7	8.1
Dec-08	6.2	6.4	6.4	4.8	5.9	7.9	7.4	5.4
Jan-09	5.0	5.6	5.7	4.3	5.4	6.8	5.8	3.8
Feb-09	3.5	4.5	4.5	3.4	4.6	5.4	4.4	2.4
Mar-09	1.2	2.1	2.8	1.1	3.4	3.2	2.1	0.0
Apr-09	1.3	3.2	2.8	0.9	2.7	3.2	1.9	0.0
May-09	1.4	1.9	2.4	0.8	2.8	3.4	2.2	0.1
Jun-09	-1.0	-1.3	0.5	0.0	2.0	2.4	0.3	-3.1
Jul-09	-0.7	-1.0	0.4	0.0	2.6	2.2	-0.6	-3.2
Aug-09	-0.2	-0.9	0.5	0.0	2.9	2.4	-0.4	-2.7
Sep-09	0.5	-1.0	0.7	0.0	3.1	2.9	0.1	-2.1
Oct-09	1.3	-0.7	1.3	0.0	3.2	3.5	1.1	-0.9
Nov-09	4.8	1.1	2.6	0.0	4.3	6.3	3.6	2.5
Financial year: 2008-09								
Range	11.6	8	5.7	5.9	4.6	8.4	10.7	13.9
Mean	8.5	6.9	6.4	5.0	6.5	8.7	8.9	8.6
Std. dev.	3.8	2.3**	1.7*	1.9*	1.5*	2.5**	3.4	4.7
Financial year: 2009-10								
Range	5.8	4.5	2.4	0.9	2.3	4.1	4.2	5.7
Mean	0.9	0.2	1.4	0.2	3.0	3.3	1.0	-1.2
Std. dev.	1.8	1.7	1.0**	0.4*	0.7*	1.3	1.5	2.0

* and ** indicate that the core inflation standard deviation is lower and significantly different from the standard deviation of headline inflation at 1 per cent and 5 per cent level of significance, respectively.

Source: RBI

increased from the old to new series from 455 to 579 in primary group and from 1391 to 4831 in the manufactured products group. A comparison of the weighting diagram and number of commodities between the old and new series for the major groups is drawn in Table 5.3.

Table 5.3: Major Changes in the Weights and Commodities in the Revised WPI Series

Items	Weights New Series (base: 2004-05)	Weights Old Series (base: 1993-94)	No. of Commodities New Series (base: 2004-05)	No. of Commodities Old Series (base: 1993-94)	New Items Added/ Revised
All Commodities	100.00	100.00	676	435	417
Primary Articles	20.12	22.03	102	98	11
Food Articles	14.34	15.40	55	54	1
Non-Food & Minerals	5.78	6.63	47	44	10
Fuel and Power	14.91	14.23	19	19	0
Manufactured Products	64.97	63.75	555	318	406
Food Products	9.97	11.54	57	41	25
Non-Food Products	55.00	52.21	498	277	381

Source: The Office of the Economic Adviser, Ministry of Commerce and Industry

Some of the important items included in primary articles in the new series basket are flowers, lemons, and crude petroleum. In manufactured products, the items added are ice cream, canned meat, palm oil, readymade/instant food powder, mineral water, computer stationery, leather products, scooter/ motorcycle tyres, polymers, petrochemical intermediates, granite, marble, gold and silver, construction machinery, refrigerators, computers, dish antenna, transformers, microwave ovens, communication equipment (telephone instruments), TV sets, VCDs, washing machines, and auto parts.

Introduction of CPI-Urban and CPI-Rural

A new initiative has been taken up by the Central Statistics Office (CSO) under which it shall compile CPI (urban), CPI (rural), and CPI (rural+urban) for all states/UTs and all India by considering all sections of the urban and rural population. It is expected that these indices would reflect the true picture of price behaviour of various goods and services consumed by the urban and rural population.

Trends in Inflation

Core inflation has moved up in fiscal 2010-11 which indicates that the inflation in food items might have spilled over into a more generalized phenomenon. Inflation in manufactured items with a weight of 65 per cent in the WPI has been above the 4 per cent mark since January 2010 and after reaching 6.4 per cent in April 2010 has evinced a moderating trend. This rise in wage goods and levels of inflation in intermediates has implications for the industrial output.

General Wholesale Price Situation

During the first half of 2009-10, the headline year-on-year inflation remained significantly low at 0.36 per cent on account of sharp increases in prices recorded in 2008-09. The second half of 2009-10 showed increasing food prices on account of unfavourable agricultural supply conditions coupled with the waning of base effect, leading to sharp increase in inflation. Thereafter, the headline WPI inflation reached 10.23 per cent in March 2010. Financial year 2010-11 started with 11 per cent headline inflation in April 2010. However, demand pressures became visible in early 2010.

At disaggregate level, the price behaviour of three major commodities groups has been in marked contrast to the previous year when inflation remained low on account of global decline

Table 5.4: Annual Average Inflation Rate—based on WPI

(Per Cent)

Year	Primary Articles	Fuel & Power	Manufactured Products	All Commodities
Weights (%)	20.12	14.91	64.97	100
2000-01	2.8	28.5	3.3	7.2
2001-02	3.6	8.9	1.8	3.6
2002-03	3.3	5.5	2.6	3.4
2003-04	4.3	6.4	5.7	5.5
2004-05	3.7	10.1	6.3	6.5
1st 5 Years' Average	3.5	11.9	3.9	5.2
2005-06	4.3	13.5	2.3	4.3
2006-07	9.6	6.5	5.6	6.5
2007-08	8.3	0.0	4.9	4.8
2008-09	11.0	11.6	6.2	8.0
2009-10	12.7	-2.1	1.8	3.6
2nd 5 Years' Average	9.2	5.9	4.1	5.5
Decadal Average	6.4	8.9	4.0	5.3
2009-10 (Apr.-Dec.)	9.8	-5.8	0.7	1.7
2010-11 (Apr.-Dec.)[P]	18.0	12.3	5.3	9.4

Source: The Office of the Economic Adviser, Ministry of Commerce and Industry

Note: P-Provisional

in commodity prices. From March to July 2010, while the headline inflation remained in double digits, the inflation in manufactured products remained in the lower range of 4.5 to 6.4 per cent.

Average Trends in WPI Inflation

The ten-year (2000-01 to 2009-10) average of headline WPI inflation comes to 5.3 per cent. Inflation was relative to the decadal average in 2000-01, 2003-04, 2004-05, 2006-07, and 2008-09. In the financial year 2010-11, the average inflation (April-December 2010) of 9.4 per cent was also much higher than the decadal rate. The years 2003-04, 2004-05, 2006-07, and 2008-09 also witnessed high inflation in manufactured products mainly on account of high prices of raw materials such as basic metal alloys and metal products, non-metallic mineral products, and machinery and machine tools. The overall average inflation from April-December 2010 at 9.4 per cent, is the highest recorded in the last ten years (Table 5.4).

Core inflation (WPI non-food inflation), which was 0.55 per cent in November 2009, reached its peak in April 2010 at 8.07 per cent (Table 5.5). Thereafter, it has moderated in response to monetary measures taken by the Reserve Bank

Table 5.5: Movement in WPI Non-food Inflation during 2010-11

(Per Cent)

	Non-food Composite Index	Non-food Articles	Minerals	Fuel & Power	Core Inflation	Non-food Manufactured
Weight	75.69	4.26	1.52	14.91	60.78	55.0
Apr. 2010	9.18	18.08	34.56	13.61	8.07	5.92
May 2010	8.71	14.76	25.34	14.42	7.27	5.77
Jun. 2010	8.47	15.83	22.08	13.92	7.09	5.55
Jul. 2010	8.43	15.30	31.60	13.26	7.16	5.41
Aug. 2010	7.97	15.81	23.77	12.55	677	5.21
Sep. 2010	7.96	20.75	26.77	11.06	7.13	5.09
Oct. 2010	8.57	25.74	29.38	11.02	7.91	5.25
Nov. 2010	8.02	23.22	21.54	10.32	7.40	5.41
Dec. 2010	8.36	22.31	27.69	11.19	7.60	5.34

Source: The Office of the Economic Adviser, Ministry of Commerce and Industry

Note: Core Index = Total WPI – (Total Food + Fuel & Power)

of India (RBI). However, inflation in non-food manufactured products (weight 55.00 per cent) had not increased much and remained in the range of 5.1 to 5.9 per cent in the financial year 2010-11. Notwithstanding, year-on-year inflation in the composite non-food index (weight 75.7 per cent) increased to 8.36 per cent in December 2010 after moderating to 7.96 per cent in September 2010 from 9.18 per cent in April 2010.

Main items of concern in non-food inflation are raw cotton, raw jute, raw silk, copra, castor seed, sunflower, raw rubber, copper ore, zinc, iron ore, cotton textiles, petrochemical intermediates and industrial machinery and machine tools.

Annual Inflation as per Different Price Indices

The inflation in terms of the consumer price index for industrial workers (CPI-IW) remained in double digits from July 2009 to July 2010. The inflation in terms of the CPI-AL (Agricultural Labourers) and CPI-RL (Rural Labourers) had reached double digits in May 2009 and continued so until July 2010. Further, inflation in terms of the CPI-AL and CPI-RL was higher than inflation based on the CPI-IW during all these

Table 5.6: Year-on-Year Inflation Based on Different Consumer Price Indices

Month	WPI (2004-05=100)		CPI(IW) (2001=100)		CPI(AL) 1986-87 =100)		CPI(RL) (1986-87 =100)	
	2009-10	2010-11	2009-10	2010-11	2009-10	2010-11	2009-10	2010-11
April	0.89	11.00	8.70	13.33	9.09	14.96	9.09	14.96
May	1.21	10.60	8.63	13.91	10.21	13.68	10.21	13.68
June	-0.71	10.28	9.29	13.73	11.52	13.02	11.26	13.02
July	-0.62	10.02	11.89	11.25	12.90	11.02	12.67	11.24
August	0.31	8.82	11.72	9.88	12.89	9.65	12.67	9.66
September	1.09	8.93	11.64	9.82	13.19	9.13	12.97	9.34
October	1.48	9.12	11.49	9.70	13.73	8.43	13.51	8.45
November	4.50	7.48P	13.51	8.33	15.65	7.14	15.65	6.95
December	6.92	8.43P	14.97	9.47	17.21	7.99	16.99	8.01
January	8.53		16.22		17.57		17.35	
February	9.68		14.86		16.45		16.45	
March	10.23		14.86		15.77		15.52	
Average (April-March)	3.57		12.37		13.91		13.76	

Source: Labour Bureau, Shimla and the Office of the Economic Adviser, Ministry of Commerce and Industry

Note: P: Provisional

months. In August 2010, the inflation in terms of all price indices had come down to single digit for the first time in 15 months. Table 5.6 shows that inflation in the CPI-IW was at its peak of 16.22 per cent in January 2010 and it declined to 9.47 per cent in December 2010.

Disaggregated Consumer Price Inflation

Besides food, housing has also been a major contributor to CPI-IW inflation. The housing sector has a 15.27 per cent weight in the CPI-IW commodities basket. The non-food inflation in CPI-IW increased during April-December 2010 to 11.64 per cent as against 8.78 per cent in the corresponding period in 2009 (Table 5.7). Inflation in the CPI-IW increased in December 2010 to 9.47 per cent as against 8.33 per cent in November 2010.

Table 5.7: Quarterly Inflation Trend in CPI-IW by Major Commodity Groups (Base: 2001=100)

		2009-10				2010-11			
	Weights	Apr.-Jun.	Jul.-Sep.	Oct.-Dec.	Apr.-Dec.	Apr.-Jun.	Jul.-Sep.	Oct.-Dec.	Apr.-Dec.
General Index	100.00	8.87	11.75	13.06	11.67	13.66	10.31	9.16	10.96
Food Group	46.20	11.47	13.97	16.56	14.70	13.99	10.34	7.01	10.29
Pan, Supari, Tobacco and Intoxicants	2.27	7.44	8.80	7.86	8.34	12.93	12.13	11.26	12.10
Fuel and Light	6.43	4.59	3.02	3.91	4.08	6.00	11.26	10.84	9.41
Housing	15.27	5.97	22.06	22.06	16.82	33.1	21.08	21.08	24.68
Clothing, Bedding and Footwear	6.57	4.14	4.38	4.22	4.34	4.51	5.51	7.05	5.70
Miscellaneous Group	23.26	7.11	5.95	4.30	6.11	5.03	4.72	5.35	5.03
Total Non-food	53.80	6.45	9.64	9.62	8.78	13.33	10.27	11.42	11.64

Source: Labour Bureau, Shimla

Housing Price Index (NHB-RESIDEX)

In India, the housing sector contributes more than nine per cent of national employment. The conditions are favourable for a vibrant housing market as it is one of the most populous and fastest growing countries in the world. While the housing sector has considerable growth potential, housing finance remains underdeveloped. As a result, though there is no lack of demand for housing, there is shortage of credit flow. The challenge in the Indian housing market is primarily in the low and moderate income segments.

In 2007, the National Housing Bank (NHB) launched RESIDEX to provide an index of residential prices in India across cities and over time. Initially, a pilot study was conducted with 2001 as base year during the period 2001-05 to capture the trend of price movements in residential property. The pilot study covered five cities, namely Bengaluru, Bhopal, Delhi, Kolkata and Mumbai. Thereafter, compilation of RESIDEX has been expanded to ten more cities, namely Ahmedabad, Faridabad, Chennai, Kochi, Hyderabad, Jaipur, Patna, Lucknow, Pune, and Surat. RESIDEX is now being updated on a quarterly basis with 2007 as base year for 15 cities.

An analysis of the movement in prices of residential properties in the 15 cities covered under the NHB RESIDEX in the first half of 2010 shows a mixed trend. Residential housing prices in ten cities, viz. Surat, Mumbai, Lucknow, Ahmedabad, Chennai, Pune, Kolkata, Patna, Faridabad and Bhopal, have shown an increasing trend compared to the base year.

RBI's Monetary Policy

The accommodative monetary policy pursued by the RBI beginning mid-September 2008 instilled confidence in market participants, mitigated the adverse impact of the global financial crisis on the economy, and ensured that it started recovering ahead of most other economies. In October 2009, the Reserve Bank embarked on the first phase of exit from the expansionary monetary policy in view of the rising food inflation and the risk of it impinging on inflationary expectations. By April 2010, available data suggested that the recovery was firmly in place, though inflationary pressures accentuated. Accordingly, repo and reverse repo rates as well as the CRR were increased by 25 bps each.

In April 2010, the RBI's monetary policy stance was guided by three considerations. There was the need to move in a calibrated manner in the direction of normalizing the policy instruments in a scenario where real policy rates were still negative. Second, the need to ensure that demand-side inflation did not become entrenched. Finally, the need to balance the monetary policy imperative of absorbing liquidity while ensuring that credit was available to both the government and private sectors.

Soon after the announcement of the monetary policy in April 2010, developments on the inflation front raised several concerns. The upward revision in administered fuel prices on 25 June 2010 was bound to influence inflation in the months ahead. Hence, the repo and reverse repo rates under the LAF were increased by 25 bps each on 2 July 2010. The changes in policy rates since 2009 are shown in Table 5.8.

Table 5.8: Revision in Policy Rates

(Per Cent)

Effective Date	Repo Rate	Reverse Repo Rate	CRR
2009			
05.01.2009	5.50	4.00	
17.01.2009			5.00
05.03.2009	5.00	3.50	
21.04.2009	4.75	3.25	
2010			
13.02.2010			5.50
27.02.2010			5.75
19.03.2010	5.00	3.50	
20.04.2010	5.25	3.75	
24.04.2010			6.00
02.07.2010	5.50	4.00	
27.07.2010	5.75	4.50	
16.09.2010	6.00	5.00	
02.11.2010	6.25	5.25	
2011			
25.01.2011	6.50	5.50	

Source: Monetary Policy Statements, RBI

Various monetary policy actions of the RBI were intended to moderate inflation by reining in demand pressures and inflationary expectations, maintain financial conditions conducive to sustaining growth, generate liquidity conditions consistent with more effective transmission of policy actions, and reduce the volatility of short-term rates in a narrower corridor.

Quarterly Reviews

Mid-quarter reviews of monetary policy in India are made in June, September, December, and March. On the basis of assessment of the macroeconomic situation, the RBI in its Mid-Quarter Review on 16 September 2010 decided to increase the repo rate under the LAF by 25 bps from 5.75 per cent to 6.0 per cent and the reverse repo rate by 50 bps from 4.5 per cent to 5.0 per cent.

The Second Quarter Review of Monetary Policy for 2010-11 (released on 2 November 2010) noted that headline inflation in India remained significantly above its medium-term trend and well above the comfort zone of the RBI. Accordingly, the RBI further increased the repo rate by 25 bps to 6.25 per cent and the reverse repo rate also by 25 bps to 5.25 per cent on 2 November 2010. The Second Quarter Review also noted that the fragile and uneven nature of the recovery and large unemployment in advanced economies raised concerns about the sustainability of the global turnaround whereas the Indian economy was operating close to the trend growth rate, driven mainly by domestic factors.

In its Third Quarter Review of the Monetary Policy on 25 January 2011, the RBI indicated that inflation is its dominant concern. Non-food articles inflation and fuel inflation were already at elevated levels. Non-food manufacturing inflation too remained sticky and there were signs of food and fuel price increases spilling over into generalised inflation. Equally important consideration was the heightened upside risks to domestic inflation due to a sharp rise in global commodity prices. The Review also noted the reduced uncertainty with regard to global recovery, and that the growth has moved close to its pre-crisis trajectory.

On the basis of the assessment of the then existing macroeconomic scenario, the RBI increased the repo rate under the LAF by 25 bps from 6.25 per cent to 6.5 per cent; and the reverse repo rate under the LAF by 25 bps from 5.25 per cent to 5.50 per cent. On the basis of an assessment of the liquidity situation, the RBI extended additional liquidity support to the SCBs under the LAF to the extent of up to 1 per cent of their NDTL, till 8 April 2011. For any shortfall in maintenance of the SLR arising out of availment of this facility, banks were allowed to seek waiver of penal interest purely as an ad hoc measure.

The RBI had raised its baseline projection of WPI inflation for March 2011 from 5.5 per cent to 7.0 per cent. This upward revision was based on several considerations. First, the upside risk to inflation, as mentioned in the mid-quarter review of December 2010, materialised and was reflected in the increase in prices of metals and non-administered fuel. Second, there were some transitory supply shocks which triggered a sharp increase in vegetable prices. Third, petroleum and aviation turbine fuel prices went up in early January which added 9 bps to WPI inflation.

Due to the fact that the food inflation remained at an elevated level for about two years, the prospect of it spilling over to the general inflation process has increased. Secondly, as global growth consolidates, imports as a means to supplement domestic availability for many commodities are becoming less of an option, thus accentuating demand-side pressures as capacity utilisation increases.

Under the prevailing conditions, the monetary policy stance of RBI is intended to contain the spill-over of high food and fuel inflation into generalised inflation and anchor inflationary expectations, while being prepared to respond to any further build-up of inflationary pressures. It is also intended to maintain an interest rate regime consistent with price, output and financial stability. The RBI manages liquidity to ensure that it remains broadly in balance, with neither a surplus diluting monetary transmission nor a deficit choking off fund flows. In short, the RBI's anti-inflationary monetary stance is determined, based on its expectation that the domestic growth momentum shall stabilise and at the same time providing comfort to banks in their liquidity management operations.

Challenges and Outlook

In the first three quarters of 2010-11, non-food manufacturing inflation remained above its medium-term trend of 4 per cent. Average headline inflation in April-December 2010-11 at 9.4 per cent is the highest ever in the decadal average. This is also true of annual average inflation based on the WPI, for primary food articles, fuel and power, and manufacturing products.

After some moderation between August and November 2010, inflation rose again in December 2010 on account of sharp increase in the prices of primary food articles and the recent spurt in global oil prices. Non-food manufacturing inflation has also remained sticky, reflecting buoyant demand conditions. However, in January 2011, headline inflation came down to 8.23 per cent.

Rising Steel Prices

The rising prices of steel are worrying the businessmen. The prices of steel products like cold and hot-rolled sheets, TMT bars and angles have spiked by almost ₹ 9,500 a tonne since mid-December 2010. There was a jump of almost ₹ 5,000 a tonne in various steel products in a single fortnight in January 2011.

The rates were still near the levels prevailing in the same period last year, but it is apprehended that in 2011, the prices may cross last year's peak. The pace at which the prices have shot up is more alarming than the year-on-year level. Last year, the rates had touched these levels over a period of time, not in just a month and a half like this time, as per traders.

This may have an adverse impact on industries like white goods, construction, automobile and so on. The manufacturers may first try to absorb the higher cost but after a point it will have to be passed on to the customers.

The cold-rolled sheets are now being quoted in the range of around ₹ 48,000 a tonne, while the hot-rolled sheets are priced in the range of ₹ 39,000 to ₹ 44,000 a tonne. There has been a jump of ₹ 9,000-9,500 in these categories. Similarly, TMT bars used in construction industry are priced at around ₹ 37,000 a tonne and ingots at ₹ 34,000, again registering a similar rise. The rates are close to or marginally higher than the previous year's level.

The peak rates were ₹ 48,000 and ₹ 44,000 per tonne for cold-rolled and hot-rolled sheets respectively, while TMT had touched a peak of ₹ 40,000 and ingots ₹ 38,000 in 2010.

The reason of rising prices of steel is the major increase in the iron ore prices. Iron ore prices have jumped to ₹ 7,500 a tonne against ₹ 4,500 a tonne in mid-December 2010. The open market rate of coal has also risen to ₹ 5,000 a tonne from ₹ 3,500, directly affecting steel prices.

The rising steel prices are not confined to India. The prices in international markets have also gone up and the inventory with domestic manufacturers is low compared to the demand. Some traders have also complained that the supply has been withheld by the distributors in the wake of rising prices as they want to increase their prices in anticipation of future high prices. Some dealers assured to adjust with lower margins till March 2011 but after that they may have to escalate the rates in fresh tenders if the high prices continue.[3]

High steel prices are having a disastrous impact on industries that consume steel, especially medium and small units. Steel consumers have pointed out that there is no justification for the increase in steel prices, as raw material costs have not gone up correspondingly. But steel producers in India warned that there is likely to be an acute shortage of coking coal following heavy floods in Australia, and are suspected to have jacked up the rates.

Some traders also pointed out that steel prices have been climbing every year towards the end of the financial year. The governments as well as bulk of the companies in India follow the April-March calendar for their fiscal period, and most government departments go on a spending spree towards the end of the fiscal, to utilize their budgets. This puts pressure on supply and results in higher prices during the period.

The spending on public projects by the public works departments of various State Governments also peaks towards the end of the fiscal, as bureaucrats and department heads fear that their future allocation in the new year would be slashed if they do not utilise the funds.

With the automotive and consumer goods sectors doing exceedingly well, the demand for steel continues to surge in India. According to the World Steel Association, India will soon emerge as the world's third largest consumer of steel after China and the US. This will naturally put pressure on supplies and therefore, prices.

According to Beni Prasad Verma, Minister of State for Steel, India was the fifth largest producer of crude steel in 2010, and the largest sponge iron producer. India's crude steel production capacity soared from 51.17 million tonnes per annum in 2005-06 to 72.96 million tonnes per annum in 2009-10. Steel remains critical for the growth of the economy, especially now that the government is focusing on infrastructure development.

Steel production has been growing by nearly 10 per cent over the past few years. But the consumption has been increasing at a faster rate and demand continues to outstrip supplies, resulting in a nearly 30 per cent growth in imports. Mr. Verma also pointed out that the steel sector is expected to grow at a minimum of 10 per cent over the next five years. Over the next 10 years, India's steel production capacity is expected to cross the 275 million tonne mark, attracting investments of over ₹ 8.7 trillion (almost $200 billion).

Tata Steel, the major steel producer in India, which acquired European steel major, Corus a few years ago, expects growing demand from the automobile sector. At present, most of the automakers import the bulk of their cold-rolled steel requirements, as Indian producers are unable to meet their demand.

According to the Managing Director of Tata Steel, Mr. Nerurkar, "The current demand in the country for auto-grade steel is close to four million tonnes per annum. Domestic steel companies are able to meet less than 50 per cent of this demand." Tata Steel plans to get into producing high-end steel products including skin panels for vehicles, which will boost supply.

Tata Steel expects to sell a million tonnes of steel to the automobile sector by next year, out of its total sales of over six million tonnes. It aims to double this to two million tonnes by 2014. The company has also entered into a joint venture with Nippon Steel, a Japanese major, to set up a 600,000 tonnes per annum auto-grade steel plant. The two companies are investing ₹ 23 billion in the new venture. In fact, all the leading steelmakers in India are investing huge amounts in expansion—both greenfield and brownfield—even as other international majors are seeking to set up massive plants. This is likely to increase supply, but as the demand is likely to be more than supply, the prices will remain high. The prices of consumer durables manufactered using steel, including electronic goods and cars are thus likely to remain high.

High Cement Prices

The cement prices are increasing fast in India. The prices of cement have been increased for the fifth time since October 2010 and have increased by about 12 per cent since then. The major reason has been the rise in the cost of materials used to make cement.

According to Shailendra Chouksey, Director JK Lakshmi Cement, while fuel input costs have risen by about 50 per cent over the last year, logistics' costs have also gone up due to indirect increase in the cost of rail transportation following an increase in demurrage and wharfage charges. Power and fuel account for nearly 60 per cent of the variable costs. The industry needed to push cement prices up to address the increase in input costs.

Since input costs for all raw materials are rising, the analysts feel it would put pressure on the operating margins of the companies from 4 to 9 per cent over the next two years. While reduced coal linkages will force companies to buy from the costlier open market and through imports, rail freight rates have gone up by four per cent from December 2010. Imported coal has also escalated by about 50 per cent in the quarter ending December 2010 and open market coal prices are surging. Besides, cost of other inputs like gypsum, fly ash and slag is also going up by about 12 per cent on a year-on-year basis.

There has been a steady drop in capacity utilization in India, from 80 per cent in the first quarter to 69 per cent in the second and 71 per cent in the third quarter of the current financial year. The average capacity utilization for financial year 2010-11 decreased to 74 per cent, against 85 per cent during the corresponding period of the previous year. The net cement capacity in the country is 265 million tonnes, with another 35 million tonnes expected to come up in 2012-13.

It was also believed that cement makers are forming cartels and pushing prices up artificially, which adds to the total cost of construction, and thus leads to an escalation in the prices of property. It was felt that there should be a separate regulator for construction material suppliers and manufacturers to keep a check on such unhealthy practices.

Cement manufacturers, on the other hand, have argued that since there has not been any major infrastructure project after the Commonwealth Games last year, the dip in capacity utilization is translating into the present demand situation.

As in many other products, the prices of cement are also different in different cities in India. In March 2011, prices in Mumbai were in the range of ₹ 257-260 per 50 kg bag, while in the rest of Maharashtra, they were slightly lower at ₹ 238-248. In Tamil Nadu and Andhra Pradesh, prices were still lower at ₹ 220-230 a bag, but in Chennai they were higher at ₹ 260-265 a bag, while in the northern part of the country, much lower at ₹ 210-215 a bag. This variation in prices in different parts of the country bears testimony to poor distribution and supply system.

Rising Aluminum Prices

During the last five years or so, metals have been adversely impacted by a combination of factors, mainly the rising oil price which has gone above US$ 100 per barrel. It is rightly believed that rising oil prices are negative for business, increasing costs like a form of tax. As costs increase, the consumer pays more and consumption falls, so why would aluminum prices continue rising and how robust are current price levels in the medium term? It was indeed a matter of surprise that although virtually no aluminum around the world is smelted from electricity generated from oil, yet aluminum prices have increased with an increase in Brent crude price.

The prices of aluminum started to fall in 2007-08 before the global economic meltdown started to spread in America, Europe, Asia and other parts of the world and to adversely impact the industry worldwide, including India. As the wider market came to realize that the true level of inventory available for consumption was only around 25 per cent of the whole and that in practice the market had little more at its disposal than the level around the middle of the decade, the price started recovering. As the forward price premium available on the LME (Dec. 2012) has recovered from $90/ton at the start of February 2011 to $120/ton now, financing deals have become more attractive, increasing the probability that current deals will be renewed when they mature.

Currently, the price is being supported by many factors beyond just prompt availability. Firstly, unrest in the Middle East is spreading slowly yet steadily from one regime to another, i.e. from Egypt to Libya to Bahrain. Among major aluminum-producing countries, only Bahrain has been seriously affected so far, but even there, aluminum production has been spared any impact. If Qatar, Dubai or Saudi Arabia witness popular unrest, it will impact some of the lowest-cost production in the world.

The greater influence to the price, though seems to be the cost of energy as reflected in the oil price. Investors' eyes have particularly been on China of late, home to 40 per cent of the world's aluminum production and consumption. According to a news report, Beijing is considering its first electricity price increase from generators to grids since 2009, which could start in April 2011 and in the news organization's opinion, could curtail aluminum output as Chinese producers find their profit margins squeezed.

Going forward, the inflation outlook will be shaped by the food price situation and the demand-side pressures in the economy. The domestic food price situation could be exacerbated by the increase in global food prices because of dependency on import of some food items like edible oils. Thus, current growth and inflation trends warrant persistence with an anti-inflationary monetary stance.

In the near term, the centre stage of policy consideration will be the issue of maintaining an environment where the cost and availability of credit is supportive of growth momentum, while ensuring that inflation falls back to more comfortable target levels. This needs to be seen in the context of more than expected inflation in the recent past, relative stickiness of prices, especially of food, and building of wider inflationary expectations in the economy. This is even as monetary policy tools are being used proactively to manage demand and dampen inflationary pressures in the economy.

The concurrent consolidation of fiscal deficits will ease the conduct of effective monetary policy in the near future. The reduced fiscal deficits will permit greater availability of credit to sustain growth. The tighter monetary policy, on the other hand, will have its impact in reducing inflationary pressures. The transmission of monetary policy, however, comes with a lag.

The policy challenge of maintaining the growth momentum in the economy with price stability is going to remain a key focus area for monetary policy and macroeconomic management. According to D. Subbarao, Governor of the Reserve Bank of India, inflation could become a global concern as the advanced economies consolidate their recovery. According to him, the inflation outlook in India will be shaped by three factors: (i) on how the food price situation, both domestic and global, evolves; (ii) how global commodity prices behave; and (iii) the extent to which demand-side pressures may manifest.[2] While the impact of transitory factors is expected to dissipate, price pressures on account of demand-supply imbalances in respect of some commodities are expected to persist.

Frederic Neumann, HSBC's co-head of Asian Economics Research is of the opinion that the worry in India, more than anywhere else in Asia, is that inflation will prove very sticky and very difficult to bring down. According to him, the growth in Asia is being driven by strong consumption but also increased investment spending. He adds that India, however, has to start to tighten its monetary policy by raising interest rates further.[4] The inflation is the first big by-product of very low interest rates and unless these rates are further increased, inflation may go up even further in 2012 and 2013.

Keeping rates too low for too long also risks generating asset bubbles and policymakers will also have to use other tools to cool down property markets and other asset markets. These steps should not be draconian, but just enough to stabilize the economies. Currency appreciation is not as important a tool to bring down inflation in India because inflation in India is driven by too strong demand locally, and not because of imported food prices or imported oil prices. Since the Indian economy is a domestically focused economy, it is not very sensitive to the change in exchange rates. If the RBI takes a cautious approach, not fully believing in the strength of the current recovery, there arises the risks that the price for erring on the side of caution shall be paid not immediately, but in the more distant future.

The Indian economy has long mired in what was called the 'Hindu rate' of growth. So the desirability of higher growth is unquestionable. However, with higher growth has come uncomfortably high inflation, one of the highest among the Group of 20 nations. Stephen Roach, chairman of Morgan Stanley Asia is of the view that India has leant too heavily on stimulus measures for too long.[5] The government has over-stimulated the economy with public spending and a monetary policy that was too loose.

In order to curb inflation, the RBI hiked its policy rate seven times during 12 months ending January 2011. But these hikes had no bearing on inflation, according to Dipankar Dasgupta, a former professor of economics at the Indian Statistical Institute. Instead, he argues, these rate hikes hamper the growth of the manufacturing sector. "The hikes in rates will increase investment cost by raising interest rates at which banks provide loan to companies. Thus, manufacturing sector growth will be less and that will lead to less employment in the sector."[6]

It is another thing, however, that the hike in policy rates may not have any bad impact on the growth as the momentum in India's national income is being driven by the booming service sector and not manufacturing sector.

Notes

1. Measures of Inflation in India: Issues and Perspectives, Speech by Deepak Mohanty, Executive Director, Reserve Bank of India, at the Conference of Indian Association for Research in National Income and Wealth (IARNIW) at the Centre for Development Studies (CDS), Thiruvananthapuram, January 9, 2010.
2. Media statement released by Dr. D. Subbarao, Governor of the Reserve Bank of India (RBI) on the Third Quarter Review of Monetary Policy 2010-11, Jan. 25, 2011.
3. *Times of India*, 1 Feb. 2011.
4. Inflation in India may prove hard to bring down: Frederic Neumann, Jan 17, 2011, Venkatesan Vembu, DNA.
5. "The economy: High plaudits tempered by inflation fears, James Lamont." *Financial Times*, January 26 2011.
6. "Central bank's rate hikes may not tame inflation: Economists." IANS, *The Economic Times*, 27 Jan. 2011.

Table A.1: Index Numbers of Wholesale Prices

(Base: 2004-05 = 100)

	Primary articles					Fuel	Manufactured products						All
	Total	Food articles Total	Food articles Food-grains	Non-food articles	Minerals	power-light & lubricants	Total	Food products	Textiles	Chemicals & chemical products	Basic metals, alloys & metal	Machinery & machine products	commodities tools
Weight-Base (1993-94)=100	22.03	15.40	5.01	6.14	0.49	14.23	63.75	11.54	9.80	11.93	8.34	8.36	100.00
Weight-Base (2004-05)=100	20.12	14.34	4.09	4.26	1.52	14.91	64.97	9.97	7.33	12.02	10.75	8.93	100.00
1	2	3	4	5	6	7	8	9	10	11	12	13	14
Last week of (1993-94 = 100)													
1994-95	121	115	119	137	104	109	117	113	128	121	116	109	116.9
1995-96	125	124	127	129	93	115	123	118	126	130	123	113	122.2
1996-97	136	138	144	133	109	130	126	130	115	136	128	117	128.8
1997-98	142	144	139	142	100	148	129	137	117	137	132	115	134.6
1998-99	153	157	167	146	118	153	135	150	114	152	133	116	141.7
1999-00	159	168	176	141	104	193	139	150	116	160	137	116	150.9
2000-01	162	168	170	149	118	223	144	145	122	167	142	127	159.2
2001-02	168	177	170	150	120	231	144	145	116	171	140	130	161.8
2002-03	178	178	176	183	118	256	152	158	128	178	150	130	172.3
2003-04	181	178	175	191	148	263	162	174	139	179	183	134	180.3
2004-05	183	184	179	177	249	290	169	174	131	186	214	144	189.5
Last month of (2004-05 = 100)													
2005-06	104	105	113	97	119	117	103	102	100	105	101	105	105.5
2006-07	118	119	126	107	135	119	110	107	101	110	116	112	112.7
2007-08	129	126	137	124	173	127	118	116	101	116	138	115	121.4
2008-09	136	136	152	125	168	123	119	123	103	116	127	118	123.2
2009-10	166	164	172	150	232	140	126	142	112	120	129	120	135.8

(Contd...)

1	2	3	4	5	6	7	8	9	10	11	12	13	14
Average of weeks (1993-94 = 100)													
1994-95	116	113	115	124	105	109	112	114	118	117	108	106	112.6
1995-96	125	122	122	135	95	115	122	118	129	127	120	112	121.6
1996-97	136	137	138	134	107	126	124	125	119	131	126	116	127.2
1997-98	139	141	139	138	100	144	128	135	115	137	131	115	132.8
1998-99	156	159	152	152	111	148	134	150	114	146	133	116	140.7
1999-00	158	165	176	143	110	162	137	151	115	155	135	116	145.3
2000-01	163	170	174	147	113	208	142	146	120	164	140	123	155.7
2001-02	168	176	172	153	119	227	144	146	119	169	141	129	161.3
2002-03	174	179	174	165	119	239	148	153	122	174	145	130	166.8
2003-04	181	181	176	186	122	255	156	167	132	177	168	133	175.9
2004-05	188	186	177	188	255	280	166	175	136	182	203	140	187.2
Average of months (2004-05 = 100)													
2005-06	104	105	107	97	115	114	102	101	99	104	101	104	104.4
2006-07	114	116	122	102	137	121	108	107	101	109	110	110	111.2
2007-08	124	124	131	114	153	121	113	110	102	113	122	114	116.5
2008-09	138	135	145	129	187	135	120	120	103	118	137	117	125.9
2009-10	155	155	166	136	203	132	122	136	107	118	126	118	130.4
2009-10													
April	141	140	155	128	183	124	120	127	103	116	124	118	124.6
May	143	142	156	131	190	125	120	128	104	117	125	118	125.5
June	147	145	157	132	202	126	120	129	105	116	124	118	126.4
July	149	150	159	132	187	131	121	130	105	117	124	118	127.8
August	153	154	161	133	201	132	121	133	105	118	124	118	129.3
September	153	155	164	133	194	133	122	136	106	117	126	117	129.9
October	155	158	167	132	197	133	122	136	106	117	126	117	130.5

(*Contd...*)

1	2	3	4	5	6	7	8	9	10	11	12	13	14
November	162	165	174	136	203	135	123	141	106	117	125	118	132.4
December	162	165	177	140	200	135	123	142	108	118	125	118	132.9
January	165	165	179	144	224	136	125	146	110	119	128	118	134.8
February	164	163	175	143	224	137	125	145	111	120	128	119	134.8
March	166	164	172	150	232	140	126	142	112	120	129	120	135.8
2010-11													
April	171	169	172	152	246	141	127	138	115	123	136	121	138.3
May	173	172	172	151	238	143	127	138	115	123	135	120	138.8
June	176	175	173	153	246	143	127	137	116	122	135	120	139.4
July	178	178	174	152	246	148	127	139	116	122	133	121	140.6
August	177	177	174	154	248	148	128	139	116	123	133	121	140.7
September	181	180	174	161	245	148	128	140	116	123	134	121	141.5
October	183	181	173	166	255	148	128	141	117	123	134	121	142.4
November P	183	180	172	168	247	149	128	142	117	123	134	121	142.3
December P	189	187	173	172	256	150	129	143	119	124	135	121	144.1

Source: Office of the Economic Adviser, Ministry of Commerce & Industry

P Provisional

Table A.2: Index Numbers of Wholesale Prices—Selected Commodities and Commodity Groups

(Base: 2004-05=100)

	Rice	Wheat	Pulses	Tea	Raw cotton	Raw jute	Ground-nut seed	Coal mining	Mineral oils	Sugar, khandsari & gur	Edible oils	Cotton yarn	Cotton cloth	Jute, hemp & mesta (Mills)	Fertili-zers textiles	Cement	Iron, steel & ferro alloys[a]
Weight-Base: (1993-94=100)	2.45	1.38	0.60	0.16	1.36	0.11	1.03	1.75	6.99	3.93	2.76	3.31	0.90	0.38	3.69	1.73	3.72
Weight-Base: (2004-05=100)	1.79	1.12	0.72	0.11	0.70	0.06	0.40	2.09	9.36	2.09	3.04	1.38	1.23	0.26	2.66	1.39	6.88
1	2	3	4	5	6	7	8	9	10	11	12	13	14	15	16	17	18
Last week of (Base: 1993-94=100)																	
1994-95	112	113	124	76	173	140	136	106	106	110	118	152	134	121	122	127	112
1995-96	120	119	147	93	131	261	130	107	106	114	111	141	141	164	130	140	119
1996-97	130	156	145	113	136	na	130	125	129	126	112	135	148	150	137	130	126
1997-98	135	137	152	162	166	117	138	144	146	134	120	143	150	152	137	121	133
1998-99	161	171	152	123	155	108	148	144	144	154	135	143	155	160	142	128	134
1999-00	166	180	169	104	145	156	139	156	204	158	111	140	155	170	155	127	136
2000-01	165	172	182	116	156	171	140	185	240	149	105	153	157	169	160	153	137
2001-02	162	177	176	91	123	187	145	181	243	145	119	139	161	184	166	146	137
2002-03	168	178	177	104	165	131	199	181	287	129	151	153	162	165	169	147	150
2003-04	165	188	172	101	185	141	180	198	287	148	161	183	168	175	169	149	201
2004-05	170	186	168	114	141	191	167	232	333	174	147	153	172	199	175	164	244
Last month of (Base: 2004-05=100)																	
2005-06	105	117	126	92	91	159	94	118	122	112	93	98	98	114	103	106	97
2006-07	115	129	147	97	99	118	132	118	123	97	107	98	97	120	105	130	111
2007-08	131	140	148	110	122	130	147	136	133	93	127	100	98	110	107	138	138
2008-09	151	151	159	156	124	142	141	151	124	126	114	102	105	125	108	148	126
2009-10	163	173	199	129	149	173	153	163	147	178	114	123	109	157	110	151	127

(Contd...)

1	2	3	4	5	6	7	8	9	10	11	12	13	14	15	16	17	18
Average of weeks (Base: 1993-94=100)																	
1994-95	111	109	122	82	154	120	123	105	106	119	111	136	120	110	116	112	106
1995-96	117	112	135	103	159	189	135	106	106	113	117	147	139	148	129	130	117
1996-97	129	137	151	105	133	189	135	118	123	119	115	137	146	153	129	134	124
1997-98	134	138	146	160	155	102	134	140	139	134	114	141	149	136	136	129	130
1998-99	146	152	160	150	167	108	151	144	143	154	139	142	156	151	138	131	133
1999-00	171	175	166	152	147	113	140	149	160	156	122	141	155	161	143	128	134
2000-01	68	177	180	128	157	150	140	161	226	153	103	150	156	163	158	137	137
2001-02	167	175	190	117	149	182	144	182	240	146	113	148	159	181	161	149	137
2002-03	166	176	181	118	142	154	169	181	255	135	138	145	162	169	168	145	143
2003-04	169	181	177	109	181	137	181	194	274	139	158	166	166	160	169	147	180
2004-05	168	184	174	131	166	160	182	223	315	163	156	167	173	181	171	153	232
Average of months (Base: 2004-05=100)																	
2005-06	105	105	113	89	90	135	97	118	117	109	94	95	99	112	102	102	100
2006-07	110	125	149	104	97	136	10	118	127	107	102	98	97	115	104	119	105
2007-08	122	134	145	104	112	122	140	122	126	91	116	101	99	111	106	138	119
2008-09	141	148	156	153	141	138	144	151	142	107	122	103	103	117	107	139	137
2009-10	158	166	191	174	139	160	148	156	136	162	114	111	107	146	108	149	124

(Contd...)

	Rice	Wheat	Pulses	Tea	Raw cotton seed	Raw jute	Ground-nut seed	Coal mining	Mineral oils	Sugar, khandsari & gur	Edible oils	Cotton yarn	Cotton cloth (Mills)	Jute, hemp & mesta textiles	Fertili-zers	Cement	Iron, steel & ferro alloys[a]
Weight-Base: (2004-05=100)	1.79	1.12	0.72	0.11	0.70	0.06	0.40	2.09	9.36	2.09	3.04	1.38	1.23	0.26	2.66	1.39	6.88
1	2	3	4	5	6	7	8	9	10	11	12	13	14	15	16	17	18
2009-10																	
April	151	156	163	181	130	146	146	151	125	131	114	102	105	134	108	148	122
May	151	158	166	222	133	154	146	151	126	135	116	104	105	137	108	148	123
June	152	158	168	214	133	155	145	151	128	138	115	108	106	139	108	149	122
July	151	158	180	205	135	153	140	151	135	140	114	106	106	143	108	150	122
August	153	157	187	167	135	152	141	151	136	153	114	106	106	143	107	150	122
September	158	159	189	171	133	152	145	151	138	162	113	105	107	145	107	149	124
October	160	163	194	169	132	178	142	157	137	164	112	108	107	146	108	150	124
November	163	174	208	168	139	168	152	163	138	177	114	110	107	149	109	149	123
December	165	181	212	166	149	163	156	163	139	179	116	114	108	152	109	147	123
January	165	182	219	152	148	164	154	163	140	193	116	121	108	152	109	148	127
February	164	179	204	144	146	167	156	163	141	193	115	120	109	153	109	151	126
March	163	173	199	129	149	173	153	163	147	178	114	123	109	157	110	151	127
2010-11																	
April	164	169	203	139	151	172	162	163	148	162	114	129	110	157	115	152	136
May	164	168	206	146	152	175	163	163	149	159	114	130	112	158	115	152	135
June	164	169	207	141	156	178	163	163	150	153	115	130	112	158	115	150	134
July	166	168	206	146	153	190	166	163	157	160	117	130	112	156	115	153	132
August	164	173	202	147	153	187	174	163	157	157	118	130	112	156	117	151	133
September	167	172	197	155	180	218	178	163	157	156	120	132	113	159	117	150	133
October	169	168	194	157	190	239	172	163	157	158	120	134	113	161	116	151	134
November[P]	166	171	191	157	190	228	161	163	158	159	120	135	113	160	117	152	134
December[P]	166	172	189	157	196	235	160	163	161	162	122	140	113	161	116	150	134

Source: Office of the Economic Adviser, Ministry of Commerce & Industry.

[P] Provisional

na: Not available

[a] Composite Index of Iron &Steel and Ferro Alloy for base 1993-94 and Iron & semis, steel long, steel flat, stainless steel & alloys and ferro alloys for base 2004-05

Table A.3: All India Consumer Price Index Numbers

	Industrial workers[a] (Base: 2001=100)		Urban non-manual employees (Base: 1984-85 =100)	Agricultural labourers (Base: 1986-87 =100)
	Food index	General index	General index	General index
1	2	3	4	5
Average of Months				
1989-90	177	173	145	746[b]
1990-91	199	193	161	803[b]
1991-92	230	219	183	958[b]
1992-93	254	240	202	1076[b]
1993-94	272	258	216	1114[b]
1994-95	304	284	237	1247[b]
1995-96	337	313	259	237
1996-97	369	342	283	256
1997-98	388	366	302	264
1998-99	445	414	337	293
1999-00	446	428	352	306
2000-01	453	444	371	305
2001-02	466	463	390	309
2002-03	477	482	405	319
2003-04	495	500	420	331
2004-05	506	520	436	340
2005-06	527	542	456	353
2006-07	126	125	486	380
2007-08	136	133	515	409
2008-09	153	145	561	450
2009-10	176	163	634	513
Last Month of				
1989-90	178	177	149	736[b]
1990-91	207	201	169	858[b]
1991-92	241	229	192	1046[b]
1992-93	253	243	205	1053[b]
1993-94	281	267	222	1175[b]
1994-95	311	293	244	1300[b]
1995-96	339	319	264	237
1996-97	373	351	291	262
1997-98	401	380	312	272
1998-99	431	414	340	296
1999-00	446	434	357	306
2000-01	446	445	377	300
2001-02	462	468	395	309
2002-03	479	487	410	324
2003-04	494	504	424	332
2004-05	502	525	441	340
2005-06	527	551	463	358
2006-07	129	127	498	392

(Contd...)

1	2	3	4	5
2007-08	141	137	528	423
2008-09	156	148	577[c]	463
2009-10	181	170	663[c]	536
2009-10				
April	159	150	583	468
May	162	151	589	475
June	165	153	595	484
July	172	160	624	499
August	174	162	631	508
September	176	163	635	515
October	181	165	643	522
November	187	168	655	532
December	188	169	657	538
January	186	172	671	542
February	183	170	666	538
March	181	170	663	536
2010-11				
April	182	170	667	538
May	184	172	672	540
June	188	174	679	547
July	192	178	696	554
August	191	178	696	557
September	193	179	701	562
October	195	181	705	566
November	197	182	710	570
December	203	185	na	581

Sources: 1. Labour Bureau, Shimla for consumer price indices for industrial workers and agricultural labourers.

2. C.S.O. for consumer price indices for urban non-manual employees.

na: Not available

a The current series of CPI for Industrial Workers with 2001 base was introduced w.e.f. January, 2006 Index. The earlier series on base 1982=100 was simultaneously discontinued. The conversion factor from the current to the old series is 4.63 in case of the General Index, and 4.58 for Food Index. CPI-IW series from 1989-90 to 2005-06 is on base 1982 = 100.

b Old base 1960-61 = 100 and the current series of CPI for agricultural labourers with 1986-87 (July 1986 to June 1987) base was introduced w.e.f. November, 1995. The earlier series on base 1960-61 (July 1960 to June 1961) was simultaneously discontinued. The conversion factor from the new to the old series is 5.89.

Note: Annual figures are yearly averages of months.

Table A.4: Index Numbers of Wholesale Prices—
Relative Prices of Manufactured and Agricultural Products

Year	General Index of Wholesale Price	Price Index of Manufactured Products	Price Index of Agricultural Products[a]	Manufactured Price Index as per cent of Agricultural Price Index
Weight (Base: 1993-94)	100.00	63.75	21.54	(Col 3/Col 4)x100
Weight (Base: 2004-05)	100.00	64.97	18.59	
1	2	3	4	5
(Base: 1993-94 = 100)				
1994-95	112.6	112.3	116.0	96.8
1995-96	121.6	121.9	126.0	96.8
1996-97	127.2	124.4	136.4	91.2
1997-98	132.8	128.0	140.3	91.2
1998-99	140.7	133.6	157.2	85.0
1999-00	145.3	137.2	159.1	86.2
2000-01	155.7	141.7	163.7	86.6
2001-02	161.3	144.3	169.5	85.1
2002-03	166.8	148.1	175.3	84.5
2003-04	175.9	156.5	182.9	85.6
2004-05	187.3	166.3	186.7	89.1
(Base: 2004-05 = 100)				
2005-06	104.4	102.3	103.4	99.0
2006-07	111.2	108.0	112.5	96.1
2007-08	116.5	113.3	121.5	93.3
2008-09	125.9	120.2	133.5	90.1
2009-10	130.4	122.4	151.0	81.2
2009-10				
April	124.6	119.7	137.4	87.1
May	125.5	120.2	139.4	86.2
June	126.4	120.4	142.0	84.8
July	127.8	120.5	146.2	82.4
August	129.3	121.4	148.9	81.5
September	129.9	122.0	149.7	81.5
October	130.5	122.2	151.9	80.4
November	132.4	122.8	158.2	77.6
December	132.9	123.4	159.0	77.6
January	134.8	125.2	160.0	78.2

(Contd...)

1	2	3	4	5
February	134.8	125.4	158.6	79.0
March	135.8	125.6	160.6	78.2
2010-11				
April	138.3	127.4	164.8	77.3
May	138.8	127.4	167.2	76.2
June	139.4	127.2	170.2	74.7
July	140.6	127.4	172.2	74.0
August	140.7	127.6	171.5	74.4
September	141.5	127.9	175.5	72.9
October	142.4	128.3	177.5	72.3
November[P]	142.3	128.4	177.3	72.4
December[P]	144.1	128.9	183.4	70.3

Source: Office of the Economic Adviser, Ministry of Commerce & Industry.

[a] Composite Index of the sub-groups—(Food Articles and Non-food Articles).

[P] Provisional

Note: Monthly figures are average of weeks.

6

Inflation and Other Issues

The discussion about inflation nowadays focuses mainly on the effects of the price increases rather than on the causes. The fact that the expansion of the uncovered money supply is to be blamed for the rising level of prices tends to be forgotten. The focus is now on the development of the basket of goods, which only highlights the symptoms of the price increase.

Inflation versus Gold

In Zimbabwe, Robert Mugabe's government has made comedic attempts to paper over the inflation with yet more paper, with an utter lack of restraint, resulting in an economy that has an inflation rate of over 100,000 per cent annually. This is the most extreme example of making currency at will or creating inflation at will.

Inflation can be created by governments by simply creating more money, whereas gold cannot be created at will. No wonder then that until the mid-20th century, gold was the basis of the world's monetary systems. Even in the 21st century, gold mining not only remains a dirty, expensive and difficult business, but it is also becoming ever harder to find new deposits below ground. Indeed, the world supply of gold has grown by barely 1.6 per cent per year since the mid-1990s. Annual output in South Africa, the world's biggest gold mining nation, has more than halved during 2000-10.

Gold is not merely a promise of payment (like currency), but simply a precious metal that people across the world have used to store wealth for more than 5,000 years. The quality that sets gold apart is its rarity. In the earth's crust, gold is six times rarer than platinum and 18 times rarer than silver. It is 75 per cent heavier than lead. Since one cubic metre of gold weighs 19.3 tonnes, all the gold ever mined, estimated at 150,000 tonnes, would fit into a cube less than 20 metres on each side. Although it is growing by 12 centimetres per year, it still would not even cover a tennis court.

While currency can be easily destroyed, it is very nearly impossible to destroy gold. Over the years, the growing demand for this rare metal and the rising inflation has led to a steady increase in the price of gold. The removal of the anchor previously provided by the gold standard, in managing monetary policies, is an important driver of the rising price inflation around the world.

The fiat monetary systems, in which monetary policies are managed based on flexible guidelines, are now in universal favour around the world. The inherent limitations and risks in this system make it difficult for the vast majority of the nations which find the task politically inexpedient and hence are losing control over their monetary policies. Hence, all nations tend to make the same errors, albeit at differing levels of failure. The result of too much money chasing too few goods is inflation.

Cancellation of Gold Standard

The situation that unleashed the tidal wave of money can be traced to the early 1970s, when the US took a policy decision to cancel the gold standard. Its impact was felt around the world because of the historic 1944 Bretton Woods agreement between representatives of over 40 countries.

As the World War II came to an end, the United States pushed forward a wide-ranging set of agreements. As a result, from that point forward, the US Dollar became the *de facto* global reserve currency, with all the nations of the world pegging their currencies to the dollar. Of course, new institutions, including the International Monetary Fund and the International Bank for Reconstruction and Development, came into being at Bretton Woods, but they only helped in ensuring that the other countries stayed in line, buying and selling dollars as needed to maintain a stable peg. For its part, the US guaranteed Dollar convertibility at a Gold Price of $35 "forever".

In the late 1960s, however, France under Charles de Gaulle decided that it would prefer to have the Gold, President Nixon cancelled convertibility, which took effect in August 1971. The world's central bankers, however, continued using the US Dollar as a key component of their reserves, not because they wanted to, but because they were left with no other immediately obvious or more viable alternative. And from that point forward the creation of US Dollars and, by extension, all of the world's currencies, was restrained by nothing more than political expediency.

Since then, in the absence of any "hard" limiting factor or defined discipline, the governmental spending across the world has not only continued apace, but significantly worsened in some countries due to compounding interest on government borrowing and many irrevocable social commitments. Under such circumstances, the only limitation to government spending is that which the politicians believe will be politically unacceptable to a population. This is, generally speaking, no real limitation at all, because the public is now apathetic about, and sometimes even numb to, the real world implications of large numbers.

Gold and Money

Undoubtedly, gold is the world's longest-serving form of money. And for times immemorial, investors have turned to gold as a hedge against unforeseen disasters. In fact, historically, gold and money have been pretty much synonymous.

Pure gold was immune from inflation, but still it did not stop currency inflation. Kings discovered very early that they could "extend" their money supply by adding just a bit of lead to the melting pot. Unfortunately, as the percentage of lead increased the value of the coins decreased. These were the first cases of inflation that also created the habit of biting coins to see how soft they were and thus how much lead they contained.

The earliest gold coins were said to be issued around 2700 BC by Egyptian Pharaohs, primarily as gifts for friends and not for commerce. For general circulation, gold coins were first issued by King Croesus (560-546 BC) of ancient Lydia.

Incidentally, every country that employed fair gold coinage prospered while the countries which inflated their coinage with "base" metals failed. For example, Spain was a world superpower when it was issuing its famous "pieces of eight", but lost that status as it debased its currency.

Gold and Inflation in the US

Although the US did not have its own gold coinage, unofficially, gold circulated as currency since the beginning. People used coins minted in other countries like the Spanish "pieces of eight". It was only in 1792 did the Coinage Act establish official US monetary units based on a world gold price of $19.39 per Troy ounce. The gold specification of money was changed by the Congress in 1834 and again in 1837 when it was set at $20.67 per ounce. It may be noted here that no gold coins were minted from 1805-37.

During the American Civil War (1861-65), the US issued paper currency called "greenbacks". During both the Revolutionary and Civil wars, periods of high inflation were witnessed. At the end of the Civil War in 1879, in its effort to control inflation, the US government made the "greenbacks" convertible into gold. This *de facto* put the US on gold standard. Subsequently in 1900, the government officially adopted the gold standard once again.

From 1913 through 1920, while inflation (as measured by the CPI) had increased by almost 98 per cent (in other words, in seven years prices had almost doubled), the price of gold remained flat (by government decree). During the next ten years, deflation set in as the US economy boomed and Europe suffered the after-effects of World War I. However, in 1929 the system could not stand the internal stresses and the stock market crashed ushering in the Great Depression. Even in 1933, gold was worth only $20.67 per ounce—a price at which foreign governments can afford to buy all the US gold.

At this juncture, President Franklin Roosevelt forced the US citizens to sell their gold at the official price of $20.67.

Once all the gold was collected into government coffers, the price of gold was adjusted to its real price of $35 per Troy ounce. Thus, the government made a handsome 69.33 per cent profit in a few months, equivalent to a 69 per cent tax on gold owners.

It may be noted here that in 1930, inflation since 1913 was up about 64 per cent and this one-time adjustment did not solve the inflation problem permanently. It only postponed it by bringing the gold price in line with inflation. In other words, it legitimized the inflation that had silently been occurring behind the scene as gold values remained fixed while prices increased. In effect, this increased the money supply and became the key factor in the emergence from the depression.

The price of gold officially remained at $35 an ounce until 1970. By this time, inflation was up 306 per cent and once again the price of gold needed adjusting. But this time the government was in a bind as there was no gold in the hands of private citizens. Foreign governments, on the other hand, could continue to present their foreign exchange tickets at the "gold window" and the US was obligated to pay up in gold. Hence, President Nixon ended the US gold standard in 1971 and allowed the price of gold bullion to float freely and find its own level.

The government was able to raise money by allowing the people to buy gold back at the new higher free market prices. The liquidation by the government of its excess gold bullion had a tempering effect on gold prices for a while. It was only when the government stopped its gold sales in the late 1970s, did the price of gold really take off. While the inflation rate declined from the peak in 1980, cumulative inflation climbed steadily upward. The price of gold—rather than keeping up with inflation—fell from the peak of $850 per ounce down to under $300 in 2001. If measured in terms of inflation adjusted dollars, the scene is even worse. The 1980 peak in current inflation adjusted dollars was over $2250 and it fell to under $370, losing a whopping 84 per cent of its value. Thus, even though inflation rose, gold fell.

Rise in Gold Prices

As seen above, inflation does not necessarily translate into higher gold prices. During the decades of 1980s and 90s, inflation was slow and steady, and was not big enough to cause fear. Fear of any sort usually does translate into higher gold prices. In 1980, for example, gold prices rose due to international crisis arising from the Soviet invasion of Afghanistan and the Islamic Revolution in Iran. In such situations of turmoil, people get scared that paper currency is not enough and start opting for gold. They put their faith in thousands of years old traditions of hoarding stores of wealth that is physical, portable, and easily divisable.

Thus, gold prices rise during times of crisis and fear and it is beyond individual governments to stop it. Of course, during more peaceful times, governments are able to maintain control and keep a lid on the price of gold. This causes gold to move up in a sort of "stair step" fashion. Crisis and fear prevail during times of war, longer term political instability, etc.

Gold prices did not rise during the 2008 global financial crisis. It was because everyone was trying to increase their liquidity at the same time. In the process, people were forced to sell their quality assets to cover the losses in their junk. This, unfortunately, dragged down the price of quality assets along with the junk.

Gold prices also rise when the demand for the metal picks up. Like all other commodities, whenever the worldwide demand for gold increases it adds pressure on the price of gold.

Gold Exchange Rate

From 1880-1914, the US dollar official gold price was \$20.67 per ounce and the UK official gold price was £4.24 per ounce. This resulted in an exchange rate of US \$4.87 per Pound Sterling. By 1914 most countries in the world were on a gold standard and the gold exchange rate was maintained by a complex system of transferring gold from New York to London. This system worked fairly well until other countries began abandoning their gold standard to finance the First World War.

Since the US entered the war late, it was able to maintain its gold standard. Despite this, inflation still occurred as other countries were able to export their inflation to the US The true value of the dollar floated because the currencies of the other countries floated against the dollar. It so occurred because at that time people spent gold and silver coins. Even though the price of gold was fixed, other prices were not fixed and so the amount of goods people could buy with their gold could still fluctuate.

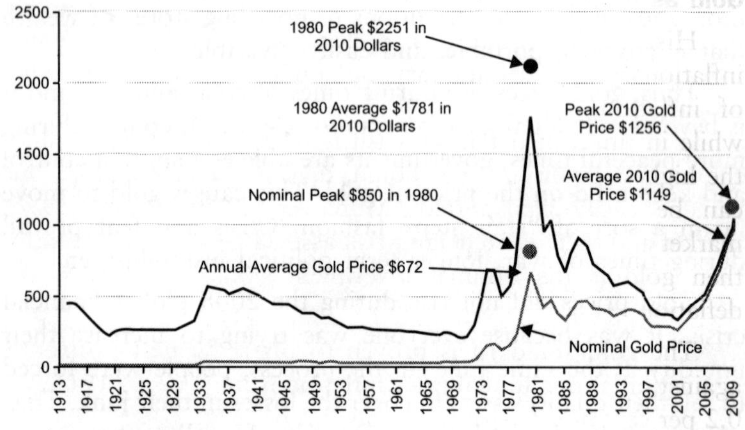

Fig. 6.1: Inflation Adjusted Annual Average Gold Prices

Source: http://inflationdata.com/inflation/images/charts/Gold/Gold_inflation_chart.htm

The graph shows that the inflation adjusted price of gold does not overlap the nominal price. It means that gold does not perfectly hedge inflation. However, gold is an excellent hedge in periods of deflation. In times of pronounced deflation, public budgets are strained, the financial sector is faced with systemic problems, currencies are depreciated in order to reflate the system, and the money supply is continuously rising. The creditworthiness of companies and countries is queried, the confidence in paper currencies falls, and gold is subjected to remonetisation. The table below shows how gold, silver and commodities have appreciated during three major times of deflation. Clearly, gold has performed better than silver and commodities.

Deflation	Gold	Silver	Commodities
1814-30	100%	89%	-50%
1864-97	40%	27%	-65%
1929-33	44%	-5%	-31%

Sources: Roy Jastram, "The Golden Constant" and "Silver, the Restless Metal", Erste Group Research

Gold as Investment

Historically, gold has performed excellently in both inflationary and deflationary economic scenarios. In periods of inflation, tangible assets are the preferred asset class, while in times of deflation, cash is preferred. Gold is cash of the highest quality as it is liquid, divisible, indestructible, and can be easily transported. Moreover, it has a worldwide market and there is no default risk associated with it. Naturally, then gold is the optimal investment both in inflation and deflation.

The gold standard is proven to offer the best protection against inflation: annual price inflation from 1879 to 1914 was 0.2 per cent at a volatility of only 2.2 per cent. Since 1971 (i.e. the end of Bretton Woods), volatility has been 2.8 per cent, with average price inflation at 4.6 per cent. An important feature of high inflation is the rapid loss of trust in one's own currency. From 1914 to 1918, the German money supply soared from 8.5 bn to 55 bn Reichsmark, which paved the way for hyperinflation of historic dimensions. The price of gold shot up to 87 trillion Mark for one ounce by November 1923 from 170 Mark in January 1919. Another example, is when the rate of inflation in the USA and Europe soared to new highs at the end of the 1970s, so did the gold price. During the period of high inflation from 1978 to 1982, the monthly correlation coefficient of gold and the inflation rate also soared.

In the words of George Bernard Shaw, "You have a choice between the natural stability of gold and the honesty and intelligence of the members of government. And with all due respect for those gentlemen, I advise you, as long as the capitalist system lasts, vote for gold".

Inflation-indexed Securities

Inflation-indexed securities are Treasury bonds that have a unique feature: the value of the principal, i.e. the par value of the bond, is adjusted daily, based on the Consumer Price Index. As a result, the value of the bond increases at the rate of inflation. In effect, the investor is guaranteed a real return over and above the inflation rate. Therefore, any money invested in these bonds should retain its purchasing power up until the time the bonds mature. Similarly, these securities provide a constant real or inflation-adjusted cost of finance for a borrower. Thus, these securities protect borrowers and investors alike from changes in the general level of prices in the real economy.

Since these are backed by the government, they have the highest credit quality. The interest rate on inflation-linked bonds is set at the time the bonds are sold at auction. That rate remains in force until the bond matures. But because the value of the principal is adjusted daily at the rate of inflation, interest income rises with inflation: the interest income is calculated based on a constantly higher base. When the numbers are estimated for a bond with a ten-year maturity, the numbers begin to look a lot more attractive.

In effect, the structure of inflation-linked bonds guarantees a rate equivalent to the real rate of return. Moreover, the structure of these bonds guarantees that the purchasing power of the principal will not erode due to inflation. In the US, the Treasury guarantees an additional layer of protection whereby, in the unlikely event of deflation, the final value of the bond will not be less than par, or the initial price paid for the bond. Although the structure of these bonds is designed to protect the value of principal, this does not eliminate market risk. An increase in interest rates may cause the price to decline. So can a lack of demand.

Markets for inflation-linked bonds around the world have developed somewhat independently. Inflation-indexed bonds were almost unknown in India until December 1997 when the Reserve Bank of India issued the 6 per cent Capital Indexed Bond, 2002. Unlike the inflation-indexed bonds issued in other countries, the Capital Indexed Bonds (CIB) issued by the RBI protected only the principal and not the interest against the inflation rate. The real cash flows on the capital indexed bonds are fixed. But the nominal cash flows (interest and principal) are increased as the Wholesale Price Index (WPI) increases. However, the RBI has not issued further CIB as the response to its first issue was muted, chiefly because interest payments were not protected against inflation.

While the interest payment that investors would receive would tend to vary from year to year, depending on the rate of inflation, investor will be protected because he would get a real rate of return on investment. Hence, inflation-indexed bonds are particularly beneficial to investors such as pension and retirement funds that want to invest funds for long periods.

I Bonds

I Bond or inflation-linked savings bond is a highly popular form of savings bond in the United States. These were launched as Series I Bonds in September 1998. This bond pays a fixed coupon plus an amount adjusted every six months according to the Consumer Price Index. These bonds are sold at face value and pay at par upon maturity, which is 30 years after purchase. Series I Bonds not held for at least five years are subject to a redemption penalty. Taxes on interest are deferred until redemption or maturity. Savings bonds are non-transferrable and must either be held or redeemed.

The I Bonds are marketed at face value. The face value for the electronic inflation linked savings bonds is US$ 25 and above and the face value of the paper inflation linked savings bonds ranges from US$ 50 to US$ 10,000. The I Bonds increase in value according to the inflation linked earnings for a maximum term of 30 years. The holders of I Bonds are entitled to receive interest once every month and the interest is accumulated or added together twice every year.

In spite of periods of deflation, the composite rate of interest is secured in such a way so that it cannot be less than zero or negative. This suggests that the redemption value of I Bonds cannot decrease. Thus, these bonds are tax-deferred investments and bear the protection against value loss.

Inflation-linked Derivatives

Derivatives in the inflation market offer many opportunities to market participants. Interest rate derivatives have been used extensively to convert between fixed and floating rates, to accommodate changes in profile and maturity, and in the construction of many other structured finance products. The addition of a third variable, the real interest rate, opens up possibilities to expand still further the range of available debt-financing solutions.

Inflation-linked (IL) derivatives are financial products used by entities such as sovereign states, local governments, financial institutions and corporations, to manage the risks associated with variable rates of inflation. IL derivatives help lower barriers of entry to the index-linked market and thereby expand the universe of market participants beyond those who invest in inflation-indexed bonds alone.

Over time IL derivatives have enhanced liquidity and made the underlying sovereign and corporate inflation-indexed bond markets more efficient. It is because derivatives in the inflation market offer many opportunities to market participants: to transfer risk, access increased liquidity, customize cash flows, optimize market timing, meet portfolio hedging requirements, effect market arbitrage, and create hybrid structures, e.g. inflation-indexed equity or credit-linked bonds, to name a few. Their existence therefore facilitates the execution of strategies that are cheaper and more efficient than those available using just the bond market and helps participants to meet needs that the bond market is unable to satisfy.

IL derivatives can be used to bridge mismatches in maturity, timing, index, profile, and size, especially when investor interests and issuer needs cannot be fully matched. For example, a financial intermediary can synthetically convert an issuer's 10-year bond into a 15-year maturity issue by swapping out the issuer's cash flows and thereby assuming the maturity mismatch risk, thus delivering to the investor the desired maturity. Hence, there is a growing demand from both market participants and end-users for increasingly complex option structures to beat the future path of inflation.

Inflation and Foreign Investment

In recent years interest in understanding the determinants of foreign direct investment (FDI) has intensified. From 1990 to 2005, the total worldwide FDI inflows increased from $203 billion to $974 billion. The volume of FDI inflows has been increasing with almost all developing countries competing to attract a major share of these inflows. In fact, the share of net FDI inflows in the gross domestic product (GDP) of middle income countries has risen from 0.74 per cent in the 1970s to 1.08 per cent between 1985 and 1994, and to 2.85 per cent between 1995 and 2005.[1]

The intensified competition to attract more FDI has even led to changes in the regulatory frameworks provided by almost all countries. During 1991-2002, around 95 per cent of the changes in worldwide laws governing FDI have been favourable to activity of multinational corporations (World Investment Report, UNCTAD 2003). Along with the improvements in local regulatory environments, investment promotion agencies have been established along with provision of fiscal incentives.

Among the factors that influence the FDI flows, the role of inflation needs to be understood. During the 1970s, inflation rates have increased from around 5 to 10 per cent on average in developing countries. The average increase among developing countries between 1985 and 1994 was 49 per cent on average. In the late 1990s, this trend of increasing inflation rates was reversed and the inflation rates in developing countries on average declined to 9.2 per cent during 1995-2004.[2] During this period, the net FDI inflows as a share of GDP more than doubled in the middle income countries.

The above data raises a question whether the increasing inflation rates in the 1970s and 1980s might have been a deterrent for FDI inflows and whether their reversal in the 1990s might have contributed to the increase in FDI inflows to these economies. The coincidences of high inflation and low FDI versus the low inflation and high FDI inflows in these developing countries points towards possible links between the two variables.

Inflation is one of the factors that is taken into consideration by multinational corporations while making an investment decision. These corporations anticipate changes in inflation rates of the domestic or foreign country and they can alter the net returns and affect optimal investment decisions. The existence of FDI opportunities is tantamount to increased hedging possibilities against inflation taxes. So, multinational corporations minimize the negative effects of policy changes, in this case expected changes occur in the inflation rate, through a shift in the location of production across home and host countries. Thus, the ability of a multinational company to invest in two alternative economies reduces the real effects of nominal shocks.

The fact is that no FDI decision is taken independently on the basis of one particular factor like inflation, and other factors including exchange rates, political stability, etc. are also considered. The effect of uncertainty is generally larger than all other effects on FDI. However, given other factors as almost equal among a group of countries, inflation certainly plays a major role in FDI decision.

Multinational corporations benefit from having the opportunity to invest abroad and the ability to finance their foreign investment activity through different financial markets. In other words, the option of diversifying the investment decision across countries and across financing means reduces the negative effect of inflation on physical investment fluctuations. The extent of reduction in the FDI financed through alternative financial markets depends on the motivation for FDI. In the case of vertical FDI, results show that both the quantitative and qualitative effects of a higher domestic inflation tax on the domestically financed portion of FDI depends on the substitutability of the factors of production. The lower the degree of substitutability between the factors of production, the higher the possibility that domestically financed FDI also decreases in response to domestic inflation.

It is a known fact that countries with lower inflation attract higher foreign direct investment. According to Schneider and Frey (1985), there seems to be a negative relationship between inflation and Foreign Direct Investment (FDI) as higher inflation pushes up prices and discourages investment by increasing interest rates and 'crowding out' productive investment. Multinational companies planning to raise money in the host country can be adversely affected by higher inflation as it increases the interest rates. Therefore, the cost of doing business, i.e. the cost of capital becomes higher.

Rodrrik (1996) states that higher inflation shakes investor confidence in an economy and curtails investment. Estrin et al. (1997) are of the view that higher inflation reduces interest of multinational corporations in the host country as it puts pressure on the currency and leads to currency depreciation. Another view holds that a large and uncontainable increase in the price level, or high inflation, might reflect instability of the macroeconomic policy of the host country, which in turn creates uncertainty in the investment environment. High inflation also discourages FDI for re-exportation since the relative costs of production in the host country rise. In contrast, falling price levels and the resulting contraction in economic activities might trigger a deflationary spiral and eventually bankrupt the host country's firms. This can induce local investors to sell off their interests in the host country's companies to foreign investors at low prices, thereby expanding the inflow of FDI.

According to the International Monetary Fund (IMF), higher inflation rates deter foreign investors. But the effect is somewhat stronger at moderate levels of inflation, that is, investors react more averse to an increase in inflation from, say, 5 to 15 per cent than to an increase from 90 to 100 per cent per year. A likely explanation is that investors believe they learn less about the stability of a possible FDI destination if the increase occurs at already very high levels of inflation.

Foreign Institutional Investment

Indian economy has been attracting billions of dollars from abroad for the last few years. But inflation due to a sharp jump in food prices threatens to put a brake on the stellar growth of India's stock market and force investors to rethink exposure to Asia's third-largest economy. In an effort to curb food price inflation, the Reserve Bank of India often raises interest rates. This could undermine growth prospects and the likely returns for foreign investors.

In the beginning of 2011, foreign institutional investors, the main drivers of Indian equities, have sold more shares than they have bought, leading to a net capital outflow of $711.5 m, according to data released by India's market regulator on January 24, 2011.

Even the annual *Economic Survey 2010-11*, released on 25 February 2011, expressed concern about inflation, a drop in foreign investment, and a potential skills and innovation shortage in the future. The survey warned that the country may face a slowdown in foreign investment unless it streamlines the management of its land and natural resources for industrial and commercial use.

Inflation versus Morality

A striking decline in both public and private morality has occurred during every period of high inflation. For example, there was a significant increase in speculation and gambling during the French inflation of 1790-96. There was widespread stock jobbing and more and more people saw the advantages of borrowing and later paying off in depreciated money. While the income and savings of the lower and middle classes evaporated, there was sudden enrichment of speculators, leading to social unrest and resentment. This led to cynicism and corruption, which in turn, led to widespread distrust and a loss of faith in patriotism and virtue.[3] A similar pattern was observed during the great German hyperinflation of 1919-23.

Inflation, by its very origin and nature, involves a redistribution of real incomes. The new money that is printed by the government goes first of all to special interest groups such as government officials, government contractors (and their employees), pensioners, and various recipients of relief and other appropriations. These groups start to spend the new money when it still retains its former purchasing power. But as they spend it they inevitably raise prices. Hence, the last to receive the new money, as one group makes purchases from the other, pays the highest prices. Thus, those who benefit by inflation, do so only at the expense of others. This again creates a sense of animosity between those who have benefited in the initial stages and others at whose expense they have benefited.

A decline in moral values can also be gauged by the increasing frequency of scandals and incidents of corruption in government circles. The chain of causation, from inflation to corruption to crime, is direct. In a free enterprise system, there is dominantly a close link between effort and productivity, on the one hand, and economic reward on the other. Inflation severs this link and reward comes to depend less and less on effort and production, and more and more on successful gambling and luck.

It is not merely that inflation breeds dishonesty in a nation. Notwithstanding all the pious pretences of the government, inflation, according to Henry Hazlitt, is practically always the result of deliberate governmental policy. Inflation itself is a dishonest act on the part of the government which sets examples for private citizens that are not exemplary. It is an immoral act on the part of modern governments to inflate by increasing the paper-money supply, directly or indirectly. In principle, this is tantamount to what kings once did when they clipped coins. In common parlance, diluting the money supply with paper is the moral equivalent of diluting the milk supply with water.

When the government itself adopts a policy that is morally wrong, it would be futile to expect people to remain morally righteous. It is well said in Hindu scriptures, 'yatha raja, tatha praja', i.e. 'As the ruler so the ruled'. In today's world, it can be translated to 'As the government, so the people'.

Inflation is the result of the political demands of special interest groups, the career desires of politicians, and ill-conceived motives of economists. It is nothing but taxation by deceit in which not only wealth is transferred from one group of citizens to another, but authority is also transferred from citizens to government. Monetary and economic decisions are increasingly taken from individuals and transferred to politicians, central bankers, and bureaucrats. In the process of enforcing this transfer of decision-making power, government officials accumulate power through legislation and regulation. Thus, coercion becomes commonplace and freedom is gradually destroyed.

Inflation is destructive and dishonest, because the government, which is the largest debtor, controls the money supply. Without honest money, a moral society cannot exist. An immoral society and dishonest money go hand in hand. Hence, if for no other reason, inflation should be rejected on the basis of morality. There is an urgent need for an alternative that rejects inflation and dishonest money. And until, a better alternative is found out, a regulation of inflation is very essential.

Effects of Unregulated Inflation

Unregulated inflation is morally disastrous. It heaps the burdens of the nation on those who are least able to bear them. It encourages extravagance and wild speculation, while it discourages thrift and labour. When senseless and extravagant luxury sets in, it spreads as a fashion. To imitate it, people resort to cheating; corruption spreads among officials and other persons at the position of authority. In course of time, a stage may come when national honour and patriotism might merely become words of fiction.

Inflation has the potential to turn laws into engines of oppression and wrong, corrupt justice, and eventually destroys the morality of the people. Businesses might become no more than a gamble in currency and exchanges. Salaried workers might be forced to speculate, barter, or steal in order to make both ends meet. Hence, inflation needs to be regulated.

Inflation and Corruption

Corruption levels vary greatly across countries. High variability of inflation can make over-invoicing by procurement officers and under-invoicing by sales persons easier because it makes auditing more expensive to the principal. High and variable inflation is also assumed to increase uncertainty about prices and therefore to increase the cost of auditing the agent's behaviour. This can lead to higher corruption and lower investment in equilibrium.

Since corruption increases the size of the unofficial economy, Al-Marhubi (2000) argues that the optimal level of inflation should increase with corruption, because the larger the size of the unofficial economy, the easier it is to raise government revenue by increasing the money stock rather than by distortionary taxation. Goel and Nelson (2005) argue that inflation lowers public salaries and increases the need for supplementary income.

In the developing countries, the cause for high rates of inflation resides in the nexus between the central bank and private sector. High rates of inflation may also be a result of political incentive to influence voters. In addition, there are rent-seekers that have private sector businesses but do business with the government. Examples are selling of goods and services to the government offices and departments, contracting and implementing development projects, producing goods and services by using subsidized loans and foreign exchanges.

When these rent-seekers lobby, especially for selling goods and services to the government and implementing public sector projects, they try to persuade the concerned officials for buying more goods and services, or approving and implementing more projects. At the same time, there are corrupt officials who benefit from this lobbying, especially those officers who are practically engaged in doing business with private sector enterprises.

When there are many independent rent-seeking and corruption bodies, there could be a destructive competition among rent-seekers to obtain more rent. When there is widespread rent-seeking and corruption, there is no coalition solution and every body of rent-seekers tries to sell more goods and services to the government as a way to collect the underlying rent. And there is only one way to guarantee the rent, i.e. to persuade the officials for more government activities and more government expenditures. These generate negative externalities and result in the government expenditures that are much higher than the optimal level.

When government expenditures are too high, it becomes difficult to finance them through tax revenues. So, budget deficit becomes the natural outcome of these higher government expenditures. Since the tax capacity is low in many developing countries, the routine way to finance government expenditures is inflation tax and seigniorage. Thus, the extent of seigniorage and inflation tax and therefore inflation rate is an increasing function of the extent of corruption and rent-seeking. Thus, rent-seeking as a profitable business drives government expenditures, more budget deficit, and higher growth rates of money supply and eventually higher inflation rates.

Rent-seeking and corruption in many developing countries, especially in the form of unnecessary increased government expenditures that is imposed on the budget, is not always the outcome of politically motivated manipulation in the allocation of resources. It is also not always a diversion to benefit a political group or party, because many rent-seekers do not belong to any political party or a group. Irrespective of the ideological background of the political party in power, they simply lobby for rents in government expenditures and their attempts cause the government expenditures to increase. Of course, when a new party or cabinet comes to power, there will be new opportunity for some people to engage in rent-seeking and corruption. However, it is important to understand the fact that rent-seekers are able to continue their connections with corrupt officials under different cabinets and different parties being in power.

As long as opportunity exists to make money through rent-seeking, there will be incentive for good talented people to allocate some of their time and other resources to create and hold connections with corrupt officials and legislators and persuade them for higher government expenditures to ensure the continuation of their rents. This is the prime reason why efforts to end corruption do not succeed. It is also the reason why corruption cannot be ended or even weakened even when there are big changes in cabinets and officials. The persistence of corruption, therefore, remains a characteristic of many developing countries.

Corruption causes inflation to increase directly by increasing government expenditures which necessitates the financing of budget deficit by printing money. In addition, there is also an indirect channel through which corruption increases inflation rate. The growth rate of GDP is lower when corruption and rent-seeking is higher and the inflationary effect of the growth in the money supply is higher when the growth rate of GDP is lower. This means, the higher the inflation rate, higher the corruption. Corruption, therefore, is not a cultural or political phenomenon, although cultural, political, institutional and even religious environment can influence its extent.

The above discussion clearly indicates that corruption is an important determinant of inflation and it is significant even after taking into account the effect of the growth in money supply. Although the main determinant of inflation in the long run is the growth of money supply in excess to potential output growth, corruption is an important factor for the explanation of inflation.

Corruption is also important in explaining the growth rate of money supply. There is more or less a negative relation between these two variables, implying that there are lower growth rates of money supply for countries that have higher index of corruption, i.e. countries that have less corruption. In short, countries with higher corruption have on average higher rates of money supply growth and higher inflation rates.

Beating Inflation

Inflation does not come out of nowhere. It is the result of something that is always within the control of the government, through monitoring the supply of money and bank credit. Governments initiate or continue inflation in the belief that it will benefit debtors at the expense of creditors, or exporters at the expense of importers, or workers at the expense of employers, or farmers at the expense of city dwellers, or the old at the expense of young, or this generation at the expense of the next. However, there is no magic in paper money, and everybody cannot get rich at the expense of everybody else.

Still, inflation exists and will continue to exist because politicians think that they can continue to hold office only as long as they spend more than they tax, as long as they redistribute income, and as long as they give subsidies on the pretext of alleviating the conditions of certain sections of the society. This has resulted in a situation where millions of people have got used to their food subsidies and other benefits to the extent that they have come to accept all these subsidies as rights. In the developed countries, high and prolonged unemployed insurance as well as the escalating social security benefits also fall under this category. The existing governments fear that any attempt to remove or reduce these benefits will set off riots.

Under such circumstances, it is futile to wait for inflation to end. It might fluctuate or temporarily deflate but may never end. Hence, it becomes the duty of every individual towards himself and his family to try to minimize the harm that inflation threatens to inflict on his own fortunes. An alert individual can do certain things to protect himself from the eroding effects of inflation, but only on the assumption that he acts both sooner and more wisely than the majority. An inexpert speculator may turn to investment trusts or mutual funds which diversify his investment for him and protect him to some extent against his own lack of expert knowledge. But always, the individuals who buy first, or at lower prices, can profit or protect themselves only at the expense of those who buy later or at the top. Few known and tested invested options are discussed below in the light of eroding value of money under inflation.

Savings

One of the worst results of inflation is that it steadily wipes out the value of savings-bank deposits, including that of bonds, mortgages, insurance benefits, pensions, and fixed-income payments of every kind. It thereby penalizes and discourages the more conservative investments. Hence, leaving money in the savings bank or mortgages or fixed-interest securities in the midst of inflation faces a certain loss in its real purchasing power. So, during times of higher inflation, especially double-digit inflation, it is advisable to take out or at least reduce the savings-bank deposits to a minimum.

Often, many schemes for issuance of government bonds and other securities are proposed, in which interest payments or redemption values would increase in the same proportion as the cost of living. Investing in such schemes, as and when they are floated help in countering the bad effects of inflation.

Stocks

In any inflation, individual prices and costs never go up at a uniform rate but at widely different relative rates and times. This makes it increasingly difficult for individual firms to guess or know what their own future costs or future selling prices are going to be. Also, demand quickly shifts from one product to another. This makes it increasingly difficult for companies to plan production ahead, or to estimate future profit margins. This increasing uncertainty tends to lower stock prices. Moreover, owing to the increasingly uncertain future of the business, corporations become more reluctant to pay out dividends. This acts as a demoralizing effect on the stockholders.

Even if the prices of equity stocks rise during inflation, the average wholesale prices would increase much more. Hence, investing in stocks is not a viable option during periods of inflation as the returns would be lower than the increasing costs of day-to-day goods. However, in exceptional cases, a single or a selected stock may outperform for some time owing to some strange circumstances and reasons. Since mutual funds too invest in stocks, they are also not expected to give returns that beat high inflation.

Gold

From a strictly economic point of view, buying gold in a major inflation and holding it until the inflation ends probably presents the least risk of capital loss of any investment or speculation. It can be cited that during the great German inflation, those Germans who consistently bought gold whenever and to the extent they could, and held it until the inflation ended, came out with at least their principal intact.

However, purchasing and holding gold is not without any serious drawbacks. Firstly, since hoarded gold yields no interest, a certain amount of gold needs to be sold from the stock at regular intervals, especially in the absence of any alternative arrangement for meeting day-to-day living expenses. Secondly, purchasing and holding gold can beat inflation only if the holder sits with the gold until the inflation is over. But technically, it is difficult to know when the inflation is over. Finally, the possibility of a discriminatory capital gains tax on gold profits, or even of outright confiscation, though remote, cannot be wholly dismissed.

Real Estate

Real estate provides a variety of choices to an individual—the purchase of a home, or perhaps of a bigger and more expensive home; the purchase of raw land; the purchase of residential property—apartments or detached houses—for the purpose of renting; and the purchase of commercial property for one's own business or for rental. Each of these choices has its own risks and its own comparative advantages and disadvantages.

In the case of purchasing one's own home or a much better home during an inflationary period, there is no immediate monetary return. However, besides an added enjoyment, there is also an added satisfaction of knowing, if the house is bought wisely, that the monetary value of property will keep on increasing. Actually, it rises as long as the inflation lasts. Once the inflation is over, the rate of increase in prices will definitely fall, but one can still expect a rise in monetary value of investment, due to other factors like population growth. So, this kind of investment is an option even during the later phase of inflation. However, there may be some problems due to rising cost of maintenance, repairs, and taxes.

Making a speculative purchase of raw land eliminates the need to worry about upkeep or repairs. Another advantage is that the selling price of the raw land tends to capitalize not only past and existing inflation, but the average expectations about future inflation. On the other hand, the owner usually gets no enjoyment or other useful value out of raw land, and it yields him no monetary return. Instead, he is out of pocket year by year for taxes, which tend to increase with inflation. Moreover, land is illiquid, that is, it cannot be sold easily and quickly. There is also a danger that it may lead to a situation where an individual may own large pieces of land, but does not have enough cash to meet current living expenses.

The purchase of residential property for rental will normally yield a net income over taxes and maintenance charges, but during the times of very high inflation, the owner may be faced with the danger of a sudden imposition of rent control.

This danger of rent control can be avoided by the purchase of commercial property. But it also involves greater risks in finding and keeping a tenant. If the owner puts up an office building or a factory on speculation, he may find that he has built the wrong size or kind of office building or factory.

Trading in Commodities

Some economists advice people to speculate in precious metals such as silver, platinum and other commodities that are traded on exchanges. These include copper, cotton, lumber, coffee, cocoa, sugar, wheat, soyabean, corn, oats, etc. While trading in these commodities, it is not only necessary for the trader to know a great deal about the special supply and demand situation of the particular commodity, but he also has to take into account all the costs of trading in and out—the costs and risks of buying on margin, paying interest on borrowed money, paying commissions, and losing because of the constant gap between bid and asked prices. Even if the general trend of the market for a commodity is upward, violent price fluctuations both ways are always possible, and the trader may find himself being "whipsawed". Moreover, the speculator must also take into account the capital gains tax. So, trading in commodities seems to be a risky proposition for common people.

Diamonds

Diamonds, like gold, have a negligible storage charge. But the investor in these may need expert advice and appraisal, which involve a cost. In case the investor is not in the business, then he must either buy at the retail price and sell at the wholesale, or pay high commissions. In addition, each diamond being unique in some degree, will not be as liquid or as readily saleable as gold, stocks, or commodities on the exchanges.

Paintings and Other Art Objects

It is often said that fortunes can be lost as well as made in paintings. The trick for the person who wants to speculate in them is either to have impeccable taste or a shrewd market sense of the next swing of an art fashion or vogue and of how long it will last. Failing this, he may need expert advice, which may not only be hard to find, but may also go wrong. Again, whosoever is not himself in the business must pay a substantial dealer's commission when he wants to buy and face the problem of finding a buyer to unload on when he wants to sell.

Investments Abroad

Investments abroad include the acquisition of foreign currencies and investment in foreign securities, businesses or property. This form of hedge against inflation is usually resorted to only by a comparatively small and sophisticated group of bankers and businessmen. One reason for this is that it is not easy to keep track of one's foreign investments, particularly when no foreign country is today exempt from a possible spurt of international inflation. Secondly, such investments lead to 'flight of capital' and at certain times the government may impose some restrictions or tax to stop such flight. On the other hand, if the country in which the investment is made happens to be a small country like Switzerland, it may become difficult to handle excessive refuge deposits and may try to discourage or penalise such investments. Of course, it would be embarrassing for any country to find itself being considered as an 'inflation-refuge' country.

No Way Out

It is clear from the above discussion that each possible inflation hedge has its own particular attractions, risks, and shortcomings. There is no one single type of hedge or purchase to be at all times preferred to any of the others. Hence, during times of inflation, where the money is invested acquires less importance compared to the time when the investment is made, the price at which the purchase is made, the capacity of the speculator to hold with the investment, and eventually, the price at which disposal is made.

In a major inflation, no one thing goes up steadily and dependably faster than anything else. At any one time, for a week or a month, say, one commodity will be going faster than any other. It is in the nature of speculative markets that the particular front-runner will be constantly changing. But it is also a fact that no person is smart or lucky enough to know just when to buy and when to sell each particular thing, and thus, reap benefits by constantly changing his investment. In short, it is impossible for everybody to protect themselves against inflation. The early buyers can profit only at the expense of the later buyers. The scramble to get out of money and into things only intensifies the inflation and accelerates the rise of prices and the fall of the value of the currency. This process could be stopped only if the monetary authorities refused to supply the added money and credit necessary to sustain successive increases.

In view of the above discussion, it can be concluded that there is only one solution or only one hedge against inflation, that is, not to have inflation at all, or halt it as soon as possible whenever it occurs.

Living with Inflation

Inflation is not a problem for which some costless panacea is likely to be found just around the corner. In fact, inflation is a period in which demagogy and an anti-business mentality are likely to be most rampant. In addition, the combination of inflation, subsidies, and taxes undermines and destroys the incentives of the middle classes to work and save. Taking advantage of the situation, tipsters, advertising their services, often lead the unsuspecting citizens to believe that inflation offers them exceptional opportunities to make a fortune. And for an overwhelming majority of people, this is exactly the opposite of what it does.

In spite of all these, people have been living with inflation for long, and many people profess to have been deeply disturbed by its adverse distributional effects. Various governments' pursuit of policies to reduce the inflation rate without increasing unemployment distracts attention from the problems of making labour markets more efficient and of making it easier for the general public to live with inflation. In other words, it seems that people have become so used to inflation that they do not see that it is a major peril. But the fact is, when inflation starts to spike, people find it difficult to maintain their present standard of living. However, the extent to which a family's standard of living will sink depends on the steps they take to protect their purchasing power.

Most consumers come to know that inflation is up when they buy their food for a week, and do not need the government to tell them. For many people living today, inflation has been a part of their lives throughout their lifetime. And people have been able to live, raise families, go on vacations and even save some money in spite of inflation. People have been able to do such things as the rate of inflation has been not very rapid. Generally, most people get exceedingly alarmed when prices double in a week or mere days. On the other hand, if the price of a certain item increases by only two per cent a week, people may hardly notice at all. People would not stop buying that item, even though they may complain. At two per cent rate of inflation, the price of that item will get doubled in several weeks.

If the government admits to an inflation rate of about five per cent per year, an average citizen would find about five per cent of his purchasing power dissolve. This affects him because his wages will not rise at the same rate as the inflation rate. When expenses increase by 100 per cent and wages do not change, one has to either increase one's income or cut one's expenses, or a combination of both. Income can be increased by getting a second or third job. To cut expenses may also mean choosing between paying one creditor or another. Some would have to stop all restaurant meals, turn off their air conditioners, or even sell off their property. But for how long? And what will a person do when all his old stuff is sold and he has used up all his assets, and he cannot earn any more. That is the reason why inflation is so evil.

In order to curtail inflation, interest rates are often raised. Up to a point, higher interest rates do not militate against investment and growth, but once that undefined limit is reached, profits are affected. While it can be argued that as long as there is sufficient demand, no factory will cut back on production, as it is its business to produce. In doing so, they ignore the fact that profits come under pressure, especially for infrastructure projects. In such situations, normally, the first axe falls on the wage earners. They can keep in mind some points in order to learn and adjust to live with inflation.

Count Inflation in the Budget

As long as wage increases outpace price increases, it is not hard to absorb increases in consumer prices. This generally happens when inflation is in the one to three per cent range. Things go awry when inflation crosses the four per cent mark. In such situations it is advisable to factor baseline inflation for household budgets as a starting point for the next year. For example, if the household expense on average is ₹ 15,000 per month this year and inflation is five per cent, ₹ 15,750 per month should be budgeted for average expenses next year.

Those who do not include inflation, this way, while calculating their budget could feel the pinch. They need to get into the habit of doing so at the earliest.

Inflate Savings

According to the 'time value of money' principle, whatever the intended purchase, it will likely cost more in the future. Those who are saving for big expenditures, including retirement, need to save even more than they were planning. That is the reason why retirement and financial planners routinely use inflation factors when figuring clients' future cash needs. Even half a percentage point change in the inflation rate may make a good plan look faulty and unsuccessful. Hence, the moment inflation rate seems to be going up; it is time to update those plans.

Cautious Investment

In the face of higher inflation, investors should be more cautious in their asset allocation, or even letting a portfolio drift past the lower end of the equity range. Investors should also consider alternative investments like retirement plans that include inflation-oriented investments or funds that invest in inflation-protected securities. Most importantly, investors should not shy away from buying in the face of inflation. Generally, purchases will cost less than they will in future, in the likely increase of inflation.

Inflation and Common Man

It is often said that a little bit of inflation is good for any economy so that business transaction takes place, otherwise there would not be any growth in the economy. But from a common man's perspective, inflation means paying more for goods than what was being paid earlier. The hike in prices is not limited to essential goods, and even non-essential items like cigarettes, etc. also cost more. Rents shot up, and savings are affected. In other words, inflation makes a hole in common man's pocket. It brings no gain to common man except for a few hoarders and investors. Thus, inflation enriches fewer while impoverishing more.

Sometimes, price of certain items may increase due to scarcity. But it is not always the case. For whatever reason, when there is a simultaneous and overall increase in the cost of products, services, taxes and fees, employees are forced to search better paying jobs or live on less or ask the employer for a raise. The common man may be forced to borrow money from banks and other financial institutions. In course of time, people might have to stand with indefinite debts, or drastically cut down on their lifestyle, or beg for hike in the face of inflation. Thus, the survival of common man becomes tougher and tougher. In short, it hurts the common man at the very place where it should not—it hurts his ego and makes it difficult for a common man to lead his life in dignity.

It is well said that crisis always leads to frustration and invention as well. During inflation, such is the instinct for survival that people bring drastic changes in their lifestyle to survive. Inflation knocks the affordability out of the common man's life. Raising a family becomes the biggest challenge of life for a common man, be it living in ordinary cities or the metropolises. In the face of inadequate governmental educational facilities and expensive private educational institutes, the poor find it difficult to educate their children. Next, shelter, which is one of the foremost necessities of human beings, becomes extremely hard to purchase as the property rates rise everywhere. The major cities become a very pricy place and become unsuitable for the low income groups to live in.

Inflation and Interest Rates

Inflation is one of the factors that affect interest rates. It is because investors try to preserve the value of their money by investing in activities that have yields that are either equivalent or higher than the inflation rate. For example, if the local inflation rate is pegged at 7.5 per cent, the money that is saved and invested should be able to, at the very least, match that rate. If the money is put in a savings bank, its value would have been eroded by that rate at the end of the year. So ₹ 100 saved at the start of the year, would be worth only ₹ 92.50 at the end of the year.

People in developed economies, however, find it easy to cope with inflation because bank savings interest rates normally equal that of the inflation rate. And if competition is fierce between banking institutions then people get higher interest rates. In effect, it is possible for people to get more yields for their money.

Normally, the central bank of the country decides on the interest rate by declaring the benchmark—a level below which it will be a losing proposition for investment. The benchmark interest rate is either increased or decreased in consonance with upward or downward movement of inflation.

Interest rates also affect inflation. When interest rates are low, they put more borrowing power in the hands of consumers. And when consumers spend more, the economy grows, naturally creating inflation. But at the same time there must be enough economic growth to keep wages up and unemployment low. On the other hand, too much growth leads to dangerously high inflation. It is here that the role of the central bank in balancing the inflation and interest rates come in.

If the central bank feels that the economy is growing too fast—that demand will greatly outpace supply—then it can raise interest rates, slowing the amount of cash entering the economy. Generally, the target inflation rate is kept somewhere between two and three per cent per year.

Inflation and Real Interest Rate

A nominal interest rate is the quoted bond yield or interest rate. The real interest, on the other hand, is calculated as difference between the nominal rate of interest and the inflation rate. If future interest rates—both nominal and real—are known with certainty, then the difference between nominal and real interest rates is exactly equal to the inflation rate over the same period. In practice, however, future interest rates are not known with certainty and many debt markets are not complete and efficient. So, it is difficult to use nominal and real interest rates to derive estimates of market participants' inflation expectations.

The prices of real and nominal bonds not only depend on expectations of real and nominal interest rates but also on other factors such as tax regimes, market liquidity, the choice of index, the indexation methods for real bonds, etc. The problem is that a person who purchases a one year bond does not know what the inflation rate will turn out to be during the period after his purchase. It is only after a certain period that it can be said with certainty what the real interest rate turned out to be depending on how much the CPI or WPI grew.

Usually, the buyer of a bond starts out with some expectation of what inflation will be during the period until the bond matures. This means both the owners and issuers of bond become a player in the inflation game. If inflation is worse than expected, bond issuers win and bond owners lose, but if inflation is lower than expected, it is the bond issuers who lose and the bond owners who win.

It is a fact that inflation will almost never turn out exactly as anyone's expectation. While the nominal interest rate can be found directly, it is difficult to find the expected inflation rate. While the real interest rate can only be expected on a nominal bond, the real interest rate on an inflation-indexed bond is known for certain at the time of purchase.

If the inflation is expected to be on a higher side than what is implied by the inflation-indexed bond yield, one can act on that opinion by purchasing the real rather than the nominal bond. This calculation becomes particularly important for managers of pension portfolios since they are large purchasers of bonds and the risk of inflation is a very important consideration. The real rate of interest is determined on the basis of what lenders earn and what borrowers pay in real, purchasing power terms. Hence, the real interest rates matter more than nominal interest rates for all—economic agents, employees and employers.

Inflation and Prosperity

The question of inflation is closely associated with prosperity, good times or booms. Some even declare that 'inflation is prosperity'. It is true to some extent as it gives a temporary good feeling. The good feeling, however, can be compared to that of a drunkard after his draught. As the frequency of draughts of paper money increases the successive periods of good feeling grow shorter.

Actually, for people who appear prosperous during inflation, their prosperity is artificial and short-lived. It is because when inflation reaches its climax, that is, when it becomes galloping inflation, it conceals in itself the seeds of destruction, which have the potential to throw the entire economy out of gear.

Good times are characterised by general prosperity. But it is accompanied by some inflation as prosperity swells demand and forces up prices faster than production can keep pace. In other words, inflation often accompanies the changes in industrial conditions which characterize good times. Eventually, the day of reckoning comes.

Extravagant spending and reckless public borrowing give a false sense of prosperity. Whenever there is reckless expansion, over enthusiasm, and ungrounded hopes, disaster, sooner or later, is inevitable. Along with inflation, there might be zoom in prices, full employment, high wages, and a great sense of hustle and bustle in business. But all these may be built on the unsound quicksand of debt, and of course inflation.

The further a country goes in inflation, the greater will be the amount of increase of the circulating medium, and the greater will be the unwarranted expansion of industry and debts. When the crash comes, everything goes down like a house of cards. This gives us the key to the cause of unnatural and excessive booms—great spurts of prosperity, not warranted by conditions.

The periods of enormous expansion are coupled with increase in debt, both public and private, as everybody borrows to take advantage of rising markets for various reasons—to get rich in the stock market, to enlarge the factory, to expand the business, or to increase the size of farm. When crash comes, the results spread like a pestilence throughout the entire economic life.

In ancient times, great credit structures were not built on a flimsy foundation that can be readily toppled over by the lightest breeze. In contrast, the present economic life is built on credit. People live on promises; and if one person fails to keep his promise, the results react through a long chain and become steadily worse. During both the great depression of 1929 and global meltdown of 2008-09, the world saw how the failure of one important customer might lead to the failure of a bank, reacting on all the bank's depositors, whose balances might be wiped out or tied up indefinitely. In such situations, depositors may be unable to pay their creditors and be forced to sell investments, breaking the price of securities and rendering insufficient the collateral which others had put up with their banks as security, thus forcing its sale; and the situation would go from bad to worse.

No doubt, borrowing, issuing paper money, printing bonds and using them as bank collateral, increase the amount of money in circulation and give a false sense of prosperity. It is all part and parcel of inflation. When everything keeps going up—from prices to salaries—it looks like a great era of prosperity; but it is all a house of cards.

In short, mild inflation often brings a short-lived pseudo-prosperity. Then, as things progress, sound money gradually disappears or commands an ever increasing premium, while the inferior money passes only at a heavy, and generally an increasing, discount. Then, finally, money almost disappears. The good money is hoarded or exported, and poorer money becomes worthless. If there is the slightest value to the discredited currency, everyone hastens to spend it anywhere for anything, seeking to turn a valueless voucher into some form of true wealth of any kind, on any terms. Finally, money passes out of use and people resort to barter. So it is folly to imagine that the inflation and false prosperity can be anything but real or substantial, to be desired and encouraged.

Notes

1. Data is obtained from the World Bank, World Development Indicators (2006). The middle income classification follows the World Bank's definition.
2. "Foreign direct investment and inflation." *Southern Economic Journal*, Oct., 2009 by Selin Sayek.
3. Hazlitt, Henry, *Inflation Crisis and How to Resolve It*, Ludwig von Mises Institute, Auburn, Alabama, 2009, pp. 138-43.

7

Inflation and Govt Schemes for the Poor

Inflation and Social Development in India

Since the adoption of the New Economic Policy in 1991, India has been making sustained progress on a scale, size and pace that is unprecedented in its own history. Real GDP growth, which had been averaging below 5 per cent until then, accelerated to touch a peak level of 9.4 per cent in 2007. This undisputed growth is, however, belied by India's consistently dismal ranking in Human Development Index (HDI).

The rise in GDP results in increased disposable income in certain sections of society, not necessarily all the sections; and more availability of money for the Indian government to spend, not necessarily more purchasing power. GDP merely reflects the increasing costs of economic change, and it does not measure the real welfare effects. It also does not take into account a decline in stocks, for example, natural gas in the earth. Moreover, the cost of certain public goods that cannot serve as an adequate measure of the benefits associated with these goods—say, defence equipments—is also covered by the GDP. Due to these and other reasons, rise in GDP and welfare or social sector development often do not coincide.

The Human Development Index, on the other hand, combines normalized measures of life expectancy, literacy, educational attainment, and GDP per capita for countries worldwide. The United Nations Development Programme (UNDP) refers to the concept of HDI as a process of widening the options of persons, giving them greater opportunities for education, health care, income, employment, etc. The HDI is claimed as a standard means of measuring human development and is basically used to measure a country's development.

The HDI combines three basic dimensions: (i) Life expectancy at birth—as an index of health and longevity. (ii) Knowledge and education—as measured by the adult literacy rate (with two-thirds weighting) and the combined primary, secondary, and tertiary gross enrolment ratio (with one-third weighting). (iii) Standard of living—as measured by the natural logarithm of gross domestic product per capita.

The HDI is restricted to the socio-economic sphere of life and the political and civil spheres are in the most part kept separate. Hence, irrespective of political strife, based on socio-economic parameters only, India does not rank very high. But other factors like gender equality, etc. are also no less important. Thus, numbers such as GDP growth and HDI rankings reflect a less ideal picture of social upliftment and delivery of public goods. Instead, the use of progress indicators like male adult and female adult literacy rates, Below Poverty Line rates (both monetary value and calorie intake), access to basic health care, primary education, etc. in line with United Nations Millennium Development Goals would make better sense.

At the same time, the usefulness of greater generic indicators like GDP and HDI should not be underestimated. We have to acknowledge the fact that they are just necessary conditions, and not sufficient conditions. So, higher GDP and lower HDI, without development means very little to India's population of 1.21 billion (2011 provisional census). Higher growth should be said to be attained when there is equivalent development of human race.

Phase of High Growth

During the two decade period of 1991-2011, India has moved on to a new phase of high growth but inflationary concerns remain. The country's 9.6 per cent GDP growth rate for 2006 reflected double-digit growth in the industrial and services sectors. India's continued high growth in 2007 resulted

Table 7.1: Key Indicators

Data categories and components	Units	2005-06	2006-07	2007-08	2008-09	2009-10	2010-11
1. GDP and Related Indicators							
GDP (current market prices)	₹ crore	3692485	4293672	4986426	5582623[PE]	6550271[QE]	7877947[AE]
Growth Rate	%	13.9	16.3	16.1	12.0	17.3	20.3
GDP (factor cost 2004-05 prices)	₹ crore	3254216	3566011	3898958	4162509[PE]	4493743[QE]	4879232[AE]
Growth Rate	%	9.5	9.6	9.3	6.8	8.0	8.6
Savings Rate	% of GDP	33.5	34.6	36.9	32.2	33.7	na
Capital Formation (rate)	% of GDP	34.7	35.7	38.1	34.5	36.5	na
Per Cap. Net National Income (factor cost at current prices)	₹	27123	31198	35820	40605	46492	54527
2. Production							
Foodgrains	Mn tonnes	208.6	217.3	230.8	234.5	218.1[a]	232.1[b]
Index of Industrial Production[c] (growth)	Per cent	8.0	11.9	8.7	3.2	10.5	na
Electricity Generation (growth)	Per cent	5.2	7.2	6.4	2.8	6.0	na
3. Prices							
Inflation (WPI) (12 month average)	% change	4.3	6.5	4.8	8.0	3.6	9.4[d]
Inflation CPI (IW) (average)	% change	4.4	6.7	6.2	9.1	12.4	11.0[d]
4. External Sector							
Export Growth (US$)	% change	23.4	22.6	29.0	13.6	-3.5	29.5[e]
Import Growth (US$)	% change	33.8	24.5	35.5	20.7	-5.0	19.0[e]
Current Account Balance (CAB)/GDP	Per cent	-1.2	-1.0	-1.3	-2.3	-2.8	na
Foreign Exchange Reserves	Us$ Bn.	151.6	199.2	309.7	252.0	279.1	297.3[f]
Average Exchange Rate	₹ / US$	44.27	45.25	40.26	45.99	47.42	45.68[g]
5. Money and Credit							
Broad Money (M3) (annual)	% change	16.9	21.7	21.4	19.3	16.8	16.5[h]
Scheduled Commercial Bank Credit (growth)	% change	30.8	28.1	22.3	17.5	16.9	24.4[h]
6. Fiscal Indicators (Centre)							
Gross Fiscal Deficit	% of GDP	4.0	3.3	2.5	6.0	6.3[i]	4.8
Revenue Deficit	% of GDP	2.5	1.9	1.1	4.5	5.1[i]	3.5
Primary Deficit	% of GDP	0.4	-0.2	-0.9	2.6	3.1[i]	1.7
7. Population	Million	1106	1122	1138	1154	1170	1186
(Year-wise projected propultion as on 1st Oct.)		(2005)	(2006)	(2007)	(2008)	(2009)	(2010)

[AE] GDP figures for 2010-11 are advance estimates; [PE] Provisional Estimates. [QE] quick estimates.

[na] not yet available/released for 2009-10.

[a] Final estimates.

[b] Second advance estimates.

[c] The annual growth rates have been recompiled from 2005-06 onwards since the indices have been recompiled from April 04 onwards using new seried of WPI for the IIP items reported in value terms.

[d] Average Apr.-Dec. 2010.

[e] Apr.-Dec. 2010.

[f] as of December 31, 2010.

[g] Average exchange rate for 2010-11 (Apr.-Dec. 2010).

[h] Provisional.

[i] fiscal indicators for 2009-10 are based on the provisional actuals for 2009-10.

from steady gains in the rate of savings and investment, consumption demand, addition of new capacity and the more intensive and efficient use of existing capacity. Strong growth in the industrial and services sectors supported the high overall rate, more than compensating for an agricultural slowdown.

This high growth rate has led to concerns about whether the country is growing beyond its growth potential, thereby straining its labour force and capital stock, and creating inflationary instabilities. The government tries to increase productivity, ameliorate skills shortages and add capacity through investments. This is done in order to maintain high growth while keeping prices fairly stable. Monetary policy plays a critical role in maintaining price stability. However, the sustainability of high economic growth with moderate inflation depends critically on fiscal prudence and high investment levels.

Inflation in India, as measured by the consumer price index for industrial workers has seen a steady rise since 2005. This is generally attributed to demand-supply gaps in the domestic production of major foodgrains and oilseeds amid rising global prices. Inflationary pressures on the demand side include elevated asset prices, high investment and consumption demand and strong growth in credit and monetary aggregates. Generally, inflationary pressures persist in India whenever international commodity prices, particularly oil prices, further increase. In the absence of appropriate policy actions, it becomes difficult to stabilize prices and anchor inflationary expectations.

Containing fiscal deficit of the central government becomes paramount in containing inflation. The government's deficit reduction strategy is essentially revenue-led and focuses on improving the efficiencies in allocating public spending. Its policy of reprioritizing expenditure has led to higher outlays for the social sector.

Another contributing factor is the deepening trade deficit. It occurs because India's imports tend to increase more than exports. Higher capital inflows can be realized when there are strong macroeconomic fundamentals, greater investor confidence and ample global liquidity. The amount of foreign exchange reserves, and the appreciation of the Indian rupee against the United States dollar also play a role in this.

High oil prices put pressure on budgets, inflation rates and the balance of payments. In such a scenario, it is a challenge for India to sustain its growth momentum. And it becomes essential for the government to contain oil imports through selective energy conservation measures.

Excessive fiscal deficit remains a serious problem and it has received relatively less attention despite its serious economic implications. Excessive reliance on debt, whether domestic or external, carries macroeconomic risks that may hinder economic and social development. High domestic public debt pushes up interest rates and crowds out private investment, which is much needed to promote economic growth. Since most government revenues get devoted to debt servicing fiscal policy cannot be used to provide basic services, such as education, health, safe drinking water and housing. When public debt level reaches a very high level, a larger fiscal deficit becomes unavoidable. As a result, inflation starts climbing, pushing domestic interest rates and raising the cost of debt servicing. Hence, pursuing vigorous macroeconomic policies to contain public debt, including domestic public debt before they become totally unmanageable, acquires importance.

Budgetary Expenditures and Fiscal Deficit

The focus of the government as well as the media is generally on the fact that India is one of the fastest growing economies in the world. The fact that is sidelined is that the Indian fiscal deficit is the highest in percentage among the other countries of the world. Fiscal deficit is essentially the difference between what the government spends and what it earns. It is expressed as a percentage of GDP.[1]

In Budget documents, the government makes realistic revenue expectations, but underestimates expenditure. This may be because expenditure to the tune of 2.0-2.5 per cent of GDP remains off budget. For example, in the Budget for 2008-09, there was no provision for the loan waiver of ₹ 71,680 crores to the farmers and huge amount of ₹ 27,145 crores for the Central sixth pay commission recommendations. While net borrowings for 2008-09 were budgeted at ₹ 1 trillion and the gross borrowing estimate was at ₹ 1.45 trillion, it did not include oil bond redemptions of ₹ 13,000 crores. The loss made by public enterprises also adds to the fiscal deficit to some extent.

The Budget document for 2008-09 estimated that the Plan expenditure is going to rise by around ₹ 38,000 crores or around 19 per cent, while the non-plan expenditure will rise by a much smaller amount, by ₹ 64,806 crores or 17 per cent. The actual figure was much higher. It is because of such reasons that the actual fiscal deficit tends to be much higher than the forecast. It is mandated by the Fiscal Responsibility and Budget Management (FRBM) Act, operationalised in 2004-05, that the fiscal deficit of the Central Government should be lower than 3 per cent of GDP.

In practice, the populist announcements made by the government, especially in view of the impending elections, and fuel inflation add pressure on the fiscal deficit. Hence, it may be argued that high fiscal deficit may not be worrisome. Instead, a high fiscal deficit may be an indication that the government is spending more on 'productive expenditures'.[2] Market borrowings finance more than half of the gross fiscal deficit and the rest of the gap is filled by small savings, provident funds, reserve funds and deposits and advances. To some extent, the loss due to rise in the oil prices is recovered by increasing the prices of petrol, diesel and gas.

In India, the Central Government share in public debt is much higher than that of State Governments. The real burden of public debt is in its servicing. In 2005, interest payments alone consumed more than 28 per cent of the revenue of the Central and State Governments, more if repayments of principal are included. The sustainability of such huge debt is crucially dependent on the size of the economy. Past experience suggests that it is difficult to bring public debt ratios down without robust economic growth. Therefore, the government vigorously tries to pursue policies that promote GDP growth.

Debt sustainability becomes an issue of growing concern when the growth of government interest payments exceeds that of government revenues. The country's debt-carrying capacity can increase only if the pace of government revenue growth continues to rise. This can happen only by strengthening the tax administration and broadening of the tax base. It is here that strengthening tax administration acquires importance. In reality, while the actual tax rates are not low, revenues are low due to inefficient tax system and corruption. The government can strengthen the tax administration by: (i) adopting a simpler tax system, with fewer exemptions, less discretion and better compliance; (ii) improving documentation of the economy; and (iii) greater use of information technology.

Public Spending Towards Priority Sectors

Inflation is indirectly caused due to excess public spending by the government than its revenue. When this excess public spending is properly utilised and diverted towards priority sectors that better the livelihood of millions, it is worthwhile. Otherwise, it may be better to curb the excessive public spending by the government. An attempt is made here to analyse as to how far the public spending by the Government of India is in sync with the social sector development needs of the country.

The demand for public spending is high in India owing to widespread poverty and lack of basic services. Hence, it is a challenge for the government to contain wasteful public spending and orient it towards priority sectors. In other words, public expenditure should promote pro-poor growth and priority should be given to basic services such as education, health, sanitation and housing.

Agriculture Sector

In the race to increase GDP, priority is given to increasing industrial productivity and agriculture is often neglected. Agriculture is the main livelihood for around 60 per cent of the country's population which inhabits the rural areas. Even though agriculture contributes substantially to the country's GDP, growth and productivity in agriculture are slowing. It is not good news as agricultural labour productivity has a significant impact on poverty reduction. It is estimated that one per cent increase in agricultural productivity can lead to 0.3-0.4 per cent drop in poverty.[3]

Hence, it should be a policy priority to revitalize agriculture and urgent steps need to be taken to raise agricultural productivity. Revitalizing agriculture requires connecting the poor to markets through improvements to rural infrastructure, the availability and management of water, agricultural technology, increasing the capacity to adapt technologies, and speeding up diversification and commercialization. It also requires improving the distribution of land and the access to agricultural credit and extension, thus making macroeconomic policy friendlier to agriculture. All these would enable the poor to make a dent on poverty by themselves. Some economists are of the view that large gains in poverty alleviation are possible through comprehensive liberalization of global agriculture trade.

Shift from Agriculture to Industry and Services

In recent years, rural poor are increasingly shifting from agriculture to industry and services, which offer them a better chance of escaping poverty. This trend is not likely to subside, even if agriculture growth helps in reducing poverty in rural areas. So, taking this aspect into account, there is a need to put in place a policy to make this migration from agriculture to industry and services easy. This requires creating opportunities in the non-farm sector as well as urban planning. Both require better opportunities for skills development and strategies for raising overall economic growth.

Inclusive Growth

The Planning Commission, in its Eleventh Five-Year Plan has sought to achieve the overall objective of achieving the 'inclusive growth', i.e. to include all those in the process of economic growth, who have remained excluded from the process of economic growth experienced by the country during the past decades. This is because the government policy of the past decades has been criticised for having lacked the human face. It is said that the government has been over-obsessed with the idea of achieving higher growth rate and fiscal and monetary management, rather than addressing the needs for equitable and inclusive growth.

In fact, the reforms process has ignored the common man and the trickle-down theory has actually failed to deliver. India is much behind countries like China and Indonesia in most of the social sector indicators. Some areas of serious concern are availability of doctor per 1000 people, availability of health institutions, quality of elementary education and literacy rate, particularly among the females. Among these, the literacy rate and poverty percentage are the two biggest embarrassments and the country still languishes in the Human Development Index of the UNDP. These issues call for a more cautious approach towards the financial sector reforms in the future.

India and Human Development Report 2010

The 2010 Human Development Report by United Nations Development Programme (UNDP), titled "The Real Wealth of Nations: Pathways to Human Development" ranks India at 119 out of 169 countries on the Human Development Index (HDI). While China moved eight places upwards between 2005 and 2010, India managed to move only one rank upwards. Although India is placed at tenth position globally in terms of HDI measured on income growth, the country reports severe inequalities. This is in contrast to several low-income nations, including Nepal, that have posted huge profits by investing in education and health.

India's life expectancy at birth is among the lowest at 64.4 years as against China's 73.5, Bangladesh's 66.9, Pakistan's 67.2 and Nepal's 67.5. In mean years of schooling too, India lags behind recording 4.4 years while China has 7.5, Pakistan 4.9 and Bangladesh 4.8. On female labour force participation too, Bangladesh with 61 per cent is much ahead of India, which has just 31 per cent. This is partly due to the fact that India has a large population and partly because of other economic factors.

India compares very poorly with countries with high level of human development on all indicators such as life expectancy, education and per capita income. For instance, life expectancy at birth is 64.4 years in India, which is less than the world average of 69.3 years. Similarly, the number of years a person has spent in school is a dismal 4.4 years for India as compared to global average of 7.4 and 4.6 for South Asia. The mean years of schooling children are expected to complete is 10.3 years in India compared to the world average of 12.3 years. Lastly, the breadth of deprivation in India, which is the average percentage of deprivation experienced by people in multi-dimensional poverty, is 54 per cent. Thus, India is a laggard compared to many other developing countries which have moved faster on the measured indicators.

Patterns and Drivers of Human Development

There is no significant correlation between economic growth and improvements in health and education, especially at low and medium levels of the HDI. In the past, only those countries that became rich were able to pay for costly advances in health and education. Today, however, technological improvements and changes in societal structures allow even poorer countries to realise significant gains. In recent times, the unprecedented flows of ideas across countries have been transformative. These range from health-saving technologies to political ideas and productive practices. In fact, many recent innovations have allowed countries to improve health and education at very low cost. Over time, this has led to the weakening of the association between the income and non-income dimensions of human development.

Generally, the growth of income can indicate that opportunities for decent work are expanding. Income is also the source of the taxes and other revenues that the government needs in order to provide services and undertake redistributive programmes. Thus, increasing income on a broad basis should remain an important policy priority. Such increase in income should be more at the lower level of one society, so that they are able to cope up with rising prices of essential goods.

Governments try to address the complex issue of the need for markets to generate income and dynamism and the need to deal with market failures in a range of ways. Markets may be necessary for sustained economic dynamism, but they do not automatically bring progress in other dimensions of human

Table 7.2: Trends in the HDI 1980-2010

HDI	Country	1980	1990	1995	2000	2005	2009	2010	Avg. Annual HDI Growth Rate (percent) 1980-2010	1990-2010	2000-2010	HDI Improvement Rank 1980-2010*
1	Norway	0.788	0.838	0.869	0.906	0.932	0.937	0.938	0.58	0.56	0.34	34
2	Australia	0.791	0.819	0.887	0.914	0.925	0.935	0.937	0.57	0.67	0.25	35
41	Poland	—	0.683	0.710	0.753	0.775	0.791	0.795	—	0.76	0.54	—
57	Malaysia	0.541	0.616	0.659	0.691	0.726	0.739	0.744	1.06	0.94	0.73	19
65	Russia	—	0.692	0.644	0.662	0.693	0.714	0.719	—	0.19	0.82	—
73	Brazil	—	—	—	0.649	0.678	0.693	0.699	—	—	0.73	—
83	Turkey	0.467	0.552	0.583	0.629	0.656	0.674	0.679	1.24	1.03	0.76	14
89	China	0.368	0.460	0.518	0.567	0.616	0.655	0.663	1.96	1.83	1.57	2
91	Sri Lanka	0.513	0.558	0.584	—	0.635	0.653	0.658	0.83	0.82	—	51
92	Thailand	0.483	0.546	0.581	0.600	0.631	0.648	0.654	1.01	0.90	0.86	29
97	Philippines	0.523	0.552	0.569	0.597	0.619	0.635	0.638	0.66	0.72	0.67	78
101	Egypt	0.393	0.484	0.523	0.566	0.587	0.614	0.620	1.52	1.23	0.90	8
108	Indonesia	0.390	0.458	0.508	0.500	0.561	0.593	0.600	1.43	1.35	1.82	12
110	South Africa	—	0.601	0.634	—	0.587	0.594	0.597	—	-0.03	—	—
113	Vietnam		0.407	0.457	0.505	0.540	0.566	0.572	—	1.70	1.24	—
119	India	0.320	0.389	0.415	0.440	0.482	0.512	0.519	1.61	1.44	1.66	6
125	Pakistan	0.311	0.359	0.389	0.416	0.468	0.487	0.490	1.52	1.55	1.64	10
128	Kenya	0.404	0.437	0.435	0.424	0.443	0.464	0.470	0.50	0.37	1.03	87
129	Bangladesh	0.259	0.313	0.350	0.390	0.432	0.463	0.469	1.99	2.03	1.86	3
	World	0.455	0.526	0.554	0.570	0.598	0.619	0.624	1.05	0.85	0.89	

Source: HDR 2010.

* Measured using deviation from fit. Lower the number, faster the improvement.

development. Development that overly favours rapid economic growth is rarely sustainable. In other words, a market economy is necessary, but not enough. It is possible for a capable and focused state to help drive development and the growth of markets. What is possible and appropriate, however, is context specific.

Truly speaking, human development involves a much broader dimension than health, education and income. It is because progress in these areas has little meaning in the absence of democracy, human rights and freedom. Even when countries progress in the HDI, they do not necessarily excel in the broader dimensions. It is possible to have a high HDI and be unsustainable, undemocratic and unequal just as it is possible to have a low HDI and be relatively sustainable, democratic and equal.

The greatest challenge in maintaining progress in human development is the unsustainable nature of production and consumption patterns that is evolving in recent years. High costs and low availability of clean energy hamper the progress of most developing countries in alleviating the worst effects. This necessitates a radical rethinking on the economics of growth and its relationship with development. Economic growth can no more be equated with development. It is futile to assume that people care only about consumption. Well-being is about much more than money. It is about the possibilities that people have to fulfil the life plans they have reason to choose and pursue.

Informed Policy-making

The vast increases in literacy and educational attainment in many parts of the world have strengthened people's ability to make informed choices and hold governments accountable. Technology and institutions have broadened the scope for empowerment. The proliferation of mobile telephony and satellite television and increased access to the Internet, in particular, has vastly increased the availability of information and the ability to voice opinions. This has made policy-making much better informed by the views and concerns of citizens. It has deepened the local democratic processes, too. The representation of traditionally marginalized people, including women, the poor, indigenous groups, and refugees has greatly expanded. But the fragility of some of the achievement has been exposed by the global financial crisis of 2008-09.

Education for All Development Index (EDI) and India

It was in April 2000 that the World Education Forum met at Dakar, Senegal with more than 1,100 participants from 164 countries to finalise the six Education for All (EFA) goals, which are as under:

1. Expanding and improving comprehensive early childhood care and education, especially for the most vulnerable and disadvantaged children.
2. Ensuring that by 2015 all children, particularly girls, children in difficult circumstances and those belonging

to ethnic minorities, have access to, and complete, free and compulsory primary education of good quality.

3. Ensuring that the learning needs of all young people and adults are met through equitable access to appropriate learning and life-skills programmes.
4. Achieving a 50 per cent improvement in levels of adult literacy by 2015, especially for women, and equitable access to basic and continuing education for all adults.
5. Eliminating gender disparities in primary and secondary education by 2005, and achieving gender equality in education by 2015, with a focus on ensuring girls' full and equal access to and achievement in basic education of good quality.
6. Improving all aspects of the quality of education and ensuring excellence of all so that recognized and measurable learning outcomes are achieved by all, especially in literacy, numeracy and essential life skills.

While each of these six EFA goals adopted in 2000 matters in its own right, the commitment undertaken by the governments at the World Education Forum in Dakar was to sustain advances on all fronts. The Education for All Development Index (EDI) provides a composite measure of progress, encompassing access, equity and quality. Because of data availability constraints, it includes only the four most easily quantifiable goals, attaching an equal weight to each: (1) universal primary education, measured by the primary adjusted net enrolment ratio (ANER); (2) adult literacy, measured by the literacy rate for those aged 15 and above; (3) gender parity and equality, measured by the Gender-specific EFA Index (GEI), an average of the gender parity indexes of the primary and secondary gross enrolment ratios and of the adult literacy rate; and (4) quality of education, measured by the survival rate to grade (5) The EDI value for a given country is the arithmetic mean of the four proxy indicators. Since these components are all expressed as percentages, the EDI value can vary from 0 to 100 per cent or, when expressed as a ratio, from 0 to 1. The higher the EDI value, the closer the country is to achieving Education for All as a whole.

India's Position

In 2007, only 123 countries had a complete set of the indicators required to calculate the EDI. They were ranked according to "high", "medium" or "low" EDI. UNESCO's EFA Global Monitoring Report 2010 ranks India among the countries with "low" EDI at position 105.[4] In 2001 also, in terms of EDI, India ranked exactly 105 among 127 countries. In terms of the EDI, India is behind in 2007 not only countries like Norway, Japan and Germany that figure on the top, but ranked below several Latin American, African and Asian developing countries, which are economically poorer than India such as Zambia, Kenya, Ghana, Bhutan, Maldives and Cambodia.

This poor scoring of India on the EDI is not in any way in consonance with the tremendous progress that India had made since 2000. No doubt, there has seen improvement in enrolment ratio in primary education—both gross and net enrolment ratios—over the years. According to both the national data reports and the Global Monitoring Report, the 'adjusted' net enrolment ratio in primary education, including children of the relevant age group enrolled in primary or secondary schools, was 94 per cent in 2007. In contrast, India's performance with respect to all the other three components of EDI, viz. adult literacy, GEI, and survival rate to grade V is indeed appalling.

The gender index is only 0.84 in India, compared to over 0.9 in all high and medium EDI countries, except Zambia. In adult literacy, only 66 per cent of the adults in India are literate compared to over 80 per cent in most countries of the high and medium EDI groups. However, the most worrisome of all is the poor survival rate of children enrolled in grade I. In India, only 66 per cent of the children enrolled in grade I survive to grade V, which means every 34 out of 100 children enrolled in grade I dropout before reaching grade V. These dropouts may not even acquire basic 3Rs of reading, writing and arithmetic. In turn, it contributes to child labour and adds to illiterate population.

Education Scenario of India

To fulfil the educational needs of the various sections of the society, the Government of India has chalked out different educational categories such as elementary education, secondary education, higher education, adult education, technical education and vocational education. India has also brought about a constitutional amendment to impart free and compulsory education to all children up to the age of fourteen years. To achieve the goal of Universalisation of Elementary Education (UEE), the government has initiated a number of programmes including the much popular Sarva Shiksha Abhiyan (SSA), which was launched in 2001. To improve universal access and quality at the secondary and higher secondary stages of education the Government of India has recently launched the Rashtriya Madhyamik Shiksha Abhiyan (RMSA). It is expected to meet the demand for secondary education generated by SSA.

Literacy in India has made remarkable strides since Independence. The literacy rate has increased from 18.33 per cent in 1951 to 74.04 per cent in 2011 (provisional). This increase is substantial when seen in the light of the fact that there has been exponential growth of the population at nearly 2 per cent per annum during the same period. The figures of expansion of elementary education system of India are also enormous. While the number of primary schools increased from 2.15 lakhs in 1950-51 to 6.1 lakhs in 1997-98, the corresponding increase in upper primary schools was from 0.14 lakhs to 1.85 lakhs. These 8.17 lakh schools together enrolled 1,110 lakh children as compared to 192 lakh in 1951.

At the primary stage, i.e. classes I-V, universal provision of education has been substantially achieved with an estimated 95 per cent of the rural population living in 8,26,000 habitations having a primary school within a walking distance of one km. About 85 per cent of the rural population has an upper primary school within a walking distance of three km. Despite such significant achievements, there are serious problems of gender, regional, sectional and caste disparities in UEE. It can be seen from the fact that nearly 30 per cent of the world's adult illiterates are in India. More than 20 per cent of the world's out-of-school children are also in India. The rapid progress in enrolment, when contrasted with 34 per cent drop-out rate, loses its significance. Rapid progress in net enrolment ratio is relatively easy compared to ensuring that the children enrolled in schools progress through the system to complete the given cycle of schooling and even beyond.

A significant proportion of children continue to drop-out due to socio-economic and cultural factors as also due to lack of adequate infrastructure, shortage of teachers and unsatisfactory quality of education provided. In many areas, the teachers are inadequately trained and have lack of motivation. Hence, there is an urgent need to mainstream the problem of drop-outs together with the quality of education at the primary, secondary and technical levels. For the cause of education, the rural sector especially needs to be mobilized and encouraged.

Further, economic development and educational development must go hand-in-hand. Experience of other countries shows that education is based on economic development; and economic development is built around educational development. Besides its social and cultural dimensions, education is also an economic and political investment yielding long-term benefits. It is for this reason that people who can afford tend to invest a substantial part of their household expenditure in education.

The Indian Government, on the other hand, has been unable to allocate the required resources for education. The present 3.6 per cent of GNP that the government sets aside for education in its budget is not sufficient to provide reasonable levels of quality education to all the students enrolled presently. The amount even falls short of the requirements of the system to provide universal elementary education of eight years for every child of the age-group 6-14, and the consequent growth in secondary and higher education.

According to the latest statistics available from the Flash Statistics and Analytical Reports on Elementary Education in India, on average there are only three classrooms per primary school in the country, and there are only three teachers on average per school. About 14 per cent of the schools have a single classroom each and a similar proportion of the schools are single-teacher schools. It may be noted here that most primary schools offer schooling from grade I to grade V. While the national norm is to have one teacher for every 40 students in primary schools, 30 per cent of the schools have a ratio above this norm of 1:40, and in some states like Bihar the average pupil-teacher ratio at the state level is 1:59.[5] This means there is a need to increase pupil teacher ratio by recruiting more teachers, which would add to the national and state exchequers.

Besides investment, attention also needs to be paid to the quality dimension at all levels of education. Another issue that is linked to the overall issue of education is value education at all levels. Industrialisation, actually, increases the need for value education. It is because the western values get automatically imbibed in students along with progress and development. Hence, at all levels of education, values such as wisdom, humility, rationality, intellectualism, etc. have to be inculcated along with India's cultural values.

The condition of physical infrastructural facilities in schools is also an important factor for school drop-outs. Drinking water facilities is available in only 85 per cent of the schools in the country; only about one-fourth of the schools have electricity connection; and only nearly six per cent of the primary schools have a computer. About 37 per cent of schools do not have toilets and only 44 per cent of the schools have separate toilet facilities for girls. While no medical facility is available in half of the schools, one-third of the primary school buildings require major or minor repairs. The list is endless. Moreover, these figures are national averages and the actual facilities could be even more disturbing in some specific areas based on social or economic groupings of population.

Certainly, there is a lot to do with respect to improvement of schooling facilities, both physical and human (teacher), and the overall functioning of the schooling system in order to improve the children's survival rate in schools in India. Having good quality teachers in sufficient numbers is a basic pre-requisite for quality primary education and to decrease the school drop-outs. This is necessary for building a strong and meaningful educational edifice in India. In most of the North American and Western European countries, where the survival rate of children to the final grade of primary education is 99-100 per cent, the pupil-teacher ratio is below 20. To bring the pupil-teacher ratio in India at par with these countries, the government would have to at least double the number of teachers than there are at present in primary schools. This indeed is a huge task but not out of reach if the government so desires. There are examples like that of petrol pumps which have been modernised to an international standard all over the country, including the interior areas. Effective monitoring and an efficient information system are essential for successful implementation of educational programme in India.

Education not only increases awareness of masses and gives people better control of their affairs but also enhances their prospects of finding jobs and increases their capacity to earn. The spread of education in India is absolutely necessary if we are to see poor people bring a positive economic change in their lives and equip themselves to meet the situations of rising prices of various types of goods and services.

Budget 2011-12 and Social Spending

In his budget speech on Feb. 28, 2011, Finance Minister Pranab Mukherjee indicated that the country's social spending would rise by 17 per cent in 2011-12. This includes health spending, which would rise 20 per cent in the fiscal year starting April 1, 2011. This additional spending is based on the government hopes of buoyant tax revenues from near-nine per cent economic growth. However, the government's calculation that the fiscal deficit would fall to 4.6 per cent of GDP in 2011-12 seems to be too optimistic.[6] The government's expectations may not materialise because it has worked out both the borrowing and fiscal deficit numbers on the most optimistic macroeconomic scenarios. In reality, the likelihood of such a scenario is negligible. In the previous year, the government enjoyed big one-time gains from the sale of 3G telecom licenses. In the absence of provision for such gains in the fiscal year, the government has to count only on a robust economy to expand its revenue.

The move to directly give some subsidies for food and fuel as cash to customers is aimed at making the subsidies system more efficient with less waste. Another focus area in 2011-12 is getting rid of supply bottlenecks in the food sector. For this, cold storage chains would be given infrastructure status, making them eligible for preferential borrowing rates to build facilities. The budget has also increased interest subsidy to farmers to 3 per cent in 2011-12, up from 2 per cent previously. The target for loans to the farm sector has been raised to 4.75 trillion rupees from 3.75 trillion rupees previously.

The subsidy burden on the government could swell, especially if oil prices stay above $100 per barrel and the government continues to subsidise diesel and cooking fuels. Food and fuel subsidies are popular with voters and hence the government is expected to continue it in some form or the other. These help offset inflation, but add to fiscal burden. Further, any slowdown in growth would make the deficit target harder to reach. It may be noted here that in the beginning of 2011, the government's net market borrowing from the bond market was to the tune of 3.43 trillion rupees.

Growth and Social Sector Projects

India's economy has been rising steadily at around 8 per cent annually. This makes it harder for India to become eligible for multilateral soft loans for social sector projects. The steady rise in India's international prestige takes away the country's eligibility for aid in the other direction. This fact poses new challenges for a country that runs large deficits, and where large sections still remain outside the mainstream. Thus, India's growth numbers act as window-dressing to mask its underlying problems.

The exponential growth rate of India's population also adds to its share of problems. The rate of increase of workforce is more rapid than that can be absorbed by India's growing economy. The growth in population means a greater demand for infrastructure, viz. power, roads and ports and housing. This makes the country struggle to invest enough to keep pace with the growing demand. The rising population increases demand for food and fuel, on the one hand, and decreases land availability for cultivation, on the other. This tends to steadily increase the prices of food items, causing inflation. Due to these factors, even if India's growth exceeds that of China, the social condition of the people may not reflect drastic improvement.

Considered in the light of above, it is no wonder then that inflation has remained a worrying issue for India in the midst of persistent high growth. The country has been caught in the classic negative spiral of high inflation, which reduces demand, leading to the flight of capital and a decline in investment. The government needs to reduce its fiscal deficit to tame inflation. However, the government lacks the necessary political will to do so, especially as every year some states in the country go to polls. On the other hand, reducing deficit would affect social infrastructure projects on employment, food security and education.

At the State and Central Government level, India runs a persistently high single- to low double-digit combined fiscal deficit. The current account deficit also remains reasonably high at more than 4 per cent of GDP. This limits the government's ability to add more social programmes. Moreover, to finance a large and growing current account deficit also requires continued capital flow from the developed world.

Thus, an embarrassment of riches at the overall level awaits India that hides several of its underlying problems. Unless the government realises sooner rather than later and tries to better utilise its existing financial resources, the country may well become a resource poor country that is considered too rich to deserve support for its future large-scale social programmes. A robust growth is only worth if the financial resources are better targeted towards social initiatives.

The government also must not forget that with increasing prestige comes increasing responsibility. It may range from contributing in aid to Less Developed Countries (LDCs) to an increase in its share of UN funds. All these, in turn, make it difficult to reduce fiscal deficit. The only way out is to harness internal capital resources and use them on those projects of development which will bring a balanced development of all the regions of the country and the benefit of which goes to all the sections of population, particularly the poor.

National Rural Employment Guarantee Act

In spite of the growing fiscal deficit the Government of India has implemented the Mahatma Gandhi National Rural Employment Guarantee Scheme—the world's largest social programme ever—with an annual budget of about $10 billion. India's National Rural Employment Guarantee Act (NREGA) of 2005 provides basic social security for rural workers: a universal and legally enforceable right to 100 days of employment per rural household on local public works at minimum wage. Labourers who are not given work within 15 days of asking for it are entitled to unemployment benefits.

The other noteworthy features of the act are:

- It encourages women's participation. One-third of employment generated is to be set aside for women and provided within 5 kilometres of their village; child care facilities (if required) must be provided at the work-site.
- It decentralises planning and implementation. At least half of allocated funds are to be spent by elected local councils; village assemblies are to select and prioritise projects.
- It creates rural assets. People are to be employed to create public assets (such as roads and check-dams) as well as assets on private lands (such as land improvement and wells).
- It imposes strict norms for transparency and accountability. All documents are to be publicly available, with proactive disclosure of essential

documents (such as attendance records), and periodic audits are to be carried out by village representatives.

In fiscal year 2009-10, India spent almost $10 billion (approximately one per cent of GDP) on the programme, and 5.26 crore households were provided employment under this scheme as against 4.51 crore during 2008-09. On average, each participating household worked for 54 days. The disadvantaged groups joined in large numbers; a majority of workers were members of Scheduled Castes (SCs) or Scheduled Tribes (STs), and more than half were women. During 2010-11, about 4.10 crore households have been provided employment till December 2010. Out of the 145 crore person days created under the scheme during this period, 23 per cent and 17 per cent were accounted for by SC and ST population respectively and 50 per cent by women.

Payments of minimum wages and improved work conditions at NREGA work-sites have created pressure for similar improvements in the private labour market, benefiting all rural workers. Distress migration to urban areas has slowed. And for many rural women programme earnings are an important source of economic independence. But the moot question is: To what extent is the scheme contributing to the social sector development of the country?

Swarnjayanti Gram Swarozgar Yojana

The Swarnjayanti Gram Swarozgar Yojana (SGSY) was launched on 1 April 1999 by the Government of India as an integrated programme for self-employment of the rural poor. The objective of the scheme is to bring the assisted poor families above the poverty line (APL) by organising them into Self-Help Groups (SHGs) through the process of social mobilisation, their training and capacity building and provision of income-generating assets through a mix of bank credit and government subsidy. The scheme emphasizes the establishment of activity clusters through selection of key activities based on aptitude and skill of the people, availability of resources and market potentiality. The scheme adopts a process approach and attempts to build the capacities of the rural poor. It provides for involvement of NGOs/CBOs/Individuals/Banks and Self Help Promoting Institutions in nurturing and development of SHGs, including skill development. The scheme provides for the cost of social intermediation and skill development training based on the local requirement. Flexibility has been given to the District Rural Development Agencies (DRDAs)/States in the utilisation of funds for training, sanction of Revolving Fund, and subsidy for economic activity based on the stage of development of groups.[7]

The programme focuses on establishing a large number of micro-enterprises in rural areas based on the ability of the poor and potential of each area, both land-based and otherwise, for sustainable income generation. Different components such as capacity building of the poor, skill development training, credit training, technology transfer, marketing and infrastructure are emphasised. The subsidy allowed under the SGSY is 30 per cent of the total project cost, subject to a ceiling of ₹ 7,500 (for SCs/STs and disabled persons subsidy limit is 50 per cent of the project cost subject to a ceiling of ₹ 10,000). For Self-Help Groups (SHGs), subsidy is 50 per cent of the project cost subject to a ceiling of ₹ 1.25 lakh or per capita subsidy of ₹ 10,000, whichever is less. There is no monetary ceiling on subsidy for minor irrigation projects for SHGs as well as individual swarozgaris. The SGSY has a special focus on the vulnerable groups among the rural poor. SCs/STs account for at least 50 per cent, women 40 per cent and the persons with physical disability constitute 3 per cent of the swarozgaris. The SGSY seeks to promote multiple credits rather than a one-time credit injection.

Under SGSY each block concentrates on 4-5 selected key activities and attends to all aspects of these activities in a cluster approach, so that swarozgaris can draw sustainable income from their investments. Since the inception of the programme, 22.52 lakh Self-Help Groups (SHGs) have been formed covering 66.97 lakh swarozgaris. These include 35.54 lakh members of the SHGs and 31.43 lakh individual swarozgaris who have been assisted with a total investment of ₹ 14403.73 crore. SCs/STs constituted 45.54 per cent and women 47.85 per cent of the swarozgaris assisted. During 2006-07, the central allocation for the scheme was ₹ 1200 crore.

If we consider only the central allocation, the sum of ₹ 1200 crore seems to be a huge amount. But when it is seen from the other side, a subsidy of maximum ₹ 7,500 seems to be meagre for any project. Any increase in the amount of subsidy would automatically increase the sum required for central allocation, which might influence inflation in a negative way.

Sarva Shiksha Abhiyan

Sarva Shiksha Abhiyan (SSA) is Government of India's flagship programme for achievement of Universalization of Elementary Education (UEE) in a time-bound manner, as mandated by 86th amendment to the Constitution of India making free and compulsory education to the children of 6-14 years age group, a Fundamental Right. The SSA is being implemented in partnership with State Governments to cover the entire country and address the needs of 192 million children in 1.1 million habitations. The programme seeks, inter alia, enrolment of all children in school; setting up of Education Guarantee Centres (EGC), Alternate Schools, 'Back-to-School' camps; retention of all children till the upper primary stage; bridging of gender and social category gaps in enrolment with retention and learning; and ensuring that there is significant enhancement in the learning achievement levels of children at the primary and upper primary stage.

The programme seeks to open new schools in those habitations which do not have schooling facilities and strengthen existing school infrastructure through provision of additional classrooms, toilets, drinking water, maintenance grant and school improvement grants. Existing schools with inadequate teacher strength are provided with additional teachers, while the capacity of existing teachers is strengthened by extensive training, grants for developing teaching-learning materials and strengthening of the academic support structure at a cluster, block and district level. Additionally, the SSA seeks to provide quality elementary education including life skills. The SSA has a special focus on girl's education and children with special needs. The SSA also seeks to provide computer education to bridge the digital divide.

The allocation of resources to the SSA depends on several factors including:

- Preparation of District Elementary Education Plans and their appraisal.
- Commitment of the State Government with regard to the state share.
- Performance of the State Government regarding resources made available earlier.
- Institutional reforms in states to facilitate decentralized management of education and as per RTE requirements.
- Reports of supervision teams regarding the quality of programme implementation.
- Availability of financial resources in a particular year.

In practice, districts with poor infrastructure require more resources. However, the release of the funds is performance linked. If an educationally backward district fails to utilise the resources in the manner intended, it is unlikely to continue to receive a priority.

The achievements under the SSA till September 2010 include 3,09,727 new schools, construction of 2,54,935 school buildings, 11,66,868 additional classrooms, 1,90,961 drinking water facilities, and 3,47,857 toilets, supply of free textbooks to 8.70 crore children, and appointment of 11.13 lakh teachers. Around 14.02 lakh teachers received in-service training under this programme. There has been a significant reduction in the number of out-of-school children on account of SSA interventions. The social sector schemes like SSA yield results because of two factors, viz. appropriate allocation of funds, and their implementation.

National Social Assistance Programme

The National Social Assistance Programme (NSAP) which came into effect from 15 August 1995 represents a significant step towards the fulfilment of the Directive Principles in Article 41 of the Constitution. The programme aims at ensuring minimum national standard for social assistance in addition to the benefits that states are currently providing or might provide in future. NSAP comprises five schemes: Indira Gandhi National Old Age Pension Scheme (IGNOAPS), Indira Gandhi National Widow Pension Scheme (IGNWPS), Indira Gandhi National Disability Pension Scheme (IGNDPS), National Family Benefit Scheme (NFBS), and Annapurna Gramin Rozgar Yogana (AGRY).

Indira Gandhi National Old Age Pension Scheme (IGNOAPS) was launched by the Ministry of Rural Development. All persons of 65 years and above, belonging to below the poverty line are eligible for the scheme. Destitute persons who do not have any kind of source of income can also avail this pension facility. The pension amount is ₹ 200 per month per person.

Indira Gandhi National Widow Pension Scheme (IGNWPS) is implemented by Ministry of Rural Development, Government of India. The pension is given to the widows aged between 45 and 64 years of age. The applicant should be a household below the poverty line as per criteria prescribed by the Government of India. The pension amount is ₹ 200 per month per beneficiary and the concerned State Government is also urged to provide an equal amount to the person. The pension is to be credited into a post office or public sector bank account of the beneficiary. The pension will be discontinued if there is the case of remarriage or once the widow moves above the poverty line.

Indira Gandhi National Disability Pension Scheme (IGNDPS) is implemented by Ministry of Rural Development, Government of India to assist disabled people in the country. The disabled person should be aged between 18-64 years of age and belong to Below the Poverty Line. The applicant should be suffering from severe or multiple disabilities. The pension amount given by the Central Government is ₹ 200 per month per person and the concerned State Government is also urged to contribute an equal amount. The pension is to be credited into a post office or public sector bank account of the beneficiary.

National Family Benefit Scheme (NFBS) is implemented by the Ministry of Rural Development, Government of India, to assist the families living under Below the Poverty Line. The financial assistance is given to the family on the death of the breadwinner in the family. The death of such primary breadwinner should have occurred whilst he or she is between 18 and 64 years of age. The amount of assistance is ₹ 10,000.

Annapurna Gramin Rozgar Yojana is launched by the Ministry of Rural Development. Indigent senior citizens aged 65 years or above, who though eligible for old age pension under the National Old Age Pension Scheme (NOAPS) but are not getting the pension, are covered under the Scheme. 10 kg of foodgrains per person per month are supplied free of cost under the scheme.

From 2002-03, the National Social Assistance Programme has been transferred to State Plan and the funds are being released by the Ministry of Finance as Additional Central Assistance (ACA) to the State Plan. The states have the requisite flexibility in the choice of beneficiaries and implementation of the Schemes. The individual benefit per person under these schemes is very meagre and it is questionable whether these schemes really contribute to social sector development.

All these schemes and programs are aimed at improving the economic condition of poor sections of population in India, so that they are not only able to get the amenities of food, clothing and shalter but are also able to face the situations of rising prices of essential commodities.

National Rural Health Mission

The National Rural Health Mission (NRHM) was launched in 2005 to provide accessible, affordable and accountable quality health services to the rural areas with emphasis on poor persons and remote areas. It is being operationalized throughout the country, with special focus on 18 states which include 8 Empowered Action Group States (Bihar, Jharkhand, Madhya

Pradesh, Chhattisgarh, Uttar Pradesh, Uttarakhand, Orissa and Rajasthan), 8 north-eastern states (Assam, Meghalaya, Tripura, Nagaland, Arunachal Pradesh, Mizoram, Manipur and Sikkim) Himachal Pradesh, and Jammu and Kashmir. The achievements under the NRHM as on September 2010, include selection of 8.33 lakh Accredited Social Health Activists (ASHAs), employment of 1,572 specialists, 8,284 MBBS doctors, 26,734 Staff Nurses, 53,552 Auxiliary Nurse Midwives (ANMs), 18,272 paramedics on contract basis and setting up a total of 16,338 additional primary health centres (PHCs), community health centres (CHCs), and other sub-district facilities made functional on 24×7 basis. All these achievements have to be considered in light of the 6 lakh odd villages that exist in India.

Health is an important matter and is directly related with the earning capacity of the people. If the health-related problems of poor people are not taken care of in time, it adversely impacts their earnings. NRHM can therefore be called an important step to give better health to people at affordable costs.

Schemes/Programmes in the Agriculture Sector

In India, agriculture being a state subject, the primary responsibility for increasing agricultural production, enhancing productivity, and exploring the vast untapped potential of the agriculture sector rests with the State Governments. The Central Government, however, supplements the efforts of the State Governments through a number of centrally sponsored schemes. The major schemes/programmes are as discussed here.

The National Food Security Mission

The National Food Security Mission (NFSM) was launched in rabi 2007-08 with a view to enhancing the production of rice, wheat, and pulses by 10 million tonnes, 8 million tonnes, and 2 million tonnes respectively by the end of the Eleventh Plan. The Mission aims to increase production through area expansion and productivity, create employment opportunities, and enhance the farm-level economy to restore confidence of farmers.

As of December 2010, the NFSM was being implemented in 476 identified districts of 17 states of the country. To intensify the pulse production programme from 2010-11, a series of activities for more vigorous promotion of pulse crops were adopted under the NFSM.

The pulse component of the Integrated Scheme of Oilseeds, Pulses, Oil Palm and Maize (ISOPOM) has been merged with the NFSM so as to increase the scope and area coverage of the pulses programme. Jharkhand and Assam have also been included under the programme since there is immense potential for pulse promotion in rice fallows.

Through a new programme under the NFSM called the Accelerated Pulses Production Programme (A3P), 1000 block demonstrations of technology have been launched from 2010-11. This programme will essentially promote plant nutrients- and plant protection-centric technologies in compact blocks of 1000 ha each for five major pulse crops, namely tur, moong, urad, gram, and lentil.

Focused and target-oriented technological intervention under the NFSM has made significant impact since its inception. It is reflected in the increase in production of rice and wheat in 2008-09 and 2009-10. From 2010-11, as a new initiative, the A3P has been launched as a part of NFSM Pulses. Under the A3P, one million ha of potential pulses area, covering tur, urad, moong, gram, and lentil, has been taken up for large-scale demonstration of technology in compact blocks. A total of 600 A3P units of tur, urad, moong, gram, and lentil have been proposed for 2010-11.

For organizing A3P units at the farmers' fields, an amount of ₹ 54.66 lakh per unit has been proposed. Further, an amount of 300 crore has been provided in the Union Budget 2010-11 for promoting dry-land farming in 60,000 pulses and oilseeds villages in rainfed areas. These funds have been provided as additional central assistance under the ongoing RKVY to the States of Andhra Pradesh, Gujarat, Karnataka, Madhya Pradesh, Maharashtra, Rajasthan, and Uttar Pradesh.

Another programme, namely Bringing Green Revolution in the Eastern States is operational in seven States—Uttar Pradesh, Jharkhand, Bihar, West Bengal, Assam, Orissa, and Chhattisgarh. The Rice Development and Organizing Pulses and Oilseeds Villages is another programme, beside the pulses promotion strategies and other initiatives undertaken to boost agricultural productivity in these states.

During the course of the implementation of the NFSM during 2007-08 to 2010-11, as many as 63,273 demonstrations of the system of rice intensification (SRI), and 32,344 demonstrations of hybrid rice have been conducted. New farm practices have been encouraged through 3.24 lakh demonstrations of improved package of practices. Nearly, 96.84 lakh quintals of high yielding variety seeds of rice, wheat, and pulses and hybrid rice have been distributed. About 72.27 lakh ha of area has been treated with soil ameliorants such as gypsum/lime/micro nutrients to restore soil fertility for higher productivity. An area of about 29.25 lakh ha has been treated under Integrated Pest Management (IPM). Further, nearly 21.27 lakh improved farm machineries, including water-saving devices have been distributed. As a capacity-building initiative, 33,205 farmers' field school-level trainings have been held. In addition, about 353 (3.53 lakh ha) block demonstrations have been conducted during the 2010 kharif under the A3P.

Rashtriya Krishi Vikas Yojana

The Rashtriya Krishi Vikas Yojana (RKVY) was launched in 2007-08 with an outlay of ₹ 25,000 crore for the Eleventh Plan to incentivize states to enhance public investment so as to achieve a 4 per cent growth rate in agriculture and allied sectors during the Plan. During the three-year period 2007-10, an amount of ₹ 7895.12 crore was released under the RKVY. Out of the budget provision of ₹ 6,722 crore for implementation of the RKVY in the states, specific allocation has to be made for the three new initiatives introduced under the RKVY in 2010-11. The first initiative is to extend the Green Revolution to the eastern region of the country, covering the States of Assam, Bihar, Chhattisgarh, Jharkhand, Orissa, eastern UP, and West Bengal, with the objective of increasing the crop productivity of the region by intensive cultivation through recommended agricultural technologies and package of practices.

The second is the special initiatives for pulses and oilseeds in dryland areas by organizing 60,000 pulses and oilseeds villages in identified watersheds where pulse and oilseed farmers are provided farm machinery and equipment on custom hiring basis. These initiatives dovetail with other schemes of the Government of India having components for promotion of oilseeds and pulses production.

The third is the implementation of the National Mission on Saffron-Economic Revival of Jammu & Kashmir Saffron Sector during 2010-11.

The RKVY has linked 50 per cent of central assistance to the percentage of State Plan expenditure on agriculture and allied sectors. This has incentivized states to step up allocation to agriculture and allied sectors, from 5.11 per cent of total State Plan Expenditure in 2006-07, to 6.29 per cent in 2009-10. The RKVY has emerged as the principal instrument in financing development of agriculture and allied sectors in the country. Its convergence with other schemes like the Mahatma Gandhi National Rural Employment Scheme (MGNREGA) is expected to boost development of the agrarian economy. The states will take up projects under the RKVY primarily from amongst those that appear in their District and State Agriculture Plans. An increased coordination between agricultural planning and implementation of schemes is necessary to promote holistic development of agriculture and allied sectors.

Integrated Scheme of Oilseeds, Pulses, Oil Palm and Maize

The Integrated Scheme of Oilseeds, Pulses, Oil Palm and Maize (ISOPM) is being implemented in 14 major states for oilseeds and pulses, 15 for maize, and 10 for oil palm. The pulses component has been merged with the NFSM with effect from 1 April 2010. The Scheme provides flexibility to the states in implementation based on a regionally differentiated approach to promoting crop diversification. Under the Scheme, assistance is provided for purchase of breeder seed, production of foundation seed, production and distribution of certified seed, distribution of seed mini-kits, plant protection chemicals, plant protection equipment, weedicides, gypsum/pyrite/liming/dolomite, sprinkler sets, and water carrying pipes, supply of rhizobium culture/phosphate solubilising bacteria and improved farm implements, publicity, etc.

The Oil Palm Development Programme under the ISOPOM is being implemented in the states of Andhra Pradesh, Karnataka, Tamil Nadu, Gujarat, Goa, Orissa, Kerala, Tripura, Assam, and Mizoram. Its Maize Development Programme is under implementation in 15 states, viz. Andhra Pradesh, Bihar, Chhattisgarh, Himachal Pradesh, Jammu and Kashmir, Gujarat, Karnataka, Madhya Pradesh, Maharashtra, Orissa, Punjab, Rajasthan, Tamil Nadu, Uttar Pradesh, and West Bengal.

Diesel Subsidy

Due to deficit rainfall during south-west monsoon 2010 in Bihar, Jharkhand, Orissa, and West Bengal, the central share of the State Disaster Response Fund (SDRF) for 2010-11 was released to enable these states to expeditiously take the necessary drought-mitigation measures. In view of drought/deficit rainfall in certain regions, a program of Diesel Subsidy was implemented during kharif 2010 (14 July 2010 to 30 September 2010) in drought/deficit rainfall areas to save the standing crops in the field.

Agriculture needs a boost to reduce food inflation. Various schemes for the development of agriculture are not only aimed at increasing yield, but also helping poor farmers to buy various inputs. More agriculture protection will ensure adequate supply of foodgains and stable prices.

ALLIED SECTORS

National Horticulture Mission

The centrally-sponsored National Horticulture Mission (NHM) is implemented by the Ministry of Agriculture for the holistic development of the horticulture sector since 2005-06. It ensures forward and backward linkages with the active participation of all the stakeholders. The scheme is being implemented in 372 districts in the country. All the states and the three Union Territories of Andaman and Nicobar Islands, Lakshadweep, and Puducherry are covered under the NHM except the eight north-eastern states including Sikkim and the States of Jammu and Kashmir, Himachal Pradesh, and Uttarakhand. The latter are covered under the Horticulture Mission for the North East and Himalayan States (HMNEH).

During 2005-06 to 2009-10, an additional 16.57 lakh ha of identified horticulture crops have been covered. Apart from establishment of 2192 nurseries for production of quality planting materials, 2.78 lakh ha have been covered under rejuvenation of old and senile orchards. Organic cultivation of horticultural crops has been adopted in an area of 1.37 lakh ha.

With the implementation of the NHM and other schemes, the production of horticulture crops has increased from 170.8 million tonnes in 2004-05 to 214.7 million tonnes in 2008-09. The per capita availability of fruits and vegetables has increased from 391 gram/day in 2004-05 to 466 gram/day in 2008-09.

Horticulture Mission for North East and Himalayan States

The Technology Mission for Integrated Development of Horticulture was launched in 2001-02 to address issues related to production and productivity, post-harvest handling, marketing, and processing of horticultural crops in the north-eastern states. The Mission was extended to the three Himalayan States, namely Himachal Pradesh, Jammu and Kashmir, and Uttarakhand in 2003-04. The Mission covers the entire spectrum of horticulture development right from production to consumption through backward and forward linkages. During the course of its implementation, some new components such as high density planting, vegetable seed production, and horticulture mechanization have been included in the Mission. Subsequently, this has been renamed as the Horticulture Mission for North East and Himalayan States (HMNEH) along with revision of the cost norms so as to incentivize investment and supplement income generation for the beneficiaries.

The HMNEH has helped bring an additional 5,12,614 ha under various horticulture crops (fruits, vegetables, spices, plantation crops, medicinal plants, aromatic plants, root crops, and tuber crops) in these states. In addition, 26,571 ha of senile and unproductive orchards have been rejuvenated to increase productivity. The Mission has succeeded in bringing 54,938 ha under organic farming. Major infrastructure which has come up under the Mission includes 974 nurseries, 10,979 community tanks, and 12,758 tube wells. Drip irrigation has been extended to 16,303 ha. Twenty-five model floriculture centres, fifty-nine herbal gardens, twenty-five tissue culture units, and twenty-two disease forecasting units have also been set up. The Mission gives special thrust to protected cultivation of high-value crops like tomato, coloured capsicum, strawberry, and flowers to ensure quality production. It also gives special attention to promoting and popularizing mechanization in horticulture. By December 2010, 5,785 power tillers, 4,64,595 manually operated machines, 12,542 power operated implements, and 12,887 diesel engines were distributed among the farmers of the region. To strengthen the hands of women farmers, Self-Help Groups (SHGs) have been promoted. About 8,527 SHGs have been formed and these are involved in the promotion of floriculture and in exports. For proper handling and marketing of horticultural produce, 47 wholesale markets, 344 rural primary/Apni Mandies, 35 cold storages, and 64 processing units have been set up. Under the Mission 2,65,435 persons, including 53,276 women, have been trained as of 2010.

National Mission on Micro Irrigation

The centrally-sponsored National Mission on Micro Irrigation (NMMI) was launched in June 2010 in addition to the earlier Micro Irrigation Scheme launched in January 2006. The Mission is being implemented during the Eleventh Plan period for enhancing water-use efficiency by adopting drip and sprinkler irrigation systems in all States and Union Territories for both horticulture and agricultural crops. The scheme provides assistance at 60 per cent of the system cost for small and marginal farmers and at 50 per cent for general farmers. Since 2005-06, a sum of ₹ 2,739 crore has been released by the

Government of India under the scheme and 2.27 lakh ha have been brought under micro-irrigation.

The system is beneficial for farmers in increasing crop productivity and water-use efficiency; reducing fertilizer consumption (fertigation through drip system) and electricity and labour consumption; and enhancing income.

National Bamboo Mission

The Ministry of Agriculture has been implementing the centrally-sponsored National Bamboo Mission (NBM) in 27 states in the country to harness the potential of the bamboo crop. With an outlay of ₹ 568.23 crore, the NBM aims to promote holistic growth of the bamboo sector by adopting an area-based, regionally differentiated strategy. It also aims to increase the area under bamboo cultivation and marketing. Under the Mission, steps have been taken to increase the availability of quality planting material by supporting the setting up of new nurseries/tissue culture units and strengthening of existing ones. To address forward integration, the Mission is taking steps to strengthen the marketing of bamboo products, especially handicraft items. During the 2010-11, 7,946 ha forest and 2,079 ha non-forest area had been covered under bamboo plantation.

CREDIT AND INSURANCE

Agricultural Credit

From kharif 2006-07 to 2008-09, crop loans up to a principal amount of ₹ 3 lakh were given to farmers at 7 per cent interest. In the year 2009-10, government provided an additional one per cent interest subvention to those farmers who repaid their short-term crop loans as per schedule. In the year 2010-11, the government raised this subvention for timely repayment of crop loans from 1 per cent to 2 per cent. Thus, the effective rate of interest for such farmers has decreased from 7 to 5 per cent per annum in 2010-11, which is much lower than the market rate.

Revamping of Cooperative Credit Structure

A package for revival of the Short-term Rural Cooperative Credit Structure involving financial assistance of ₹ 13,596 crore was announced by the government in January 2006. The National Bank for Agriculture and Rural Development (NABARD) is the implementing agency for this purpose. Under the Structure, states are required to sign memorandums of understanding (MoUs) with the Government of India and NABARD, committing to implementation of the legal, institutional and other reforms as envisaged in the revival package. Twenty-five states have already executed such MoUs. This covers 96 per cent of the primary agricultural cooperative societies (PACS) and 96 per cent of the central cooperative banks (CCBs) in the country. As of November 2010, an amount of ₹ 8,009.75 crore was released by NABARD as Government of India share for recapitalization of 49,983 PACS.

Rehabilitation Package for Distressed Farmers

During 2010-11, the government implemented a rehabilitation package for 31 suicide-prone districts in the States of Andhra Pradesh, Karnataka, Kerala, and Maharashtra involving a financial outlay of ₹ 16,978.69 crore. Special packages were implemented in Kerala for the development of Kuttanad wetland ecosystem and mitigation of agrarian distress in Idukki district with an outlay of ₹ 1840.75 crore and ₹ 764.45 crore, respectively.

Kisan Credit Card Scheme

Since its introduction in August 1998, about 970.64 lakh Kisan Credit Cards (KCCs) have been issued up to September 2010. The KCC scheme includes reasonable components of consumption credit and investment credit within the overall credit limit sanctioned to the borrowers to provide adequate and timely credit support to the farmers for their cultivation needs.

Agricultural Insurance

Four crop insurance schemes, namely the National Agricultural Insurance Scheme (NAIS), Pilot Modified NAIS

Table 7.3: Agency-wise KCCs Issued and Amount Sanctioned

(As on 31 August 2010)

Agency	Cards Issued (lakh)					Amount Sanctioned (₹ crore)				
	2007-08	2008-09	2009-10	2010-11	Total*	2007-08	2008-09	2009-10	2010-11	Total*
Co-operative Banks	20.91	13.44	17.43	12.31	391.19	19,991	8428	7606	5164	1,45,758
RRBs	17.73	14.15	19.49	6.73	140.94	8783	5648	10,132	4329	58,293
Commercial Banks	46.06	58.34	53.13	—	423.64	59,530	39,009	39,940	—	2,33,190
Total	84.70	85.93	90.05	19.04	955.77	88,264	53,085	57,678	9493	4,37,241

Source: NABARD

Note: *Since inception of the scheme (1998). —: Not available.

(MNAIS), Pilot Weather Based Crop Insurance Scheme (WBCIS), and Pilot Coconut Palm Insurance Scheme (CPIS) are under implementation in the country.

National Agricultural Insurance Scheme (NAIS)

It was floated in rabi 1999-2000 season and is being implemented by 25 States and two UTs. The Agriculture Insurance Company of India Ltd. (AIC) is the implementing agency for the Scheme. The main objective of the scheme is to protect farmers against crop losses suffered on account of natural calamities. The scheme is available to all the farmers—loanee and non-loanee—irrespective of their size of holding. It operates on the basis of an area approach. It envisages coverage of all the food crops, oilseeds, and annual commercial/horticultural crops in respect of which past yield data are available for adequate number of years. Premium rates for food and oilseeds crops range between 1.5 per cent and 3.5 per cent. In case of annual commercial/horticultural crops, actuarial premiums are charged. A 10 per cent subsidy is available for small and marginal farmers. All financial liabilities under the scheme are shared by the Central and State Governments on 50:50 basis.

The Pilot Modified NAIS (MNAIS)

The implementation of this scheme has been approved by the government on pilot basis in 50 districts from rabi 2010-11 season. The major improvements made in the MNAIS are: actuarial premium with subsidy in premium at different rates, i.e. 40 per cent to 75 per cent depending upon the slab, provided to farmers, all claims liability on the insurer, unit area of insurance reduced to village panchayat level for major crops, indemnity for prevented/sowing/planting risk and for post-harvest losses due to cyclone, payment up to 25 per cent advance of likely claims as immediate relief, more proficient basis for calculation of threshold yield, minimum indemnity level of 70 per cent instead of 60 per cent, and private sector insurers with adequate infrastructure allowed (at present, ICICILombard, IFFCO-Tokio and Cholamandalam-MS). Only upfront premium subsidy is shared by the Central and State Governments on 50:50 basis and claims are the liability of the insurance companies. Seven states have already notified the areas for implementation of the scheme and it is expected that the scheme will be notified by more states.

Weather Based Crop Insurance Scheme (WBCIS)

To bring more farmers under the fold of crop insurance, this Scheme has been introduced in selected areas on pilot basis. The WBCIS intends to provide insurance protection to farmers against adverse weather incidences, which are deemed to unfavourably impact crop production. It has the advantage of settling claims within the shortest possible time. The WBCIS is based on actuarial rates of premium but to make the scheme attractive, premium actually charged from farmers have been restricted on a par with the NAIS. In addition to the Agriculture Insurance Company of India Ltd., private insurers have also been included for implementing the scheme in selected areas. During kharif 2007 to kharif 2010, about 81 lakh farmers were covered under the pilot scheme.

Coconut Palm Insurance Scheme (CPIS)

Since 2009-10, the CPIS is being implemented on pilot basis in selected areas of Andhra Pradesh, Goa, Karnataka, Kerala, Maharashtra, Orissa, Tamil Nadu, and West Bengal. The scheme is administered by the Coconut Development Board (CDB) through the AIC. As on 30 July 2010, 14.33 lakh palms of about 27,023 farmers were covered under the scheme.

Agricultural Marketing

Most of the States and Union Territories have enacted the Agriculture Produce Marketing Committee (APMC) Act to provide for regulation of agricultural produce markets. As on 31 March 2010, there were 7,157 regulated markets in the country. Besides, there are 21,221 rural periodical markets, about 15 per cent of which function under the ambit of regulation. The advent of regulated markets has helped mitigate the market handicaps of producers/sellers at wholesale assembling level. Internet connectivity is being provided to important agricultural markets in the country to establish a nationwide information network for speedy collection of prices and market-related information.

The Agricultural Marketing Information Network (AGMARKNET) portal provides wholesale prices of 300 commodities and about 2000 varieties from more than 1900 markets. However, rural periodic markets in general and tribal markets in particular have remained outside the ambit of the APMC Act. Other major initiatives include setting up of terminal market complexes (TMC) for fruits, vegetables, and other perishables in important urban centres in those states which provide for market reforms as per the Model Act. These markets will provide state-of-the-art infrastructure facilities for electronic auction, cold chain and logistics, and operate through primary collection centres conveniently located in producing areas to allow easy access to farmers.

Extension Services

A scheme called Support to State Extension Programmes for Extension Reforms was launched in 2005-06, with the aim of making the extension system farmer driven and farmer accountable. For this purpose, new institutional arrangements are being made for technology dissemination in the form of an Agricultural Technology Management Agency (ATMA) at district level to operationalize the extension reforms. It will involve the active participation of farmers/farmer groups, non-government organizations (NGOs), Krishi Vigyan Kendras, Panchayati Raj Institutions (PRIs) and other stakeholders operating at district level and below. Up to October 2010, over 590 district-level ATMAs were established. Gender concerns are being mainstreamed by mandating that 30 per cent of resources on programmes and activities are allocated for women farmers and extension functionaries.

The Mass Media Support to Agriculture Scheme focuses on use of Doordarshan infrastructure for providing agriculture-related information and knowledge to the farming community. The mass media initiative includes the use of 96 All India Radio FM transmitters to broadcast 30-minute area-specific agricultural programmes six days a week. With a view to creating awareness about assistance available under various schemes, a 'Focused Publicity Campaign' was launched during 2010-11. Under this campaign, publicity through newspapers as well as electronic media was carried out.

The Kisan Call Centre scheme, launched in 2004, provides agricultural information to the farming community through toll-free telephone lines. A country-wide common 11-digit number—1800-180-1551—has been allocated for these Call Centres. Replies to the queries of the farming community are provided in 22 local languages. Calls are attended to from 6.00 am to 10.00 pm on all seven days of the week.

The Agri-clinic and Agri-business Centres Scheme, launched in 2002, provides extension services to farmers on payment basis through setting up of economically viable self-employment ventures. Selected trainees are provided agri-preneurship training. NABARD monitors the credit support to Agri-Clinics through commercial banks. Provision of credit-linked back-ended subsidy at 33 per cent of the capital cost of the project funded through bank loan as well as full interest subsidy for the first two years on the bank credit has been approved under the scheme. From the inception of the scheme 22,158 unemployed agriculture graduates have been trained up to September 2010.

In addition to the above, agri fairs are promoted/organized at national, state, district, and block levels. Information dissemination through agri fairs/exhibitions is an excellent mechanism for showcasing latest technological advancements and dissemination of information to the farming community and also promoting business opportunities in agriculture and allied sectors.

Food Subsidy

The twin objectives of the food security system are provision of minimum nutritional support to the poor through subsidized foodgrains and ensuing price stability in different states. The food subsidy is given by the government to fulfil its obligation towards distributive justice. The issue price of wheat and rice has been kept unchanged since 1 July 2002, although the economic cost of these commodities has continuously gone up. Therefore, the food subsidy bill has increased substantially in the past few years. This adds to the budget deficit and consequently inflation.

TPDS Allocation

The government is providing large and growing amounts of subsidy on foodgrains for distribution under the Targeted Public Distribution System (TPDS), other nutrition-based welfare schemes, and open market operations. Allocations of foodgrains for the BPL and Antyodaya Anna Yojana (AAY) categories are made at 35 kg per family per month for all accepted 6.52 crore BPL (including 2.43 crore AAY) families in the country as per 1993-94 poverty estimates of the Planning Commission and March 2000 population estimates of the Registrar General of India (RGI). For the APL category, allocations to different States/UTs are made depending upon the availability of stocks of foodgrains in the central pool and past off-take by the states. The allocation for the APL category was temporarily increased from 10 kg to 15 kg per family per month from August 2010 for six months. Accordingly, these allocations ranged between 15 kg and 35 kg per family per month.

Wheat and rice are issued by the Central Government at uniform CIPs to States and Union Territories for distribution under the TPDS. The difference between wholesale prices of wheat and rice in the open market and the CIPs at which food-grains are issued to cardholders has widened in the last five years due to non-revision of the latter, as a result of which off-take under the TPDS, particularly by APL families has gone up substantially. During 2010-11, the government released a quantity of 470.80 lakh tonnes under the TPDS covering AAY, BPL and APL families. In addition, 5.90 lakh tonnes of foodgrains were released to states as calamity relief, etc. Further, special ad hoc allocation of 30.66 lakh tonnes of foodgrains was made to States/UTs in May 2010 for all accepted numbers of BPL/AAY/APL families in the country. The issue price of this allocation was ₹ 8.45 per kg for wheat and ₹ 11.85 per kg for rice. A total quantity of 25.00 lakh tonnes was allocated as special ad hoc/additional allocation for BPL families at BPL prices to all States/UTs in September 2010 for distribution over next six months. Further, during 2010-11, an allocation of 47.55 lakh tonnes of foodgrains had been made till November 2010 for other welfare schemes such as the Mid-day Meal Scheme, Integrated Child Development Services (ICDS), Welfare Institutions, and the Emergency Feeding Programme.

Open Market Sale Scheme (Domestic)

The Food Corporation of India (FCI) on behalf of the Government of India has been undertaking sale of wheat and rice at pre-determined prices in the open market from time to time to enhance the supply so as to have a moderating influence on open market prices. The disposal of rice and wheat under the Open Market Sale Scheme (Domestic) (OMSS [D]) is in addition to maintaining buffer stocks and providing foodgrain stocks to meet the requirement of the TPDS and other welfare schemes.

Allocation for Social Sector Schemes

India's social sector spending has progressively been stepped up and it stood at 37 per cent of the total plan outlay in 2010-11. The government is continuously providing higher budgetary allocations for projects in rural areas like rural development, education, medical and public health, family welfare, water supply and sanitation, housing, urban development, and welfare of Scheduled Castes (SCs) and Scheduled Tribes (STs), and Other Backward Classes (OBCs).

This is reflected in the fact that the share of Central Government expenditure on social services including rural development in total expenditure (Plan and Non-Plan) has increased from 13.75 per cent in 2005-06 to 19.27 per cent in 2010-11 (Budget Estimates). There was also a 24 per cent rise in education spending to 520 billion rupees (11.5 billion dollars) and a 20 per cent rise in funds for health to 267 billion rupees. However, mere focus on *aam aadmi* and putting aside higher funds for flagship programmes is not enough. The increasing central allocation of funds for social sector schemes would not yield the desired results unless they are implemented properly.

Countering Inflation Through Pro-Active Measures

President Pratibha Devisingh Patil, in her address to the Budget session of the Parliament on Feb. 21, 2011 said that the government's foremost priority in 2011-12 will be to combat inflation, and in particular, to protect the common man from the impact of rising food prices. Some of the pro-active measures taken by the government to counter the ill-effects of inflation were cited by her. Pulses are supplied at subsidized prices through the public distribution system. Public sector units have been directed to open more retail outlets for selling vegetables to individual consumers. The issue prices for rice and wheat for the public distribution system have not been changed for the last eight years, i.e. since 2003.

As a long-term measure, the government is trying to increase productivity and production by providing huge incentives to farmers. The government has raised the minimum support price for paddy from 550 to 1,000 per quintal and that of wheat from 630 to 1,100 per quintal over a six year period. The support price for sugarcane has also been increased. Incentives are also given through the supply of fertilizers at subsidized prices. Further, around 35,000 crore has been invested in agriculture under a scheme called the Rashtriya Krishi Vikas Yojana. Credit flows to agriculture have reached record levels. Nearly one crore hectares have been brought under assured irrigation since 2005-06. Water conservation measures have been taken up on a war footing under the

Mahatma Gandhi National Rural Employment Guarantee Act. Moreover, the new nutrient based system is likely to enhance the rational use of fertilisers.

The government is in the process of introducing a long-awaited food security bill that guarantees subsidised food for low-income families. The success of the programme, however, hinges critically on the commitment of the states to implementing reforms in the public distribution system. Although the National Food Security Mission has taken the Green Revolution to Eastern India, many parts are yet to see such a revolution. The government has not only to commit but also ensure that farmers get remunerative prices for their produce.

PRESENT AND FUTURE CHALLENGES

Agricultural Sector

Since the mid-sixties, India has made great strides towards increasing production of foodgrains like rice and wheat as well as milk, fruits, and vegetables. Yet the rising demand for food items and relatively slower supply response in many commodities result in frequent spikes in food inflation. It seems that the technological breakthrough achieved due to Green Revolution in the 1960s is gradually waning and the need for a second Green Revolution is being experienced more than ever before.

For ensuring national food security, nutritional security, and for sustaining high levels of growth, increasing agriculture production and productivity is a necessary condition. But this remains a challenge due to very little increase in cultivable area and marginal growth in yields of many crops during 2000-10. The stagnating productivity levels in agriculture need to be addressed through concerted and focused efforts. The critical levels of productivity needed can be achieved through a holistic approach, which involves simultaneous working on agricultural research, development, dissemination of technology, and provision of agricultural inputs such as quality seed, fertilizers, pesticides, and irrigation. Moreover, to ensure optimum results, effective coordination and monitoring of the ongoing agriculture and allied sector programmes is required.

Since the government embraced the New Economic Policy, capital investment in agriculture as a percentage of the GDP has been stagnating, although the capital expenditure in agriculture as a percentage of the GDP in agriculture has shown some improvement in the Eleventh Five Year Plan. Another point of concern is the fact that the agriculture sector GDP has itself stagnated during 2007-08 to 2009-10. Hence, the real challenge for the government in agriculture sector is to enhance capital investment in the sector both by public and private sector in a sustained way.

Any irregular or untimely monsoon leads to rise in prices of foodgrains because 60 per cent of India's net sown area is still rainfed. It is high time that the government gives priority to a targeted development of rainfed areas in the country.

The successful experience of cooperatives in the milk sector in managing the supply chain and providing remunerative prices to the producers has not been emulated in the case of agricultural products. For this to become a reality, it is essential that the farmers are given incentives to produce more. This can be done by enhancing the returns that the farmers get on their production. They should be able to realise the market price for their produce. In order to link farmers to the market, efficient supply chains need to be set up so that adequate supplies of essential items at reasonable prices are ensured while adequately compensating the producers.

The demand for processed food is likely to increase with the rise in income and population. The present level of secondary food processing in India is very low compared to many western countries. The focus in food management needs to be shifted from cereals like rice and wheat to processed food. It is necessary to cater to this changing demand and at the same time enhance the income of farmers. Hence, the government has to encourage investment in food processing, cold chains, handling, and packaging of processed food.

A major concern is the declining per capita availability of foodgrains. The government has to frame strategies not only to increase the per capita availability of foodgrains but also to ensure that right quantities of food items are there in the food basket of a common man. Also required is a thrust on horticulture products for enhancing per capita availability of food items. Otherwise, nutritional security will be in jeopardy.

Another priority of the government should be to address infrastructure requirements in the agriculture sector, especially storage, communication, roads, and markets. For the growth of agriculture sector, Public Private Partnership models can be of help in ensuring faster development of these vital requirements.

There is pressure on products from the livestock sector too due to a higher growth rate of the economy and rising levels of income. The upward pressure in the prices of many items such as meat, milk, and poultry add to the wholesale food price inflation. It becomes imperative for the government to prepare a long-term strategy to increase the production of these items. Such steps would also supplement the livelihood options of the rural populace and thus enhance rural income.

A substantial increase in the MSPs of various crops is considered necessary for incentivizing farmers to increase production and productivity. But this, in turn, increases the floor price for the produce which has the potential of increasing the prices. Hence, the challenge is to address the welfare of the agricultural producers and of the consumers simultaneously. Also, it is doubtful whether the increases in MSP actually benefit small and marginal farmers, as a large number of them do not have a direct access to agri-market.

To increase its buffer stock and strategic reserve of wheat and rice, the government has to go for more procurement which involves a huge cost. This cost is met through budgetary sources in the form of food subsidy which leads to fiscal stress. Hence, urgent attention is needed to address the issue of efficient food stocks management and offloading of stocks in time.

All procurement is waste unless the grains are properly conserved. For the purpose, laws need to be enacted to lay ecological foundations for climate resilient agriculture, management of agricultural waste, building carbon sequestration of soil and overall natural resource management. Thus, substantial investments are necessary to not only increase farm productivity and create adequate infrastructure for transport, storage and distribution of agricultural produce, but also to address environmental concerns. These investments, however, should not be made in a manner that can take inflation haywire.

Anti-Poverty Programmes

The government has definitely undertaken a large increase in budgetary allocations for anti-poverty programmes and employment generation schemes. But in order to facilitate the effective implementation of these programmes, the delivery mechanism needs to be bolstered and streamlined. The government has to ensure that allocations result in outputs and outcomes.

The widening gap between the rich and the poor is another worrisome trend. Actually, the benefits of economic growth are not getting equally distributed between different sectors, regions and income groups. Improving the country's business environment may enable the country to not only achieve but even sustain a 10 per cent GDP growth rate. But that would only worsen the social situation if it results in widening of the gap between the rich and the poor.

Education

In India, a large number of children such as the street children, destitute children, and children of sex workers do not have access to quality education. It is because there are no formal schemes to bring them into the mainstream.

Secondly, the skills and motivation of teachers is an area of concern which needs to be improved. Thirdly, enrolling and retaining children in schools, especially girls, working children of urban poor and children with special needs is important. Hence, it is important to understand the quantitative requirements of the education sector concerning issues of enrolment, school infrastructure, and teacher availability, etc.

There has to be absolutely no compromise with respect to enrolment and retention of children in schools. For this to happen, however, there has to be 100 per cent literacy and 100 per cent enrolment at primary, secondary and technical levels. This acquires supreme importance due to the fact that economic development of a country is built around educational development. This means that the state has to increase its financial commitments towards education, which are already substantial.

Notes

1. India's Fiscal Deficit is the Highest in the World, TheIndiaStreet, May 26, 2008, by Bharat Ratna.
2. Dr. Ashima Goyal, Professor at Indira Gandhi Institute of Development Research.
3. http://www.unescap.org/survey2008/notes/india.asp
4. http://www.norrag.org/issues/article/1302/en/india-ranked-at-105-in-the-education-for-all-development-index.html?PHPSESSID=a02be85225d91552f39b23b1370009ee
5. Reports of the DISE—District Information System for Education, published by the National University of Educational Planning and Administration, New Delhi in 2009 and 2010.
6. http://timesofindia.indiatimes.com/home/union-budget-2011/Social-sector-allocation-up-by-17/articleshow/7594359.cms
7. http://india.gov.in/sectors/rural/swarna_jayanti.php

Table A.1: India's Global Position in Human Development 2010

Country	HDI 2010	GNI per capita (PPP2008 US $) 2010	Life Expectancy at birth(yrs) 2010	Mean Yrs of Schooling 2010	Expected Yrs of Schooling 2010*
Norway	0.938(1)	58,810	81.0	12.6	17.3
Australia	0.937(2)	38,692	81.9	12.0	20.5
Poland	0.795 (41)	17,803	76	10.0	15.2
Malaysia	0.744 (57)	13,927	74.7	9.5	12.5
Russia	0.719 (65)	15,258	67.2	8.8	14.1
Brazil	0.699 (73)	10,607	72.9	7.2	13.8
Turkey	0.679 (83)	13,359	72.2	6.5	11.8
China	0.663 (89)	7258	73.5	7.5	11.4
Sri Lanka	0.658 (91)	4486	74.4	8.2	12.0
Thailand	0.654 (92)	8001	69.3	6.6	13.5
Philippines	0.638 (97)	4002	72.3	8.7	11.5
Egypt	0.620 (101)	5889	70.5	6.5	11.0
Indonesia	0.600 (108)	3957	71.5	5.7	12.7
South Africa	0.597 (110)	9812	52.0	8.2	13.4
Vietnam	0.572 (113)	2995	74.9	5.5	10.4
India	0.519 (119)	3337	64.4	4.4	10.3
Pakistan	0.490(125)	2678	67.2	4.9	6.8
Kenya	0.470(128)	1,628	55.6	7.0	9.6
Bangladesh	0.469(129)	1587	66.9	4.8	8.1
World	0.624	10,631	69.3	7.4	12.3

Source: HDR 2010

Note: * Refers to an earlier year than specified.

Figures in parentheses in Column 2 give ranking among 169 countries.

Table A.2: Trends in Social Services Expenditure by General Government (Central and State Governments combined)

(₹ crore)

Items	2005-06 (Actual)	2006-07 (Actual)	2007-08 (Actual)	2008-09 (Actual)	2009-10 (RE)	2010-11 (BE)
Total Expenditure	9,59,855	11,09,174	13,16,246	15,95,110	19,09,380	20,71,147
	2,02,672	2,39,340	2,94,584	3,80,269	4,76,351	5,22,492
Expenditure on Social Services of which:						
(i) Education	96,365	1,14,744	1,29,366	1,61,360	2,04,986	2,35,035
(ii) Health	45,428	52,126	63,226	73,898	90,700	99,738
(iii) Others	60,879	72,470	1,01,992	1,45,011	1,80,665	1,87,719
As Per Cent of GDP						
Total Expenditure	25.99	25.83	26.40	28.57	29.15	26.29
Expenditure on Social Services of which:	5.49	5.57	5.91	6.81	7.27	6.63
(i) Education	2.61	2.67	2.59	2.89	3.13	2.98
(ii) Health	1.23	1.21	1.27	1.32	1.38	1.27
(iii) Others	1.65	1.69	2.05	2.60	2.76	2.38
As Per Cent of Total Expenditure						
Expenditure on Social Services of which:	21.1	21.6	22.4	23.8	24.9	25.2
(i) Education	10.0	10.3	9.8	10.1	10.7	11.3
(ii) Health	4.7	4.7	4.8	4.6	4.8	4.8
(iii) Others	6.3	6.5	7.7	9.1	9.5	9.1
As Per Cent of Social Services Expenditure						
(i) Education	47.5	47.9	43.9	42.4	43.0	45.0
(ii) Health	22.4	21.8	21.5	19.4	19.0	19.1
(iii) Others	30.0	30.3	34.6	38.1	37.9	35.9

Source: RBI as obtained from Budget Documents of Union and State Governments.

BE: budget estimates; RE: revised estimates.

8

Inflation-Growth Trade-off

Inflation-growth trade-off is always an interesting empirical question for the economists and the policymakers. Some of the important questions relating to the link between inflation and growth are: (a) How much inflation can an economy tolerate? (b) After what level of inflation does growth start to decline? (c) Is there a robust negative relationship between inflation and growth? (d) Is there a kink in the relationship such that at very low levels of inflation the relationship is positive, but at higher levels of inflation the relationship is negative? and (e) Does inflation have to reach some minimum threshold before the growth effects become serious?

A.W. Phillips was the first to propose that there may be a trade-off between inflation and real economic performance, which was encapsulated in the so-called Phillips curve. The original Phillips curve was an empirical relationship between the rate of change of money wages and unemployment in Britain from 1861 to 1957.[1] This concept was taken up and propagated by economists in other countries all over the world. Therefore, through the 1960s and early 1970s, it was widely believed that there existed a permanent and stable negative trade-off between inflation and unemployment, which could be exploited for policy purposes. In such case, either monetary or fiscal policy will reduce unemployment permanently, but only at the cost of a permanently higher inflation rates, or vice versa. Following this concept, each society will have to assess the relative costs of inflation and unemployment and choose some optimal mix of the two.

A linear version of the price-inflation Phillips curve can be given by

$$p = a(\bar{u} - u_i); \qquad a > 0 \qquad \text{... (1)}$$

where,

p = price-inflation,
a = constant,
$\bar{u}$ = natural rate of unemployment, and
u_i = unemployment rate.

The natural rate of unemployment is the level of unemployment that would exist when the economy is also growing at its natural rate. It implies that an economy can experience a maximum rate of growth in any period of time based on technology, the skill of the labour force, resources, etc. This determines the natural rate of economic growth and associated with this is a natural rate of unemployment, which constitutes the "full employment". This is not the zero unemployment, but the minimum unemployment rate attainable,

Fig. 8.1: Linear version of Price-inflation Phillips Curve

given the current state of technology and development, without putting pressure on the labour market. The Phillips curve can be represented diagrammatically as shown in Fig. 8.1.

The above figure shows that the unemployment rate can be held down permanently even below the natural rate (e.g. u_1), as long as the inflation rate is high enough. However, the Phillips curve approach is criticized on the following two main grounds:

(a) The idea of Phillips curve is in basic conflict with the main presumptions of classical and neoclassical economics, i.e. the economic decisions should be based on real (adjusted inflation) magnitudes rather than on nominal magnitudes.

(b) In particular, during the 1970s, the idea of a Phillips curve trade-off seemed to be actively misleading due to the occurrence of stagflation in the real world data during that decade. There were cases in which both inflation and unemployment increased in various jurisdictions.

One point worth mentioning here is that the apparent empirical failures of the Phillips curve came well after the basic theoretical challenge. This led to the decline in the belief in permanent trade-off between inflation and unemployment. It was argued that the short-run or expectations-augmented Phillips curve could shift bodily whenever there was a change in inflationary expectations. Therefore, in the mainstream macroeconomic models of the later 20th century and up to the present day, any postulated trade-off between inflation and unemployment was held explicitly to be short-term. In the long run, any rate of inflation at all was thought compatible with the natural rate of unemployment, which later came to be called the non-accelerating inflation rate of unemployment. The long-run Phillips curve was assumed to be vertical. The expectations-augmented version of the Phillips curve can be illustrated as

$$p = a(\bar{u} - u_i) + p^e \qquad \text{... (2)}$$

where p^e is the expected inflation.

Equation (1) shows that inflation will increase not only whenever unemployment falls below the natural rate, but also due to increase in inflation expectations. According to Equation (1), whenever actual and expected inflation are equal, unemployment will be at the natural rate, i.e. when $p = p^e$, we have $\bar{u} = u_i$. Thus, there is no long-run trade-off between actual inflation and unemployment, only a temporary, or short-run, trade-off that only exists when actual and expected inflation are not equal. This is because in the short-run an increase in inflation will lead to a lasting reduction in unemployment which can be shown by a movement along the short-run Phillips curve (SRPC). However, over time, the economy cannot sustain this level of economic activity, which is reflected by a shift of the short-run Phillips curve. In the long-run, output goes back to its natural level, but with a higher rate of inflation. Figure 8.2 shows the set of expectations-augmented Phillips curve, and the way they shift over time.

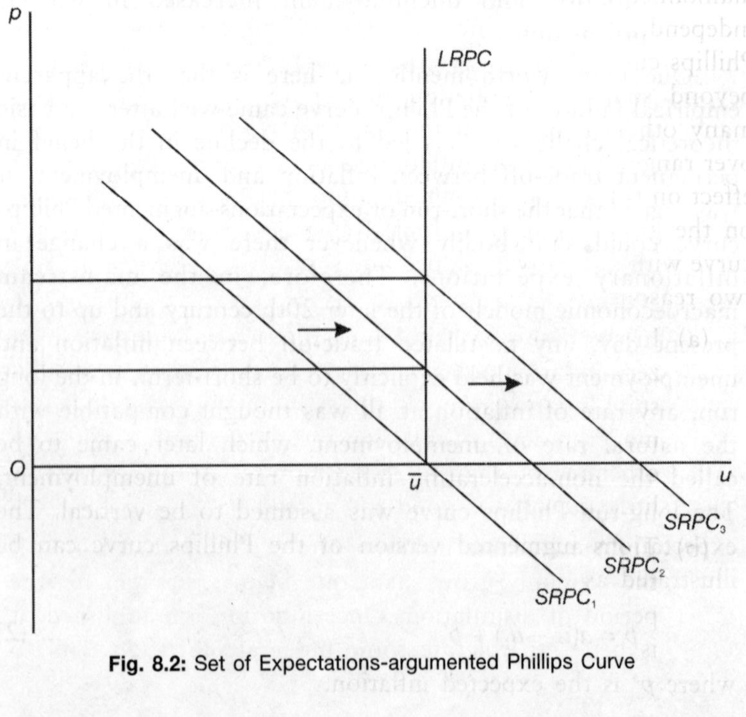

Fig. 8.2: Set of Expectations-argumented Phillips Curve

There must be some relationship between growth relative to trend and the unemployment gap along the lines of the so-called Okun's Law[2] which states that there must be some quantitative relationship between changes in the growth rate of the economy and the unemployment rate. For example, for the advanced industrialised countries, for the unemployment rate to fall by 1 percentage point, the growth rate would have to increase by about 2.5 percentage points. Thus, whatever the exact number is, there will be a relationship between the unemployment and growth of the form:

$$u_i - \bar{u} = (b/a)(\bar{y} - y); \qquad b>0 \qquad \ldots (3)$$

where, $\bar{y}$ is the natural rate of GDP growth.

Many economists believed that lower rates of inflation could be obtained only by reducing output. In the late 1960s, Milton Friedman and Edmund Phelps demonstrated that, if economic agents are rational, the trade-off could not be maintained indefinitely, i.e. the steady-state level of output is independent of the rate of inflation, so that the long-run Phillips curve (LRPC) is vertical. Most economists believe that beyond some rate, inflation does reduce output. However, many others believe that the long-run relationship is vertical over range of moderate inflation. If inflation has no permanent effect on the level of output, it cannot have a permanent effect on the growth rate of output. Replacing the vertical Phillips curve with a negatively sloped one is not reasonable for at least two reasons:

(a) In the case of vertical long-run relationship, pursuing zero inflation policy is not reasonable. Any low steady-state inflation rate will do as well. Consequently, some moderate level of inflation rate is acceptable, if for no other reason than to appease those who believe that a little inflation is good for growth.

(b) The steady-state inflation rate can be reduced only if the economy grows at a rate below potential for the period of disinflation. Once inflation is established, it is better to tolerate some moderate inflation than to bear the economic costs of reducing the inflation rate to zero.

There has been an enduring debate between structuralists and monetarists. According to structuralists, inflation is essential for economic growth, whereas the monetarists see inflation as detrimental to economic progress. This debate has two aspects: (a) the nature of the relationship if one exists, and (b) the direction of causality. Friedman has summarised the inconclusive nature of the relationship between inflation and economic growth as, "Historically, all possible combinations have occurred: inflation with and without development, no inflation with and without development".[3]

Theoretical models such as Orphanides and Solow, in the money and growth literature analyse the impact of inflation on growth focusing on the effects of inflation on the steady-state equilibrium of capital per capita and ouput. There are three possible results regarding the impact of inflation on output and growth: (a) none, (b) positive, and (c) negative. The first impact was established by Sidrauski who showed that money is neutral and superneutral in an optimal control framework considering real money balances in the utility function. Tobin assumed money as substitute to capital and established the positive impact of inflation on growth, his result being known as the Tobin effect. Anti-Tobin effect, which shows the negative impact of inflation on growth, is associated mainly with cash in advance models which consider money as complementary to capital.

To examine the extent to which economic growth is related to inflation and vice versa, we shall use three models: (a) cointegration and error correction model, (b) an endogenous growth model, and (c) generalised autoregressive conditionally heteroskedastic (GARCH) model.

Cointegration and Error Correction Model

With the help of cointegration and error correction model, it is possible to examine the short-run and long-run relationships between two variables—growth and inflation. The Engle-Granger two steps cointegration procedure is used to test the presence of cointegration between the two variables. If both the time series variables are integrated of the same order then it is possible to proceed with the estimation of the following cointegration regression.

$$y_t = \alpha_{11} + \beta_{11} p_t + \mu_t \qquad \dots (4)$$

$$p_t = \alpha_{21} + \beta_{21} y_t + \eta_t \qquad \dots (5)$$

where,

y_t = economic growth rate at time t,
p_t = inflation rate at time t,
α = intercept coefficient,
β = slope coefficient, and
μ_t, η_t = random error terms.

Residuals μ_t and η_t measure the extent to which y_t and p_t are out of equilibrium. If μ_t and η_t are integrated of order zero, I(0), then y_t and p_t are cointegrated and not expected to remain apart in the long-run. If cointegration exists, then information on one variable can be used to predict the other, and there can be a long-run or equilibrium relationship between two series in a bivariate relationship only if they are stationary or if each series is at least integrated of the same order.[4] Thus, if two series are integrated of the same order, I(d) for d = 0, 1, 2, ... then the two series are said to be cointegrated and the regression on the same levels of the two variables is meaningful. Now our first task is to check for the existence of stationary property in the series for growth rate (y) and inflation rate (p).

We shall use Dickey and Fuller (DF) test[5] first and then the ADF test[6] with and without a time trend. The latter allows for higher autocorrelation in residuals.

$$\Delta X_t = \gamma_1 + \delta_1 X_{t-1} + \sum_{i=1}^{n} \omega_1 X_{t-i} + \varepsilon_{1t} \qquad \dots (6)$$

It has been found that the ADF tests are unable to discriminate well between non-stationary and stationary series with a high degree of autoregression. Inflation which is highly autocorrelated, is in fact stationary whereas the ADF tests show that it is non-stationary. The ADF tests may also incorrectly indicate that the inflation series contain a unit root when there is a structural break in the series.[7] Therefore, Phillips-Perron (PP) test is applied.[8] The PP test is better than the ADF tests because it gives robust estimates when the series has serial correlation and time-dependent heteroskedasticity, and there is a structural break. For the PP test we have to estimate the equation of the form:

$$\Delta X_t = \tau + \delta_2 X_{t-1} + \Phi_{(t-T/2)} + \sum_{i-1}^{m} \Phi_i \Delta X_{t-I} + \varepsilon_{2t} \qquad \text{... (7)}$$

In Equations (6) and (7), Δ is the first difference operator and ε_{1t} and ε_{2t} are covariance stationary random error terms. The lag length n in Equation (6) is determined by Akaike's information criteria[9] to ensure serially uncorrelated residuals and m (for PP test) is decided according to Newley-West's[10] suggestions.

The null hypothesis of non-stationarity is tested using the t-statistic with critical values calculated by MacKinnon. The null hypothesis that y_t and p_t are non-stationary time series is rejected if δ_1 and δ_2 are less than zero and statistically significant for each. Given the inherent weakness of the unit root test to distinguish between the null and alternative hypotheses, both DF and ADF tests are applied following Engle and Granger (1987) and Granger (1986), and subsequently supplemented by the PP test following West (1988) and Culver and Papell (1997). These tests are carried out for both variables by replacing X_t with y_t and p_t in Equations (6) (for the DF-ADF tests) and (7) (for the PP test). DF-ADF-PP unit root tests are also applied for residuals μ_t and η_t [from Equations (4) and (5)] by respecifying Equations (6) and (7) in terms of μ_t and η_t instead of X_t. When μ_t and η_t are found to be integrated of order zero then it can be concluded that these two series are cointegrated. If the hypothesis of no integration is rejected, a stable long-run relationship exists between economic growth and inflation. According to Engle and Granger, when y_t and p_t are found to be cointegrated then there must exist an associated error correction mechanism that may take the following form:

$$\Delta y_t = \Phi_{10} + \sum_{j=0}^{s} \Phi_{11}\, \Delta p_{t-j} + \sum_{i=1}^{q} \Phi_{12}\, \Delta y_{t-i} + \omega_1 \mu_{t-1} + \varepsilon_{3t} \quad \dots (8)$$

$$\Delta p_t = \Phi_{20} + \sum_{j=0}^{s} \Phi_{21}\, \Delta y_{t-j} + \sum_{i=1}^{q} \Phi_{22} \Delta p_{t-i} + \omega_2 \eta_{t-1} + \varepsilon_{4t} \quad \dots (9)$$

where,

Δ = first difference operator,

μ_{t-1}, η_{t-1} = error correction terms,

s, q = number of lag lengths, and

ε_{3t}, ε_{4t} = random disturbance terms.

In Equations (8) and (9), i begins at one and j begins at zero in order for the series to be related within a structural error correction model.[11] The error correction terms μ_{t-1} and η_{t-1}, which are the residual series of the cointegrating vector normalised for y_t and p_t, measure deviations of the series from the long-run equilibrium relations. For the series to converge to the long-run equilibrium relation, $\omega_1 \geq 0$ and $\omega_2 \leq 1$ must hold. However, cointegration implies that not all ω_1 and ω_2 should be zero.

From the above discussion it can be concluded that inflation is harmful rather than helpful to growth, since higher inflation may trigger inflationary spirals beyond a safe level as implied by larger inflation elasticities. As Bruno puts it, "chronic inflation tends to resemble smoking; once you get the habit, it is very difficult to escape a worsening addiction".

The most important preconditions for sustained growth are necessary infrastructure and macroeconomic stability. Therefore, one of the most important avenues through which inflation can affect growth is the effect of inflation on investment. Low or moderate inflation is an indicator of macroeconomic stability and creates an environment conducive for investment. The cross-country evidence indicates a negative relationship between inflation and long-term growth. Countries with low or moderate rates of inflation have higher growth rates over the long-term, compared with countries with high inflation rates. However, low inflation does not constitute a sufficient condition for growth. Evidence from investment behaviour in private manufacturing suggests that an increase in the rate of inflation has a negative impact on private investment in manufacturing. The regression for private investment in agriculture points towards complementarities between public and private investment. Taking economy-wide linkages into account, the analysis suggests that higher growth can be achieved by controlling inflation and raising public investment. To promote growth and keep inflation low, the government needs to control budget deficits. While simulations indicate that this can be achieved by switching public expenditure from consumption to investment, this may be a difficult policy to pursue, especially in a developing country with a multiparty democracy. Using deficit-financed public investment, it will be more realistic to choose tolerable levels of inflation rate and achieve the maximum possible growth.

Endogenous Growth Model of Trade-off

Let us consider an endogenous growth model with transitional dynamics. In this model, allocation of resources matters for growth, and money growth and inflation can affect the allocation of resources. We consider the accumulation of human capital as externality. One of the crucial assumptions of this model is that productivity growth depends on the level of employment, so that exogenous changes that affect the allocation of time between leisure and work will affect the rate of growth. We also assume that individual agents do not take into account the effects of their actions on productivity growth. However, changes in government policy, especially changes in rates of distortionary taxation, including the inflation tax, can affect the economy's growth rate. We shall discuss the objectives and constraints facing households, firms, and the government, and describe the productivity growth and dynamic maximisation problem of the households.

Households

Intertemporal utility function of the household is given by

$$u = \sum_{i=0}^{\infty} \beta_i \, u_t(c_{t+i}, l_{t+i}) \qquad \text{... (10)}$$

where,

β_i = subjective discount rate,

c_t = household's consumption expenditure at time t, and

l_t = leisure.

Period utility function of the household is given by

$$u_t(c_t, l_t) = \ln c_t + \frac{\phi}{(1-\gamma)} \cdot l_t^{(1-\gamma)} \qquad \text{... (11)}$$

The maximisation problem is subject to the sequence of budget constraints

$$(1-\tau^n_{t+i}) W_{t+i} \, n_{t+i} + (1-\tau^k_{t+i}) R_{t+i} \, k_{t+i} + \tau^k_{t+i} \, \delta k_{t+i}$$

$$+ \frac{m_{t+i}}{P_{t+i}} + \chi_{t+i} = (1+\tau^c_{t+i}) c_{t+i} + i_{t+i} + \frac{m_{t+i+1}}{P_{t+i}} + T_{t+i} + \psi_{t+i} \qquad \text{... (12)}$$

where,

W_{t+i} = real wage rate,

R_{t+i} = real rental rate of capital,

n_{t+i} = number of hours worked by the household,

k_{t+i} = household's holdings of capital at time $t + i$,

δ = constant rate of depreciation of capital,

m_{t+i} = household's holdings of nominal money balances,

P_{t+i} = price level,

i_{t+i} = household's investment expenditure,

T_{t+i} = lump-sum taxes,

τ^n_{t+i} = proportional tax rates on labour income,

τ^k_{t+i} = proportional tax rates on income from renting capital to firms,

τ^c_{t+i} = proportional tax rates on consumption,

χ_{t+i} = real value of monetary balances transferred to households through the costless deposit expansion mechanism, and

ψ_{t+i} = pecuniary transactions costs.

The transactions costs at time t are given by

$$\psi_t = a_0 \left\{\left(1+\tau^c_t\right)c_t\right\}^{a_1} \left(\frac{m_t}{P_t}\right)^{(1-a_1)} ;$$

$$a_0 > 0 \text{ and } a_1 > 1 \qquad \text{... (13)}$$

Increasing real money balances lead to a reduction in real pecuniary transactions costs and this transactions cost specification leads to a standard long-run demand for money function and that the standard cash-in-advance constraint emerges as a_1 approaches infinity. The maximisation is also subjected to:

The law of motion for the household's capital stock,

$$k_{t+i+1} = (1-\delta)k_{t+i} + i_{t+i} \qquad \text{... (14)}$$

and to the total time endowment of the household which has been normalised to equal 1 as

$$n_{t+i} + l_{t+i} = 1 \qquad \text{... (15)}$$

Firms

Households provide capital and labour to the firms. Aggregate production function of the firm at time t is given by

$$Y_t = Z_t\,(H_t\,N_t)^{\alpha}\,K_t^{(1-\alpha)} \qquad \text{... (16)}$$

where,

Y_t = output,

Z_t = level of technology,

H_t = level of human capital in the economy,

N_t = aggregate employment, and

K_t = aggregate capital stock.

Here, one point should be kept in mind that, when variables appear in both upper and lower case form, the lower-case versions indicate variables that are choice vriables or state variables from the individual household's point of view, and the upper case versions are their aggregate or per capita equivalents. The law of motion of the technology is given by

$$\ln(Z_t) = \rho \ln(Z_{t-1}) + (1-\rho)\ln(\bar{Z}) + \varepsilon_{Zt};$$

$$\text{with } 0 < \rho < 1 \qquad \text{... (17)}$$

where,

$\bar{Z}$ = long-run average level of Z_t, and

ε_{Zt} = a shock to production technology.

Since the capital stock is held by the households and they rent it to firms, the profit maximisation problems of firms are static. Therefore, profit maximisation by competitive firms implies

$$W_t = \alpha Z_t H_t^{\alpha} N_t^{(\alpha-1)} K_t^{(1-\alpha)} \qquad \text{... (18)}$$

$$\text{and} \quad R_t = (1-\alpha) Z_t (H_t N_t)^{\alpha} K_t^{-\alpha} \qquad \text{... (19)}$$

Government

The government finances a stream of expenditures via distortionary taxation on labour income, capital income, and consumption via money creation and via lump-sum taxation and thus its behaviour is exogenous. The budget constraint of the government is

$$G_t = \tau_t^k (R_t - \delta) K_t + \tau_t^n N_t + \tau_t^c C_t + \frac{MB_{t+1} - MB_t}{P_t} + T_t \qquad \text{... (20)}$$

where MB_t is the monetary base at time t.

Since in this model we have considered infinite horizons, lump-sum taxation has the same effect as deficit financing, holding constant all distortionary tax rates and inflation, so we do not model debt financing explicitly. The law of motion for the monetary base is given by

$$MB_{t+1} - MB_t = \mu_t MB_t \quad \text{... (21)}$$

where μ_t is the net rate of growth of the base money supply.

Government spending, tax rates, and the rate of growth of the money supply are determined by a multivariate stochastic process, which is also allowed to depend on the level of technology. Given the rate of creation of money and the rates of taxation on capital income, labour income, and consumption, the level of lump-sum taxes is determined residually to ensure that the government budget is balanced in each period. This assumption implies that a change in the inflation tax rate has no impact on other marginal tax rates in the model. Money balances are related to the base money supply as

$$M_t = \frac{MB_t}{rr} \quad \text{... (22)}$$

where rr is the constant ratio of base money to nominal money balances.

Equation (22) can be used to distinguish between the monetary aggregate relevant for measuring seigniorage revenues and the aggregate that is used to reduce transactions costs. The transfer of resources to private households via deposit creation is given by

$$\chi_t P_t = \left(M_{t+1} - M_t\right) - (MB_{t+1} - MB_t)$$

$$\text{or,} \quad \chi_t = (1 - rr)\frac{M_{t+1} - M_t}{M_t}\frac{M_t}{P_t}$$

$$\text{Therefore,} \quad \chi_t = (1 - rr)\mu_t \frac{M_t}{P_t} \quad \text{... (23)}$$

Growth in Productivity

In this model, we assume that the growth in productivity is a by-product of the production process, and arise from learning by doing. Neither households nor firms take into account this externality in their maximisation problems. The law of motion for the human capital is given by

$$H_{t+1} = (1 - \delta_h)H_t + \theta_0 H_t \ln(1 + N_t) \quad \text{... (24)}$$

Equation (24) represents a simplest possible set-up, in which the allocation of resources in general, and employment in our particualr model, matter for growth, and in which monetary policy may affect the economy's growth rate.

Trade-off between Growth and Inflation

In our model, the equilibrium solution for the growth and inflation depend on the model's state variables, and are of the form

$$\frac{P_t - P_{t-1}}{P_{t-1}} = \pi_t = \pi\left(Z_t, \tau_t^k, \tau_t^n, \tau_t^c, \tilde{G}_t, \mu_t, \tilde{K}_t\right) \quad \text{... (25)}$$

$$\theta_t = \theta\left(Z_t, \tau_t^k, \tau_t^n, \tau_t^c, \tilde{G}_t, \mu_t, \tilde{K}_t\right) \quad \text{... (26)}$$

The solutions for growth and inflation in the long-run are of the same form and depend on the long-run levels of the exogenous variables. From the empirical data it has been found that there is a very slight negative trade-off between inflation and growth induced by changes in the rate of monetary expansion.[12] An increase in the rate of monetray expansion acts as a tax on consumption via the transactions cost equation and in such situation agents substitute leisure for consumption, employment goes down in the steady-state, and so does the rate of growth, which depends directly on employment. The welfare of the representative household increases because of a reduction in monetary expansion (or a reduction in the inflation tax), which leads to an increase in steady-state growth.

Leaving the level of technology, changes in all the other exogenous variables of the model induce a sharp negative trade-off between growth and inflation, because changes in technology in the long-run leave employment unaffected and therefore, neither growth nor inflation depends on the level of technology in the long-run. Except technology, all the other exogenous variables lead to the same trade-off because there is a simple identity that links growth and inflation in the long-run if velocity is stationary. Since the normalised price level in the steady-state is constant, we have the following relation:

$$\frac{M'}{P'H'} = \frac{M}{PH}$$

Here, the prime symbol denotes next-period values, such that

$$\frac{M'}{M} = 1 + \mu = \frac{P'}{P} \cdot \frac{H'}{H}$$

or, $$\pi = \mu - (\theta - 1) \quad \text{... (26)}$$

Thus, from Equation (26) we find that in the steady-state, the inflation rate is just the difference between the rate of money growth and the net real rate of growth of the economy. For a constant rate of monetary expansion, for any exogenous variable x other than μ, we have

$$\frac{\partial \pi}{\partial x} = -\frac{\partial \theta}{\partial x} \quad \text{... (27)}$$

From Equation (27), we find that the trade-off has a slope of −1. In response to a change in the rate of monetary expansion, we get

$$\frac{\partial \pi}{\partial \mu} = 1 - \frac{\partial \theta}{\partial \mu} \quad \text{... (28)}$$

Since the value of $\partial \theta / \partial \mu$ is quite small, changes in monetary policy have a large positive impact on inflation and a small impact on growth. Here, we have made an assumption that the endogenous element of the government's budget constraint is the level of lump-sum taxation. If lump-sum taxation is not feasible and the government must adjust other marginal tax rates to satisfy its intertemporal budget constraint, monetary and fiscal policy are not independent, and the effects of a monetary policy change on growth could be stronger because of the induced effects on other tax rates.

This model has the following implications:

(a) Both growth and inflation are endogenous in the steady-state, and depend on underlying variables that affect the allocation of resources in the long-run. The signs of the coefficients in reduced-form Equations (24) and (25) show the conditional correlation between growth and inflation—that is to say, conditional on the cross-sectional variations of the determinants of inflation and growth. Permanent changes in all the explanatory variables lead to a negative trade-off between growth and inflation.

(b) The absolute size of the coefficient in regression of growth on inflation will depend on which explanatory variables are responsible for the cross-sectional variation of growth and inflation. If cross-sectional variations in money growth dominate the sample, we would expect that the absolute value of the coefficient on inflation would be relatively small. If cross-sectional variations in other variables dominate the sample, the coefficient on inflation should be close to −1.

(c) The effects of variables other than money growth on growth and inflation may be sufficient to change the sign of the conditional correlation induced by variation in money growth. Increase in μ reduces the equilibrium rate of growth because agents substitute leisure for consumption. In case human capital accumulation is a separate activity, when the inflation is increased, agents may substitute time spent investing in human capital for time spent in the labour market. This would lead to a positive effect of money growth on inflation. This implies that the coefficient estimates from the empirical literature tell us little or nothing about the trade-off between inflation and growth that is relevant from the point of view of the monetary policy authorities. Noise from other exogenous variables will always exaggerate the negative trade-off between inflation and growth, and would lead us to conclude that there is a negative trade-off even if an exogenous reduction in money growth has a mild negative effect on economic growth.

(d) Variables such as average tax rates, differentiated according to type (consumption, labour, and capital) may have important qualitative effects on inflation and growth.

(e) The prediction that higher money growth reduces growth in the long-run depends on the assumption that changes in the inflation rate are made up for by changes in the level of lump-sum taxation. If lump-sum taxation is not an available policy instrument, the policy for the trade-off between inflation and growth may be very different.

GARCH Model of Inflation and Growth

In this section, we shall use a bivariate generalised autoregressive conditionally heteroskedastic (GARCH) model of inflation and output growth to examine the causality relationship among nominal uncertainty, real uncertainty and macroeconomic performance measured by the inflation and output growth rates. Here, we shall examine the theoretical issues raised above with the use of a bivariate GARCH model that allows for the measurement of uncertainty about inflation and output growth by the respective conditional variances.

The objectives of monetary policy are inflation and output stabilisation around some target levels. Exogenous shocks to the economy that generate uncertainty about the inflation rate and growth rate tend to cause a deviation of these variables from their desired values and hence necessitate some policy response. In the view of Friedman, inflation uncertainty causes an adverse output effect, which is based on the idea that uncertainty about future inflation distorts the allocative efficiency aspects of the price mechanism. More specifically, inflation uncertainty affects both the intertemporal and intratemporal allocation of resources.

The effect of inflation uncertainty on output growth works through its impact on investment and the current investment gives the option to invest in the future. The value of the lost option represents the opportunity cost of an investment project. Inflation uncertainty increases the uncertainty regarding the potential returns of investment projects and therefore provides an incentive to delay these projects, thus contributing to lower investment and output growth. In contrast, using a cash-in-advance framework, Dotsey and Sarte obtained a rather puzzling result—more inflation uncertainty can increase output. This result is based on a precautionary motive and the assumption of risk-averse agents—more inflation uncertainty raises savings and hence investment and growth.

Output growth and inflation are interrelated. Although the traditional short-run Phillips curve implies that an increase in output above its natural level would result in inflationary pressures, another strand of the literature analyses how a rise in the output growth can affect the rate of inflation. In the view of Briault, there is a positive relationship between growth and inflation, at least over the short-run, with the direction of causation running from higher growth to higher inflation.[13] This positive effect is referred as the Phillips curve effect.

Economists of the structuralist tradition argue that moderate inflation rates are potentially beneficial for the growth. However, the theoretical studies generally find that a rise in inflation either results in slower growth or has no impact on the growth rate. Some models have produced insignificant long-run inflation-output growth effects (e.g. Dotsey and Sarte, 2000), while at least an equally diverse group of models have produced significant and negative inflation-growth effects. A simple model of the interaction of inflation and output growth was presented by Gylfason and Herbertsson. Their model indicates that, although a wide variety of outcomes is possible, inflation via saving, financial development and the government budget deficit tends to deter growth in the long run.[14] In the view of Klump, inflation can lead to a reduction of the aggregate elasticity of factor substitution. He suggests several microeconomic justifications for such an influence, which in turn can help to explain the negative link between inflation and growth.[15] Gillman and Kejak showed that endogenous growth models, with different use of physical and human capital and different exchange technologies, can generate significant negative effects of inflation on growth.

Now, we shall use a bivariate GARCH model to simultaneously estimate the conditional means, variances and covariances of inflation and output growth. Let π_t and y_t denote the inflation rate and real output growth, respectively, and define the residual vector ε_t as $\varepsilon_t = \left(\varepsilon_{\pi t}\, \varepsilon_{yt}\right)'$. A general bivariate vector autoregressive, VAR(p), model can be represented as

$$x_t = \Phi_0 + \sum_{i=1}^{p} \Phi_i \, x_{t-i} + \varepsilon_t \qquad \text{... (29)}$$

with

$$\Phi_0 = \begin{bmatrix} \phi_{\pi 0} \\ \phi_{y0} \end{bmatrix} \quad \text{and} \quad \Phi_i = \begin{bmatrix} \phi_{\pi\pi,i} & \phi_{\pi y,i} \\ \phi_{y\pi,i} & \phi_{yy,i} \end{bmatrix}$$

where,

x_t = 2×1 column vector given by $x_t = (\pi_t \; y_t)'$,

Φ_0 = 2×1 vector of constants, and

Φ_i = 2×2 matrix of autoregressive parameters with $i = 1, 2, \ldots\ldots, p$

Several bivariate vector autoregressive (VAR) specifications are estimated for inflation and output growth. VAR models of order up to 12 are estimated. The order of the VAR process is determined by using the optimal lag-length algorithm of the Akaike and Schwarz information criteria. ε_t is conditionally normal with mean vector 0 and covariance matrix H_t, that is, $\left(\varepsilon_t | \Omega_{t-1}\right) \sim N(0, H_t)$, where Ω_{t-1} is the information set up to time $t-1$. VAR models are also estimated where the Φ_i matrix is either lower triangular $\left(\phi_{\pi y,i} = 0\right)$, or upper triangular $\left(\phi_{y\pi,i} = 0\right)$, or diagonal $\left(\phi_{y\pi,i} = \phi_{\pi y,i} = 0\right)$. Then the best model is chosen on the basis of Granger-causality tests, which is based on the least squares and states that when conditional heteroskedasticity is ignored, least squares causality tests exhibit considerable size distortion if the conditional variances are correlated.[16] The Granger-causality tests can be performed by imposing the constant conditional correlation (ccc) GARCH(1, 1) structure on the conditional covariance matrix H_t as

$$h_{\pi t} = \omega_{\pi} + \beta_{\pi} h_{\pi,t-1} + a_{\pi} \varepsilon^2_{\pi,t-1} \quad \text{... (30)}$$

$$h_{yt} = \omega_{y} + \beta_{y} h_{y,t-1} + a_{y} \varepsilon^2_{y,t-1} \quad \text{... (31)}$$

$$h_{\pi y,t} = \rho\sqrt{h_{\pi t}}\sqrt{h_{yt}} \quad \text{... (32)}$$

with $\omega_i > 0, a_i > 0, \beta_i \geq 0$, for $i = \pi, y$ and $-1 \leq \rho \leq 1$,

where,

$h_{\pi t}$ = conditional variance of the inflation rate,
h_{yt} = conditional variance of the output growth, and
$h_{\pi y,t}$ = conditional covariance between $\varepsilon_{\pi t}$ and ε_{yt}.

In this model, we measure inflation and output uncertainty by their respective estimated conditional variances. Depending on model specification, causation in mean can exist with or without the presence of causality in variance and vice versa.[17]

An alternative approach, called simultaneous approach, can be used to test for the causal relationships among inflation, growth, inflation uncertainty and growth uncertainty. Under this approach, a bivariate GARCH-in-mean model is estimated where each conditional variance equation incorporates the lagged values of both inflation rate and the real growth rate.

To conclude, nominal uncertainty is detrimental to the growth prospects of most countries and a higher rate of average inflation has a negative effect on growth in nearly all the countries. In short, inflation tends to exert an adverse impact on real growth both directly and indirectly via changes in nominal uncertainty. The findings of empirical studies based on the GARCH approach shows that inflation uncertainty is a negative determinant of growth.

Notes

1. A.W. Phillips, "The relation between unemployment and the rate of change of money wages in the United Kingdom, 1861-1957", *Economica* (1958).

2. Arthur Okun, "Potential GNP: Its measurement and significance", *Proceedings of the American Statistical Association* (1962); 98-111.
3. Friedman, 1973: 41.
4. Campbell and Perron, 1991.
5. Dickey and Fuller, 1979.
6. *Ibid.*, 1981.
7. Culver and Papell, 1997.
8. Phillips and Perron, 1988.
9. Akaike, 1973.
10. Newley and West, 1987.
11. Engle and Yoo, 1991.
12. Love and Wen, 1996.
13. Briault, 1995.
14. Gylfason and Herbertsson, 2001.
15. Klump, 2003.
16. Vilasuso, 2001.
17. Cheung, 1996.

decadal rate at 9.4 per cent. A major portion of high inflation of 2000-01 was contributed by high fuel prices. The years 2003-04, 2004-05, 2006-07, and 2008-09 witnessed high inflation in manufactured products mainly on account of high prices of raw materials such as basic metal alloys and metal products, non-metallic mineral products, and machinery and machine tools. However, the year 2008-09 was different from the previous three years as inflation in all the three sectors remained high. The year 2009-10 turned out to be abnormal owing to global slowdown and unfavourable monsoon. The overall average inflation of 9.4 per cent in April-December 2010 was the highest recorded inflation in the last ten years.

Trends in Food Inflation

A sharp rise in food price inflation remained a major concern in the domestic economy during 2010-11. If we look at WPI, the composite food index has an overall weight of 24.31 per cent. Of this, the weight of primary food articles is 14.34 per cent and the remaining 9.97 per cent is of manufactured food products.

The WPI food inflation, i.e. 24.31 per cent of WPI, moderated to 8.59 per cent in December 2010 after reaching its peak of 20.22 per cent in February 2010. The primary food price inflation touched a historic high at 21.9 per cent in February 2010, and then declined to 9.4 per cent in November 2010 before rising again to 13.6 per cent in December 2010. Manufactured food products, on the other hand, exhibited a decline in inflation from 19.3 per cent in December 2009 to 0.4 per cent in December 2010.

In 2010-11, inflation in primary food articles was mainly driven by rice, vegetables, potatoes, onions, fruits, milk, eggs, meat and fish, condiments and spices, and tea. The WPI of manufactured food products showed a marginal increase due to the rise in prices of vanaspati oil, groundnut oil, sunflower oil, rice bran extraction, tea and coffee process, and malt liquor.

Trends in Core Inflation

Core inflation is a preferred tool for framing long-term policy as it measures inflation that excludes items that face volatile price movement, notably food and energy. Core inflation reached its peak at 8.07 per cent in April 2010 from a mere 0.55 per cent in November 2009. Thereafter, it moderated owing to monetary measures taken by the RBI.

Non-food manufactured products, which have a weight of 55 per cent in WPI, have not increased much and remained in the range of 5.1 to 5.9 per cent in 2010-11. The composite non-food index—which has a weight of 75.7 per cent in WPI—increased to 8.36 per cent in December 2010 taken at year-on-year basis, after moderating to 7.96 per cent in September 2010 from 9.18 per cent in April 2010. The main non-food items which have shown an increase in price are raw cotton, raw jute, raw silk, copra, castor seed, sunflower, raw rubber, copper ore, zinc, iron ore, cotton textiles, petrochemical intermediate, and industrial machinery and machine tools.

Consumer Price Inflation

In India, inflation can also be seen in terms of the consumer price index for industrial workers (CPI-IW), for agricultural labourers (CPI-AL), and for rural labourers (CPI-RL). CPI-IW remained in double digits from July 2009 to July 2010, while the inflation in terms of the CPI-AL and CPI-RL had reached double digits in May 2009 and continued so until July 2010. Further, during all these months, inflation in terms of the CPI-AL and CPI-RL was found to be higher than inflation based on the CPI-IW. Inflation in the CPI-IW substantially declined to 9.47 per cent in December 2010 from its peak of 16.22 per cent in January 2010. The inflation in terms of all the three price indices came down to single digit in August 2010, after hovering in double digits for nearly 15 months.

Relative to the WPI, the CPI maintained higher levels in 2010-11, mainly because of the larger weight assigned to food items. In consumer price indices, food items contribute a weight of 46.20 per cent in the CPI-IW and 69.15 per cent in the CPI-AL as against 24.31 per cent in the WPI. The food inflation has decelerated after reaching its peak in January 2010. As a result, CPI inflation rates have gone down substantially since the food inflation started decelerating after reaching its peak in January 2010.

Inflation in the CPI-IW increased in December 2010 to 9.47 per cent as against 8.33 per cent in November 2010. Food inflation in the CPI-IW has also increased to 7.98 per cent in December 2010 from 5.35 per cent in November 2010. The non-food inflation in CPI-IW has increased during April-December 2010 to 11.64 per cent as against 8.78 per cent in the corresponding period the previous year. During April-December 2010, food inflation declined to 10.29 per cent as compared to 14.70 per cent during the corresponding period of the previous year. Inflation in fruits and vegetables and onions based on the CPI-IW in December 2010 was 15.3 per cent and 77.6 per cent respectively as against 22.77 per cent and 45.82 per cent respectively, based on the WPI.

The phase of relatively high inflation seen since the beginning of the recovery from the global financial crisis is concentrated in food, pan, supari, tobacco and intoxicants, and housing. Of these, the two major contributors to high CPI-IW inflation were food and housing. The housing sector, which has a 15.3 per cent weight in the CPI-IW commodities basket, is the third major contributor after food and the miscellaneous group.

Housing Price Index

India has a considerable growth potential for a vibrant housing market. The fact that India is one of the most populous and fastest growing countries in the world ensures that there is no lack of demand for housing. However, there is shortage of credit flow, and housing finance still remains underdeveloped. The challenge in the Indian housing market primarily remains in the low and moderate income segments. Since the housing sector contributes more than 9 per cent of national employment, a measure of price movements in this sector should give an indication of people's purchasing power.

In 2007, the National Housing Bank (NHB) launched RESIDEX—an index of residential prices in India across cities and over time. After completion of a pilot study to capture the trend of price movements in residential property across five cities—Bengaluru, Bhopal, Delhi, Kolkata, and Mumbai, the compilation of RESIDEX has been expanded to ten more cities, namely Ahmedabad, Faridabad, Chennai, Kochi, Hyderabad, Jaipur, Patna, Lucknow, Pune, and Surat. At present, RESIDEX is being updated on a quarterly basis with 2007 as base year for the above 15 cities.

The NHB RESIDEX in the first half of 2010 showed that the residential housing prices increased in 10 of the 15 cities compared to the base year, i.e. 2007. The remaining five cities—Jaipur, Bengaluru, Kochi, Delhi and Hyderabad—have shown price correction in residential property prices. This means that the effect of inflation is not uniform throughout the country.

Improvements in the Standard of Living

Standard of living is often correlated to the country's gross domestic product (GDP) or gross domestic income (GDI), which is the market value of all final goods and services produced within a country in a given period. However, GDP does not show the pattern in which the consumers have switched from buying one good to another, which occurs due to price change. The fixed basket CPI also does not account for altered spending habits caused by price changes.

The movement of the consumption pattern can be analysed through a deflator generated by the Private Final Consumption Expenditure (PFCE) at current prices over constant prices base 2004-05. The PCFE Deflator is a preferred measure of inflation as it takes into account the substitutions in product made by the consumers due to price change.

The fact that price indices in CPI-RL are higher than the CPI-IW points to improvements in purchasing power and consumption pattern in rural areas. To an extent, this may be due to various employment generation schemes of the government, of which the Mahatma Gandhi National Rural Employment Guarantee Scheme (MNREGS) is the prominent. Otherwise also, a general analysis of the annual price indices data for the CPI-RL, CPI-IW and PFCED from 2004-05 onwards indicate an upward swing in the standard of living.

Volatility in Global and Domestic Inflation

There was much higher volatility in global food prices from April 2009 compared to the WPI-based domestic food inflation. The scenario altered in September 2010 and since then a higher volatility is seen in international food inflation as compared to domestic food inflation in India. The higher food inflation in 2010-11 is widespread and not unique to India. Since India depends on imports for some food items like edible oils, the increase in domestic food prices could lead to costlier imports which might push up domestic inflation. Hence, the global inflation is an ominous portent for domestic inflation, which warrants that the government persist with its anti-inflationary monetary stance.

Measures to Contain Inflation

The Government in India, irrespective of the party in power, has always shown a commitment to ensuring availability of cooking fuels to the common man at affordable prices. Since long, all governments have continued with the subsidies on kerosene and domestic liquefied petroleum gas (LPG) in view of their importance as household fuels. The present government has also extended the PDS Kerosene and Domestic LPG Subsidy Scheme 2002 as well as the Freight Subsidy (for Far-flung Areas) Scheme 2002 till 31 March 2014.

While continuing with these subsides, the government has to do a delicate act of balancing the recoveries. In February 2011, in order to reduce the burden of under-recoveries, the government announced its decision to increase the retail price of public distribution system (PDS) Kerosene by ₹ 3 per litre and of domestic LPG by ₹ 35 per cylinder, at Delhi, with corresponding increases in other parts of the country. Further, it was announced that the prices of petrol and diesel, both at the refinery gate and retail level, will be market-determined. This would impact everyone, especially the poor and the vulnerable. Hence, in order to minimise the impact, the government has proposed that increase in prices of diesel will be staggered over time. Moreover, in case of a high rise and volatility in international oil prices, the government will suitably intervene in the pricing of petrol and diesel.

From time to time, the government takes measures to contain prices of essential commodities. These measures are taken on the basis of the price situation which is constantly monitored by the government. Some of the measures taken to contain prices of essential commodities are: (i) selective ban on exports and futures trading in foodgrains, (ii) zero import duty on select food items, (iii) permitting import of pulses and sugar by public-sector undertakings, (iv) distribution of imported pulses and edible oils through the PDS, and (v) release of higher quota of non-levy sugar. In addition, State Governments are empowered to act against hoarders of food items by holding in abeyance the removal of restrictions on licensing, stock limits, and movement of food articles under the Essential Commodities Act, 1955. Some other important anti-inflationary measures, particularly to contain food inflation, taken by the government are mentioned below.

Monetary Measures

As a part of its monetary policy review, the RBI has taken suitable measures to moderate demand to levels consistent with the capacity of the economy to maintain its growth without provoking price rise. In doing so, the RBI has already raised its key policy rates several times. To reduce the volatility of rates, the RBI has narrowed the liquidity adjustment facility (LAF) corridor. Since March 2010, the Indian economy has witnessed aggressive tightening.

Fiscal Measures

The government has reduced the import duties to zero on rice, wheat, pulses, edible oils (crude), butter, and ghee. It has also reduced the import duties to 7.5 per cent on refined and hydrogenated oils and vegetable oils. The government has allowed import of raw sugar at zero duty under open general licence (OGL).

Administrative Measures

The prominent administrative measures taken by the government to contain inflation are:

1. It has removed levy obligation in respect of all imported raw sugar and white/refined sugar.
2. It has banned export of non-basmati rice, edible oils (except coconut oil and forest-based oil) and pulses (except Kabuli chana).
3. To regulate exports, minimum export price (MEP) has been issued for onion and basmati rice.
4. The Forward Market Commission suspended futures trading in rice, urad, and tur.
5. Stock limit orders were occasionally extended in the case of pulses, paddy, rice, edible oil and edible oilseeds.
6. Export of onion (all varieties) was stopped till further orders.
7. Full exemption from basic custom duty, special additional duty and education cess was provided to onions and shallots to combat the rising prices.
8. NAFED and NCCF undertook sale of onions at ₹ 35 per kg from their retail outlets at various locations. The government provided suitable budgetary support for this purpose.

Besides these, there are some other measures that are being considered by the government. These include:

(a) Introducing a scheme to support the State Governments in the setting up of farmers' mandis and mobile bazaars and improve the functioning of civil supplies corporations and cooperatives.

(b) Strengthening the existing PDS through computerization and other steps, including opening more procurement windows across the country.

(c) Urging the State Governments to review the APMC Acts and, in particular, considering exempting horticultural products from their purview, thereby mitigating marketing and distribution bottlenecks in this crucial sector.

(d) Urging the State Governments to consider waiving mandi tax, octroi, and other local levies which impede smooth movement of essential commodities, as well as to reduce commission agent charges.

(e) Encouraging investment in supply chains, including provisions for cold storages, which will be dovetailed with organized retail chains for quicker and more efficient distribution of farm products, and minimizing wastage. The schemes for this purpose would be jointly worked out by DIPP, Department of Food and Public Distribution, Ministry of Food Processing Industries, and the Planning Commission.

(f) Setting up of an Inter-Ministerial Group (IMG) under the Chief Economic Adviser, Ministry of Finance, to review the overall inflation situation, with particular reference to primary food articles. The IMG will, inter alia, review production/rainfall trends and build an institutional machinery to read warning signals, assess international trends, recommend action on the fiscal, monetary, production, marketing, distribution, and infrastructure fronts to prevent price spikes, and suggest measures to strengthen collection and analysis of data and forecasting.

(g) The Committee of Secretaries under the Cabinet Secretary will review the prices situation with individual States, and advise the Departments concerned of the Central Government to maintain close coordination with State agencies to get direct feedback with a view to taking suitable remedial measures on a fast track.

Monetary Developments

Beginning mid-September 2008, the RBI adopted an accommodative monetary policy stance in response to the global financial crisis. This helped instil confidence among market participants and ensured that the economy recovered as quickly as possible. As a result, during the course of 2009-10, the Indian economy exhibited acceleration in the momentum of recovery. Due to the expansionary monetary and fiscal stance adopted in response to the global crisis, the process of recovery turned out to be less difficult despite a deficit monsoon.

The RBI made a clear shift in stance from 'managing the crisis' to 'managing the recovery' and announced the first phase of exit from the expansionary monetary policy in its Second Quarter Review of October 2009 by terminating some sector-specific facilities and restoring the statutory liquidity ratio (SLR) of scheduled commercial banks (SCBs) to its pre-crisis level. This was done in view of rising food inflation and the risk of it impinging on inflationary expectations. As soon as clear signs were evident that the recovery was consolidating, the RBI decided to carry forward the process of exit from an accommodative policy stance. At that moment, it was being felt that the main policy instruments were at levels more consistent with a fast recovering economy than a crisis economy.

During 2010-11, taking the above into consideration, the RBI raised the policy rates six times whereby the repo rate under the LAF was cumulatively increased by 175 basis points (bps) to stand at 6.5 per cent and the reverse repo rate by 225 bps to 5.5 per cent as on 28 February 2011. Moreover, the RBI retained the cash reserve ratio (CRR) at 6 per cent of the net demand and time liabilities (NDTL) of banks. Thus, in 2010-11, the persistently high inflation above the comfort level of the RBI, together with growth buoyancy, necessitated that the monetary policy focus should remain on containing inflation and inflationary expectations.

In order to take the surprise element out of off-cycle actions, the RBI has been undertaking mid-quarter reviews roughly at the interval of one and half months after each quarterly review since 16 October 2010. Consistent with the objective of price and financial stability, the RBI is continuing its policy of maintaining adequate liquidity in the system so that all legitimate credit requirements for productive purposes were met. The management of liquidity was achieved through appropriate use of open market operations (OMOs), the Market Stabilization Scheme (MSS), LAF, and a slew of special facilities.

Consistent with the policy stance, the overall liquidity in the system has remained in deficit. However, the extent of tightness has been beyond the comfort level of the RBI of (+)/(–) 1 per cent of NDTL, mainly due to the persistence of large government cash balances. In addition, the liquidity deficit was accentuated by structural factors such as significantly above-trend currency expansion and relatively sluggish growth in bank deposits.

During 2010-11, several banks raised deposit and lending interest rates even as the credit growth accelerated. It became difficult for the banking system to sustain credit delivery, as excessive deficits induced unpredictability in both availability and cost of funds. The liquidity deficit, however, improved transmission of monetary policy signals. The persistent liquidity pressures prompted the RBI to implement some measures in November 2010 such as additional liquidity support to SCBs under the LAF up to two per cent of their NDTL, continuation of the second LAF (SLAF), and OMO purchase of government securities.

Subsequently in its mid-quarter review on 16 December 2010, the RBI reduced the SLR of SCBs from 25 per cent of their NDTL to 24 per cent with effect from 18 December 2010. Furthermore, it conducted OMO auctions for purchase of government securities for an aggregate amount of ₹ 48,000 crore in one month. The RBI did not mince words in communicating that as the economy expands, it needs primary liquidity, which will have to be provided in a manner consistent with the monetary policy stance. It further added that such provision of liquidity should not be construed as a change in the monetary policy stance since inflation continues to remain a major concern.

Thus, the underlying growth momentum of the Indian economy remains strong, in spite of the fact that inflation remains significantly above the comfort level of the RBI. Also, risks to inflation remain on the upside, both from domestic demand and higher global commodity prices. This necessitates a need for continued vigilance on the inflation front against the build-up of demand-side pressures.

Liquidity management has remained a major challenge for the RBI owing to inflationary pressures. This is being alleviated by the RBI in a manner consistent with the monetary policy stance of containing inflation and anchoring inflationary expectations. The monetary policy stance of the RBI as indicated in its Second Quarter Review (November 2010) was as follows:

(a) To contain inflation and to anchor inflationary expectations while being prepared to respond to any further build-up of inflationary pressures;

(b) To maintain an interest rate regime consistent with price, output, and financial stability;

(c) To actively manage liquidity to ensure that it remains broadly in balance, with neither a surplus diluting monetary transmission nor a deficit choking off fund flows; and

(d) To take further policy actions if required, and, in an uncertain world, to be prepared to respond appropriately to shocks that may emanate from either the global or domestic environment.

Monetary Aggregates

During the year 2010-11 (up to 3 December 2010), the growth rates of reserve money (M0) and narrow money (M1) have been higher as compared to the preceding year, while broad money (M3) growth has been lower. This moderation in growth of narrow and broad money is attributed largely to the deceleration in growth of deposits, both demand and time.

Reserve Money (M0)

According to the RBI figures, during 2010-11, on a financial-year basis, M0 expanded by 8.4 per cent (up to 10 December 2010), compared to an increase of 1.6 per cent during the corresponding period of the preceding year. During this period, the net foreign assets (NFA) of the RBI increased by 6.1 per cent as against an increase of 1.5 per cent during the corresponding period of the previous year. On a year-on-year basis, as on 11 December 2010, the NFA of the RBI marginally increased by 0.6 per cent compared to a 6.8 per cent increase a year earlier. During the financial year (up to 10 December 2010), net RBI credit to the Central Government increased by ₹ 70,856 crore. This was mainly on account of increase in repo operations under the LAF and open market purchases of the Bank, partly offset by increase in the cash balances of the Central Government. On a year-on-year basis, increase in the net RBI credit to the Central Government, as on 10 December 2010, was ₹ 2,10,714 crore as against an increase of ₹ 98,273 crore a year earlier.

Narrow Money (M1)

In 2009-10, narrow money (M1) increased by 18.6 per cent as compared to an expansion of 9.0 per cent the previous year. During 2010-11, M1 growth was generally higher than in 2009-10. On a financial-year basis, M1 increased by 3.1 per cent during 2010-11 (up to 3 December 2010) compared to an increase of 5.1 per cent during the corresponding period of the previous year. On a year-on-year basis, as on 3 December 2010, M1 growth was 16.5 per cent as compared to 18.3 per cent a year earlier. During the same period, currency with the public expanded by 12.9 per cent (₹ 99,324 crore), compared to an increase of 9.8 per cent (₹ 64,962 crore) during the corresponding period of the previous year.

Demand deposits with banks, the other important component of M1, decreased by 7.3 per cent during the period up to 3 December 2010 as against a marginal increase of 0.1 per cent during the corresponding period of the previous year. On a year-on-year basis, as on 3 December 2010, the growth of currency with the public was higher at 18.7 per cent as compared to 17.2 per cent a year earlier. For the same period, growth in demand deposits was 13.7 per cent as compared to 19.9 per cent a year earlier.

Broad Money (M3)

During 2009-10, broad money (M3) supply increased by 16.8 per cent which was lower than the 17.0 per cent indicative growth envisaged in the Annual Policy Statement of the RBI for 2009-10. Time deposits with banks during 2010-11 grew at a lower rate of 10.1 per cent (up to 3 December 2010) as compared to 11.2 per cent during the corresponding period of the previous year. On a year-on-year basis also, as on 3 December 2010, the growth in time deposits moderated to 14.9 per cent from 18.7 per cent a year earlier.

During the 2010-11 (up to 3 December 2010), the growth in M3 was 8.2 per cent as compared to 9.6 per cent during the corresponding period of the previous year. On a year-on-year basis, M3 grew by 15.3 per cent on 3 December 2010, as against growth of 18.6 per cent on the corresponding date of the previous year. This is lower than the indicative 17.0 per cent target set in the Second Quarter Review of the Annual Policy Statement for 2010-11. Since November 2009, however, bank credit to the commercial sector has been accelerating.

Money Multiplier (M3:M0)

Money multiplier is the ratio of M3 to M0, i.e. broad money to reserve money. Since the expansion in M0 was higher than that in M3 during 2009-10, there was a decrease in money multiplier. At the end of March 2010, this ratio was 4.8, marginally lower than the end-March 2009 figure of 4.11. The decreasing trend shown by the money multiplier during 2010-11 was because the reserve money registered a higher growth than broad money supply.

Monetary Deepening

Monetary deepening is measured by the ratio of average M3 to the GDP. Its increase from 43.8 per cent in 1990-91 to 83.1 per cent in 2009-10 could be attributed to the spread of banking services in the country and development of the financial sector.

Monetization of the Economy

The monetization of the economy is measured by the ratio of average M1 to the GDP. It has also shown an upward trend, albeit at a slower rate, and the ratio increased from 15.3 per cent in 1990-91 to 21.2 per cent in 2009-10.

Other Monetary Indicators

While the year-on-year non-food credit growth at 24.4 per cent in December 2010 was much above the indicative projection of 20 per cent, money supply (M3) growth at 16.5 per cent was close to the indicative projection of 17 per cent. During the period, credit expansion has been rather sharp, far outpacing the expansion in deposits. This means that banks have to rely on borrowing from the central bank. Therefore, rapid credit growth without commensurate increase in deposits is not sustainable. However, the structural liquidity deficit in the system declined significantly since early November 2010 as a result of injection of primary liquidity of over ₹ 67,000 crore through OMO auctions.

Liquidity Management

During 2010-11, the RBI continued its active policy of liquidity management through the LAF, CRR, and OMOs. In fact, the Centre's surplus balance with the RBI and currency in circulation are the two key drivers of autonomous liquidity. The LAF window of the Reserve Bank remained in surplus mode for nearly 18 months, but switched into deficit mode towards the end of May 2010. This was mainly on account of 3G (third generation spectrum) and BWA (broadband wireless access) auctions and the consequent migration of liquidity to the Central Government's cash balance account with the RBI. The trend largely continued during the remaining part of the financial year 2010-11.

During the first quarter, April-June, of 2010-11, there was a significant change in the liquidity conditions. The gradual moderation in the volume of surplus liquidity in the system since February 2010 reflected the calibrated normalization of the monetary policy by the RBI. Accordingly, the LAF remained in the absorption mode, though the absorption volume declined gradually. The surplus liquidity in the domestic market gradually declined after the RBI increased the repo and reverse repo rates as well as CRR by 25 bps each in April 2010 in the Annual Monetary Policy for 2010-11. This was done to anchor inflation and prevent further build-up of inflationary pressure. The average daily liquidity injection under the LAF during June 2010 was around ₹ 47,000 crore in contrast to the average daily absorption of around ₹ 33,000 crore in May 2010.

During the second quarter, July-September, of 2010-11, the liquidity conditions generally remained in deficit mode. Hence, the RBI extended the liquidity-easing measures introduced earlier. The SCBs were permitted to avail of additional liquidity support under the LAF to the extent of up to 0.5 per cent of their NDTL. Further, for any shortfall in maintenance of the SLR arising out of availment of this facility, banks were allowed seek waiver of penal interest. On an assessment of the prevailing overall liquidity conditions and with a view to providing flexibility to SCBs in liquidity management, the RBI further extended the SLAF on a daily basis till 30 July 2010. The average daily liquidity injection under the LAF remained at around ₹ 47,000 crore during July 2010.

The liquidity conditions improved in August 2010, mainly on account of large pre-scheduled public debt redemptions on 28 July 2010, and the average daily net injection of liquidity declined to around ₹ 1,000 crore during the month. After a brief period of surplus liquidity from the end of August to early September 2010, the liquidity conditions again switched to injection mode as liquidity migrated to government account with the RBI on account of quarterly advance tax outflows. The liquidity conditions remained tight in the second half of September 2010 as the surplus cash balances of the Centre started building up, and the average daily net outstanding liquidity injection was around ₹ 24,000 crore during the month.

During the third quarter, October-December, of 2010-11, the liquidity conditions tightened further, especially in October 2010 on account of increase in government surplus balances and currency in circulation due to festive season demand. For the entire month of October 2010, the average daily net outstanding liquidity injection was around ₹ 62,000 crore. Subsequently, the RBI announced certain temporary measures in order to ease the frictional liquidity pressure. The RBI also increased the repo and reverse repo rates by 25 bps each in the Second Quarter Review of Monetary Policy on 2 November 2010 to contain inflation and anchor inflationary expectations.

Further, the RBI conducted purchase of government securities under its OMOs for an aggregate amount of ₹ 12,000 crore on 4 November 2010 and accepted an aggregate amount of ₹ 8352 crore in that auction. This was consistent with the stance of monetary policy and based on the assessment of prevailing and evolving liquidity conditions.

In November 2010, the high deficit liquidity conditions continued with the persistence of high government balances and rise in currency in circulation. The RBI has temporarily re-introduced liquidity-easing measures such as SLAF on a daily basis, the waiver of penal interest on shortfall in maintenance of the SLR to the extent of 1 per cent of NDTL for availing of additional liquidity support under the LAF. The average daily net liquidity injection during the month of November 2010 was around ₹ 99,300 crore.

In December 2010 too, the liquidity conditions remained in high deficit (till 20 December). This was because of the increased liquidity stress in the system owing to huge quarterly advance tax payments. As part of its OMOs, the RBI conducted purchase of government securities through auction for an aggregate amount of ₹ 12,000 crore each on 9 December 2010 and 15 December 2010; and accepted an aggregate amount of ₹ 10,120 crore and ₹ 11,706 crore respectively in the auctions. The average daily net outstanding liquidity injection was around ₹ 1,10,000 crore during 1 to 20 December 2010.

Thus, while the overall liquidity in the system has remained in deficit, consistent with the policy stance, the extent of tightness has been beyond the comfort level of the RBI.

Money Market

During 2010-11, the money market generally remained orderly. Since the commencement of the financial year up to May 2010, the call rate mostly remained around the lower bound of the informal LAF corridor. Since end-May 2010, however, the call rate firmed up with the tightening of liquidity conditions, reflecting migration of liquidity to the Central Government account with the RBI on account of 3G auction/ advance tax payments. The average daily call rate for the first quarter was at 4.16 per cent. It hovered around the upper bound of the LAF corridor till July 2010 as deficit liquidity conditions persisted due to the high Central Government cash balances.

Towards the end of August and early September 2010, the call rate declined with the change in liquidity conditions. However, it again firmed up from the middle of September and breached the upper bound of the informal LAF corridor in the second half of the month reflecting the onset of high deficit liquidity conditions. The average call rate increased to 5.40 per cent in the second quarter. In the third quarter too, the call rate mostly remained above the upper bound of the corridor, reflecting the increased liquidity stress in the system. The average call rate was 6.59 per cent in the third quarter of 2010-11 (till 20 December 2010).

The collateralized segment of the money market continued to remain the dominant segment, accounting for more than 80 per cent of the total volume during 2010-11. During the period, the rates in the collateralized segments continued to move in tandem with the call rate, albeit below it. The weighted average interest rate in the collateralized segment of the money market increased to 5.20 per cent during the second quarter from 3.97 per cent in the first quarter of 2010-11. Transaction volumes in the collateralized borrowing and lending obligation (CBLO) and market repo segments remained high during this period, reflecting active market conditions. While banks continued to remain the major group of borrowers in the collateralized segments, mutual funds (MFs) remained the major group of lenders of funds in these segments.

Certificates of Deposit (CDs)

During 2010-11, though the average gross issuance of CDs was high, the amount of CDs outstanding declined. This indicates a decline in net issuances. The amount of outstanding CDs issued by scheduled commercial banks (SCBs) declined marginally from ₹ 3,41,054 crore at the end of March 2010 to ₹ 3,32,982 crore at the end of November 2010. During April-November 2010, the average issuance was of the order of around ₹ 22,000 crore as compared to around ₹ 11,000 crore during the same period of the previous financial year. The effective interest rate in respect of aggregate CD issuances increased from 6.07 per cent at the end of March 2010 to 8.16 per cent as on 19 November 2010.

Commercial Paper (CP)

The commercial paper (CP) market also picked up and the size of fortnightly issuance increased significantly during 2010-11. The outstanding amount of CP issued by corporates showed an increasing trend from ₹ 75,506 crore at the end of March 2010 to ₹ 1,12,003 crore at the end of September 2010 and ₹ 1,17,793 crore at the end of November 2010. The weighted average discount rate (WADR) of aggregate CP issuances increased from 6.29 per cent at the end of March 2010 to 7.82 per cent at the end of September 2010, and reached 12.22 per cent at the end of November 2010. At the end of November 2010, the shares of 'leasing and finance companies', 'manufacturing companies', and 'other financial institutions' in total outstanding CPs were at around 50 per cent, 39 per cent, and 11 per cent respectively.

Treasury Bills (T-Bills)

T-Bills issuances were modulated according to the cash management requirements of the government as well as evolving market conditions during 2010-11. During the first two quarters of the fiscal year, the notified amounts for competitive auctions of T-Bills were reduced. The outstanding stock of T-Bills went down from ₹ 1,34,500 crore on 31 March 2010 to ₹ 1,26,269 crore on 31 December 2010, after taking into account a rise in non-competitive allotment. The liquidity conditions and monetary policy action by the RBI influenced the primary market yields for T-Bills of different tenors (91 days, 182 days, and 364 days), which moved up during the year.

Cash Management Bill (CMB)

In May 2010, a new short-term instrument, named cash management bill (CMB), was introduced. CMBs were issued for an aggregate of ₹ 12,000 crore. These are non-standard, discounted instruments issued for maturities of less than 91 days. These were issued to meet the temporary cash-flow mismatches of the government.

Central Government Borrowing

The Union Budget 2010-11 placed the net market borrowings (through dated securities) requirement of the Central Government at ₹ 3,45,010 crore as against ₹ 3,97,957 crore raised during the previous year. Including repayments of ₹ 1,12,133 crore, gross market borrowings were estimated at ₹ 4,57,143 crore as compared to ₹ 4,51,000 crore raised in the previous year, including MSS de-sequestering of ₹ 33,000 crore. The actual issuances during the first half of 2010-11 amounted to ₹ 2,84,000 crore as against issuances of ₹ 2,95,000 crore, excluding MSS de-sequestering of ₹ 28,000 crore, during the corresponding period of the previous year. The issuance calendar for dated securities released on 23 September 2010 proposed to raise ₹ 1,63,000 crore during the second half of the year. This indicated a reduction of ₹ 10,000 crore from the budget estimate.

The gross borrowings requirement in 2010-11 remained high as in the previous year and the government undertook buy-back operations whereby securities worth ₹ 11,767 crore were bought back. The market borrowings programme is, however, carried out in a smooth and non-disruptive manner. Gross market borrowings raised through dated securities by the Central Government up to 31 December 2010 were ₹ 3,84,000 crore (net ₹ 2,98,342 crore) as against ₹ 3,83,000 crore (excluding issuances under the MSS) (net ₹ 3,46,911 crore) raised during the corresponding period of the previous year. The weighted average maturity of dated securities issued during the year (up to 31 December 2010) was moderately higher at 11.54 years as compared to 11.15 years for issues during the corresponding period of the previous year. The weighted average yield of dated securities during 2010-11 (up to 31 December 2010) increased to 7.87 per cent from 7.21 per cent during the corresponding period of the previous year.

Yields on 10-year Government Securities

Monetary policy, inflation concerns, and supply issues were the major factors influencing yields on government securities during 2010-11. Secondary market yields on government securities remained in a broad range during the year. Intra-year movements in yields on government securities could be attributed to various factors. The upward movement in the month of April 2010 was mainly on account of supply pressure in the wake of front-loading of the market borrowings programme. Subsequently, in May 2010, concerns regarding high fiscal deficit receded due to higher-than-budgeted collections from auction of 3G and BWA licences. This improved sentiment was offset by concerns of high inflation and policy tightening by the Reserve Bank. In the third quarter, tight liquidity conditions remained a major factor putting upward pressure on yields and the 10-year yield, which was at 7.87 per cent on 31 March 2010, went up to 7.94 per cent on 31 December 2010.

State Government Borrowing

An aggregate amount of ₹ 74,104 crore was raised by twenty-two State Governments on a gross basis up to end-December 2010 as compared to ₹ 1,00,085 crore raised by 25 State Governments during the corresponding period of the previous year. The cut-off yields have ranged between 8.05 and 8.58 per cent as compared to 7.04 and 8.49 per cent during the corresponding period of the previous year. The weighted average yield worked out to 8.36 per cent up to end-December 2010 as compared to 8.02 per cent during the corresponding period of 2009-10 and 8.11 per cent for the year as a whole. The spread between the yield on State Development Loans (SDLs) and the 10-year benchmark Government of India securities stood lower at 32-69 bps up to December 2010 as compared to 45-129 bps during the corresponding period of the previous year.

Analysis of Situation

In addition to domestic factors, inflation in India is also affected by the rising international prices. In a global economy, domestic prices cannot remain fully insulated and some spillovers of global prices to Indian markets are inevitable. Actually, the high food inflation during 2010-11 was unexpected because the rainfall was good. While the good monsoon indeed brought down prices for cereals, the prices of vegetables, fruits, dairy, oilseeds, and spices surged.

The surge in global food prices since 2009 is led by sugar, oils and fats, and cereals, but not dairy and meat. Some analysts attribute this to factors such as rise in prices of oil, which in turn is said to be due to high liquidity and a falling dollar. The factors do not seem to include: a rising demand in emerging markets such as China and India, and a shift to bio-fuels. Climate change is also blamed for the surge in global food prices, chiefly the floods in Australia, earthquake and tsunami in Japan, poor summer in Russia, flooding in Indonesia, and dry spell in Argentina. Thus, the food price rise is not due to any one specific reason and is an outcome of several complex factors.

The volatility of global prices is far greater than that of domestic prices, and India's prices have been much more stable, avoiding the highs and lows. Recently, cereals prices have been declining in India relative to global ones. The rising prices of non-cereal foods in India, to an extent, may be due to a shift in consumers' preference to greater quantity of non-cereals. Irrespective of the underlying reason, inflation clearly remains the dominant concern.

While ensuring that inflation falls back to more comfortable target levels, the government has to maintain an environment where the cost and availability of credit is supportive of growth momentum. In spite of proactive use of monetary policy tools, prices relatively remained high and the concurrent consolidation of fiscal deficits will be essential to ease the conduct of effective monetary policy. At the same time, to sustain the current growth momentum of the Indian economy, the reduction of fiscal deficit is highly necessary.

